Stratification

Why are the social backgrounds of friends so strongly related? Why is falling in love apparently constrained by our occupational position?

Stratification: Social division and inequality is about who gets what, and how. It is concerned with the patterning of inequality and its enduring consequences for the lives of those who experience it. It offers a fresh perspective on the stratification debate, looking at how our most personal choices (of sexual partners, friends, consumption items and lifestyle) are influenced by hierarchy and pressures towards social similarity.

Exploring how hierarchy affects our tastes and leisure-time activities, and who we choose (and hang on to) as our friends and partners, *Stratification: Social division and inequality* considers how ordinary, everyday activities – going to work, spending time with our friends, pursuing hobbies and interests, socialising with family – help to reproduce inequalities in social position and resources.

This book:

- Relates class inequalities to broader processes of social division and cultural differentiation, exploring the associational and cultural aspects of hierarchy;
- Explores how groups draw on social, economic and cultural resources, using cultural 'cues', to admit some and exclude others from their social circle;
- Provides an accessible and lively introduction to classical and contemporary theories of stratification and hierarchy, relating theoretical debates to students' own life experience.

Offering a radically different approach to existing texts, *Stratification: Social division and inequality* will be an invaluable resource for social science students.

Wendy Bottero is a Lecturer in Sociology at the University of Southampton. Her research interests centre on the social reproduction of inequality and hierarchy.

Stratification

Social division and inequality

Wendy Bottero

Routledge
Taylor & Francis Group

LONDON AND NEW YORK

First published 2005
by Routledge
2 Park Square, Milton Park, Abingdon, Oxon, OX14 4RN

Simultaneously published in the USA and Canada
by Routledge
270 Madison Ave, New York NY 10016

Routledge is an imprint of the Taylor & Francis Group

Transferred to Digital Printing 2010

Typeset in Baskerville by
Taylor & Francis Books

British Library Cataloguing in Publication Data
A catalogue record for this book is available from the British Library

Library of Congress Cataloging in Publication Data
Bottero, Wendy, 1965–
    Stratification: Social division and inequality / Wendy Bottero.
        p. cm.
    Includes bibliographical references and index.
    ISBN 0–415–28178–4 (hardcover) –
    ISBN 0–415–28179–2 (softcover)
    1. Stratification: Social division and inequality.   I. Title.
    HM821.B68 2005
    305–dc22   2004013653

ISBN 0–415–28178–4 (hbk)
ISBN 0–415–28179–2 (pbk)

Contents

Part 3
Re-orderings **145**

Illustrations

Acknowledgements

As befits a work on stratification, I must acknowledge a series of intellectual debts. By far the biggest debt is owed to the members of the Cambridge Stratification Group: Ken Prandy, Sandy Stewart, Bob Blackburn, John Holmwood and Janet Siltanen. Their work has had a profound impact on the shaping of this book, and their intellectual rigour, originality and comradeship have been an – admittedly rather daunting! – inspiration throughout my career. I hope I have done their ideas justice. I must also particularly thank another member of the group, my friend Sarah Irwin, who has worked with me on many of the arguments developed here, and whose scholarship has always been a spur to my own work. This book certainly could not have been written without them, although no one should blame them for that.

Many friends and colleagues provided support in the early stages of the book, and I must thank Fiona Devine, Mel Semple, Kate Reed, Ellie Lee, Paul Sweetman and Rachel Brooks for their encouraging remarks, which got me into the project in the first place, and kept me going once I had begun. Some brave friends read chapters, often at very short notice, and for their forbearance, insight and suggestions, I thank Sue Heath, Graham Crow, Paul Bridgen, Traute Meyer and Caroline Knowles. Many people suffered with me during the long writing process, and I must particularly thank two friends: Derek McGhee, for allowing me to talk 'at' him, for reading every word, for many cups of tea, and for being a general marvel; and Claire Alexander, whose pep talks were bracing and to the point, who gave inscrutable advice (Cordelia, the spatula!), and just, generally, for being a distraction.

I must also thank friends and family, who saw very little of me during the last stages of the book, and yet who never complained. Strange that. Finally, the book is dedicated to my Aunt Toni, who waited a long time (rather impatiently) for it to be finished.

Part 1

Foundations

1 Stratification and social distance

Persistence and transmission

This book is about who gets what, and how. Social stratification is concerned with the patterning of inequality and its enduring consequences on the lives of those who experience it. All of us live within pre-existing relations of unequal power, status or economic resources; and these unequal relations surround and constrain us, providing the context of our interactions, inevitably affecting the choices we make in life, opening some channels of opportunity, and closing off others. This is a condition of social life (individual choice is always limited by the choices of those around us), but stratification is concerned with how some have more freedom and choice than others. Money, power or influence give those who possess them greater control over the external forces which affect us all, and open doors which might otherwise be closed. The point of stratification analysis is to see how such inequalities persist and endure – over lifetimes and between generations. Going to university, for example, opens the door to higher-level, better-paid jobs. So someone who cannot take up a university place because they cannot afford the fees will be affected by this throughout their life, in the sort of career they can get, and in the level of their lifetime earnings. If we start off as unequal, these disadvantages are likely to accumulate and be reinforced over our lifetimes. As the old phrase has it: 'the rich get richer, and the poor get poorer'.

The study of stratification is therefore the study of how inequalities between individuals at any given point in time are reproduced between and across generations. As Otis Duncan argues, the difference between *inequality* and *stratification* is that 'social *stratification* refers to the persistence of positions in a hierarchy of inequality, either over the life time of a birth cohort of individuals or, more particularly, between generations' (1968: 681). The notion of *inter-generational transmission* is important here. Inequality in one generation affects inequality in the next. The resources that are available to us growing up as children affect the success of our schooling, and so our eventual occupational careers, and the lifestyles we adopt as adults. However, this means there is also an impact on the *next* generation, since our social position influences the resources to which our children have access, and so their life-chances too. Here the social location of children constrains the choices of their adult lives, and the choices of *their* children, quite independent of their individual efforts. So social stratification also looks at the extent to which advantage (or disadvantage) is handed down from one generation to the next, reproducing the pattern of inequalities between individuals and groups over time.

Stratification analysis looks at how where we *start* in life affects where we *end up*, and the impact of parents' social position on that of their children. However, the persistence of inequality is represented in more ways than inter-generational transmission, since stratification also has an important impact on our *social relations*. Whom we fall in love and settle down with, and the friends and social contacts that we make throughout our life, are all affected by our hierarchical position. This process, called *differential association*, is an essential feature of stratification. People sharing a similar social position, in terms of social class or status group membership, are more likely to interact socially with members of the same group than with members of other groups. So, acquaintances, friends and sexual partners all tend to be chosen much more frequently from within the same group than from without. There are many reasons why this occurs, but all of them result from living within stratified social arrangements. So people may actively seek to exclude certain groups from their social circles, for reasons of prejudice or snobbery, but this is bound up with the uneven levels of prestige, resources and social standing of different groups. However, differential association is not just based on the deliberate exclusion of others. It also happens because people with different social resources (whether economic, social or cultural) tend to travel in different social circles, and have different lifestyles, so they are less likely to bump into those from different social groups and, when they do, they often don't have much in common.

The lives of social unequals are often lived in different places, with different sorts of people, who have different lifestyles, tastes and interests. This is a *consequence* of the impact on stratification of social arrangements, but it also helps to reproduce stratification. If individual and family decisions – about the choice of a partner, the raising of children or the choice of a career – are choices influenced by our (stratified) social location, then such patterned choices help to maintain differences in the outcomes of people's lives. Friends and family are important sources of financial help, useful contacts and social support. They help us to 'get on' in life. But differential association means that disadvantaged people tend to associate with people who are similarly disadvantaged, whilst the privileged likewise draw more of their contacts from the privileged. If two people settling down are both from privileged backgrounds, this will reinforce (rather than dissipate) the pattern of economic privilege in such families. Similarly, if working-class people rarely make friends with upper-middle-class people, their friends will only be able to help them get working-class jobs. Differential association acts as a conservative force on the distribution of opportunities and resources, circulating them within groups rather than across them.

What this means is that the persistence of inequality is not simply a matter of material advantage and disadvantage; along with it goes a range of attitudes, social relationships and styles of life, so the persistence of inequality over time is partly about the continual reproduction of these social relationships and styles of life. Because social hierarchy acts as a constraint on all close social relationships, in turn, the patterning of such relationships helps to transmit and reproduce hierarchy itself.

The stratification space

To understand stratification as a process of enduring, unequal, social relations, we have to think about the nature of the social hierarchies in which people live their lives. Stratified social relations occur when social differences are organised hierarchically along some dimension of inequality. There are many dimensions to inequality, because we value many different resources and attributes (cultural, social, and economic) which all serve to stratify our social relations. Unequal social relations occur along lines of prestige, reputation, property, income, occupation, education, skill, gender, race, ethnicity, age, disability, and sexuality, to name just a few. And to complicate things, these dimensions of inequality do not straightforwardly map onto each other, but nor are they completely independent. This gives us a series of highly differentiated and stratified social relations which intersect and combine to influence an individual's overall stratification position. Our social position, then, is the product of all our social relations, of our gender, age, race, class, sexuality, and so on. But how do these combine to produce an all-embracing stratification order, an overall space of unequal social relations – and how is this ordering best understood?

As the writer Pierre Bourdieu argues, because of the complex differentiation of social relations, the same experience of the social world can be 'constructed in different ways ... according to different principles of vision and division' (1985: 726), and this is true for both stratification theorists and the people they study. There are a series of different approaches to stratification, which all picture it differently. Many of these approaches will be examined during the course of this book. However, these approaches can – very schematically – be divided into two main ways of thinking about stratification: *structural* approaches and *relational* or *interaction* approaches. Both of them use the notion of social distance, albeit in contrasting ways. The first sees social distance in terms of the different locations of people within an external structure of stratification. The second sees social distance in terms of social relations of closeness and distance, in which stratification is composed of the patterned nature of these social relations.

Social structure

The term 'social distance' is part of the language of spatial metaphor which has dominated stratification theory (Ossowski 1963: 9). Social distance, for most stratification writers, refers to the relative position of individuals within a structure, and is a metaphor for the degree of separation between groups placed by other criteria (so, the 'distance' between the rich and the poor refers to the extent of their difference economically). One early approach, by Pitirim Sorokin (1927), emphasises distance within an overall social space, in which an individual's overall location is determined by the values of many coordinates, among them 'family status, the state in which he [sic] is a citizen, his nationality, his religious group, his occupational group, his political party, his economic status, his race, and so on' (1927: 5). Therefore, the level of social distance between individuals depends on how different they are in terms of various attributes. People from different ethnic backgrounds, and with different religions, would be regarded as 'socially distant' from each other, whereas people with different ethnic backgrounds, but the same religion (or vice versa), might be seen as somewhat closer to each other in social space.

> The greater the resemblance of the positions of the different men [*sic*], the nearer they are towards each other in social space. The greater and more numerous are their differences in these respects, the greater is the social distance between them.
>
> (Sorokin 1927: 6)

Because theorists of stratification are interested in the constraining and enduring nature of unequal social relations they have naturally been drawn to *structural* accounts of social behaviour, which usually focus on one main dimension of stratification, whilst recognising other, complicating, factors. Structural approaches then investigate this dominant dimension of inequality (usually, the economic) as an external structure, which – to a greater or lesser extent – determines people's lives. In this method, the identification of the social structure comes first. The best-known approach of this kind is class analysis, which sees economic inequality as the main dimension of stratification, and so defines a structure of economic positions. Structural approaches see differential association (the impact of hierarchical location on our social relationships) as a key aspect of stratification. However, their method first defines the main dimension of stratification (as a set of classes or status groups) and then investigates patterns of social interaction *between* these groups.

Structural accounts of stratification are much the better known, and have dominated work in the area, with their models of social behaviour proving to be powerful analytical tools. However, in recent years a disillusionment with structural approaches in social analysis more generally has led to a declining interest in stratification. In this book I argue that these attacks are misguided and dramatically overstate the difficulties of structural analysis. Stratification remains a key force structuring our social experience, and structural approaches still have much to tell us about the nature of these processes. However, certain weaknesses in structural approaches have opened the door to such charges.

There are two related problems. First, there is the problem of how the structure of stratification relates to other dimensions of difference. Usually 'structure' is defined in terms of the valued resource that is seen to be the *most* important in people's lives, and then analysts look at how inequalities in that resource affect social relations. This inevitably separates 'structure' from 'action', since – because there are always other, acknowledged, dimensions of difference – the 'dominant' structural location will only explain *part* of people's social behaviour. Recent attacks have focused on this gap. It is argued that structural accounts are necessarily incomplete explanations, which make exaggerated claims. Second, therefore, structural accounts have been accused of determinism, placing too much emphasis on structural locations (the membership of class or status groups) which cannot explain the diversity of people's lives. Structural accounts, it is claimed, see stratification as a mould into which we must pour our behaviour, whether we wish to or not, denying the freedom, choice and agency of individuals. Recent postmodern accounts of social 'difference' have stressed the hyper-differentiated nature of social relations, arguing that actors can slice up the social order in different ways, in much the same way as stratification theorists. That is, that highly differentiated social relations can be interpreted in different ways. Such accounts have argued that the internal differences within, and across, the categories of structural accounts simply undermine the usefulness of stratification theory altogether.

Relations in social space

However, there is another way of thinking about stratification and social distance, a parallel, less well-known tradition, which is less susceptible to charges of determinism or essentialism, but which still stresses the constraining nature of stratified social relations. Some of these approaches (particularly the work of Pierre Bourdieu) have come into greater prominence as a way of defending stratification analysis from the incursions of postmodernism. In the second tradition – known as relational or interaction approaches – the concept of social distance refers to closeness in social interactions.

> According to an interaction notion of social distance, low distances should be assigned between individuals or groups who are likely to be involved in such social interactions as living near each other, seeing each other socially, intermarriage, having friends or relatives in the other group, moving from one group to the other, or merely approving of each other. High distances should be assigned where such social interactions are unlikely.
>
> (McFarland and Brown 1973: 227)

In structural approaches, groups are defined as socially distant if they are very *different* to each other (in terms of class, gender, or race categories), in relational approaches groups are defined as socially distant if they rarely *associate* with each other. Groups can be very different (belonging to different class or racial categories) but can still be socially close if they engage in friendship and sexual partnership on a regular basis. The pattern of social relationships between categories (how similar their social behaviour is) is used to map the relative social distance between all the various categories.

Although they are less well known, relational accounts of social distance have a long history. One early approach, by Bogardus (1925), emphasises *subjective* social distance, and refers to the social approval for various social groups, as measured by the level of intimacy (neighbourliness, friendship, marriage, and so on) that respondents would find acceptable with individuals from different national, ethnic and religious groups. The urban sociologist Robert E. Park used the concept of social distance to describe the crowded urban neighbourhoods of Chicago in the early twentieth century, where different racial, ethnic and class groups lived in close physical proximity, rubbing up against each other in the normal course of their working and community lives. However:

> Amongst the dense, diverse and transient populations of large and rapidly growing cities, one could no longer presume social affiliations and relationships from the mere fact of propinquity. People might live alongside each other, cheek by jowl, but the social distance separating them could still be a chasm of class, ethnic, occupational and age differences, a 'mosaic of little worlds that touch but do not interpenetrate'.
>
> (Amit and Rapport 2002: 42–43)

These early perspectives have given way to modern accounts which look at the patterning of social relationships to determine the stratification order (Blau 1977: 32). These approaches identify a 'social space of relationships' by empirically mapping relations of proximity. Such approaches use the patterning of actual social relationships (either of relations of intimacy, or through similar relations to cultural lifestyle) to identify the ordered (and stratified) nature of social life. The most famous approach in this tradition, that of Bourdieu (1984 [1979]), argues that people living the same cultural lifestyles occupy the same location in social space. He places groups with similar tastes close to each other in the space, whilst groups with very different tastes are more distant. Bourdieu focuses on lifestyle, but sees lifestyle emerging from processes of social interaction and differential association, since those who interact socially tend to be similar in terms of lifestyle (Prandy 1999a: 229). Other approaches, such as that of the Cambridge Stratification Group, have focused more directly on interaction patterns (such as friendship and marriage) (Stewart *et al.* 1980). The idea behind such approaches is that looking at patterns of intimate social interaction allows us to conceptualise 'social distance' in terms of both the gap that separates people with dissimilar social and cultural relations, and also the proximity of those with similar social and cultural relationships (Bottero and Prandy 2003).

So if the usual approach to stratification is to define a structure of groups and then look at the relations between them, relational approaches reverse this method, and use patterned social relations to determine the nature of the stratification order. Differential association is seen as a way of defining distances within a social space. If social interaction occurs frequently between categories they are socially close to one another, if social interaction is infrequent between them then they are socially distant.

Underlying such approaches is the notion that 'structure' isn't something that determines people's choices, rather 'structure' is better understood as consisting of the (patterned) choices that people do in fact make. Of course, all accounts of structural forces accept that the 'social structure' is really only the sum of the relations between individuals, but there is always a problem in specifying which dimensions of difference and inequality constitute 'structure'. Rather than establishing a structure of positions and then looking at the nature of social relations within it, relational approaches look at how the range of different valued resources (social, cultural and economic) and dimensions of inequality *combine* within practical social relations to create ranked social groupings. Such approaches make no division between the economic and the social aspects of stratification, and cultural lifestyle is not seen as an effect of structure, but rather is one of the means by which stratification position is constituted. Such accounts therefore attempt to reconnect difference and inequality.

This is possible because of the way in which social similarity (along many dimensions of difference) structures social networks, so that 'contact between similar people occurs at a higher rate than among dissimilar people' (McPherson *et al.* 2001: 416). This of course reconnects structural accounts (which see social distance in terms of degrees of difference along categories of class, race, ethnicity, etc.) and relational accounts (which see social distance in terms of infrequent interaction) because people who interact socially also tend to be socially similar. This means that 'distance in terms of social characteristics translates into network distance' (McPherson *et al.* 2001: 416).

> Similarity breeds connection. This principle – the homophily principle – structures network ties of every type, including marriage, friendship, work, advice, support, information transfer, exchange, co-membership, and other types of relationship. The result is that people's personal networks are homogenous with regard to many sociodemographic, behavioural, and intrapersonal characteristics. . . . Ties between non-similar individuals also dissolve at a higher rate, which sets the stage for the formation of niches (localized positions) within social space.
>
> (McPherson *et al.* 2001: 415)

We all sit at the centre of a spider's web of relationships, in which we connect to a range of different sorts of people, directly and indirectly. These individual webs build up into very complex *networks* of relations, in which some people are closely connected, whilst others are more distant. However, social characteristics (class, gender, race, etc.) are systematically embedded in these social networks, so that the people closest to us also tend to be socially similar to us, along a range of characteristics.

A series of relational approaches to stratification have therefore shown that differential association is crucial as both an effect and also a cause of stratification. Social network approaches to stratification demonstrate that the network of social relationships and affiliations within each individual sits affects their access to resources and opportunities (Lin 1999). Put simply, often our opportunities in life depend as much on *who* we know, as on what we know. And because our networks are strongly affected by differential association and social similarity, overall they create a pattern of highly unequal social relations. In relational approaches, stratification resides in the network of people's social relations, which structure differential access to resources, information, people and places in ways which help to organise unequal class and status relations. But such networks are not 'structures', since they are simply patterned social relations (but are no less constraining and structuring, for all that). Stratification networks are highly differentiated, yet at the same time also highly ordered.

This book explores these different ways of understanding stratification, and shows the impact of thinking about stratification in terms of differential association and social distance. It shows how our most personal choices (of sexual partners, friends, consumption items and lifestyle) are influenced by hierarchy and social difference, but are also crucial elements in how hierarchy and social difference are maintained. Because stratification is embedded in our everyday lives, all of us, in our daily routine activities, help to reproduce stratification.

The 'structure' of the book

The first part of the book, 'Foundations', looks at how different models of stratification have emerged historically, through the popular imagination and in the early accounts of the classical sociologists.

Chapter 2, 'Images of inequality', explores how descriptions of inequality are also social claims: about our relations with unequal others, and the relative worth of different social groups. The social order can be mapped and divided in various ways, and different 'pictures' of inequality have emerged from the claims and struggles of unequally placed groups. However, whilst the social pictures we draw upon are related to our own social identity and to the alliances (and oppositions) in which we are engaged, social imagery is no simple reflection of social location. Imagery shifts and the same people often draw upon different images depending upon the point (and the connections) that they wish to make. This raises a fundamental question about the relationship between social identity and social location or, more simply, between where we stand in the world and how we see ourselves, and others, which is a recurring theme of the book.

This is certainly a preoccupation of the classical sociological theories of stratification, introduced in Chapter 3, 'Founding ideas'. Emerging as a major area of academic analysis in the nineteenth century, the classical sociologists moved beyond the simple social pictures of the popular imagination to map patterns of inequality. These 'foundational' accounts established key themes which continue to be central to contemporary stratification theory. However, as Chapter 4, 'Sins of the fathers', shows, the classical foundations left an ambiguous and divided inheritance, creating an unravelling legacy of problems for later writers. The classical authors struggled with the 'duality' of social life, in thinking about the relationship between individuals and the wider social arrangements in which they live, and these problems have led to a fracturing of subsequent social analysis. The problems centre around the binary divisions which have bedevilled social analysis: between structure and action, the individual and society, the economic and the social, inequality and difference. The classical authors attempted to explain social life as both externally constraining and also the product of individual actions, but it is often argued that they failed in this attempt, emphasising one side of the equation at the expense of the other, developing unbalanced explanations of social life. Later work has tried to recombine the insights of the classical authors in an attempt to resolve these difficulties, but such attempts to theorise the *relationship* between structure and action, economic and social, have been unstable, with a tendency to collapse back into one term of the equation. Because of this legacy, stratification theory has increasingly emerged as a discipline focused on the structural, economic sphere, and has had difficulty accounting for symbolic, social divisions (such as issues of race, gender, and cultural identity). Such 'social' divisions have been studied as areas of social life quite separate from conventional stratification.

Stratification refers to hierarchically organised social relationships, and so entails the analysis of structured social inequality in *all* its aspects: economic, social and cultural. However, stratification has been dominated by work focusing on economic inequality. Chapter 5, 'Name, rank and number', examines the rise of class analysis, and the criticisms that class analysis has become increasingly specialised and restricted in focus. The narrowing aim of conventional stratification research can be seen by comparison to early 'community studies' approaches, which looked at economic resources, cultural activities, networks and social cliques, and reputation, as a linked set of stratified interpersonal social relations. However, these approaches have been eclipsed by more abstract, quantitative traditions with a tighter focus on the labour market as the arena of structural stratification, which influences – to a greater or lesser extent – the lives of the people who pass through it. The task of contemporary class analysis has been the exploration of patterned inequalities in life-chances, whilst neglecting issues of cultural identity and lifestyle. In recent years class has been accused of being of diminishing relevance as a source of social identity, and attention has shifted to social divisions, with an apparently tangential relationship to economic relations, which are more straightforwardly self-conscious and 'claimed' forms of identification (such as race, ethnicity or gender).

The founding accounts of conventional stratification analysis have provided an important legacy of theory and research, but key conceptual divisions within them have led to a fractured modern inheritance. The second part of the book, 'Deconstructions', looks at these divisions, showing how many contemporary writers now see the areas under-explored by conventional analysis (gender, ethnicity, the cultural and the subjective) as more important areas of social life. This has led to claims that stratification analysis is outdated and increasingly irrelevant. Chapters 6 and 7 focus on the emergence of these claims in response to problems of theorising race and gender, within the 'structural' and 'economic' models of conventional stratification theory. Chapter 6, 'Racialised relations', explores how early accounts of racial divisions saw them as a form of 'cultural' difference (based on community, tradition and religion), but struggled to explain racial difference as a form of material inequality. Later accounts presented racial divisions as unequal power relations, but struggled to avoid reducing 'race' to a by-product of economic structures and class inequalities. The divisions between racial groups clearly extend beyond their economic differences and, rejecting the 'economic reductionism' of materialist accounts, there has been a return to analysing 'race' as a form of cultural difference.

A similar set of problems is identified in Chapter 7, 'A woman's place', which shows that accounts of gender have struggled to locate gender difference as both materially situated and as discursively constructed, and to reconcile gender, race and ethnicity as both relations of differences and as relations of inequality. However, this partly arises out of the weaknesses of conventional understandings of stratification (understood as primarily economic, objective, orderly systems of external determination). Gender, race and ethnicity have increasingly been seen as divisions which undermine economic class identities and groupings, and which call into question conventional structural theories of identity. These chapters look at how the emphasis on newer social divisions has undermined the very idea of structural forces or cohesive social groups, giving rise to a new emphasis on fragmentation and fluidity in social arrangements.

These arguments have been carried to the very heart of class analysis by critics who suggest that social change has led to a 'fragmentation of stratification', amid the increasing importance of consumption, status and lifestyle as markers of identity. Chapter 8, 'Culture and anarchy', looks at arguments that material inequality no longer shapes our social identities as it once did. For some writers, the 'decline' of class is part of a general fragmentation and individualisation of social life. These attacks – and the 'cultural turn' within sociology – have resulted in a waning interest in stratification. However, class theorists have rallied by calling for a broadening of the scope of class analysis to address issues of cultural identity, gender, race and ethnicity. In rejecting both arguments of the 'death of class', and the increasingly minimalist positions of class traditionalists, a newer generation of stratification theorist has transformed the scope and analytical framework of class analysis: inflating 'class' to include social and cultural formations, reconfiguring the causal model that has underpinned class analysis, and moving beyond the notion of distinct class identities or groups, focusing instead on individualised hierarchical differentiation.

Part 3 of the book, 'Re-orderings', looks at how this model of stratification helps illuminate a range of social relations, rebutting postmodern claims of chaotic disorder in social experience, and showing how ordinary, everyday life is an essential aspect reproducing stratification. Chapter 9, 'Social space', introduces approaches to stratification which emphasise the fused cultural and social aspects of hierarchy, using a model of social distance and social interaction within a social space. The chapter shows how exploring relationships of social *closeness* – patterns of friendship and partnership, social and cultural similarity and contiguity – allows us to see which groups interact at a distance, or in terms of dissimilarity. The extent and consequences of stratification conceived in terms of differential association are explored in Chapter 10, 'Someone like me', which shows how our most personal social relationships are deeply embedded within relations of hierarchical differentiation. This chapter explores how our choices of friendship networks and sociability, neighbourhood and association, and our use of culture and style to 'mark' ourselves and to 'mark off' others, are all affected by hierarchy. But what this means is that the ordinary routines of social life – going to school or work, hanging out with friends, spending time with family – all reflect and help to reproduce differences in social position and resources.

Chapter 11, 'Hierarchy makes you sick', explores the health consequences of social hierarchies, looking not only at the 'health gap' between rich and poor, but also showing how a relatively worse position – at every level of the hierarchy – is associated with worse ill health, even when statistically controlling for factors associated with inequality (such as poverty, bad nutrition, etc.). Social position continues to be important for health even when a society's living standards are high, and it has been argued that it is not just the absolute level of our material resources that affect our health, but also our position relative to others. The chapter introduces 'psychosocial' theories which suggest that high levels of hierarchy influence social cohesion, and feelings of social control, empowerment and self-worth, and it is this which also affects our health. It also shows how lifestyle differences bound up with differential association help to maintain health differences between groups.

Chapter 12, 'Movements in space', looks at social movement across social distances and at the consequences of movement, for those who move and for those who are left behind. The study of 'social mobility' has long been a cornerstone of class analysis because of the evidence it presents on the potential formation of classes and the openness of society. However, information on the *amount* of social movement needs to be balanced by an account of the meaning of such movements for the individuals concerned. In fact, movement is so widespread, that any view of stratification as the straightforward inheritance of social location must be rejected. Because social movement is so common it has meant that large numbers of individuals have seen their positions improve in relation to their parents'. In addition, these widespread patterns of social movement have occurred within the context of rising standards of living, and more affluent consumption-based lifestyles. So whilst the less advantaged have improved their position over time, the opportunities for the more advantaged have also improved, and at about the same rate, meaning that differentials between them have been maintained.

This raises the issue of social boundaries in the stratification order. For although differential patterns of movement clearly do amount to substantial and enduring inequality, because this consists of unequal patterns of movement (rather than in attachment to fixed and unequal positions), there is a question of how such inequalities are perceived by the people concerned. Once stratification is conceived as a structuring of movement (rather than movement within a structure) there are major questions about how social distance creates boundaries between groups, and why people draw the lines that they do, in some places and not others? Chapter 13, '"Us" and "them"', looks at how – and where – such divisions have been drawn by exploring debates about the underclass, and classed and racialised identities. Researchers have often sought to discover social gulfs – to find the gaps in people's social relations and experience – which might explain the fissures in people's perceptions of each other. The problem, however, is that there do not seem to be sharp breaks in the relations, lifestyles, or even in the social prospects of unequal groups. The chapter explores the difficulty of establishing clear-cut boundaries, and shows how relations of social distance (where there is relatively little social interaction or shared cultural tastes between people) can be the basis for group divisions and exclusionary boundaries to emerge, but also how – because of the differentiated nature of the social order – such boundaries may be ill-defined or shifting. However, it is important to trace out the links between social identities, and practical social relations, rather than see the formation of identities as somehow arbitrary, or as a simple act of will.

The concluding chapter, 'Reproducing hierarchy', draws together the strands of the analysis to look at arguments that hierarchy not only affects everyday relationships, but is also routinely reproduced by ordinary actions (such as marriage, friendship, consumption choices, etc.). The analysis explores the ways in which hierarchy emerges as an unintended consequence, or by-product, of routine social relationships, and the consequences of such a model on how we understand the relations between inequality and difference, the structuring of social action, and the role of agency and values in the reproduction of inequality.

2   Images of inequality

When people describe their unequal worlds, they are often engaged in making claims about the relative worth of different groups, and the fairness (or otherwise) of social arrangements. All accounts of hierarchy contain 'images of inequality', social pictures which classify, categorise and grade the members of society: making statements about similarity or difference, generating distinctions of social worth, establishing our own social position relative to others. These are politically loaded descriptions, and the images we draw partly depend on our own social location, our attitudes and relations towards social unequals, and the agenda (and alliances) that we are pursuing.

Popular accounts draw upon common 'social pictures' of stratification: simplified models of how resources are distributed between groups, and of how those unequal groups relate to each other. This chapter looks at the images of inequality which have emerged in historical popular debates, and how different models have been used by groups to locate themselves (and others) within a hierarchically ordered social space. It explores how representations of social distance emerge from claims and struggles between unequally placed individuals, and can act to reinforce social distance by helping to create stereotyped and negative depictions of unequals.

Social pictures

David Cannadine sees three basic and enduring models with which people attempt to 'make sense of the unequal social worlds they have inhabited': 'the hierarchical view of society as a seamless web; the triadic version with upper, middle and lower collective groups; and the dichotomous, adversarial picture, where society is sundered between "us" and "them"' (1998: 19–20). These three models make different assumptions about the nature of inequality.

Hierarchical models picture inequality as layered ranks with each succeeding layer slightly better off than the rest. Such 'ladder' images of inequality, with small distinctions between each layer, do not convey a sense of major divisions within a society; and are often related to claims of a moral or divine basis to inequality. The 'Great Chain of Being', a common image of the social order in the early modern period, imagined society as a hierarchy of finely graded social ranks, 'from the senseless clod to the brightest genius of human kind' (wrote Soame Jenyns in 1782; quoted in Cannadine 1998: 27), in which:

> A well-ordered sequence of ranks and degrees in human society was deemed part of a divinely ordained hierarchy that embraced the whole of creation. [. . .] It offered a model of an interlinked society, in which all components had an allotted role, of equal importance to the grand design but not necessarily of equal power, wealth or prominence in terrestrial terms.
>
> (Corfield 1991: 103–104)

In the Chain all 'degrees' of people had a pre-assigned social position – a hierarchy ordained by God. Sir John Fortescue, writing in the 1400s, described inequality as the divine law of nature:

> God created as many different kinds of things as he did creatures, so that there is no creature which does not differ in some respect from all other creatures and by which it is in some respect superior or inferior to all the rest. So that from the highest angel down to the lowest of his kind there is absolutely not found an angel that has not a superior and an inferior; nor from man down to the meanest worm is there any creature which is not in some respect superior to one creature and inferior to another.
>
> (quoted in Tillyard 1963 [1943]: 39)

This image 'contained no connotations of collective social categories or shared group identities, still less of deeply rooted social antagonisms: using this model of society, and putting men into classes, literally meant classifying them individually according to the prestige of their social rank' (Cannadine 1998: 27). Hierarchical models thus contain the notion of functional interdependence, in which all the parts contribute harmoniously to the whole.

The Chain of Being was a formal social picture, used by scholars and the powerful; however, 'for everyday purposes . . . people appeared to have employed a much simpler, cruder, and more effective vocabulary . . . the language of "sorts"' (Wrightson 1991: 44–45). This was a dichotomous conception of society, 'us' against 'them':

> Unlike the vocabulary of degrees, it was a language pregnant with conflict, aligning the 'richer' against the 'poorer', the 'better' against the 'meaner', 'vulgar', 'common', 'ruder', or 'inferior' sorts . . . it was a language of dissociation, usually employed by those who identified themselves with the 'better' sort of people and stigmatized those whom they excluded from that company with a barrage of pejorative adjectives.
>
> (Wrightson 1991: 47)

Images of 'us and them' shift, depending on the social identity of the person who claims to be 'one of us'. In radical models 'us' is taken to refer to the virtuous, hard-working common people, exploited by the decadent and corrupt 'them' of the aristocratic elite. The eighteenth-century radical, Tom Paine, denounced aristocratic government in a classic 'us and them' dichotomy: 'There are two distinct classes of men in the nation, those who pay taxes, and those who receive and live upon the taxes' (quoted in Corfield 1991: 119). However, dichotomous conceptions are also used by higher-level groups to mark off their social superiority from those below (the 'vulgar', the 'rabble', 'bumpkins', the 'great unwashed', the 'swinish multitude'), 'stressing the natural and legitimate right of a certain minority to lead' (Giddens 1981: 74). In distinguishing 'us' from 'them', people are making a case about the justice of their own situation, but 'us and them' is a flexible tool:

> those who embraced the binary model of society, and who were on the side of 'the people' invariably stressed that they were virtuous, respectable, independent, and predominantly consisted of 'the middling sorts' [. . .] And it often provoked the predictable counter-assertion from those at the top that, on the contrary, it was they who were virtuous, decent, public-spirited and high-minded, compared with whom 'the people' were merely 'the rabble', or 'the mob', drawn from the 'lower sorts'.
>
> (Cannadine 1998: 33)

Triadic models of inequality see society as divided into three unequal groupings: with upper, middle and lower (or 'inferior') classes or orders, or, more simply: the rich, the poor and those in between. This viewpoint tends to take a favourable view of the middle class, distinguished both from the upper class (characterised as self-serving, corrupt and decadent), and the lower class (characterised as disorderly, drunken, and of low conduct). The 'middling sort' is set up, in contrast, as honest, hard-working, sober, industrious, and thrifty: the class 'who bridged the gap between those above and those beneath' who are 'moderately placed between the two extremes, thereby holding society together' (Cannadine 1998: 30). The use of the third term, 'the middling sort', emerged during the English Civil War, as a way of defending the social basis of parliamentarian support against royalist accusations that the king's opponents were drawn from 'the rabble' (Wrightson 1991: 49).

Unlike the binary, dichotomous, model which tends to cleave society into two opposed camps, the triadic model offers more permutations for cooperation (and conflict) – as the middle class may ally or distinguish itself from both its inferiors and superiors. Because of the positive way in which the middle class is characterised in the triadic model, it was often employed by middle-class individuals themselves (Cannadine 1998). However, it could also be used to disparage the 'middling sort'. From the viewpoint of the upper class, the middle class might be characterised as ill-bred upstarts who had made their money in trade, and forced their way into the landed classes in the vain hope of acquiring high social standing. Alternatively, from the viewpoint of the working class, the middle class might have been seen as people who gave themselves 'airs and graces' and thought themselves better than 'ordinary, decent folk'.

Images and interventions

Such images contain different assumptions about the nature of stratification, and social relations within an unequal society. However, as David Cannadine argues, whilst three very distinct models have dominated discourses of inequality, 'for much of the time they have easily co-existed in people's minds and imaginations' (1998: 166). People tend to slip from one model to another, collapsing the gradations of a hierarchy into two or three groups, or sub-dividing the categories of group models to then form a hierarchy. The binary distinctions of 'us and them' are easily converted into hierarchies, by talking about the 'working class*es*' or the 'higher order*s*' in the plural; or transmuted into triadic models by the use of such terms as 'upper working class'. Such shifts are common. Historians of social imagery argue that the language of social description is fluid, and ambiguous, with frequent mixing of models (Himmelfarb 1983; Crossick 1991; Corfield 1991). It is the imprecision of the imagery which is so useful, allowing people to move 'easily and effortlessly from one model to another, recasting their vision of British society to suit their particular purpose and perspective' (Cannadine 1998: 20).

Indeed, the language of *class* has been used 'for describing all three models of contemporary British society: class as hierarchy; class as "upper", "middle" and "lower"; and class as just "upper" and "lower"' (Cannadine 1998: 20). Ossowski (1963) sees the term 'class' (and, by implication, other imagery of inequality) as metaphorical, enabling people to draw on shared understandings, but with a very wide range of possible meanings or allusions. The ambiguity of such terms gives them their political appeal – rather than identifying an objective social structure or precise social group, the language(s) of 'class', 'orders', 'us and them', or the 'people', reflect the shifting politics for which they were used (Crossick 1991). It is important to remember that images of inequality are 'no mere reflection of external reality, but an intervention within it', they are not simple attempts to describe the world, but are 'at the same time an attempt to shape it' (Crossick 1991: 152, 153).

If people shift from one social picture to another, it is because they wish to highlight different aspects of inequality, to forge particular alliances. Images of inequality are *claims*: about whose interests align with each other; who should be grouped together as virtuous or decent members of society; who deserve power or are unjustly excluded. They are campaigning strategies in the competition over social recognition, power, and resources which help form the structure of inequality. This means we have to look closely at how images of inequality have been used in attempts to justify or transform social arrangements. The social descriptions that people use to represent patterns of inequality also contain assumptions about *why* inequality exists and how rewards and resources come to be allocated in an unequal fashion.

From divine order to social inequality

In pre-industrial society, inequality was regarded as natural, and the fact of inequality was not questioned. To refuse to accept your station in life was to go against God, threatening chaos and discord in the universe. This understanding of inequality as divinely ordained, and so inevitable, began to change during the eighteenth century, as Enlightenment thinkers (such as Voltaire and Rousseau) questioned the institutions of their society, arguing that practices based on superstition, or unthinking tradition, should be replaced by rational principles. Central to these ideas was a belief in the possibility of social progress, which was based on a notion of a universal human nature, in which all individuals are equal, and share the same capacities for reason. But this meant that Enlightenment thinkers had to distinguish between natural inequality and social inequality. For Rousseau:

> the first I call natural or physical because it is established by nature, and consists of differences in age, health, strength of body and qualities of the mind and soul; the second we might call moral or political equality because it derives from a sort of convention, and is established, or at least authorised, by the consent of men. This latter inequality consists of the different privileges which some enjoy to the prejudice of others – such as their being richer, more honoured, more powerful than others, and even getting themselves obeyed by others.
>
> (Rousseau 1984 [1770]: 77)

Prior to the Enlightenment, hierarchical pictures of inequality contained little sense of either social change or conflict. Hierarchy was functional, with all the unequal elements contributing differently to the orderly operation of a Godly society. Inequality was not regarded as the result of social conflict, nor was it seen as inevitable that unequal outcomes should give rise to conflict. It was assumed that a well-ordered society was inevitably unequal, and that people accepted their lot in life.

For Enlightenment thinkers, however, inequality was the product of corruption, unearned privilege and patronage, and unfair restrictions on liberty. The emergence of social, rather than divine, explanations of inequality can be linked to the increasing use of binary and triadic 'class' pictures of the social order. These images lent themselves more readily to a view of social inequality as changeable, emerging from the corrupt, disreputable, and self-interested nature of the various social classes: 'The Great Chain did not envisage structural contest or competition within society. "Rank struggle" would have been a contradiction in terms. "Class", on the other hand, contained a potential for change, whether by cooperation, competition or conflict' (Corfield 1991: 114).

Historians used to argue that hierarchical accounts of inequality were replaced by class accounts, reflecting the move to a 'class' society. The orthodox position, as Cannadine notes, was that 'the Industrial and French Revolutions together transformed social structures and social relations, destroying the old, individualistic, hierarchical world of ranks, orders and degrees, and bringing about an entirely new social system, based on collective and conflicting identities, which resulted from the making of the working class and the making of the middle class' (1998: 57). This model now seems 'too over-determined', in part because we cannot treat shifts in imagery as an unproblematic reflection of social structure. In fact, hierarchical imagery and language persisted alongside the newer 'class' models, 'the significant difference was that these visions of society were now more consciously and contentiously politicised than before' (Cannadine 1998: 58). However, social transformations did lead to the social order being 'described, debated and discussed with unprecedented urgency, intensity and anxiety' (ibid.: 60) and to the increasing use of the language of 'class', but this did not represent the emergence of a class society out of a hierarchical one, nor even the eclipse of hierarchical images of society. In fact, the period gave rise to new hierarchical images of social inequality, with society pictured as a biological ranking.

The modern period thus saw new ideas emerging about inequality as the product of political oppression, vested interests and social conflict. If inequality was socially produced it could also be removed by social action, by rationally reforming the institutions of society. The eighteenth century saw the development of greater political and economic liberty (with the transition from the bonded feudal serf to the formally free wage worker of market capitalism, and the granting of greater civil rights), as well as the up-rooting of aristocratic hierarchies, with the American and French revolutions. However, social inequality did not disappear: 'At the time when the founding fathers of the American republic were declaring all men to be equal, they denied that same equality to millions of black slaves' (Malik 1996: 38). This stubborn persistence of deep social inequalities in the face of reform or revolution gave rise to new and more sophisticated accounts of the natural or biological basis of inequality.

Natural inequality

The egalitarian ideals of the radical and democratic movements of the eighteenth and nineteenth centuries gave rise to a curious paradox: the emergence of theories which stressed the biological basis of social inequality. Unequal relations were now seen as the result of natural differences creating biological superiors and inferiors, with the same model used to characterise inequalities between classes, racial and ethnic groups, and also between women and men.

> Naturalistic views hold that the capabilities and constraints of human bodies define individuals, and generate the social, political and economic relations which characterize national and international standards of living. Inequalities in material wealth, legal rights and political power are not socially constructed, contingent and reversible, but are given, or at the very least legitimized, by the determining power of the biological body.
>
> (Shilling 1993: 44)

Such theories are a form of 'biological determinism: the notion that people at the bottom are constructed of intrinsically inferior material (poor brains, bad genes, or whatever)' (Gould 1984: 31). Inequalities were increasingly recast as racial differences, innate and biological. It is important to remember that, in the nineteenth century, 'race' was a loose term 'used of any ethnic, national, religious, or cultural group, and sometimes in a biological sense' (Himmelfarb 1983: 324). 'For the Victorians race was a description of social distinctions, not colour differences. Indeed . . . the view of non-Europeans as an inferior race was but an extension of the already existing view of the working class at home' (Malik 1996: 91). However, '"Race", even in its loose Victorian usage, signified a distinctive physical, mental and moral constitution, a "disposition", "propensity", or "physiognomy" which was "natural" and "innate"' (Himmelfarb 1983: 329). Scientific arguments were used to suggest that differences between races, classes and sexes arose from inherited, inborn distinctions.

The discourse of 'race' was used to explain the persistence of inequality in societies which had apparently opened up their social institutions to competition on the basis of merit and achievement. Nineteenth-century thinkers drew on Darwin's theories of natural selection to explain social inequality. Evolutionary theory 'had resurrected a graduated chain of development from ape to man and it was possible to combine this with theories of inherent difference and inferiority' (Jones 1980: 141). *Social* Darwinists, such as Francis Galton, believed the structure of society reflected the principle of the survival of the fittest: 'It follows that the men who achieve eminence, and those who are naturally capable, are, to a large extent, identical' (Galton 1892 [1869]: 38).

There were several scientific versions of this theme: the notion of polygeny (the idea that the black, white and Asian 'races' were separate species of unequal development); the notions of racial and sexual evolution (the idea that 'non-white races' and women represented earlier stages of evolutionary development); and the notion of recapitulation and degeneration (the idea that 'non-white races', the poor, criminals and prostitutes were evolutionary 'throwbacks' to more 'primitive' types of humanity).

> What Darwinism did was to allow racial science to create a dynamic concept of hierarchy. The pre-Enlightenment Great Chain of Being was static – the result of divine ordination. Indeed it was anti-evolutionist. In appropriating the concept of evolution by natural selection racial science married the idea of a fixed hierarchy with that of progress – those at the top of the hierarchy arrived there on merit, because of natural superiority in the struggle for existence.
>
> (Malik 1996: 91)

However, Social Darwinism, which stressed evolutionary selection, was also closely related to the discipline of eugenics, which argued that intellectual and cultural characteristics are determined by heredity. This raised the possibility that biological inferiority not only placed the poor at the bottom of social hierarchies, but also condemned their children and grandchildren to the same fate. Hereditarian theories of inequality give a static and pessimistic view of a permanent and self-reproducing group of social and biological inferiors.

The problem with biological approaches to social inequality is that they tend to be inherently conservative (Gould 1984). For the biological determinist, whatever state of hierarchy, or degree of inequality, that currently obtains is given in our physical natures. In the nineteenth century such arguments were used to oppose the end of black slavery, the education of women, and the extension of the vote to the working classes, all because of the supposed 'natural' inferiority of these groups. Eugenicist models raised serious questions about the capacity of social reform to affect the extent and nature of inequality. Eugenicists, including many social reformers, argued that preventing the lower orders from breeding was the most progressive way of dealing with poverty:

> The superficially sympathetic man flings a coin to a beggar; the more deeply sympathetic man builds an almshouse for him so he need no longer beg; but perhaps most radically sympathetic of all is the man who arranges that the beggar should not be born.
>
> (Havelock Ellis, quoted in Malik 1996: 102)

Eugenicists proposed policies to increase middle-class fertility, but also to discourage child-rearing by the 'worst stocks'. The most extreme versions argued that the socially 'unfit' should be compulsorily sterilised, and state policies of sterilisation of epileptics, the blind and deaf, the mentally 'unfit', unwed mothers, prostitutes, and criminals, were pursued in many Western countries; in some, as recently as the 1970s.

Theories of biological degeneration contain very negative depictions of those at the bottom of social hierarchies and reflect powerful fears of the working classes – the 'mob', 'masses' or 'crowd', and their degraded and unruly nature. Eugenicists believed the working class was out-breeding the middle classes, and so 'Eugenics was able to integrate two aspects of late nineteenth century culture – fear of working class disorder and discontent and the rise in their numbers' (Jones 1980: 103). Eugenics 'meant the preservation and increase of the middle class' (ibid.: 113), and was related to middle-class concerns about the growing influence of the working classes on society through democratic enfranchisement and collective political organisation. Assumptions of biological degeneration were often used to express pessimism about social progress, and opposition to democratic and egalitarian ideals. For example, the historian, Hippolyte Taine, argued that democrats found their support among 'the human cast-offs who infest the capitals, amongst the epileptic and scrophulous rabble, heirs of a vicious blood, who . . . bring *degenerescence* into civilisation, imbecility, the distraction of an enfeebled temperament, retrograde instincts and an ill-constructed brain' (quoted in Pick 1989: 68). Given such views of the lower classes, hierarchy was seen as essential to the stability of society.

Moral capacity

Models of the natural basis of inequality held such a negative physiological view of the poor that the privileges of the middle and upper classes seemed both biologically inevitable and morally justified. Such views 'proclaimed the fitness of the capitalist class to rule over the working classes and of the white race to rule over the black . . . not in the name of divine will or aristocratic reaction but of science and progress' (Malik 1996: 100).

Biological arguments easily shifted into moral arguments, partly because social and moral propensities were also seen as hereditary traits. Accounts of the poor as physically unfit were closely linked to accounts of their moral degeneration. The Eugenics Education Society argued, in 1911, that pauperism was the result of 'inherent defects which are hereditarily transmitted' including:

> drunkenness, theft, persistent laziness, a tubercule diathesis, mental deficiency, deliberate moral obliquity, or general weakness of character manifested by want of initiative or energy or stamina and an inclination to attribute their misfortune to their own too great generosity or too great goodness, and generally to bad luck. Inquiry into nature of the bad luck or too great generosity usually resolved the matter into one of stupidity or folly on the part of the complaining victim.
>
> (quoted in Jones 1980: 114)

In linking inequality to the moral capacities of individuals, the problem was not poverty but the personal characteristics of the poor. Even social reformers characterised the poor as less than fully human: drunken, criminal, work-shy. Poverty resulted from 'demoralisation'. Henry Mayhew, a nineteenth-century journalist, attempted to inform his readers of the shocking nature of Victorian poverty, by describing the 'street folk' of London. But these tinkers, beggars, street sellers and performers were 'socially, morally and perhaps even physically considered', seen as a distinct race from settled citizens, with Mayhew characterising them as 'wanderers', 'vagabonds' and 'nomads' (Mayhew 1968 [1861] I: 1). Mayhew believed they had a distinctive 'moral physiognomy', in which poverty and a moral lack of responsibility were inextricably linked.

Mayhew campaigned against poverty, but his description of the poor implies that their poverty is their own fault. He described street folk as sharing 'a greater development of the animal than of the intellectual or moral nature', 'high cheekbones and protruding jaws', 'lax ideas about property', 'general improvidence', 'repugnance to continuous labour', 'disregard of female honour', 'love of cruelty', 'pugnacity', 'an utter want of religion', 'extreme animal fondness for the Opposite sex' (quoted in Himmelfarb 1983: 325). Mayhew saw this moral degradation as the inevitable result of privation and insecurity (that is *caused by* poverty), but also as too deeply rooted to be susceptible to reform (and so, a *cause of* poverty) (1968 [1861] I: 326–329). Immoral habits (and so poverty) were handed down from generation to generation: 'imbibing the habits and the morals of the gutters almost with their mother's milk . . . the child without training goes back to its parent stock the vagabond savage' (Mayhew 1968 [1861] I: 320).

Even Karl Marx, the revolutionary socialist, identified a group amongst the poor – the lumpen proletariat – which he sharply differentiated from the proletariat by their immorality. This group, the 'scum of the demoralised elements of all classes', was 'a recruiting ground for thieves and criminals of all kinds living on the crumbs of society' and would never be capable of improvement or revolutionary action (quoted in Himmelfarb 1983: 391).

Moral views of inequality identified a group whose social and moral habits were the cause of their poverty. This distances the problem of poverty, representing it as a problem not of society, but as a feature of groups who stand apart from society. Such viewpoints were common in the eighteenth and nineteenth centuries, even amongst social reformers, and contained highly emotive and condemnatory views of the poor. The poor were the outcasts of society, the 'other' in 'us and them' images of inequality. However, in categorising and labelling 'others' we also serve to define ourselves.

Images of the Other

In picturing others as inferior to 'us', people are implicitly describing themselves as the reverse: superior (respectable, moral and civilised). Negative views of the lower orders partly reflect the social distance that exists between different classes, and the way in which inequality can create a sense of social gulfs – with the poor literally seen as a separate and lower form of life. Descriptions of the poor as 'other' emphasise this sense of a dramatic social fissure. For example, in 1845 the Victorian politician Disraeli described the rich and poor as:

> Two nations between whom there is no intercourse and no sympathy; who are ignorant of each other's habits, thoughts and feelings, as if they were dwellers in different zones or inhabitants of different planets; who are formed by different breeding, are fed by different food, are ordered by different manners, and are not governed by the same laws.
>
> (Disraeli 1969 [1845]: 67)

Even Mayhew saw himself as a 'traveller in the undiscovered country of the poor' reporting on a people about whom less was known than 'the most distant tribes of the earth' (quoted in Himmelfarb 1983: 332).

Negative views of the 'Other' express the social distance that actually exists between unequal groups, and their lack of understanding of, or sympathy for, each other. Lack of social contact can lead to an exaggerated sense of difference, in which gross stereotypes and misconceptions can emerge. The philosopher Alfred Schütz has pointed out that our sense of others partly depends on whether our knowledge of them is achieved directly – through concrete, immediate, face-to-face interaction – or indirectly – through the stereotypes and public representations we draw upon to account for people we have never met, and are unlikely to meet.

An interesting example of this is given by the community sociologists Davis, Gardner and Gardner, in their classic investigation of perceptions of the social class structure of a small Mississippi town in the 1930s (Davis *et al.* 1941).

Upper-upper class   *Lower-upper class*

'old aristocracy'	UU	'old aristocracy'
'aristocracy' but not 'old'	LU	**'aristocracy' but not 'old'**
'nice, respectable people'	UM	'nice, respectable people'
'good people but "nobody"'	LM	'good people but "nobody"'
'po' whites'	UU	'po' whites'
	LL	

Upper-middle class   *Lower-middle class*

'society'	'old families'	UU	'old aristocracy'	'broken-down aristocracy'
	'society' but not old families	LU		
'people who should be upper class'		UM	'people who think they are somebody'	
'people who don't have much money'		LM	**'we poor folk'**	
'no 'count lot'		UU	'people poorer than us'	
		LL	'no 'count lot'	

Upper-lower class   *Lower-lower class*

'society' or the 'folks with money'	UU	'society' or the 'folks with money'
	LU	
	UM	
'people who are up because they have a little money'	LM	'way-high-ups' but not 'society'
'poor but honest folk'	UL	'snobs trying to push up'
'shiftless people'	LL	**'people just as good as anybody'**

Figure 2.1 The different social perspectives of the social classes
Source: Adapted from Davis *et al.* 1941: 65
Note: Descriptions of own class in bold.

Figure 2.1 shows people at different levels of the social hierarchy producing different class 'maps'. People at the top made finer social distinctions between people in the top half of their community, whilst crudely lumping together people at the bottom; whilst the people at the bottom tended not to see fine distinctions at the top, but were concerned to establish the decent and ordinary nature of people at their level. We can see this as partly the result of cognitive distance: that is, we have a better understanding of people (and differences) that we are familiar with at our own social level, with our knowledge becoming vaguer, the further we move from our own position. However, we can also see something else going on here – the attempt of groups to establish their own worth, particularly in the face of the negative perceptions of others.

The view from where I stand

Some commentators suggest that how we view inequality partly depends on our own social location *within* a structure of inequality. It has already been established that binary, 'us and them' images of inequality have been used more by working-class groups, whereas three class models are drawn upon by middle-class individuals, and hierarchical models of functional inter-dependence are often used by the elite. Historical evidence on this is necessarily impressionistic, but the notion that social imagery is itself socially differentiated has been widely investigated in the present day. The classic statement, by David Lockwood, argues that our social consciousness is influenced by our immediate social context, so that people's 'perceptions of the larger society will vary according to their experiences of social inequality in the smaller societies in which they live out their daily lives' (1975: 16). Lockwood suggests different work and community relationships led to different images of inequality. So, within the working class, the occupational and community solidarity of traditional, proletarian workers (such as miners) leads to a power, 'us and them' model of society; privatised factory workers with low group affiliations and instrumental attitudes to work have a hierarchical 'money' model of society, whilst agricultural workers' individual face-to-face relations with paternalistic employers result in a 'deferential' image of a functional status hierarchy of social 'betters'.

However, subsequent research has revealed that people's images of inequality do not appear to be so clear-cut, and workers are not consistent in their attitudes, with 'different kinds of views . . . "wheeled on" in different situations' (Savage 2000: 27). Cannadine also argues that different models are often used to describe the *same* social structures by the *same* speaker, with slippage from one model to another within the same accounts (Cannadine 1998). Historical evidence shows that whilst working-class groups have drawn upon 'us and them' models of inequality, they have also at various times aligned themselves with the middle classes (in a claim to represent the virtuous 'people' against a corrupt aristocracy); distanced themselves from the 'comfortable' middle classes (in claims to be the hard-working, under-privileged 'masses'); and attempted to distinguish themselves as the 'respectable' working class (distinct from the disreputable 'roughs' at the very bottom). The model used partly depends on what point the speaker is trying to make (and in relationship to whom).

Just as images of inequality are never simple descriptions of social structure, so we cannot just 'read off' an individual's social imagery from their social position. In a six-nation study of subjective class identification, Kelley and Evans found that a 'middling' self-image 'holds at all levels of the objective stratification hierarchy. Rich and poor, well-educated and poorly educated, high status and low status, all see themselves near the middle of the class system, rarely at the top or bottom' (Kelley and Evans 1995: 166). Their conclusion: 'in all societies . . . people's subjective class identification is with the middle classes or just below, with very few people identifying with the top or bottom classes'. So despite big differences in people's social position, most people located themselves as 'average' or 'middling' in the social order. But this doesn't mean that hierarchical social location has *no* effect on images of the social order. In fact, quite the contrary. As Kelley and Evans argue, claims to being 'ordinary' or 'middling' are strongly related to the hierarchical nature of general social networks. The reason is that 'reference-group forces restrict the subjective arena to a narrow range in the middle of the class hierarchy' (Kelley and Evans 1995: 166). 'Reference-group forces' refers to the way in which '[i]ndividuals assess their class location in light of the distribution of education, occupations, authority, and income among the people around them. As a consequence, even very high status people see many others above themselves, and very low status people see others even lower. [. . .] This tendency to perceive everyone as similar to oneself is reinforced by the tendency for one's spouse and friends to be similar to oneself in education, occupational status and income' (Evans *et al.* 1992: 465).

Our picture of the overall social hierarchy is affected by our position within it, but in a complicated way. Because we tend to see our own social milieu as 'typical' and 'middling', high-status people tend to exaggerate the size of the higher classes and minimise the size of the lower classes, resulting in a relatively egalitarian image of society, whilst low-status people exaggerate the size of the lower classes, resulting in a more elitist image (Evans *et al.* 1992: 477). This means that public debates over issues of equality and the politicisation of images of society are likely to emerge from, and affect, unequally located groups differently.

Moral and physical disgust

Images of the Other don't just reflect social distance – they are also ammunition in strategies attempting to create or reinforce social distance. It is not just a lack of interaction with and social knowledge of social inferiors which provides stereotyped images of the 'Other'. Even when there is close contact between groups, social inferiors are often still marked out as physically and morally distinct. Here images of the 'Other' emerge out of the attempt to regulate close contact between groups who were not interacting on the basis of equality.

Domestic servants in nineteenth-century middle-class households, for example, lived cheek by jowl with their employers, caring for their most intimate needs, but a rigid social gulf existed between them, and was reflected in the way in which servants were viewed. It was important to ensure that when social contact did occur between inferiors and superiors that it did so in a managed way. The many ritual humiliations of the servant's place served to mark out the social distance between master and servant, and stressed the social superiority of the master. Servants were expected to kneel to remove their employers' boots, to avoid eye contact, and even to turn their faces to the wall when unexpectedly encountering their employer – so as to avoid the master or mistress the embarrassment of having to acknowledge a social inferior. Servants were associated with degradation, reflecting the hard and dirty nature of their job (for example, cleaning fires and emptying chamber pots), but also as a metaphor of their social humiliation. Servants were often stripped of their own names and given a generic servant's name, and the most common – 'John Thomas' and 'Mary Anne' – both became euphemisms for male and female genitals. Similarly, the servants' corridor in the household was called the 'back passage': a euphemism for the anus (Davidoff *et al.* 1999: 170–173). With servants characterised in this degraded and humiliating way, the difference between servant and master, however close their physical proximity, was clearly marked.

The marking of inequality through the use of 'images of the other' does not only occur between the privileged and their servants, however. It can also be observed between groups in very similar social positions, as people attempt to avoid the negative collective labels attributed to them by invoking finer social distinctions. Certain sections of the working classes, for example, attempted to distance themselves from stigmatised images of the poor as 'rough', disreputable, and debased: with skilled workers making claims to be a 'labour aristocracy', whilst unskilled workers made a distinction between the 'respectable' poor (to which they belonged) and the morally reprehensible 'residuum'. 'Respectability' entailed a neat and clean appearance, and a tidy house, which were seen as the signs of regularity, hard work, good manners, and self-reliance:

> such moral concepts were an important part of the social reality for people of all classes and persuasions. 'Respectability', for example – the public analogue of private morality – was not confined to the middle classes or the 'labour aristocracy' but was just as much a fact of life for the poor. And the distinction between the 'respectable' and the 'rough' was even more critical at the lower rungs of society, where any misstep, any misfortune or imprudence, could be catastrophic.
>
> (Himmelfarb 1983: 399)

People attempted to maintain their own social value by establishing differences from social inferiors with negative social images. However, such distinctions are claims rather than clear-cut social divisions.

> Everyone knew the difference between 'rough' and 'respectable', but since the boundaries were not fixed they could be subjectively interpreted. Almost no-one saw themselves as not respectable. The factory girl whose bold and gaudy style made domestic servants look down on her as rough, saw herself as respectable so long as she observed the conventions of her group.
>
> (Davin 1996: 70)

It is unsurprising that people made such strenuous attempts to mark their social difference from the groups below them, because of the stigma which attached to those at the bottom of social hierarchies. As Himmelfarb notes, 'the same words – "residuum", "refuse", "offal" – were used to denote the sewage waste that constituted the sanitary problem and the human waste that constituted the social problem' (1983: 357). With social inferiors seen in such terms, it is no wonder that people shrank from being associated with them, to avoid the 'contamination' of their contact. For George Orwell, social barriers are powerfully reinforced by such feelings:

> That was what we were taught – *the lower classes smell*. And here, obviously, you are at an impassable barrier. For no feeling of like or dislike is quite so fundamental as a physical feeling. Race-hatred, religious hatred, differences of education or temperament, of intellect, even differences of moral code, can be got over; but physical repulsion cannot. [. . .] And in my childhood we *were* brought up to believe that they were dirty. Very early in life you acquired the idea that there was something subtly repulsive about a working-class body; you would not get nearer to it than you could help. You watched a great sweaty navvy walking down the road with his pick over his shoulder; you looked at his discoloured shirt and his corduroy trousers stiff with the dirt of a decade; you thought of those nests and layers of greasy rags below; and, under all; the unwashed body, brown all over (that was how I used to imagine it), with its strong, bacon-like reek. [. . .] And even 'lower class' people whom you knew to be quite clean – servants, for instance – were faintly unappetising. The smell of their sweat, the very texture of their skins, were mysteriously different from yours.
>
> (Orwell 1970 [1937]: 112–113)

Of course, in the nineteenth century the poor *were* less clean than their social superiors, but such stylised contrasts between clean and dirty were part of highly charged symbolic evocations of purity versus corruption, man versus beast. These are ideological constructions, not reflections of reality, and are often double-edged. Take the powerful feelings of repulsion expressed by those who saw 'interracial' sexual unions as dangerous. The assumption that 'races' were different species often led to claims that miscegenation ('racial interbreeding') would lead to the degeneration and declining fertility of the 'hybrid' offspring of such unions. In 1890, the evolutionary biologist E. D. Cope warned that the 'mixing of blood' would lead to the decline of (white) civilisation:

> With a few distinguished exceptions, the hybrid is not as good a race as the white, and in some respects it often falls below the black especially in the sturdy qualities that accompany vigorous physique. The highest race of man cannot afford to lose or even to compromise the advantages it has acquired by hundreds of centuries of toil and hardship, by mingling its blood with the lowest.
>
> (Cope, quoted in Young 1995: 117)

This was the dominant view in racial biology from the 1850s to the 1930s and in the USA, laws were passed in 40 states outlawing sex between different 'races', and were only declared unconstitutional in 1967. Similar laws were proposed for Britain in the 1920s (Young 1995: 18, 148).

However, the fears expressed about miscegenation by white writers reveal ambivalence and contradiction. It was claimed that there was an instinctive aversion between races, and their offspring would be infertile ('mulattos' referring to the sterile mule, offspring of horse and donkey). For Joseph Le Conte, writing in 1892, racial prejudice was 'an instinct necessary to preserve the blood purity of the higher race' (quoted in Hawkins 1997: 202). Similarly, Louis Agassiz, Harvard professor of zoology, wrote (before the abolition of slavery):

> The production of halfbreeds is as much a sin against nature, as incest in a civilised community is a sin against purity of character . . . the idea of amalgamation is most repugnant to my feelings, I hold it to be a perversion of every natural sentiment.
>
> (quoted in Young 1995: 149)

Yet the large numbers of children produced from inter-racial unions flew in the face of such theories. The claim of sterility could only be made by arguing that infertility (and degeneration) increased down the embarrassingly expanding generations. Even more of a problem was explaining why – if inter-racial sexual liaisons were so unnatural – so many took place. Accounts of miscegenation represented it as naturally repugnant yet also dwelt on the animalistic sensuality and bestial nature of the 'lesser races'. Such negative constructions are both a representation of social distance and a mechanism for maintaining it. Yet such strategies are also highly contradictory.

The characterisation of racial (and class) 'Others' as dark, dangerous, animalistic and forbidden also made them seem *more* sexual, so often more attractive rather than less. The nineteenth-century characterisation of working-class individuals as coarser, earthier, and more sensual was part of a middle-class discourse establishing their lower moral and physical worth, but it also played a part in making them seem more sexually adventurous, with many Victorian gentleman preying on the factory girls or female servants (seen as more 'saucy' or 'a bit of rough'). Of course, they never married them.

The images of hierarchy which we can see played out in such accounts present class and racial differences as illicitly and perversely attractive, but always within a context of *unequal* social relations. Sexual liaisons between social unequals could be contemplated, but never if they threatened to undo the hierarchy. 'Repugnant' miscegenation, for example, was normally characterised as black men defiling white womanhood. In the American South, a selective version of racial sexual segregation was brutally enforced, with black men at risk of being lynched for any suspicion of sexual impropriety with white women. Yet liaisons between white men and black women were frequent, and never subject to regulation. Such encounters were, again, almost always on terms of inequality, with black women suitable for illicit casual sexual encounters or as mistresses, but never for public viewing, as wives. The issue here, of course, is the intersection of class, racial and gender hierarchies. White women engaged in inter-racial liaisons were seen to be compromising their hierarchical advantage, whereas white men engaged in the same activity were simply reinforcing their position (and in many cases directly exploiting it to forcibly prey on black women who were in no position to refuse). So whilst 'distance' constructions which represented social inferiors as abhorrently 'Other' could lead to the perverse eroticisation of class and racial differences, they were also successful in keeping such liaisons as illicit, shameful, dangerous, and thus preventing *interaction on the basis of equality*.

Conclusion

Our sense of ourselves is partly formed by our sense of difference from other people, and how we represent ourselves in relation to 'others'. The nature of the 'others' we construct helps to define ourselves, or rather, ourselves as we *wish* to be seen. 'Us and them' images of society often produce very negative accounts of 'them', whilst hierarchical views of society can lead to highly emotive descriptions of those at the very bottom of society, who are seen as 'other' – not part of the society which contains 'us'.

The fact that degraded pictures of the 'Other' recur in images of inequality has sometimes been explained through psychoanalytic theories which argue that the establishment of a sense of 'self' occurs through the emotionally charged distinction of 'others', or through theories of group formation which see group unity and security formed out of the erection of symbolic boundaries which exclude despised others (J. Young 2003). However, the problem with such theorisation

> is that it tends to depict such othering or demonization as a cultural universal, a product of ever-present problems of human psychology or group formation. Instead we need to locate such a process in time and social context, we need to specify who is more likely to demonise, to explain the context of the labels applied to outsiders, to understand the mechanisms of exclusion and describe the likely outcome of such othering. In short, we need to know the when, why, who, what, how and whether of demonization.
>
> (J. Young 2003: 456)

This chapter has explored images of inequality and how they relate to the social location and social conflicts of the people who use such images in their daily lives. The social pictures of inequality that we draw upon are a way of taking stock of our location relative to others, and must also be seen as ammunition in the claims and struggles between unequally placed individuals. Never simply representations, such images also act to reinforce social distance by helping to create stereotyped and negative depictions of unequals. The maps people draw of (unequal) social relations are linked, albeit in complicated ways, to the patterns of association and disassociation between unequally placed groups. Sharply demarcated images of 'us and them' do emerge as part of the claims people make about their own worth relative to others, but such imagery constantly shifts, and often dissolves into finer social distinctions and gradations.

Subsequent chapters will explore more closely the relationship between social location, and the divisions and distinctions that people consciously (and unconsciously) make in establishing a sense of relative social identity. We now move to look at academic attempts to describe and explain stratification. These generate more complex images of inequality, but share many of the themes of popular accounts offering, in their own way, maps of the stratification order.

3 Founding ideas

Early accounts of social hierarchy saw inequality as natural and thus self-evident. But, by the eighteenth century, social transformations had led to growing disagreement about the nature of that social order, and an increasing awareness of the possibility – and desirability – of change. Social explanations of inequality emerged out of the collapse of notions of divine order in which 'social life and moral life were no longer inextricable dimensions of God's plan for humanity, but became objects of rational reflection and, in some cases, arenas for human design and intervention' (Shilling and Mellor 2001: 2). Part of this shift can be linked to the Enlightenment philosophers' suggestions that inequality resulted from the corruption of the powerful. However, the persistence of inequality in the face of political reform meant the re-emergence of accounts stressing the natural inequalities between people. Popular accounts saw inequality arising from a division between better and worse, good or bad, sorts of people (with the identity of these social betters depending on the standpoint of the observer), ideas which hardened into nineteenth-century scientific accounts of the biological inferiority of social subordinates. These views were rejected by the early sociologists, whose account of the socially constructed nature of inequality helped establish sociology as a distinct discipline. For them, social inequality was no mere reflection of natural difference, since the inequalities between people vary, and reflect the wider social groups, and time and place, in which people must live. The times – and the people who live within them – change. This chapter examines the contribution of these 'founding fathers' of sociology.

For these sociologists, the dramatic transformations of modernity revealed the mutable, inherently social nature of inequality. The classical writers explored how stratification emerges from the struggles between different groups, but they stressed that such struggles must be understood in terms of the wider social context within which they occur. Inequality does not just result from one group imposing its will upon another, as people's ability to act depends on external social forces which constrain them in various ways. People may not be fully conscious of these constraints, or of how their actions affect others; and it is the job of the sociologist to place individual behaviour in a broader social landscape, to reveal the taken-for-granted meanings underlying behaviour, and to uncover the orderly social patterns beneath the chaos of modern life.

Inequality became an area for academic study and theoretical analysis in the late nineteenth and early twentieth centuries, as classical sociology established stratification as a contingent, socially constructed arena. This chapter explores four key writers: the 'classical' figures, Marx, Weber and Durkheim, and a later author, Talcott Parsons, whose ideas provided the foundations for modern theoretical accounts of stratification and social distance. In their different ways, they generated the key divisions which dominate current thinking. Marx saw stratification in terms of a class society, founded upon economic relations of class conflict. Weber placed much greater emphasis on stratification as the intersection of different spheres of power, but shared Marx's stress on stratification as a process of conflict and struggle. For Durkheim and Parsons, however, the order and stability of unequal societies had to be explained, which meant that stratification reflected shared beliefs about the value of different positions and qualities.

Class society: Karl Marx

Karl Marx (1818–1883) was not a sociologist but a political activist – he argued that we study the world in order to change it – however, his views influenced both academic analysis and political practice. Marx saw inequality deriving from economic divisions, but was less interested in the distribution of income and wealth, than in the economic relations (to the dominant way of organising production) which generated that distribution. Marx argued that subsistence – the need to make a living – was the most basic aspect of life which affects the whole structure of society. This *materialist* position argues that the material conditions of our life determine how we think and act, since

> the economic structure of society, [is] the real foundation on which rises a legal and political superstructure and to which correspond definite forms of social consciousness. The mode of production of material life conditions the social, political and intellectual life process in general. It is not the consciousness of men that determines their being, but on the contrary, their social being that determines their consciousness.
>
> (Marx 1859/2000: 425)

As Figure 3.1 shows Marx distinguished an economic base underpinning social relations, with developments in the economic base explaining social change. If this economic underpinning could be grasped then unequal societies could be transformed. But how exactly does the economic base affect social behaviour and explain historical change? Marx's theory argued that developments in the economic base give rise to conflict and inequality in the social system, leading to crises and, ultimately, to revolution and the creation of a new system.

Marx believed all previous social systems had been based on the exploitation of the many by the few. Under capitalism, for example, the proletariat, the great mass of ordinary wage labourers, are exploited by the bourgeoisie, the factory owners. The source of profit for the employer rests in extracting surplus value

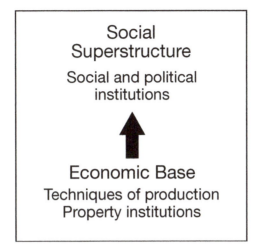

Figure 3.1 Marx's model of base and superstructure

(ensuring that the value of what the employer pays for the labour of the worker is less than the value of the goods the worker produces). For Marx, this is exploitative and leads to class conflict. As the economic system of capitalism develops, strains and tensions emerge. Together, exploitation and contradictions in economic relations lead to a revolutionary change of the system. Marx believed the same pattern had occurred in previous social systems (such as feudalism, ancient society, etc.).

Class-in-itself and class-for-itself

The motor of this social change is class conflict. Classes are economic categories, defined by their shared production relations and economic interests. Because the economic system is based on exploitation, the members of different classes have opposed economic interests and an antagonistic relationship. It is in the interests of the capitalist to force the wages of the proletariat down to the lowest possible level to ensure high profits. Employers have no choice but to behave in this way, if – in the cut-throat competition of capitalism – they want their businesses to survive. Of course people do not always realise where their true interests lie, nor do they always act upon them. Marx calls the people who share a class position a 'class-in-itself', by which he means that they fall into the same objective economic category but may never be a cohesive social group, capable of common action. However, under certain conditions a 'class-in-itself' turns into a 'class-for-itself': as members become aware of their shared interests, and act in a concerted way to achieve the same goals. If the proletariat, which shares the same objective, economic interests, becomes a 'class-for-itself', it becomes capable of collective revolutionary action.

Marx believed the economic development of capitalism was creating the conditions for the proletariat to become a 'class-for-itself'. Revolution does not occur because people are poor and oppressed alone (indeed, it may not be the most oppressed who revolt) but rather out of a new economic order emerging which creates the conditions for class consciousness. Marx argued the economic conditions for socialism were growing in embryo within capitalism. Capitalism, Marx argued, produces a massive productive surplus, which meant that for the first time a decent standard of living was possible for all. Yet under capitalist relations of production (private property ownership and the exploitation of wage labour) a tiny minority had untold wealth, whilst the majority lived in poverty. For Marx, this was because the relations of production (private property) are at odds with the forces of production (industrial factory production creating enough surplus to improve everybody's standard of living).

The competitive nature of capitalist property relations undermines capitalist development from within, leading to crises of production. This is because the pressure for profits causes both a downward pressure on wages and the over-production of goods. Effectively, the poverty of the workers undercuts the market for the goods, meaning that they cannot be sold, leading to economic slumps. Marx argued that capitalist relations of production (private property) were holding back economic development and, eventually, this would lead to their overthrow.

Marx identified processes modifying the capitalist system from within, pre-paring for its transcendence by socialism. He saw a creeping socialisation of market forces, in the monopolisation of capital (the erosion of market competition) and the development of 'joint-stock' companies, that is, companies owned by share-holders ('capitalism without the capitalist'). For Marx this signified a trans-formation of the principles upon which capitalism is based (the individualistic pursuit of profit in the free market). Since capitalist business was increasingly centralised and concentrated, and run by managers rather than owners, Marx argued that this was only a short step from socialism, where production is com-munally owned and run for the benefit of all. All that is required in this model is for new socialist relations of production – the abolition of private property – to be declared, bringing the forces and relations of production into alignment once again. To achieve this the masses must seize control of the means of production and run them to the advantage of all.

Marx believed it was possible to transform a capitalist system, based on private property, into a system of socialism, with common ownership, because capitalism has already transformed itself 'from within'. Unlike previous trans-formations this will not involve the replacement of one elite by another. Instead, with the advent of socialism both private property and class antagonisms come to an end. However, there still have to be *agents* of this change who will take action to bring about socialism. Marx also sets out a model by which revolutionary action emerges.

As Figure 3.2 shows Marx's account of revolution sees social identity and consciousness developing out of economic relationships. A series of economic transformations result in the working class becoming a 'class-for-itself'. The

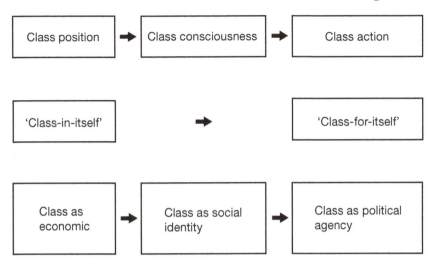

Figure 3.2 The Marxist model of class formation

intensely competitive nature of capitalism results in a 'boom and bust' economy, in which intermediate groups (the self-employed, small-business owners) are wiped out by economic crises and competition from big business. They 'sink down' into the proletariat, becoming wage labourers. Capital becomes concentrated into a few huge businesses which dominate the market, undermining competition. The capitalist pursuit for profit eliminates skill divisions amongst the working class, as all workers are reduced to the cheapest form of unskilled labour. The proletariat are homogenised, and also concentrated in larger and larger working units, whilst intermediate classes which 'complicate' the class system disappear. A polarised gap develops between an increasingly large working class, trapped in shared conditions of miserable poverty, working alongside each other in large factories; and a tiny group of capitalists, running a handful of enormous monopolistic enterprises. 'Society as a whole is more and more splitting up into two great hostile camps, into two great classes, directly facing each other: Bourgeoisie and Proletariat' (Marx and Engels 1848/2000: 246).

These processes make the conditions of capitalist exploitation increasingly clear and transparent and, Marx believed, will lead to the working class becoming aware of their shared identity. The working class are transformed into a self-aware social group with the ability to act in their own interests. Marx's model is of developments in *economic* relationships bringing about *social* change. The simplification of economic relationships leads to people in the same economic position forming a distinct social identity and acting collectively. This is the classic Marxist formulation: class position leads to class consciousness leads to class action.

Marx's theory makes concrete predictions of social trends. However, time has not been kind to Marx and has revealed problems with his model. Class polarisation and pauperisation has not occurred, as rising affluence and the expansion of middle-order groups has complicated not simplified the class structure; and class consciousness when it has emerged has done so in a very limited, intermittent and generally non-revolutionary fashion. This has cast doubt on Marx's *economic* account of social relations.

Spheres of power: Max Weber

The work of Max Weber (1864–1920) has had the greatest influence on modern accounts of stratification, partly because his theories explore the gaps which the passage of time has revealed in Marx's account. Although Weber accepts that economic divisions are an important element of inequality, he also sees other sources of social power giving rise to a very different picture of stratification. Weber, like Marx, believed that capitalist society was best defined as a 'class' society, but had a different vision of 'classes' as economic categories conferring similar life-chances. By 'life-chances', Weber means differences in opportunities, lifestyles and general prospects.

Weber argues that people's life-chances are affected by property ownership, but emphasises that occupational skill divisions (amongst the property-less working and middle-level groups in the labour market) also affect their life-chances, creating differences in incomes and lifestyles, health and welfare. He therefore defines class in relation to the property *and* labour markets, leading to a more finely graded view of class based on occupation. This more differentiated model opens the possibility of a large number of 'classes' – as many as there are different locations in the market. However, Weber resolves this diversity of possible market classes by distinguishing 'class situations' from 'social class'. A social class 'makes up the totality of those class situations within which individual and generational mobility is easy and typical' (1978 [1922]: 302).

Social classes are clumps of occupations with similar life-chances, linked by common mobility patterns. If people routinely move from white-collar work into managerial work in the course of their careers, those jobs belong in the same social class (because the people in them will have shared life-chances); however, if such movements are unusual, then those jobs belong in different social classes. Weber doesn't actually measure mobility patterns but, instead, using his own judgement of mobility links in the labour market, he identifies four distinct social classes:

- 'classes privileged through property and education';
- technicians, specialists and lower-level management;
- the petty bourgeoisie (small shopkeepers, self-employed artisans, etc.); and
- the working class.

However, Weber sees social class as a potentially unstable basis for social group-ings (class-for-itself) since 'mobility among, and stability of, class positions differs greatly; hence the unity of a social class is highly variable' (1978 [1922]: 302).

For Weber, 'classes are not communities; they merely represent possible, and frequent, bases for social action' (1978 [1922]: 927). Marx believed that class position *would* lead to class consciousness and action (given certain tendencies in economic relations), Weber believed this *could* happen, but was only a contingent possibility:

> Associations of class members – class organisations – may arise on the basis of all . . . classes. However, this does not necessarily happen. . . . The mere differentiation of property classes is not 'dynamic', that is, it need not result in class struggles and revolutions.
>
> (Weber 1978 [1922]: 302–303)

Whilst people's objective economic class situation affects their life-chances, they need not be aware of this and may never band together to further their own interests. Because of this, Weber rejected Marx's prediction of class revolution. For Weber, economic position and social identity are not identical, so there can be no 'theory of history' based on economic class relations. This is partly because of the internally differentiated and unstable basis of social classes, but also because Weber believed there were other bases of association and group action which cross-cut economic interests and undermine the formation of 'class' organisations.

Class, status and party

As Figure 3.3 shows, for Weber, class is only one aspect of stratification. 'Status' and 'party' are distinct dimensions of inequality which – unlike class – *always* manifest as self-conscious social groups. Status is a phenomenon of the social order, and refers to the actual groupings of individuals: '*status groups* are normally groups', although 'often of an amorphous kind' (Weber 1978 [1922]: 932). As opposed to the economic determination of class, status is associated with evaluations of honour and prestige. The status situation of an individual refers to the judgements which other people make about their social esteem and which affect that individual's life-chances. We value many social characteristics other than economic resources, and these valued qualities can affect the power and influence that individuals have. Such value judgements 'may be connected with any quality shared by a plurality' (Weber 1978 [1922]: 932), such as education, ethnicity, religion, gender, or even physical beauty or strength.

Status groups are people who share the same status situation (groupings which arise on the basis of ethnicity, religion, etc.). Status groups are aware of their common position and of their difference from groups of a different status, since status honour 'always rests upon distance and exclusiveness' (Weber 1978 [1922]: 935). Status groups show their distinctiveness by following a particular lifestyle – dressing in a particular way, or living in particular areas – and also by placing restrictions on how others interact with them. There may be restrictions on the sorts of friends or sexual partners that people may have and, at its most extreme form, status groups are distinct 'castes' – who only marry and make friends with members of the same group.

Party: a third, and distinct, source of inequality, refers to any voluntary association which sets up an organisation to achieve certain policies or ends (such as political parties, or even sports or social clubs, with more mundane objectives). Parties aim at 'the acquisition of social "power", that is to say, toward influencing a communal action no matter what its content may be. . . . For party actions are always directed toward a goal which is striven for in a planned manner' (Weber 1948 [1922]: 194). Parties mobilise members and resources to achieve common goals, and membership gives individuals access to contacts, resources, and a collective organisation, increasing their ability to achieve their ends.

As Figure 3.4 (see p. 48) shows in this *multi-dimensional model* of stratification the three orders of stratification are linked (with high status related to economic privilege and political power, for example), but are governed by different principles so do not straightforwardly map onto each other. An individual's stratification position depends on their *overall* location in all three orders, but their class, status and party positions may not be identical. So 'classes and status groups frequently overlap' (Weber 1978 [1922]: 937), but there are often discrepancies between the two. Status and class operate under different principles, with status concerned with 'honour' whilst class position is determined by the market. So success in the market may not receive a high-status evaluation: it may be seen as dishonourable or 'vulgar'. Weber suggests high-status groups will not allow high ranking on the basis of wealth *alone*, since this undermines the importance of status characteristics central to status stratification. He gives the example of the newly rich 'parvenus' who are not accepted into 'high society' because their education and lifestyle lack the necessary status, but whose *children* are accepted, once they have acquired the right schooling, accent, manners and style of life.

Someone may be of high status even if their economic position is weak (the impoverished aristocrat) or have low social honour even though their economic

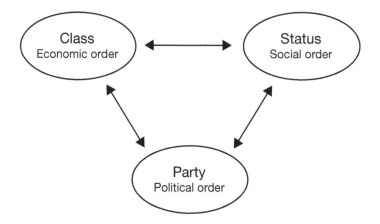

Figure 3.3 Weber's multi-dimensional model of stratification

position is high (the 'slum' landlord, or the arms dealer). Because status operates as an independent dimension to stratification, related, but not reducible to economic class, an individual's overall position can be improved by acquiring high-status characteristics (the right education or social connections) even if their economic position is poor. In the same way, party as a third source of power is related but irreducible to status and class. Parties may form on a class or status basis; however, this is not always so. 'Left-wing' political groups can have middle-class members, and the members of sporting or social clubs (the Rotarians or Freemasons) often come from diverse status and class backgrounds. Indeed, party members from humble class or status position use the contacts and resources of such clubs to help them access greater power and influence than they could otherwise achieve.

Table 3.1 Spheres of power: class, status and party

Class	Economic order	Economically determined market situation	Economic interests affecting life-chances – a possible basis for action	May give rise to social groups
Status	Social order	Social prestige or honour (lifestyle and consumption)	Social judgements of taste and prestige as basis of association and social distance – may be linked to class – but need not be	Actual groupings
Party	Political order	Political parties, clubs	Acquisition of power – may be linked to class and/or status – but need not be	Actual groupings

In this model, resources in one dimension of stratification can be converted into resources in the other two. As a general rule, high (or low) class, status and party position *tend* to go together: the rich tend to be powerful, the powerful to be wealthy, and access to high-status social circles tends to accompany both. But, as Table 3.1 shows, different principles of organisation govern the economic, social and political orders, so high status, or high party, position can sometimes be achieved without great economic resources (and vice versa). This is quite different from Marx's model, where social position and power derive from an individual's economic relationships. For Weber, the question of which dimension of stratification (class, status or party) matters most is historically contingent.

Social closure

Weber's concept of status entails the notion of distinct social groups, who reinforce their internal solidarity by drawing distinct boundaries (in intimate interaction and lifestyle) between those who fall inside and outside the group.

> Status relations revolve around the identification with a specific 'reference group' and its distinctive style of life. Identification as a 'member' of a particular reference group is the basis for exclusive networks of interaction within which social actions are geared to stressing the distinctiveness of its style of life. These actions involve attitudes of acceptance and rejection, recognition and denial, or approval and disapproval by others in terms of their conformity to the preferred style of life.
>
> (Scott 1996: 31)

This is similar to the distinct boundaries, communal relations and collective agenda that Marx envisaged for a 'class-for-itself', but extended to the status order. For Weber, status is always 'status-for-itself' – based on self-aware, collective groups – and this is bound up with *social closure*, the erection of social boundaries in order to restrict access to valued resources. This is Marx's model of class conflict extended to a general account of the struggles of groups over a diversity of scarce resources. 'He presents status groups as collectivities that mobilise their members for competitive struggles of all kinds, material and symbolic' (Parkin 1982: 97).

Social closure occurs as groups seek to increase the advantages of their situation by monopolising resources to their group and restricting access to outsiders. In the economic order principles of open competition are 'closed off' by groups who monopolise sections of the market, controlling the sale of goods or services. Occupational groups often monopolise the provision of a service or skill, preventing others from practising the trade unless they join the group by acquiring the right training, professional qualification or licence (which the group controls). And closure strategies extend to the political order, in bureaucracies, as positions become monopolised by specialists, who use 'expert knowledge' to establish their own power-base quite independent of economic resources (although they may use their position to command economic resources). Closure takes place in all three dimensions of stratification, and the resources fought over can be cultural resources, prestige, valued lifestyle items, acceptance into social circles, or legal, political and citizenship rights.

Monopolisation, for Weber, is a form of 'domination' (1978 [1922]: 943) and its purpose is 'always the closure of social and economic opportunities to *outsiders*' (1978 [1922]: 342). But to do this successfully groups have to have some form of economic, political or social advantage over the people they exclude. Social closure is therefore a process of *subordination within a hierarchy*, in which a group closes off 'opportunities to another group of outsiders beneath it which it defines as inferior and ineligible' (Murphy 1988: 8). Of course, excluded groups may also engage in social closure against the groups below *them*, so closure can occur between groups all the way down a hierarchy. Also, closure may provoke a 'corresponding reaction on the part of those against whom it is directed' (Weber 1978 [1922]: 342), as excluded groups erect defensive barriers of distance and exclusiveness upwards – restricting contact with the groups which demean and exclude them. An alternative reaction to closure is 'usurpation', in which subordinates try to usurp the privileges of those above by imitating their style of life to gain access to the group, and by distancing themselves from groups at the same level (in order to appear more select and 'exclusive').

Weber's description of social closure (like Marx's theory of class conflict) sees stratification as the competitive struggle over scarce resources. However, Weber sees closure occurring in the social and political orders, in addition to the economic, with group conflict over a variety of resources, 'ideal and material' (1948: 190). Social closure is also expressed through a range of social actions, such as restrictions on friendship and intermarriage, by distinct consumption patterns and leisure activities; and through the 'symbolic degradation of "outsiders"' by 'residential segregation and physical expulsion' (Scott 1996: 31). 'In all these ways, groups are able to establish the distance and exclusiveness from others that allows them to assert and defend their claims to social honour' (Scott 1996: 32).

Weber's complex, multi-dimensional account provides flexible, 'history proof' conceptual tools for analysing a wide array of stratification arrangements. The current popularity of Weberian models lies in their adaptability. But, like Marx, Weber concentrates on stratification as the outcome of social conflict, in which self-interested groups struggle over valued resources. Whilst this is clearly a very important aspect of stratification processes, it leaves a fundamental question unanswered. That is, why is it that unequal societies founded on the clash of interests are actually so stable, orderly, and – comparatively – free from conflict?

Social ordering: Durkheim and Parsons

Marx and Weber are concerned with the divisions of interest and conflict between *the groups* in a society. However, another way of thinking about stratification emerges in Emile Durkheim's emphasis on the relationship between *the individual and society*, and how diverse individual interests are reconciled. Instead of focusing on group conflict he addresses 'the problem of order' (Parsons 1968 [1937]: 89), the integration of individuals into a larger social whole. This emphasis gives a very different account of stratification from that of Marx and Weber. Durkheim's own writings on stratification are brief, but the extension of his ideas by Talcott Parsons can be seen as a 'third tradition' in stratification, normative functionalism.

Durkheim (1858–1917) characterises modern societies in terms of their specialised occupational division of labour. The focus is less on inequality and conflict than on the functional integration that such specialisation brings. This is not because Durkheim thought divisions of interest were unimportant, but because he believed that economic divisions were always organised within a wider moral framework.

> He was as realistic as Marx in seeing that the economic structures were the dominant structures of industrial society, but he also believed that they had to be more than just economic if they were to produce social stability and integration.
>
> (Thompson 1982: 74)

Durkheim recognised that the labour market was an arena of conflict. However, he did not believe that stratification could be explained in terms of conflict alone, because he believed that order based on coercion always breaks down. If stratification is a stable ordering this is because groups *accept* their position within a hierarchy:

> although the vanquished can for a while resign themselves to an enforced domination, they do not concur in it, and consequently such a state can provide no stable equilibrium. Truces imposed by violence are never anything other than temporary, and pacify no one. Men's passions are only stayed by a moral presence they respect.
>
> (Durkheim 1984 [1892]: xxxii–xxxiii)

Durkheim argues that highly differentiated societies are integrated through a common value system of shared beliefs and norms. In modern societies, people are increasingly differentiated, with distinct functions, skills and different aptitudes. However, these increasing differences act to bring people together, creating interdependence and 'organic solidarity'. Durkheim saw society as a moral ordering, arguing that social institutions are a 'crystallisation' of a society's moral rules and shared values. Durkheim therefore believed stratification was also a *moral classification*, a status ordering reflecting shared values about the worth of different positions:

> at every moment of history there is a dim perception, in the moral consciousness of societies, of the respective values of different services, the relative reward due to each, and the consequent degree of comfort appropriate on the average to workers in each occupation. The different functions are graded in public opinion and a certain coefficient of well-being assigned to each, according to its place in the social hierarchy.
>
> (Durkheim 1972 [1897]: 249)

As Lockwood argues, 'Durkheim takes it for granted that in normal circumstances the status hierarchy is generally regarded as legitimate because it is based on a broad consensus about the "respective value of different social services"' (Lockwood 1992: 76). Because people share the same evaluation of the worth of different social positions, the unequal rewards of such positions are also generally accepted. Weber, by contrast, saw 'status' ranking in terms of the competitive struggle over resources, rather than any general agreement about the rewards due to different positions. In Weber's account, labour-market inequality is a result of conflict between sectional interest groups rather than the result of consensual moral rankings; certain groups are able to *impose* negative status rankings on subordinates, but this is a continual process of struggle, and is inherently unstable.

By contrast, Durkheim was interested in the stability of hierarchies, and argues that all forms of competition presuppose a shared moral framework.

Even economic competition (seen as the nakedly impersonal pursuit of economic interest by Weber and Marx) is governed by moral agreement by the parties in competition. People do engage in economic struggle, but they normally compete within certain agreed bounds (they honour contracts, and have standards of acceptable – and unacceptable – behaviour). For Durkheim, the stability of the stratification system rests not in coercion, but in the way in which such shared norms regulate ambition and competition.

> What is needed if social order is to reign is that the mass of men be contented with their lot. But what is needed for them to be content is not that they have more or less, but that they be convinced that they have no right to more.
>
> (Durkheim 1962: 242)

The wants and interests of particular groups are always socially regulated. That is, an individual's position in a hierarchical stratification system affects the level of demands they can legitimately make, and expect to receive. The claims for resources that groups make are always *relative* to their stratification position, rather than being completely unrestrained. So Durkheim saw the stratification system of a society as both 'the major structural embodiment of common values and beliefs and, more particularly, as major determinant of wants or interests' (Lockwood 1992: x).

> According to accepted ideas, for example, a certain way of living is considered the upper limit to which a workman may aspire in his efforts to improve his existence, and there is another limit below which he is not willingly permitted to fall unless he has seriously demeaned himself. [. . .] A genuine regimen exists, therefore, although not always legally formulated, which fixes with relative precision the maximum degree of ease of living to which each social class may legitimately aspire. Under this pressure, each in his sphere vaguely realises the extreme limit set to his ambitions and aspires to nothing beyond. [. . .] This relative limitation and the moderation it involves, make men contented with their lot while stimulating them moderately to improve it.
>
> (Durkheim 1972 [1897]: 249–250)

Durkheim points out that ambition is always relative, measured against the achievements and possessions of others, and that the sorts of comparisons we make depend on broader societal notions of fairness and equivalence. The moral regulation of wants and ambition is strictly contained within 'legitimate' bounds, maintaining the order of the status hierarchy. This means that the competition over economic resources, which Weber and Marx see in terms of conflict and power struggle alone, is also socially regulated, with ambitions and claims set relative to wider social notions of legitimacy and reference groups. For example, when occupational groups make pay claims, they tend to use the pay of other occupational groups, who are regarded as roughly equivalent in skill or productivity, as the yardstick for their claims. Thus the pay rise of one group tends to be repeated step-wise throughout the occupational structure, maintaining the rank ordering of groups (Routh 1980).

Durkheim believed conflict occurred if a society's moral regulation was disturbed. So industrial conflict was the result of the 'abnormal' or 'forced' division of labour:

> if the institution of class or caste sometimes gives rise to miserable squabbling instead of producing solidarity, it is because the distribution of social functions on which it rests does not correspond . . . to the distribution of natural abilities.
>
> (Durkheim 1984 [1892]: 311)

This is the result of 'external constraint' which prevents individuals from occupying positions 'commensurate to their abilities' (1984 [1892]: 312–313). If people cannot compete freely for positions (because of inequalities in wealth or access to education) then the division of labour is 'forced' and will not lead to solidarity. Durkheim argues that the stratification of positions cannot be seen as fair and legitimate if the competition for *allocation* to those positions is not free and fair. Of course, a fair basis to allocation is itself morally regulated and subject to change. Durkheim argues that, in the past, birth and lineage were the legitimate basis of allocation, whereas, in modern society, skills and qualifications are the socially legitimate criteria of entry to positions (that is, like Marx and Weber before him, he saw the labour market as the key arena of modern stratification).

However, the forced division of labour is not the only basis for social conflict. Durkheim also believed that if the structure of legitimate expectations (the moral classification) is disturbed, then disorder will result. Sudden shifts in a society, such as economic disasters or an abrupt growth in power and wealth, can upset the moral classification, leading to 'anomic declassification' in which there is a mismatch between (formerly) legitimate claims to reward and the actual opportunities open to groups.

> Some particular class especially favoured by the crisis is no longer resigned to its former lot, and, on the other hand, the examples of its greater good fortune arouse all sorts of jealousy below and around it. Appetites, not being controlled by public opinion, become disoriented, no longer recognise the limits proper to them. [. . .] The state of deregulation or anomie is thus further heightened by passions being less disciplined, precisely when they need disciplining. . . . All classes contend among themselves because no established classification any longer exists.
>
> (Durkheim 1972 [1897]: 253)

So conflict does not just emerge out of inequality, but through a destabilisation of the hierarchy of legitimate expectation. The moral classification, which sets levels of social equivalence and limits social ambition, is upset, leading to more intensive competition and conflict. This helps to explain a puzzling problem faced by Marx and Weber: if stratification is based around competition over resources, why is there not more conflict in society and why does it only emerge at certain times? For Durkheim, this is because ambition and competition are regulated and always relative to position in the hierarchy: conflict emerges when this regulation breaks down.

Normative integration

Talcott Parsons (1902–1979) also believed that a key element to the stable operations of a society are the norms which regulate people's behaviour. However, Parsons wanted to reconcile Durkheim's view of society as an external, constraining force with Weber's stress on the subjective motivations of individual action. For Parsons, the existence of shared rules and values allows people to know what is expected of them, and others, and to co-ordinate their actions in a predictable and orderly manner. Shared moral values channel the actor's behaviour towards socially approved goals.

For normative functionalists, individual actions become integrated with the values embedded in social structure in two ways. External sanctions (punishments and social pressure) enforce individual conformity with institutional arrangements. However, 'introjection' – where individuals internalise the values of the wider society – is more important. Through socialisation, individuals come to value the beliefs and behaviour of the society they live in, so that they choose to conform. Here the internalisation of socialised desires and beliefs means that the apparently self-interested actions of individual actors are, in fact, actions that reflect the goals of others as well.

In looking at inequality, Parsons is concerned with the *normative* character of such arrangements, that is with the shared values and expectations that they embody. Parsons's interest is in 'social stratification' which he defines as 'the differential ranking of the human individuals who compose a given social system and their treatment as superior and inferior relative to one another in certain socially important respects' (1954a [1940]: 69). Parsons sees the moral evaluation of others (through 'respect' and 'disapproval') as the 'central criterion of the ranking involved in stratification' (1954a [1940]: 70). So the hierarchy of positions is a status ranking, in which positions vary in their prestige and social honour. Whilst, for Weber, status stratification is ultimately a structure of power, for Parsons it is a structure of normative consensus. But on what basis are different social positions given a status evaluation? Parsons argues that we value a range of characteristics and resources, so individuals can be ranked on: kinship (family position); personal qualities (sex, age, personal beauty, intelligence); achievements (qualifications, skills); possessions; authority (the right to influence the action of others, held by virtue of holding particular offices or statuses, such as doctor or parent); and power (the ability to influence others in ways not institutionally sanctioned, that is, to get our own way regardless of others). 'The status of any given individual in the system of stratification in a society may be regarded as a resultant of the common valuations underlying the distribution of status to him in each of these six respects' (1954a [1940]: 76).

Parsons argues that societies vary according to which aspects are most valued. In traditional societies, 'ascribed' status is the most important element in stratification, and kinship is the key (but never the only) element determining an individual's ranking. In modern society, 'achieved' status is the dominant aspect in stratification, and 'achievement' but also 'personal qualities', 'authority' and 'possessions' (insofar as they are taken as evidence of achievement) are the central elements in the evaluation of status. For Parsons as for the other classical sociologists, this means that the labour market is the primary arena of stratification in modern societies.

Of course, these different sources of status raise the possibility that ranking on one basis (say possessions) may be inconsistent with ranking on another (such as power), since they use different criteria of evaluation. The different dimensions may not directly relate to each other, so it is difficult to establish overall status position. When comparing one person's power with another person's achievements we may not be able to establish whose status is higher (since we are not comparing like with like). However, Parsons believed that a mechanism of 'interlarding' (1954b [1953]) 'allows status in one dimension to be "translated" into status in other dimensions and so allows comparison of relative standing to be made' (Scott 1996: 109). Money and the mass media (which establish 'reputation') serve as 'translation' mechanisms, establishing the relative equivalence of different status rankings. These serve as generalised proxies of overall social standing across dimensions.

For Parsons, stratification results from general *agreement* about which positions to value more highly. The positions we most value are rewarded more highly.

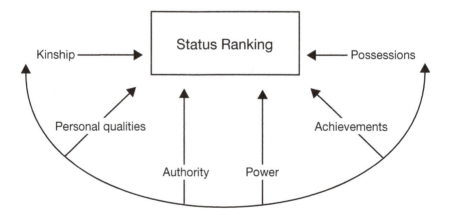

Figure 3.4 Stratification as status ranking

However, he recognises that the actual working out of stratification patterns is more complicated than this, since there is always 'an interplay [. . .] between moral patterns and the self-interested elements of motivation' (1954a [1940]: 73). People may not always agree with the general valuation of social positions, but

> if any given individual can be said to seek his own 'self-interest' in this sense, it follows that he can do so only by conforming in some degree to the institutionalized definition of the situation. But this in turn means that he must to a large degree be oriented to the scale of stratification. Thus his motivation almost certainly becomes focussed to a considerable extent on the attainment of 'distinction' or recognition by comparison with his fellows. This becomes a most important symbol, both to himself and to others, of the success or lack of success of his efforts in living up to his own and others' expectations in his attempts to conform with value patterns.
>
> (Parsons 1954a [1940]: 74)

People have little choice but to accept the general value placed on the different positions in a hierarchy. They may not like it, but – if they want to get on – they have to live with it and play by the rules.

Conclusion

This chapter sets out the basic elements of three very different models of stratification. The next chapter evaluates how the respective strengths and weaknesses of these 'foundational' accounts have influenced subsequent work. However, it is worth noting here that these strengths and weaknesses are intertwined. Their distinctive emphases (on the economic, on the multi-dimensional nature of inequality, and on the role of values) offer unique angles on stratification (a strength), but also channel analysis in a very single-minded fashion (and so, a weakness).

Marx's linking of economic relations to social identity, and his stress on the role of conflict in shaping society, has been enormously influential. However, his economic model has increasingly been questioned. The problem is that capitalist class relations did not erupt into conflict in the way that Marx predicted, and his suggestion that capitalist development simplifies class relations now seems just plain wrong. The rising affluence of Western capitalist societies and the growth of 'intermediate' professional and managerial occupations (neither capitalist nor proletariat) directly contradict Marx's prediction of class polarisation and pauperisation (Giddens 1981). Marx believed the simplification of class relations was an essential step in the development of revolutionary class consciousness, and so the absence of the former may explain the failure of the latter. But, regardless, advanced industrial societies have not experienced class conflict as predicted, so Marx's emphasis on class divisions as the defining aspect of industrial capitalism looks overstated. Of the conflict that *has* occurred, much of it has not been of a class kind, and has instead revolved around ethnic, racial and religious divisions (Parkin 1979). Subsequent writers have placed greater stress on additional, non-economic, sources of conflict.

Weber's multi-layered model stresses the diverse motivations of social behaviour, seeing stratification emerging from a variety of social strategies and interests. Rejecting mono-causal models of social behaviour, he argues the links between material location and social consciousness are contingent. This is both a strength and a weakness. Unlike Marx, Weber is unwilling to make any *systematic* statement of the links between economic position and status, or status and party allegiance. But this stress on *contingency* as a feature of social arrangements means that Weber has no developed account of the *actual* (as opposed to the potential) link between structured inequality and conscious, cohesive groups. This can be seen in his account of status group formation. Weber argues that any status characteristic may be the basis of social closure: 'it does not matter what characteristic is chosen . . . whatever suggests itself most easily is seized upon' (1978 [1922]: 342). However, closure on status characteristics can never be arbitrary, since the status identifiers people seize upon must be systematically embedded in patterned inequalities (of power, status, etc.) if closure is to be successful. Yet Weber has no real model of how status *groups* emerge out of patterned social differences. Weber stresses the divisions that people themselves consciously choose to emphasise (rather than on some notion of hidden 'objective' structure). However, his reluctance to make determinate, systematic links means that he tends to underplay the relationship between conscious social groupings and differentiated social relations. This means that Weber is sometimes accused 'of being concerned with the world of mere appearances – patterns of social inequality and distribution – instead of with the real essence of things' (Parkin 1982: 94–95).

The normative functionalist approach to stratification argues that the regulation of the stratification system is based on a general agreement about rules and social expectations. This notion – that the stability of hierarchy inevitably entails a degree of consent and acceptance on the part of subordinate groups – is an important one. We all (whether high or low) rank and rate others in society, and this is an important part of stratification. Similarly, the normative functionalist stress on the regulated, relative nature of ambition and competition stands as a useful corrective to the emphasis on stratification as a structure of 'conflict' found in Marx and Weber. However, normative functionalism stands accused of underplaying issues of conflict. These criticisms were most famously levelled at the normative functionalist writers Davis and Moore (1944), who extended Parsons's ideas by arguing that unequal rewards are the means by which a society ensures that the most important positions are filled by the most talented individuals. Davis and Moore were criticised for ignoring the fact that stratification also operates as a system of power. Power inequalities not only influence access to positions and rewards, but also affect the distribution of reward itself. To see unequal rewards solely in terms of the best people getting the most important jobs underestimates the extent to which powerful groups can make sure they receive high rewards, *regardless* of what function they serve, or how they are esteemed.

Parsons and Durkheim argue stratification systems are stable because people follow generally agreed social rules. However, even normative functionalists accept that 'rule-following' behaviour does not necessarily mean that stratification rankings are *consensual*. Parsons's own notion of 'self-interested' conformity raises the possibility that large numbers of people in a stratification system might be pragmatically accepting the rules rather than actually endorsing them. Parsons sees pragmatic acceptance as less important than genuine value consensus (Parsons 1951: 37), because he regards consensus as a more central element in stratification than conflict or coercion. However, whilst it may be right to question conflict as the defining element of stratification, it is not clear that consensus (as opposed to acceptance) can be set up in its place. Parsons and Durkheim do not ignore conflict, and spend considerable time addressing how conflict arises in normatively integrated systems. However, they do see conflict as secondary and parasitic upon processes of social order and consensus. As a result, critics of normative functionalism feel that it does not give a *convincing* account of the extent and nature of conflict and, so, inadequately describes the stratification system.

The next chapter further explores the limitations of these 'foundational' accounts, and their continuing legacy (good and ill) for contemporary understandings of stratification.

4   Sins of the fathers

The previous chapter explored how the 'founding fathers' of sociology helped establish the study of stratification. These early writers defined stratification analysis in its modern form, and identified a number of key questions that recur in contemporary discussions. These questions are:

- How do social conditions relate to individual social actions and perceptions?
- How do differences in hierarchical position relate to the drawing of subjective boundaries?
- What range of factors influence hierarchical social behaviour (and how are we to conceptualise their inter-relationship)?
- How does hierarchical inequality relate to cultural differentiation?
- By what range of social processes is the stratification order renewed and sustained over time? And how does the stability of the stratification order relate to processes of consensus, conflict and disorder within the stratification system? (Or, the question of social reproduction.)

The classical authors' answers to these questions have had a major impact on contemporary understandings of stratification, but this influence has not been entirely benign. The solutions of the classic authors are flawed, so contemporary accounts of stratification have attempted to blend their different insights, to correct their oversights and weaknesses. However, despite their differences, the classical authors shared common fault-lines in their thinking, and so cherry-picking their ideas is no guarantee of more successful solutions. In fact, the same fault-lines and problems of the classical authors are still in evidence in the work of their successors. Indeed, these fault-lines have widened into rifts which, as we shall see, have threatened to undermine the study of stratification altogether.

A series of conceptual divisions emerge in the classic accounts. These are:

- the separation of structure from action, with a concomitant stress on the 'structural' as a material, underlying realm that influences or determines action, to a greater or lesser degree, whilst 'action' is conceived in terms of meanings, intentionality and the exercise of values;

- a corresponding division between the 'economic' (seen as an impersonal structural realm) and the 'social' (seen as the realm of evaluation and cultural difference).

Contemporary stratification analysis has been strongly shaped by these divisions, emerging as a form of structural analysis, with that structure seen as an economic realm. However, difficulties in tracing the links between 'structure' and 'action', the 'economic' and the 'social', have led to increasing criticisms of this model, amid charges of determinism and economic reductionism. Critics have turned from economic and structural accounts to focus on agency, subjective meaning and social and cultural difference, all seen as increasingly independent of economic, structural divisions. In the process, social analysis has increasingly neglected issues of stratification and inequality altogether. Indeed what were tensions *within* the work of individual authors have become distinct schools of analysis, with a separation into conventional stratification approaches focusing on the structural inequalities in life-chances, on the one hand, and on the other hand, approaches influenced by postmodernism, which focus on agency, discursive identity and cultural differentiation, unencumbered by 'materialist' concerns.

As Shilling and Mellor (2001) argue, the postmodern rejection of structural, materialist social explanation often shows an amnesia about the history of social analysis. Many of the attacks caricature the work of the classical (and more recent) theorists, and ignore their efforts to battle the very problems raised by the critics. In the face of the limitations of structural and materialist models, postmodern approaches have retreated into an emphasis on indeterminate agency and the cultural, but this, of course, merely reproduces the same divisions which troubled the classical authors.

The rejection of stratification and the ordered nature of social life is unwarranted. This book shows that social location continues to be an important factor in the construction of cultural identities and social difference, and that economic inequalities remain as relevant as ever in shaping destinies, and in providing the materials for social and cultural differentiation. The concept of stratification remains a vital tool in understanding how individuals shape their lives. However, this does not mean that the attacks on structural, material explanation are simply mistaken. There are substantial problems, rapidly proliferating in recent times, which can be traced back to the classical authors' conception of stratification. Indeed, part of the reason that contemporary arrangements appear so 'chaotic' and 'fluid' is that we lack the conceptual tools to make sense of them. But the problem does not lie in the inherently disordered nature of social life. Rather the problem lies in the limiting ways in which the structured, 'material' nature of social life has been conceived, so that social life always appears to escape the limiting categories of theory. There are ways of conceiving stratification which are less encumbered with the problems of 'structural' accounts, and which correspond better to postmodern accounts of social experience as highly differentiated, and based around cultural and social lifestyles, whilst retaining an emphasis on inequality, and the patterned, orderly, and constraining nature of social relations.

However, before we think about possible solutions we have to understand the nature of the problem. This chapter sets this out: establishing the legacy of conceptual division (and explanatory difficulty) that the classical authors handed down to their intellectual heirs; and the fracturing of that inheritance into distinct areas of analysis, yet all troubled by the same explanatory problems.

A fractured legacy

All three classical statements of stratification argue that the social conditions of our existence constrain our lives, affecting how we view ourselves and others. Such a statement is basic to any theory of stratification. However, the classical authors vary in how they view the link between social conditions and individual actions and perceptions. Marx, Durkheim and Parsons make the strong claim that an external social structure *generates* social behaviour. It is generally argued that these traditions overstate their case, and that their models of structure cannot fully account for variations in behaviour. Weber's position – partly a response to the failures of Marxism – is more pessimistic about the explanatory possibilities of social location since, as he notes, sometimes people act in concert with people in the same social position, but at other times they do not. For Weber, social position is a *factor* explaining people's behaviour but is not determinative.

However, all the classical sociologists acknowledge the duality of social life, as an external constraint on the individual, but also constituted from the mass of individual actions. Each of them agrees that, on the one hand, individuals are constrained in their actions by wider social forces, but that on the other hand, the source of these external constraints lies precisely in the actions of ourselves and others. That is, we all of us actively create the social world, as purposive agents, interpreting and shaping our lives. However, this recognition of the duality of social life also gives rise to a conceptual separation, a binary division between 'structure' and 'action', seen as mutually implicated concepts (with the one constituted in the other). This division is, in turn, bound up with a series of other binaries: between the 'economic' and the 'social', 'inequality' and 'difference', which have been a key feature of stratification analysis, and of sociology more widely. As Holmwood and Stewart have pointed out (1991), a series of analysts have argued that the key to understanding social life lies in the mutuality of the links between these binary divisions, stressing that social life always contains both external constraint *and* individual agency and choice, economic *and* social elements, inequality *and* difference. Explanations which favour one or other of the terms have therefore been accused of reductionism, fitting the complexity of social life within too narrow bounds. However, the history of social analysis is a graveyard of failed attempts to balance the terms of these binaries. In practice, one side or the other has become dominant.

The structure/action divide can be compared to a game of table-tennis – once you accept there are two sides to social life then you have to keep the ball going back and forth for explanations to work, but somehow, in almost all social analysis, the ball ends up stuck on one side of the net. This results in incomplete explanations of social life. But nobody sets out to do this. Neither Marx, Durkheim nor Parsons *set out* to provide 'structural' accounts, and the problem of one-sidedness recurs in social explanations which attempt to 'correct' the limitations of the classical authors. One reason for this is because it is the *failure* of social explanations which appears to divide behaviour from its social location (Holmwood and Stewart 1991). Take the problems of accounts which are accused of determinism, that is, of making over-ambitious claims for their explanatory structural categories. Marx, for example, is accused of 'economism', placing too much importance on economic factors to explain social behaviour. However, the charge of 'determinism' is never used when social action appears to correspond to social location (when people act as the theory predicts that they will). In such cases, there seems to be no division between 'structure' and 'action'. The division only arises in those instances when people do not behave in the ways that the theory predicts (when people in the same class behave differently, for example). In such cases, social location and social behaviour appear dislocated.

There are a number of possible responses to this situation. One has been to argue that there are other influences on social behaviour (that, for example, it is not only our class that influences our actions but also our gender and ethnicity, and so on), in which case the problem is to explain the inter-relationship of these different explanatory factors. Structural categories (like 'class') appear to explain some of the variation in social behaviour, but not all of it, so the question arises why class processes sometimes appear to influence behaviour, whilst at other times gender or race and ethnicity are more decisive. This often turns into a stress on the agency of individuals, that is, stressing the 'action' side of the structure/action equation. It is commonly argued that we are always more than the product of our social location, because we have agency in how we respond to it. There are multiple influences on our behaviour, and individuals can interpret these influences in different ways (if I choose to regard my ethnic identity as more important than my gender or my class, this will affect my behaviour accordingly), just as they can decide to break the accepted rules of social behaviour. The implication is that individual behaviour can never be fully understood in terms of its social location, because the subjective meanings that individuals place on their position, and their motives and intentions, also shape their actions in unpredictable ways. This introduces an element of contingency and indeterminacy into social analysis. Some writers see the acceptance of indeterminacy as a feature of human action as rather too convenient. Indeed, Holmwood and Stewart (1991) suggest that the very notion of 'action' is in fact a residual category, and that the stress on the indeterminacy of action only emerges to help explain the messy inconsistencies of behaviour which escape the orderly categories of social explanation. They are suspicious of claims that the problem lies in the inherently 'chaotic' nature of social life rather than in explanatory deficiency.

However, structural accounts of behaviour do appear deficient, and their limitations have led, in more recent work, to a further process of division, with arguments that no reconciliation of structure and action is possible. It has been widely argued that continuing social change has made the analytical models of the classical sociologists increasingly irrelevant with a widening gap between 'structure' and 'action', the 'economic' and the 'social', as structural economic explanations no longer have the force they once did. It has variously been suggested that social divisions are increasingly 'free-floating', that culture and consumption have eclipsed economic production as the key arenas of social life; that economic divisions and inequalities have diminishing consequences for the formation of cultural lifestyles; that individuals have now become 'agents of their own fate', reflexively fashioning their biographies with increasing personal choice; and that the coherence of social divisions and inequalities has been undermined as progressive individualisation has led to increasingly fragmented, chaotic, and fluid social relations. A series of influential approaches has stressed agency in social affairs, arguing for a weakening of social structural constraints and codes of behaviour.

Although there is a recognition that patterned inequalities still exist, they are seen as an increasingly less significant aspect of people's cultural identity (so that there has been a de-coupling of action from structure, of the social from the economic). Alternatively, the rise of postmodern and post-structuralist approaches have increasingly abandoned the 'grand narratives' of structural inequality altogether. So problems with 'structure' have led to a retreat into agency. People are seen as active agents, reflexively shaping their destinies. Social relations are seen as fluid, fragmented, shifting, and, above all, *discursive*, with the formation of identities regulated by ideas and meanings, rather than by material structures. This amounts to the abandonment of the very idea of stratification and inequality in favour of accounts of the discursive construction of difference.

By definition, the problem with the retreat into action is that there is no sense of structured social relations. Social life is seen as patternless, or rather such patterned social relations that do exist are presented as inherently unstable, subject to constant change and revision. Just as the collapse into structure leads to the problem of determinism, so the retreat into agency leads to the problem of *voluntarism*. Voluntarism rests on the assumption that individual choices and decisions are the decisive element in social action. However, whilst it is clear that social relations *do* emerge out of the intentional, meaningful activity of the actors involved in them, there is a danger in assuming that social relations *only* emerge on this basis. Voluntaristic approaches disregard those influences on social behaviour that go beyond the subjective awareness or intent of the actors involved. This wilfully ignores the constraints within which people must continue to live. Structured inequalities continue to set substantial limits on choice and agency for all and create situations in which some are more free to act than others.

As we shall see, postmodern and post-structural approaches have been criticised in their turn for denying issues of inequality, and for emphasising relations of difference as symbolic, discursive constructions, thereby underplaying the ways in which 'difference' emerges through practical, lived relations in material social locations. One of the things I want to argue in this book is that this constant batting between agentic and structural accounts is neither necessary nor inevitable. There can be a reconciliation between 'difference' and 'inequality', 'action' and 'structure', the 'material' and the 'social', but we need to address problems in how the 'structural' and the 'economic' have been conceived, by both advocates and critics of such approaches.

'Structure' and 'action'

All the classical authors start out from the premise of duality of social life, yet all their explanations eventually collapse back on one side of the division that they make. Marx insists on both agency and constraint: 'Men make their own history, but they do not make it just as they please; they do not make it under circumstances chosen by themselves, but under circumstances directly encountered, given and transmitted from the past' (1852/2000: 329). Marx sets out reasons why people choose to behave in the way that they do, but they still have to choose. Marx does see objective social conditions as important regardless of the consciousness of the actors who experience those conditions, because economic relations limit our lives in ways which we may not fully recognise. But his whole argument is that particular conditions will lead to recognition, as shifts in class structure (the simplification of 'class-in-itself' relations) result in the conscious realisation of 'class-for-itself'. The problem is that the failure of revolutionary class consciousness means that the conditions of inequality and social actions appear permanently disconnected in the Marxist model. Despite their communal position, Marx's proletariat failed to act in concert as a self-aware group. Whilst it is important to stress the independent and constraining effect of social location, if structural conditions never impinge as meaningful or significant on the consciousness of the actors involved, then structure and agency are disconnected.

The same apparent problem – emphasising structure at the expense of action – emerges out of the explanatory failures of the normative functionalists. Again, the initial statement is of the duality of social life, with Durkheim arguing that social structure is really only action which has become habitual and 'crystallised'. However, these solidified actions become external and constraining: 'a totality of definite rules like so many moulds with limiting boundaries, into which we pour our behaviour' (1961: 24). This seems to remove actors as thinking, purposive agents from the picture. Parsons recognises this problem and initially aims to modify Durkheim's concern with external constraints on action with Weber's 'subjective' approach (concerned with the meanings of action) (Holmwood 1996: 31). Yet Parsons is also criticised for his system-determined account of individual action, in which 'actors only perform according to scripts which have already been written out for them' (Giddens 1976: 16). Ironically, this attempt to state the *links* between structure and action ends up describing individual actors as the expression of structures.

Part of the problem with 'over-structural' accounts lies in the particular and restrictive way they conceive social structure. Marx sees the structural arena in terms of economic relations, and is often accused of neglecting the independent effect of wider social elements on behaviour. Durkheim and Parsons provide a useful corrective in seeing the structural in social terms, of which the economic is but one component. However, they then narrowly define *social structure* as a system of institutionalised *common values*. This provides no sense of how differences in social resources affect consent to common values, nor of how the common value system might be generated by inequalities in power, status or economic resources. The structural, in both sets of accounts, is either conceived of as economic or as a value structure, and so appears 'thin' and one-sided as an explanation of social action.

The difficulty for both is in establishing a coherent relationship between 'social' and 'economic' processes. This legacy continues into the present day, as contemporary stratification theory has experienced considerable difficulty in theorising the relationship between economic and social processes in the stratification order. In all the classical accounts of stratification, the instrumental and contractual nature of economic relationships is stressed. For Marx, modernity is characterised by the rise of impersonal economic labour markets. Weber shares Marx's view of capitalism as a class-society, and stresses the market nature of class, arguing that 'the market and its processes "knows no personal distinctions"' (1948: 192). The normative functionalists also see the economic as an arena dominated by self-interested instrumental motivations, and so distinguish 'economic' from 'social' principles in much the same way. The 'social' in all these accounts, therefore, is the arena of values.

The 'economic' and the 'social'

Following the classical sociologists, the separation of the economic from the social has been a common feature of stratification theory, usually in the form of a division between class, seen as the sphere of the impersonally economic, and status, seen as the sphere of social evaluation. 'Class focuses on the divisions which result from the brute facts of economic organisation. Status relates to more subtle distinctions which stem from the values that men set on each other's activities' (Lockwood 1958: 208).

However, it is difficult to maintain a coherent distinction between the 'economic' and the 'social', because 'status' divisions also have an economic dimension, and 'economic' processes are also structured by social evaluations. But if you can't maintain the *distinction* between the economic and the social it is even more difficult to theorise their *relationship*. These divisions 'are particular manifestations of the fact/value, structure/action distinction so characteristic of modern sociology, a false opposition, though extremely difficult to dispense with' (Stewart *et al.* 1980: 5).

In dividing the economic from the social, Marx and the normative functionalists were attempting to state the nature of their relationship in stratification processes, rather than prioritise one over the other. However, in practice, the economic has increasingly become dominant in accounts of stratification. Marx is accused of reducing complex social processes to over-simplified economic factors, but he was actually attempting to unite them through the linkage of property relations. His is a '*sociological* economic theory at the centre of which are the social relations entailed by the division of labour and private property' (Craib 1997: 95). His account looks like economic 'reductionism', because his stress on property relations is too crude to link the economic and the social, ignores finer distinctions within and across property relations, and so fails to explain the subjective boundaries regarded as important by people themselves. Important divisions (such as gender or ethnicity) do not correspond well with Marx's vertical economic categories, and so these appear as a relatively independent 'social' ordering. Because the explanation fails, the social appears detached from the economic.

The normative functionalists start from the other end of the problem, arguing that self-interested 'economic' motivations are constrained and regulated *within* wider, normative, social structures. Parsons believed that self-interested 'economic rationality' was an important factor in social action, but argued that, since economic systems (and motivations) varied, they had to be explained in terms of 'other, non-economic elements' (1968 [1937]: 730). Similarly, Durkheim argued that to understand social life we must look beyond its 'material foundation' because 'the principal social phenomena, religion, ethics, law, economy, and aesthetics, are nothing else but a system of values' (quoted in Thompson 1982: 84). The difficulty is that while institutions clearly do reflect social values, they are formed by other, non-normative influences as well. Not all rewards are determined by shared evaluations of people's worth, since power and economic clout are factors too. People have varying degrees of acceptance of the stratification order, and of their own place within it, but from a normative functionalist perspective there can be no systematic explanation of why people at different levels of the stratification structure vary in their support for the ranking order, because the stratification order is itself defined as a structure of shared values. As a result, actors reflect the stratification structure, but do not reflect *upon* it. The normative functionalist account doesn't see values as deeply differentiated, so there is no systematic account of how variations in structural conditions (or the institutionalised value system) shape the actions of different groups or bring them into conflict. The problem with seeing the economic 'structure' as one based on values is that it fails to acknowledge the extent to which unequal resources create divisions of interest, and generate different and conflicting social evaluations. That is, in focusing on how the economic is shaped by social values, the normative functionalists ignore how 'brute economic facts' can shape social values.

However, it is also worth noting that whilst the normative functionalists conceive of the structural as a value system, they still see the main arena of modern stratification as being the (primarily) 'economic' realm of the labour market. They may conceive that occupational order, in value terms, is a ranking of prestige and functional importance, but it is still the occupational order which is the main determinant of social status in modern societies.

The difficulties in theorising the relationship between 'action' and 'structure', 'social' and 'economic', give rise to a third approach, that adopted by Weber, which argues there can be no systematic statement of their relationship. Weber argues that individual actions are never fully determined by social position, because 'economic' and 'social' processes are linked but always relatively autonomous. This position simply accepts that 'action' and 'structure' can never be reconciled in social analysis, and is thus a precursor of the widening gap between agentic and structural accounts in contemporary social analysis.

Weber shares Marx's view of capitalism as a class-society, and stresses the market nature of class, but divides 'class' from 'status' in a more marked way, arguing that there can be no consistent statement of their relationship. For Weber, social behaviour cannot be 'read off' from economic location, since allegiances are affected by other, non-class, factors. Economic differences are never enough to explain social divisions – a statement of the semi-autonomous nature of the 'social' from the 'economic'. However, Weber also argues that social groups introduce closure into the market through monopolisation – representing the intrusion of status elements into economic principles. This, of course, undermines the distinction between economic and social processes, because restricting allocation to positions helps structure the rewards of those positions. This means that economic locations are partly constituted through processes of status evaluation and, therefore, that 'economic' structural arrangements are also 'social'.

However, Weber avoids the problem of specifying the links between 'economic' structure and 'social' action by retreating into 'agency'. Weber is less concerned with structural relations, and refuses to identify a social *system*, instead focusing on those social divisions that are stressed by the people concerned. Weber rejects the idea of a systematic account of the link between social location and social behaviour, seeing their relationship as contingent. For Weber, 'the existence of common qualities does not imply the existence of communal relationships between the people who share these qualities; he has no conception of people belonging to a "class-in-itself", independently of their consciousness' (Craib 1997: 122). The main thrust of his work is on subjective perceptions of division, and on self-conscious groupings. This has become the template for subsequent approaches experiencing difficulties with structural determinism. Whilst acknowledging structural relations, their importance has been reckoned in terms of whether people themselves regard such distinctions as important.

The divided inheritors

Problems in mapping the relations between the 'economic' and the 'social' has led to the fracturing of contemporary accounts into approaches which focus on one or the other. There has been a division between those emphasising agency, and the 'social' as cultural and symbolic, and between those emphasising the structural and the economic. All sides acknowledge the importance of the relationship between the two, but the difficulty specifying the relationship leads to omissions and accusations of determinism or voluntarism.

Most contemporary stratification analysis has adopted a mix of Marx and Weber, stressing the labour market as a realm of structural constraint, but investigating the degree to which individual behaviour is influenced by such structures. One approach, neo-Weberian class analysis, emphasises the structural, economic, constraints on social behaviour. Here the stress is on how structural factors shape life-chances and limit opportunities. The focus is on the enduring legacy of inherited economic position, that is, on how people are limited by the structural location they are born into, over and above their individual agency or efforts. Here class occurs 'behind our backs', shaping life-chances and social behaviour in ways of which we might not fully be aware. However, it has been argued that there is a loss of agency in such accounts, and an undue prioritisation of economic relations, with social and cultural divisions seen as mere 'effects'. In their focus on patterned inequalities in life-chances such approaches have been criticised for downplaying issues of subjective identity or cultural lifestyle. In particular, it has been argued that stratification theory has ignored divisions which are not straightforwardly 'economic', such as racial, ethnic and gender divisions.

All the classical sociologists saw the separation out of the economic as a distinct (and dominant) sphere within society as one of the defining features of 'modernity'. Because of their assumption that modern life is organised around increasingly impersonal market or rationalistic criteria (Marx and Weber) or reflects the triumph of individualisation and achievement over ascription as the basis of social organisation (Durkheim and Parsons), the classical sociologists therefore saw status distinctions as peripheral in modern life. They did not ignore racial or gender divisions, but did sideline them, seeing them as the by-product of other processes (for example, the competition over economic resources). Their founding assumptions meant they shared the 'belief that racial and ethnic social bonds, divisions, and conflicts were remnants of a preindustrial order which would decline in significance in the modern period' (Omi and Winant 1994: 9). Yet, far from being an aberration or residue of the past, slavery and colonialism were *central* to the development of modern societies, and racial divisions remain an enduring basis of conflict. The 'market' also clearly differentiates on the basis of gender and other social statuses, and the persistence of gender inequality is a considerable challenge to the economic model of 'class' society and the dissolution of status constraints. In marginalising gender and race in their accounts of modernity, the classical sociologists were, at best, 'sex' and 'colour' blind and, at worst, guilty of reproducing sexist and racist categories (prioritising men over women, and 'the West' over 'the rest'). To be fair, as Shilling and Mellor note, one reason for their neglect was because they 'sought to distance sociology from the claims of evolutionary biologists' (2001: 146). But in rejecting 'biological' explanations of inequality, the classical sociologists located race and gender in the 'social' sphere (since the economic was 'impersonal'). They therefore saw race and gender as 'ideological' constructs, easily swept away by more rational evaluations. If race (and gender) are based on 'status' evaluations, they should be increasingly outmoded in societies based on 'class' processes. However, 'status' divisions have not disappeared, so it is the 'economic' model of stratification which has begun to look outmoded.

Weber's emphasis on status divisions does allow more space for the discussion of race and gender, but his account is narrowly focused on their symbolic aspects.

> Weber is moving away from a position that privileges economic relationships. However, his account of gender and ethnicity as aspects of status did not carry this insight far enough. Gender, ethnic and age divisions reflect more than differential social evaluation, also encompassing divisions of labour and differential material resources. Status does not seem a robust enough concept to encompass all of these.
>
> (Bradley 1996: 54)

This division (locating class in the 'economic' and race and gender in the 'social') has continued to the present day:

> class is seen to be a division marked by material difference, and inequality of positioning around material resources, whether conceived in the area of production or distribution, determined by relations of exploitation or by relations to the market. Ethnicity, on the other hand, is treated as relating to being positioned in terms of culture, or in the symbolic and identificational realm, with particular behavioural or action elements flowing from this. . . . The lasting effect of these traditions of exploring social inequality, through the primacy of the economic realm have seriously skewered academic conceptions of inequalities and social stratification. They have been impediments to thinking about inequalities in a more holistic and multidimensional way, and are premised on the ontological and epistemological primacy of economic/ material needs and their social organisation in human life.
>
> (Anthias 2001: 375)

From 'inequality' to 'difference'

It is usually pointed out that there are racial divisions within class categories, so that individuals in the same economic position but with different racial identities will have different lifestyles and life-chances. Racial (and gender) divisions cannot be 'read off' from economic divisions. This seems, at first sight, to suggest that the vertical dimension of economic stratification is complicated by a lateral 'cultural' (or 'social') dimension of racial difference. However, a straightforward division between 'inequality' (economic and hierarchical) and 'difference' (cultural and lateral) cannot be maintained. The 'social' dimension of difference is not independent of economic divisions, and racial differences are not 'free-floating' of economic inequality. Whilst racial and gender divisions clearly entail cultural and symbolic aspects, they are also bound up with material inequalities. Racial divisions are not simply 'cultural', since the construction of racial difference is bound up with systematic inequalities in access to social and material resources (that is, they are also vertical). So 'economic' and 'social' processes are not independent of each, but they are not identical. The difficulty is in then explaining 'racial' divisions which are not straightforwardly 'economic', but cannot be understood solely in terms of cultural 'difference'.

> [T]he analysis of social divisions as forms of stratification has tended to mean, traditionally at least, a focus on class relations. Despite the recognition that gender and ethnic processes entail subordination and inequality, the tendency has been to incorporate them into social analysis through the notion of 'difference', rather than through analysing them as forms of stratification without reducing them to class divisions.
>
> (Anthias 1998: 506)

In practice, accounts of racial divisions have tended to flip back and forth between 'material' (economic) and 'cultural' explanations, with each side accusing the other of explanatory inadequacy. 'Cultural' accounts of race have been criticised for ignoring the material inequalities that run alongside racial divisions, whilst 'materialist' approaches have been accused of economic reductionism.

Accounts of gender are riven with similar difficulties. Early attempts to explain gender inequality within the categories of class failed, as it became apparent that gender divisions cross-cut class categories. However, attempts to argue that the source of gender divisions lay outside the economic, with women's inequality located in the family and domestic relations, also ran into difficulties, because of the way in which gender divisions are both domestic and labour-market relations (so 'social' and 'economic'). Again, disillusionment with the problems of theorising different structures of inequality (patriarchy and capitalism) has led to a shift in focus to the discursive construction of gender difference.

Here we can see the same uneasy cycling between structure and action, the economic and the social, which has characterised conventional stratification analysis. The latest turn of the wheel has been a rejection of the materialist, structural side of the equation altogether.

> The notion of 'difference' and its significance in distinguishing 'self' from various culturally defined 'others' has dominated debates in many disciplines. In this work – loosely grouped under the heading of 'postmodern' or 'poststructuralist' – earlier notions of a stable, immutable sense of identity, typically rooted in social class position, have been disrupted. The significance of other dimensions of identity, especially gender and ethnicity, and their interconnections, has been recognised, as well as the provisional, tentative nature of identity which is theorised as an ongoing performance, variable in space and time ... This approach to identity is sometimes termed a 'relational perspective' in which identity is theorised as a contingently defined social process, as a discursively constituted social relation, articulated through complex narratives.
>
> (McDowell 2003: 78)

Such claims bear the mark of post-structuralist approaches which suggest 'that the ways in which humans speak about the world creates the world, yet that this speech is itself determined by discourses based on exclusions and differences', so 'that neither society nor the subject have any meaning other than that created arbitrarily within language, and that "reality" is characterised by indeterminacy, instability and the impossibility of agreed meaning' (Shilling and Mellor 2001: 188).

A range of writers, influenced by postmodern arguments, have suggested that the 'increasing social diversity and plurality' of contemporary life has led to a 'fragmentation and erosion of collective social identity' (S. Hall 1991: 44). The collective categories of 'gender', 'class' and 'race' 'cannot any longer be thought in the same homogenous form. We are as attentive to their inner differences, their inner contradictions, their segmentations and their fragmentations as we are to their already-completed homogeneity, their unity' (S. Hall 1991: 45). This is the triumph of agency over structure, and of the 'social' over the economic in social analysis. Because our social ties are so multiplex and differentiated, it is argued that subjective identity is increasingly 'free-floating'.

This rejection of any structured or material basis to identity is not limited to 'lateral' gender, or racial and ethnic differences, but now extends to the vertical divisions of class. It is argued that whilst economic inequalities still prevail, they no longer systematically relate to lifestyle differences or identity. The postmodern claim of the 'death of class' is that consumption is increasingly important for how we order our lives and define ourselves, in ways quite independent of economic divisions. Increasing affluence, and the huge array of consumption choices, mean that people at the same economic level are increasingly culturally differentiated from each other. This argument sees social relations as inchoate and shifting, in which identity is not determined in any patterned way by structural relations, but rather centres on the active construction of individualised lifestyles.

Such accounts emphasise the way in which discursive categories (ways of thinking and speaking) provide a shifting framework for our social relations, without exploring how practical and material social relations influence the formation of discursive identities. But this, of course, simply reinscribes the stress on the symbolic and cultural (rather than material) nature of racial and gender divisions. Naturally, there have been rejections of such accounts, by those who are suspicious of the abandonment of issues of inequality, and who question whether we really have that much freedom to choose who we want to be.

As we shall see, it has also been suggested that the organisation of 'difference' cannot be understood without examining its social context, that is, how differences are employed and modified in patterned social relations. This directs attention back to the role played by practical social relations in the formation of 'difference', and thus how 'difference' is bound up in 'inequality'. This will be discussed in Part 2 of this book, 'Deconstructions'.

'Objective' and 'subjective'

Part of the difficulty in thinking about the relationship between difference and in-equality is that within conventional stratification theory there has been a tendency to characterise *difference* as *vertical differentiation*, that is, as the result of structural economic inequality. This is apparent in the work of the classical sociologists. For Marx, social differentiation is the result of economic relations (which promote or undermine social differences, creating homogeneity or diversity). Durkheim, by contrast, conceives stratification in terms of functional differentiation, yet this differentiation is still primarily in terms of the division of labour (and so vertically, and economically, organised). For Weber, and for those influenced by post-modernism, the existence of cross-cutting, lateral, social divisions has therefore been seen as something which undermines the unity of economic 'groups'. The intersection of multiple dimensions of 'difference' is regarded as under-mining structural determination, because we are subject to such a range of conflicting social influences.

The difficulty is not only that we have to consider subjective perceptions of difference that are not straightforwardly economic or 'vertical' (along lines of ethnicity, race or gender, for example); but also that there are problems explaining how and why people draw lines across economic 'vertical' differentiation. This, of course, is the problem of understanding how variations in social experience relate to perceptions of social difference.

Within 'structural' accounts, subjective perceptions of difference should map onto differences in material location, but given the highly differentiated nature of unequal relations, where exactly should the lines be drawn? Ossowski (1963) argues that there are two distinct ways of viewing stratification. The first approach sees the stratification order as an unbroken, graduated *hierarchy*; a highly differentiated ordering of people or positions, with relatively fine inter-vening gaps between them. The second approach sees the stratification order as *categorical*, composed of distinct groups with the same social or economic posi-tion. Here stratification is discontinuous, comprised of internally homogenous groups with clear-cut boundaries.

The second approach places more emphasis on discontinuities and gaps in structural relations as the basis of group formation and subjective identities. Marx's main emphasis is on class *groups* defined in terms of common relations to property ownership. Whilst acknowledging that there are more differentiated gradations *within* class grouping ('intermediate strata' and class fractions), Marx argues that the polarisation of classes would eliminate such gradations within and across class groups. In the absence of polarisation, however, the occupa-tional inequalities *within* classes defined by property relations have come to seem increasingly significant. So the distinction between categorical and gradational schemes is hard to maintain because categories tend to contain hierarchical differences within them. The problem for class accounts (and indeed all categor-ical stratification schemes) is why the division *between* categories should be more important than the divisions *within* categories. Conventional class theory has spent a long time looking for gulfs in social experience to explain the sharp symbolic boundaries that people draw, but has always run up against the internal differentiation within categories, and the overlap across them.

Gradational approaches place much less emphasis on collective social cate-gories, shared group identities, or any sense of rooted social divisions. This is because although there may be discontinuities, or 'breaks', in this ladder-like hierarchy, the finely graded differences between positions means that any group-ings are likely to be heterogeneous, with many differences *within* a group. This is very much the approach of normative functionalist accounts which give com-paratively little emphasis to the role of subjective 'groups' or boundary-drawing, instead seeing the stratification order as a graduated hierarchy of status rankings (that is, functional differentiation without conflicting groups).

The problem is that the people who inhabit highly differentiated stratification orders often do draw sharp lines of demarcation across apparently fine hierar-chical differences, establishing clear-cut boundaries. The issue, then, is how groups and hierarchies, difference and inequality, are related to each other within the stratification order.

Weber stresses the self-conscious boundaries that the members of status groups draw across what may be quite fine status and power distinctions, seeing such groups as defined by how they draw a subjective line of difference to other groups. For Weber (and Marx) solidarity *within* social groups is often reinforced by conflict *between* groups. Weber's account – based as it is on self-aware status groups, parties, and on social closure – sees the antagonistic relations between groups as the key element in processes of stratification and group formation. Weber also recognises that processes of group conflict and subordination take form in a variety of routine and everyday social activities, such as the choice of lifestyle items, place of residence, friends, or marriage partners, and allow for social subordination to occur through a *range* of competitive struggles, which often fall far short of overt conflict. Weber's account offers the possibility of seeing how processes of cultural and social differentiation might prompt, or at least help to support, processes of group demarcation. But Weber's approach tends to stop short at people's subjective perceptions of social division, ignoring those elements of stratification that go beyond the subjective awareness of actors, forces that may influence us regardless of whether we fully perceive or understand them. And there is still the difficulty of explaining why people draw the boundaries in the places they do. Weber appears to think that since bound-aries are often drawn across relatively small 'objective' differences in status, power or economic resources, that such divisions are 'arbitrary'. As a result, Weber has often been accused of focusing on surface appearances, at the expense of the structural relations which help to generate them. There is no sustained account of structure, instead 'Weber offers us a pattern of groups which are always on the edge of collapsing into chaos' (Craib 1997: 129).

Chaotic fluidity, of course, is the solution that has been proposed by post-modern critics of stratification. However, this ignores the way in which differential association, and practical social relations, create an orderly, albeit highly differentiated, set of stratification arrangements. The final parts of this book argue that our experience of social life is not as fragmented, or fluid, as current conceptions of it might suggest. Each individual doubtless possesses multiple social identities, along intersecting dimensions of difference, but these arise through substantive, material (though not exclusively economic) social relations and are frequently not experienced as contradictory or fragmented. If we can have a better understanding of how identities emerge through patterns of social interaction and in turn help to demarcate and limit interaction, then we will be in a much better position to reject the metaphor of fragmentation which dominates current analysis. This however involves more than a discursive under-standing of identity, it involves the mapping of practical social relations of interaction, cultural and social dissimilarity onto an understanding of symbolic identification and demarcation.

Before we get to this, however, we have to explore in greater detail how the social divisions, and exclusions, of the classical foundations have led to problems in contemporary accounts, and the claim that social life is disorderly and fragmented.

5   Name, rank and number
Measuring stratification

This chapter looks at one strand in the modern stratification 'inheritance': the influential quantitative research tradition. In producing increasingly sophisticated measures of stratification, enabling the development of national and cross-national research programmes, these approaches have built an impressively detailed picture of how stratification affects individual prospects and collective fates. Because of this influence, stratification research has developed a reputation as an essentially quantitative discipline, wedded to structural models of social life, and adopting the most sophisticated statistical techniques. However, this reputation is not wholly positive, and quantitative approaches have been criticised for their increasingly narrow focus.

Following Marx and Weber, a *class tradition* in quantitative stratification research has looked to the market, and to production relations, as an arena of external, objective inequality. Researchers investigate the extent to which the (by implication) more ephemeral and subjective aspects of social behaviour relate to these enduring economic structures. The stratification ordering is pictured as being composed of discontinuous, class categories. The *status tradition*, influenced by normative functionalist accounts, presents stratification as a status structure, with overall social position derived from a mix of valued economic and cultural resources. This tradition pictures the stratification ordering as a finely graded status hierarchy with no sharp breaks or clearly defined groupings.

By contrast, another, earlier, research tradition – the *community studies* approach – combines the different elements found in other approaches, attempting to look at stratified relationships in their entirety; by directly investigating the status relations of whole communities. This approach maps stratification position in terms of economic position, lifestyle and cultural activities, and interaction and association; as measured by the overall status reputation that individuals have acquired on the basis of all these characteristics. The technique produces a map of the social hierarchy from the subjective perceptions of those located within it, and the approach is unusual in stratification research for the way in which it derives quantitative measures of class from qualitative methods of analysis. The stratification ordering is pictured as a hierarchy of distinct classes with differential lifestyles and interaction, but is also seen as consensually ordered. This approach looked at stratification 'in the round', drawing on the many ways in which social relationships are affected by hierarchy to develop an overall measure of stratification arrangements. As we shall see, this ambitious approach was ultimately rooted in failure, in part because of the sheer difficulty of integrating these disparate elements into a single overall measure. Subsequent research has focused on developing specialised stratification measures which are more tightly defined. In the process, there has been a considerable narrowing of focus, and a shift to a much more quantitative form of analysis.

Lifestyle, association and reputation

The 'community studies' tradition, influential in American sociology from the 1920s–1950s, used anthropological accounts of small-town communities to explore stratification as expressed through face-to-face interaction, social cliques and 'styles of life'. Lloyd Warner's studies of 'Yankee City' (Warner *et al.* 1949; Warner and Lunt 1959a [1941], 1959b [1942]; Warner and Srole 1959 [1945]) are the best example of the approach. Warner used community rankings (devised from status evaluations) to develop a measure of 'social class' (although it can also be seen as a measure of social distance) expressed through the perceived limits on social interaction.

Warner noticed that people in a community 'evaluate the participation of those around them', ranking the status of the people with whom they interact. In 'Yankee City', informants continually referred to the reputation of their neighbours, and Warner saw that this could be translated into 'social class' rankings, creating a map of the status structure of the community. This approach sees stratification position resulting from a combination of economic and status factors, since: 'Money must be translated into socially approved behavior and possessions, and they in turn must be translated into intimate participation with, and acceptance by, members of a superior class' (Warner *et al.* 1949: 21). The approach stresses subjective perceptions of 'status' as they are reflected in interaction patterns and social cliques:

> it is not the objective position a person occupies on an income or occupation scale, for example, that is being ranked; it is the way that position is *evaluated* by the members of the society and the way in which the person occupying the position behaves in other ways as well, that is being ranked.
>
> (Kornhauser 1953: 227)

Community members were used to identify the 'social participation' and 'status reputation' of their fellows. In interviews, people referred to other members of the community in terms of 'inferior' and 'superior' economic positions, talked about whether others 'acted right' (in terms of styles of life), whether they belonged to the 'right families', or associated with the 'right kind of people', placing people above and below them in social cliques. As Table 5.1 shows these perceptions were used to aggregate a status structure of a limited number of social classes.

Warner's 'classes' have distinct styles of life, based on differences in occupation and income, but also different attitudes and values, expressed through different consumption patterns and tastes. Their class also shapes their social participation, with differential association in family ties, clubs and cliques. And since the members of the same class share lifestyles and associate as intimate equals, this can be traced in the subjective evaluations that the members of a community make of each other.

> The 'right' kind of house, the 'right' neighborhood, the 'right' furniture, the proper behavior – all are symbols that can ultimately be translated into social acceptance by those who have sufficient money to aspire to higher levels than they presently enjoy. To belong to a particular level in the social-class system of America means that a family or individual has gained acceptance as an equal by those who belong in the class. The behavior in this class and the participation of those in it must be rated by the rest of the community as being at a particular place in the social scale.
>
> (Warner *et al.* 1949: 23)

Warner's approach combines all the key aspects of the stratification order identified by the classical authors: economic resources, lifestyle and consumption, interaction and association, and subjective perceptions of value. It uses the subjective experience of stratification to derive a measure of the objective, external stratification structure. However, there is a major question as to how successfully these disparate elements are integrated. Take the attempt to reconcile objective categories with subjective experience. Warner claimed that his six social classes were 'not categories invented by social scientists to help explain what they have to say; they are groups recognised by the people of the community as being higher or lower in the life of the city' (quoted in Kornhauser 1953: 227). The intention was to explore stratification in terms of how it is *meaningful* in the everyday lives of the people who experience it, and 'a central methodological assumption is that one builds up a picture of stratification inductively by examining the lives of ordinary members of society in the round', so it 'is grounded in how members of these communities understand their own activities' (Travers 1999: 7.3, 7.4).

Critics argue Warner's composite class structure lumps together quite different individual perceptions and criteria of ranking.

> For example, in the Jonesville study one panel member who was a professional man named the following categories during the course of the interviews: 'the society class' or 'the 400 class', 'the fringe of society', 'the upper-middle class', 'the working class', and the 'lulus'; another panel member who was a mill worker viewed the class hierarchy as being divided into three groups: a top group composed of powerful landowners, wealthy industrialists, and professional people, a second level of ordinary, poor people like himself, and a third group of people poorer than himself.
>
> (Kornhauser 1953: 229)

The implication is that Warner *imposed* a class structure on the rank evaluations he collected. Warner's method (aggregating subjective evaluations of rank) rests

Table 5.1 Warner's social classes (with a selection of the social evaluations used to compile the classes)

1	The upper class	'The 400', 'The Top Class', 'The Fancy Crowd', 'Snobs', 'People who look down on everyone else in town', 'the silk stockings', 'The Mainstreeters'
2	The upper middle class	'Good, substantial people, but not in the top group', 'a notch or two below The Fancy Crowd', 'people who are working to get somewhere', 'above average, but not tops'
3	The lower middle class	'top of the common people', 'Baptists', 'people with nice families who don't rate', 'working people but respectable'
4	The upper lower class	'the little people', 'poor but hard working', 'poor but respectable', 'poor people but nothing the matter with them', 'the Mill people'
5	The lower lower class	'people who live like animals', 'people who live like pigs', 'chronic reliefers', 'tobacco roaders', 'lulus', 'the poor and unfortunate', 'the people back of the tannery', 'Hill-billies'

Source: Adapted from Warner *et al.* 1949: 66–71

on the assumption that perceptions of status straightforwardly *reflect* the stratification structure. However, this ignores the extent to which perceptions differ by social position. Yet Warner's own research found that perceptions of social structure systematically vary. Individuals at different levels of the hierarchy did not make rankings on the *same basis*, with upper-level groups using criteria of prestige and style of life to rank, whilst lower-level groups ranked on income, wealth and economic superiority (Davis *et al.* 1941).

> Why, it is asked, does Warner describe a large number of classes, when only the upper strata recognise that many? Why are six divisions more 'real' than the three or four that are recognised by the lower strata? Why has Warner adopted the view that class is based on style of life and social reputation when members of the lower-middle, upper-lower and lower-lower classes (the vast majority of the population) are said to base *their* rankings *solely* on money?
>
> (Kornhauser 1953: 249)

Critics suggest that the ranking Warner developed was skewed towards the views of elite groups, emphasising consensual status rather than the power nature of rankings (Pfautz and Duncan 1950). This raises questions about the extent to which quite different perceptions and evaluations can be used to derive a single rank ordering (and therefore the extent to which this ordering is subjectively grounded rather than objectively imposed).

Warner's synthetic approach also prevents any analysis of the independent role of power and economic resources, or the relative strength of different factors in determining social position (Mills 1942). The common criticism is that stratification position is reduced to reputation ranking, ignoring the independent influence of economic and power relations. Put simply, my stratification position may not just depend on how others view me, since my economic or strategic clout may allow me to achieve my aims regardless of my status reputation, whether others approve or not. By characterising social position as a prestige ordering, Warner tended to downplay these non-consensual, non-reputational aspects of stratification.

By equating 'class' with 'class-awareness' (Mills 1942: 41), Warner ignores those hidden or non-subjective aspects of stratification which can influence social participation without people's awareness of it. The stratification system extends beyond the limits of subjects' awareness, but Warner's method stops at actors' perceptions. This is built into the approach, since Warner's anthropological technique (using members' accounts to build up a picture of social structure) required a community 'where the social organisation had become firmly organised and the relations of the various members of the society exactly placed and known by the individuals who made up the group'; so Warner did not want to study a community 'where the ordinary daily relations of the inhabitants were in confusion or conflict' (Warner and Lunt 1959a [1941]: 39). This choice inevitably minimises conflict and disagreement in status evaluations, as well as the 'hidden' (or non-perceived) features of status reputation and stratified social interaction.

The community studies approach is based on status evaluations in a small community, where the inhabitants of different status positions are personally known to each other. Status rankings are not based on occupation *per se*, but on the *overall* reputation and associated lifestyle and group membership that individuals possess. However, such multi-dimensional rankings of prestige (which are strongly linked to actual interaction patterns) can only be produced in small-scale settings of considerable social stability. As soon as we want to look at more anonymous and fluid social settings, or to consider the national picture of social status, the limitation of the community studies approach becomes apparent.

In urban settings 'social relations stretch far beyond direct face-to-face encounters and status becomes an "attributional" rather than an interactional matter. . . . In the city, then, people acquire their status from their social positions, rather than directly from their personal actions' (Scott 1996: 118). This need to investigate more generalised or impersonal rankings resulted in a shift in focus towards the national setting (Grimes 1991: 21), and a change in how stratification was conceived and measured. Stratification position was still seen as multi-dimensional, but the emphasis changed from the mapping of status relations in concrete locations (status as played out in interaction cliques and styles of life) to a more narrowly focused attempt to rank national lists of occupations by abstract prestige evaluations or by objective socio-economic measures.

Status as prestige

Prestige scales derive from the notion that the stratification structure can be mapped by looking at the general reputation of occupational positions. However, this is not reputation as it emerges from interpersonal relations and lifestyle, but rather the reputation of occupational categories, considered in the abstract:

> the reputational approach attempts to derive a description of the stratification system from evaluations or perceptions of positions (usually occupations) within that system, made by a set of respondents. In most forms of the approach, each respondent is presented with a list of occupations, chosen for their spread through an assumed social structure, and is then asked to place them in order, or to rate them on a specified scale, say from poor to excellent. The ranking or rating is performed according to some principle which is regarded as a general feature of stratification – usually some variation on the theme of 'occupational prestige' or 'social standing'.
>
> (Stewart and Blackburn 1975: 486)

The resulting prestige scores (which average individual ratings) give rise to a finely graded hierarchy of occupations. Prestige measures assume that objective measures of stratification can be derived from the subjective perceptions of those at different levels. In support of this it is argued that there is apparently a high level of agreement in the population over the ranking of occupations:

> the educated and uneducated, the rich and poor, the urban and rural, the old and young, all on the average have the same perceptions of the prestige hierarchy. There is no systematic subgroup variation in the relative ratings of jobs.
>
> (Treiman 1994: 209)

This similarity has been taken as evidence of a consensus about the worth of occupations, supporting functionalist claims of shared values about social rewards. Prestige-ranking exercises are therefore treated as a 'moral referendum' (Parkin 1972) over the legitimacy of the stratification system. It is argued that occupations at the top of the hierarchy are ranked highly in public opinion because of their functional importance to society, and because they require the most training, and are highly rewarded:

> prestige must be viewed as a measure of moral worth, that is, of the extent to which an occupation embodies that which is valued by members of society. Since power and privilege are universally valued and since hierarchies of power and privilege are relatively invariant, prestige will also be relatively invariant.
>
> (Treiman 1994: 211)

Cross-national agreement over prestige rankings is taken as evidence that inequality reflects the functional 'needs' of all societies, and receives moral support from the population as a whole (Barber 1957).

However, such conclusions are contested. Critics argue there is more disagreement over occupational prestige than most studies admit, and that the level of agreement that does exist does not actually indicate any *support* for inequality. Important variations in the ranking of particular occupations tend to be minimised by the methods and statistical techniques of comparison in prestige studies (Pawson 1989). Critics suggest that this artificially increases the level of agreement in such studies:

> cross-national, cross-cultural agreement is artefactual, depending as it does upon the set of stereotype occupational names that survive cross-national and translational comparison, and upon the crudest method of aggregating rating scale measurements.
>
> (Coxon *et al.* 1986: 47)

There is, for example, in many countries a general agreement that skilled jobs should be ranked higher than unskilled jobs. But this general, very abstract, level of agreement tends to swamp the finer details that emerge of disagreement about the ranking of *specific* occupations (Coxon and Jones 1978: 40–41).

There is also controversy about what prestige scales are actually *measuring*. The proponents of prestige scales assume that the 'goodness' of occupations is seen in terms of 'fairness' or 'justice'; however, for critics, prestige ratings do not reflect any general agreement on the *worth* of different occupations, but rather simply assess the various objective attributes (skill, income, etc.) that make jobs more or less *advantaged* (Goldthorpe and Hope 1972). When someone rates a bank manager as having higher 'social standing' than a plumber, they are not necessarily indicating that they think a bank manager is more socially useful, or deserving of higher rewards, than a plumber. Instead they are simply recognising that bank managers are in fact better paid than plumbers. A respondent need not agree with this state of affairs (they may fundamentally disagree with it), since the prestige rating they give the job merely acknowledges its advantage. This is an important rebuttal of functionalist theories of value consensus about stratification. If prestige ratings are cognitive rather than evaluative, then the differential rankings of occupations they produce are statements of fact (based on the respondent's assessment of the general income, education and training associated with particular occupations) rather than any indication of moral approval for those rewards.

However, if prestige ratings are simply 'error prone estimates' (Featherman and Hauser 1976) of the objective socio-economic characteristics of jobs, it makes more sense to measure socio-economic position directly (Goldthorpe and Hope 1972). This is what subsequent research has done, representing a move from subjective to objective measures of stratification.

Socio-economic position and status attainment

Prestige scales (like Warner's 'evaluated participation' classes) map stratification through the subjective perceptions of the population. Critics argue such approaches rest on a fundamental mistake, the false assumption 'that a single structure pervades the social consciousness' (Coxon *et al.* 1986: 13).

> Sociologists have tried to talk about, and even to quantify, a whole linear continuum of occupational status, while the 'people in the street' have for most of their time been unconcerned with this 'big picture' [. . .] people on the street are most concerned with the myriad complexities of day-to-day discussion of relatively short orderings within small segments of a set of social roles.
>
> (Coxon *et al.* 1986: 40)

Whilst individuals may be concerned with distinctions and differences in the occupations that they encounter on a daily basis (at work, through friends and family), the differences between occupations that they rarely encounter, or simply hear about in the abstract, may not mean much to them. Just because respondents can rank occupations in a linear hierarchy at the prompting of sociologists does not mean this is terribly meaningful for them, and may not relate to how they usually think of the differences between occupations. The rankings may, therefore, be an artefact of the sociological exercise, rather than a deep-seated feature of the social consciousness.

Objective scales of stratification, by contrast, do not depend on perceptions of prestige or social standing. Instead, socio-economic status is conceptualised in terms of the objective conditions affecting the general lifestyle associated with holding a particular occupation. There is no direct measurement of occupational lifestyles; instead, education and income are taken as the best predictors of lifestyle, with some weighted combination of the average education and income level of an occupational group used to place the job in an overall gradational scale. Such methods represent an attempt to capture not simply the labour-market characteristics of occupations, but their wider socio-economic advantage.

Although derived in different ways, both socio-economic and prestige scales give an index of a multi-dimensional hierarchy, in which a social dimension is stressed in addition to economic inequality. They provide a synthetic occupational measure of overall social position, the result of many different factors. Both also provide a gradational picture of the stratification order, with the social system composed of many finely differentiated social strata. Prestige scales tend to be well correlated with socio-economic scales, share similar assumptions about the underlying nature of the stratification order, and are used in very similar types of analysis. In particular, both have been used in *status attainment* approaches to stratification.

Status attainment approaches, the most influential strand in American stratification research during the 1960s–1970s, are strongly associated with the pre-eminence of Parsons's normative functionalism. These approaches to stratification view it as a finely graded hierarchy of positions, each with differing amounts of prestige or socioeconomic status. [. . .] These studies also contained at least an implicit belief in the legitimacy of the distribution of the various rewards that are attached to these positions, be they material or symbolic.

(Grimes 1991: 128)

The best example of such research, Blau and Duncan's *The American Occupational Structure* (1967), measured the relative importance of the various factors affecting how well individuals fared in the status hierarchy. The study weighed up a range of factors affecting individual occupational success, ranging from so-called 'ascribed characteristics' (social background, measured by parental occupation and education) to 'achieved characteristics' (educational level), as well as 'career effects' (first job, indicating the entry level into the labour market). The conclusion of the study, a finding confirmed by others in the same tradition, was that individual success *was* affected by social background, but educational achievement played a greater role. They therefore argued that unequal social status in modern industrial societies was increasingly the result of differences in individual achievement rather than social background.

This approach generates essentially optimistic conclusions about the nature of stratification. The picture that emerges is of a highly stratified, but relatively open, society, where people broadly agree about the justice of the processes generating inequality. There are ample opportunities to move out of disadvantaged positions and few barriers to achievement. This chimes with normative functionalist theories about the functionalist 'needs' and integration of highly technical and complex modern societies.

These conclusions were attacked for giving a distorted, unduly positive account of stratification. In particular, status-attainment research was criticised for its individualistic assumptions: emphasising how individual characteristics affect success rather than investigating structural opportunities and constraints. Where structural factors do enter the analysis, they do so only as measured at the individual level (by parental social background, for example). But, of course, success is not just determined by our individual characteristics, but also by the overall range of opportunities that are available for us to succeed (or fail) within. No matter how bright you are, or how hard you work, your chances of success will always partly depend on how many high-level jobs there are in the labour market, and whether or not you get the opportunity to apply for them.

Class analysts argue that individualist assumptions are built into the methodology of the status-attainment approach, by seeing social position as the result of movement up (or down) a finely graded status hierarchy. The common objection is that this presents stratification as a fluid, open system, with little sense that there might be structural barriers to achievement: such as internal labour markets and job ladders, which provide greater opportunities for advancement in certain jobs than others; or more general factors, such as the overall expansion or contraction of different labour-market sectors (Goldthorpe *et al.* 1980; Sorenson 1994).

An increasingly widespread reaction against normative functionalism, by the 1970s, led to a revival of class and conflict theories. With the new prominence of class analysis, a different picture of stratification emerged: no longer a seamless open hierarchy, through which individuals moved freely, but rather a divided structure of unequal and opposing groups. For class theorists, structural inequalities generate conflicts of interest and social boundaries, and stratification rests on conflict, with groups competing for and monopolising unequal resources.

Resources and class

Class approaches emphasise economic relations as the basis of the stratification order, exploring how economic location translates into unequal life-chances and affects subjective perceptions and social groupings. Approaches vary in how they define 'economic location', but share a concern with how discontinuities in economic experience relate to social boundaries and conscious identity. Such approaches emphasise classes as discrete groups (potential and actual), emerging out of differential access to economic resources.

Class theorists rejected hierarchical status schemes for merely mapping the distribution of rewards, without indicating the underlying structures which give rise to that hierarchy. Gradational status schemes were seen as descriptive, whilst class schemes were 'theoretical' (Crompton 1996), because class schemes group occupations in terms of the theories of the market or production relations which are held to explain hierarchy and this explanatory framework is built more explicitly into the categories of class schemes.

The key difference is that status approaches measure overall social position ('status'), whereas class approaches stress the economic resources and relations that are seen to give rise to that social position (Sorenson 1994: 232). Class schemes do not rank according to the general lifestyle associated with an occupational position, but rather from the production and market situation of people in different class relationships. It is not how high (or low) we stand in some abstract and synthetic social scale, but rather how our specific class location places us in definite social relations (of control, subordination, or exploitation, for example) with others in different class locations.

Class analysis has always generated diverse frameworks. Rosemary Crompton distinguishes 'case-study' approaches from what she calls the 'employment-aggregate' method of analysis (Crompton 1996, 1998). Case-studies focus on class processes in particular workplace or community locales, and explore how workplace structures are interrelated with non-class 'contextual' factors, such as local status systems or the family life-cycle (Crompton 1996: 59). 'Employment-aggregate' approaches attempt to map the stratification order at a national and cross-national level, by grouping together occupations with similar labour-market and employment relations. Central to the employment-aggregate approach is the notion that classes have distinct life-chances, as a result of their different employment and ownership opportunities. In contrast to the more qualitative, contextual approach of case-studies, the 'employment-aggregate' approach uses primarily quantitative survey methods, and has 'an empirical focus upon "class" (defined as employment) to the *exclusion* of other factors' (Crompton 1996: 59).

'Employment-aggregate' class schemes came to prominence in the 1970s. One, developed by Wright, uses neo-Marxist categories and groups labour-market positions on the basis of their differing relations of exploitation (Wright 1985, 1997). Another, neo-Weberian scheme, developed by Goldthorpe and colleagues, distinguishes jobs in terms of their employment relations (Erikson and Goldthorpe 1992: 37; Goldthorpe *et al.* 1980). Despite theoretical differences, in practical terms the schemes are similar. Both aim to identify the extent to which class resources (as measured by grouping together occupations with similar property or labour-market conditions) affect the life-chances and social relations of the people who fall into those categories. The second approach (the Nuffield or CASMIN scheme) is discussed here.

Since the 1970s, class analysis has been increasingly identified with 'employment-aggregate' approaches (Crompton 1998; Savage 2000; Scott 2001). This is partly because they generate national measures of the class structure, which can be used by other (non-class) researchers employing 'class' as a variable. However, these theoretically based measures of class have also given rise to extensive and ambitious programmes of research, in which cross-national teams of researchers, using increasingly sophisticated methods of statistical analysis, have mapped out how class location affects social behaviour. The coordinated and cumulative nature of these programmes has had a greater impact than the more piecemeal approach of case-studies.

The Nuffield 'employment-aggregate' approach

The Nuffield approach maps the stratification order by looking at the objective aggregate employment relations of different jobs. As Table 5.2 shows occupations are grouped by their employment status relations: distinguishing employers, the self-employed and employees. There are big differences between employees, however, so the scheme divides this group by the nature of their contract with their employer. A 'labour' contract of employment (which might apply to a factory worker or a shop assistant) involves the straightforward exchange of labour for money, under direct supervision, with wages calculated on a piece or time basis. By contrast, some workers (such as professionals or managers) have a 'service' relationship with their employer, and are rewarded not only for the work done, but also have additional perks such as employment security, pension rights, and career opportunities. Employees in a service relationship can exercise autonomy and discretion, have delegated authority, and dispense their expertise *on behalf* of their employers, who trust them to make decisions for the good of the organisation. Other workers sit somewhere between these two models, and therefore have an 'intermediate' position. Clerical and lower-grade technical workers, for example, may exercise some supervisory functions, but they also work alongside rank-and-file manual workers and share some of their conditions of employment.

Underlying this careful separation of occupations with different employment relations is the idea that how we make a living (and the economic resources and opportunities that this brings) fundamentally affects our life-chances. This unites the Marxist emphasis on economic structure with the Weberian emphasis on the multiple influences on social behaviour, by investigating the *extent* to which economic class position influences life-chances, identity and action. The Nuffield research programme has shown that inequalities of income and wealth affect almost every aspect of our lives. To take just a few examples, your class location is related to: your life expectancy and chances of serious illness, how you are likely to vote, your chances of falling victim to crime, and your prospects of educational success. In addition, the impact of class location continues into the next generation, affecting, for example, the likelihood of your children being born underweight or dying young, and patterning their chances of educational or occupational success.

This last question – the extent to which economic class is an *enduring* structure of inequality – has been central to the Nuffield approach, with research focusing on the extent to which class advantage or disadvantage is passed on from one generation to the next. The standard method of analysis, the social mobility table, explores how the class position of parents relates to that of their children. This concern with social mobility is different from the status-attainment approach, since the emphasis is not on the determinants of *individual* success, but rather on how mobility flows *between* economic classes affect the formation of social groupings with 'demographic' continuity of personnel over time. There are two questions explored here: (i) what is the long-term attachment to particular economic positions? (ii) how does this attachment affect the formation of distinct class *groups* with clear-cut boundaries, and different class beliefs, cultural practices, or political activity?

The Nuffield occupational ordering 'closely resembles that of conventional hierarchical schemes reflecting prestige and/or lifestyle' (Crompton 1998: 66), but Goldthorpe insists his scheme is not hierarchical, because it reflects the employment *relations* of classes. He argues that categories with distinct employment relations are not necessarily 'higher' or 'lower' on some synthetic social scale (Goldthorpe *et al.* 1987: 43). This claim has been treated with some scepticism, since there are strong hierarchical elements within the Nuffield class scheme (Marsh 1986; Prandy 1990). The significant point, however, is that the class approach makes a rigid conceptual and methodological separation of the economic and status aspects of stratification.

Class analysts are critical of status scales because, as composite measures, they group occupations with very different employment circumstances at the same general status 'level'. This confounds the effects of social and economic factors in stratification processes, preventing the independent consideration of the *varying* impact of different employment conditions on life-chances. For example, whilst small shopkeepers and skilled technicians may have broadly the same overall social 'status', their access to market and property resources is quite different. This has an impact on intergenerational mobility patterns in such jobs, for example, with the sons of small shopkeepers being much more likely to inherit the same occupation as their fathers than the sons of technicians.

Table 5.2 The Nuffield class scheme

Classes	Collapsed seven-class scheme	Employment relations	Collapsed three-class scheme
I + II	*Service class* 1. large proprietors, professionals, administrators, and managers 2. higher-grade technicians, supervisors of non-manual workers	Employer or service relationship	Service class
IIIa + b	*Routine non-manual workers* 3. routine non-manual workers in administration and commerce 4. sales personnel, other rank-and-file service workers	Intermediate	Intermediate class
IVa + b	*Petty bourgeoisie* 5. small proprietors and artisans with employees 6. small proprietors and artisans without employees	Employer or self-employed	Intermediate class
IVc	*Farmers* 7. farmers and smallholders and other self-employed workers in primary production	Employer or self-employed	Intermediate class
V + VI	*Skilled workers* 8. lower-grade technicians, supervisors of manual workers 9. skilled manual workers	Intermediate or labour contract	Working class
VIIa	*Non-skilled workers* 10. semi- and unskilled manual workers	Labour contract	Working class
VIIb	*Agricultural labourers* 11. agricultural and other workers in primary production	Labour contract	Working class

Source: Adapted from Erikson and Goldthorpe 1992, Table 2.1, pp. 38–9

A more limited project

The Nuffield programme is justly famous for its methodological sophistication and conceptual rigour yet, ironically, it is this very caution and precision which has come under attack. For the Nuffield approach:

> the empirical investigation of the 'class structure' – as they see it – requires the systematic exclusion of other aspects contributing to stratification processes. In their efforts to achieve this objective, it is true that the Nuffield

programme has become highly attenuated. It must be stressed, however, that this has come about as a process of the conscious development of the programme, and not through accident or oversight. This has resulted in strengths – a rigorous standard of empirical proof – as well as weaknesses – a progressive narrowing of focus.

(Crompton 1996: 64)

Since the 1980s, class analysis has come under increasing attack amid claims of the 'death of class'. This reflects arguments that *economic* relations have become increasingly less important in shaping people's social and cultural destinies. Yet those who defend the continuing importance of class processes suggest that the narrowing focus of 'employment-aggregate' approaches is also a problem. From within class theory it is suggested that the 'minimalist' nature (Devine 1998) of employment-aggregate analysis has led to an 'attenuation' of aims (Morris and Scott 1996), resulting in class analysis being seen as an 'increasingly arcane and technical specialism' (Savage 2000: 149).

Critics of 'employment-aggregate' class analysis have made three main points: (1) that class analysis has sidelined issues of cultural identity and the subjective meaning of class location; (2) that too great a priority has been given to economic relations in explanations of stratification, downplaying the importance of status, gender and ethnicity; (3) that the economic cannot be rigidly demarcated as an independent factor determining stratification position, since it is inextricably intertwined with social and cultural factors. These charges all relate to problems with the conceptual separation class analysis makes between, on the one hand, economic relations as underlying causal structures and, on the other hand, subjective and cultural identity as causal 'effects'. Nuffield researchers have always argued that this rigid distinction is necessary in order to establish a clear causal model for empirical analysis. Critics see it as unduly restrictive.

Take the question of subjective meaning. The Nuffield approach deliberately first defines class in terms of 'objective', external criteria and only then explores subjective meanings as a class 'effect'. Social mobility is defined from the 'outside', with no reference to whether or not people themselves believe they have changed location. But the *experience* of mobility (or inequality) depends in large part on how we *perceive* that experience. Critics question whether it makes sense to relegate subjective meaning to such a secondary role, since 'to talk about subjectivity as only an "effect" – a dependent variable – is to ignore the way in which subjective processes are tied up with the strategies and actions which produce mobility itself' (Savage 1997: 317). In other words, there is a fundamental question over whether class analysis adequately addresses the relation between stratification as an *external and objective* set of relations, and actors' *perceptions* of that structure.

The Nuffield approach has been accused of defining 'class' minimally in terms of employment relations, effectively abandoning any notion of classes as 'collectivities of people who share identities and practices' (Devine 1998: 23). Claims about the 'death of class' have dwelt on the failure of class consciousness and action to emerge, yet in defending class analysis, Nuffield researchers have only emphasised the enduring nature of patterned inequalities in life-chances, and have said very little about issues of class consciousness or identity. Cultural identity and subjective meaning are apparently no longer a 'core' aspect of the class project.

Research on social stratification has become increasingly focused on social mobility, 'and technical questions of defining class schema and allocating individuals to class categories' (Scott 2001: 129). As a result:

> there [is] little concern with using the concept of class to explain social divisions and processes of social exclusion. In the mainstream of class analysis, class became, to all intents and purposes, an empirical indicator of occupational position that – all too often – failed to yield the predictive power expected of it.
>
> (Scott 2001: 129)

Critics suggest that what is required is a 'closer investigation of interests and identities' (Crompton and Scott 2000: 5) to give issues of status, culture and identity a more prominent place within class analysis.

A related argument is that other forms of social division and identity – such as gender and ethnicity – have been ignored by class analysis, which has tended to see economic relations as more central. Proponents of the Nuffield approach protest that there is 'no assumption of the pre-eminence of class' in class analysis, since its aim lies in 'examining the importance of class (relative to that of other factors) in shaping life chances and patterns of social action' (Goldthorpe and Marshall 1992: 385). That is, there is no necessary reason why other forms of social division, such as gender or ethnicity, should not be incorporated into class accounts. This is slightly disingenuous, however, since class analysis has placed employment relations at the heart of its explanatory framework, and – historically – has devoted much less attention to other sources of hierarchy.

> Goldthorpe has restricted the remit of his theory to the mobilisation of economic resources (itself narrowly defined in terms of income) and the importance of cultural and social resources in the reproduction of advantage has been dropped from view.
>
> (Devine 1998: 24)

Goldthorpe has argued that 'class concepts must be as sharply defined as is operationally feasible, in order to avoid any confounding of class with other factors of possible relevance' (Goldthorpe and Marshall 1992: 385). In practice, this means that the class structure is defined quite *independently* of the education, status, prestige, lifestyle, gender or ethnic composition of occupations, even though these factors are acknowledged to affect an occupation's overall position in the stratification order. Increasingly, however, theorists have questioned whether this conceptual separation is desirable, or even feasible. Instead it has been argued that class can only be understood through its complex inter-relationships with 'status' factors, which also entails rethinking the *methods* of class analysis:

> Class is a complicated mixture of the material, the discursive, psychological predispositions and sociological dispositions that quantitative work on class location and class identity cannot hope to capture. . . . Now what is required are British based ethnographic examination of how class is 'lived' in gendered and raced ways to complement the macro versions that have monopolised our ways of envisaging social class for far too long.
>
> (Reay 1998a: 272)

Crompton, for example, advocates '*social* class analysis which, rather than seeking to distance themselves from the status concept, are premised upon the interrelationship of the "economic" and the "social"' (1998: 119). So class analysis needs to concern itself with the processes of class *formation* (in which prestige, association and lifestyle, and status claims are entwined with economic class) as well as the investigation of class *effects*. As Chapter 8 shows, however, this entails rejecting the analytical model in which economic class structure *gives rise to* status (or cultural) differences.

Conclusion

Despite their varying principles of construction, the socio-economic, prestige and class approaches have essentially the same understanding of the stratification order, which is conceived as an external structure of positions. The common element in all these approaches is to first establish a stratification structure (whether it be a prestige, socio-economic or class ordering) and then measure the extent to which social relations are affected by position within it. The method straightforwardly derives from the classical legacy on stratification, in dividing structure from action, the economic from the social, and investigating the influence of the former on the latter.

This, of course, is the opposite of the method used by the community studies approach to stratification. Rather than establishing a structure of positions and then looking at the nature of social relations within it, Warner reverses this procedure, looking at how different valued resources (social, cultural and economic) combine within practical social relations to create ranked social groupings. Warner makes no division between the economic and the social aspects of stratification, and does not see cultural lifestyle as an effect of structure, but rather as a means by which stratification position is constituted. That is, the *combination* of lifestyle, reputation, and economic resources within interaction patterns is used to identify the stratification ordering. However, Warner is also influenced by functionalism, so his emphasis on social interaction patterns is filtered by a reliance on subjective prestige evaluations of these patterns. As we have seen, this emphasis on the prestige aspect of stratification undermines Warner's approach.

Following Warner, and with the shift to a national focus, attempts to map stratification abandoned the notion of looking at actual status relations. Instead, mapping exercises have looked only at perceptions of the social standing of occupational titles considered in the abstract, or else have turned to the objective socio-economic characteristics of jobs. Both have produced scales of occupations quite independent of the actual social relationships of the people in the jobs. These 'conventional' approaches to stratification, whilst tightly defined, have also become very narrowly focused, as the measurement of stratification position has become centred on selected aspects of the occupational structure. There is no direct measurement of lifestyle, and status in its associational sense has dropped from the picture. These aspects of hierarchical social experience are now studied as effects of stratification position. So lifestyle and association, which in the community studies approach were used to identify the stratification order, are reduced to causal effects of a stratification structure defined in broad labour-market terms. Stratification in such approaches has increasingly been character-ised as an external structure, independent of individual perceptions of it, and measured in terms of objective labour-market characteristics.

What is striking is how the wheel has again turned. Conventional approaches to stratification have been increasingly criticised for their prioritisation of labour-market relations (effectively sidelining social divisions such as gender and ethnicity), and for concentrating on the effects of stratification on life-chances and broad social trends, whilst downplaying issues of subjective consciousness, social identity and cultural lifestyles. Indeed, as we have seen, critics of conventional class theory have called for a rethink of the conventional division between the economic and the social, structure and action. All this takes us back to the princi-ples in Warner's approach to stratification. Whilst the community studies tradition has not been revived, later chapters explore alternative approaches to stratifica-tion which embody many of Warner's principles, and focus on stratification as a process of cultural and interaction differentiation.

The first part of this book has argued that the classical theoretical foundations of stratification created an ambiguous and divided inheritance, creating an unravelling legacy of problems for later writers. Because stratification has increasingly emerged as a discipline focused on the structural, economic sphere, it has had difficulty accounting for symbolic, 'social' divisions (such as issues of race and ethnicity, gender, and cultural identity). The second part of the book, 'Deconstructions', now turns to look at these divisions, and explores recent claims that stratification analysis is outdated and increasingly irrelevant. In some recent accounts, the areas under-explored by conventional stratification analysis (gender, race and ethnicity, the cultural and the subjective) have come to over-shadow economic inequalities; and – for some – these areas of social life are increasingly disconnected from economic or class constraints. Chapters 6 and 7 explore the emergence of these claims, in response to problems of theorising race and gender within the 'structural' and 'economic' models of conventional stratification theory. Race, ethnicity and gender have increasingly been seen as divisions which undermine economic class identities and groupings, and call into question conventional structural theories of identity. These chapters look at how the emphasis on newer social divisions has undermined the very idea of structural forces or cohesive social groups, giving rise to a new emphasis on fragmentation and fluidity in social arrangements. Chapter 8 critically explores how such arguments have been used to deconstruct the very idea of 'stratification' (as the impact of ordered, enduring inequalities on individual lives), with the claim that material inequality no longer shapes our social identities as it once did. For some writers, the 'decline' of class is part of a general fragmentation and individualisation of social life.

Part 2

Deconstructions

6   Racialised relations

Whereas the popular 'narrative of race' is the story of how 'social inequalities became regarded as natural ones' (Malik 1996: 71), the sociological treatment of 'race' has been based around the effort to uncover the *social organisation* of 'racial' differentiation, deconstructing 'naturalistic' accounts of racial divisions. Sociological accounts stress that racial categories are not biologically 'real', but rather are essentially fictional, socially constructed divisions. However, in stressing the 'symbolic' nature of racial differentiation, analysts have always struggled to reconcile 'race' as relations of 'cultural' difference with 'race' as relations of material inequality. As this chapter shows, in practice, accounts have cycled back and forth between *either* cultural *or* economic accounts, with neither set of approaches entirely satisfactory. Whilst the material inequalities of 'race' are undeniable, there have been difficulties in establishing 'race' as more than the by-product of economic inequalities. In rejecting the 'economic reductionism' of materialist accounts, there has been a post-structural turn to analysing 'race' as a form of cultural difference, in which racial divisions have been seen as increasingly fluid and contingent, floating free of structural determination. But by recasting 'race' as relations of symbolic, discursive difference such approaches have themselves been criticised for denying issues of inequality, and for underplaying the ways in which 'difference' emerges through practical, lived relations in material social locations.

Racial categories

Racial characteristics are seen as marked on the body, but 'racial' divisions now regarded as self-evident were not so obvious to people in the past. Racial categorisation is a fluid process of social construction and ascription, and markers of racial difference have shifted, with groups emerging with quite different 'racial' boundaries and labels. In America, European settlers did not regard Native-Americans as significantly different in colour from themselves until the mid-1700s, and 'not until the nineteenth century did red become the universally accepted colour label for American Indians' (Bonnett 1998b: 1037). The practice of slavery coalesced the racial category of 'black', as it 'created the "black" where once there had been Asante or Ovimbundu, Yoruba or Bakonga' (Omi and Winant 1994: 66).

> Classifications of 'racial otherness' also became increasingly complex in the
> United States, where people of 'mixed race', even if they looked white, were
> not allowed to vote or inherit significant property . . . the belief [was] that
> these people were contaminated by 'dark blood' that could be smelt.
>
> (Shilling and Mellor 2001: 150)

The label 'white' is notoriously shifting, with certain groups only claiming it
after a long struggle to win social acceptance. The Irish, as colonial subjects,
were characterised as 'Black celts' in race science, and popularly represented as
non-civilised and primitive in the nineteenth century (Bonnett 1998a, b). The
story of 'How the Irish Became White' (Ignatiev 1996) (and how other groups
came to be seen as 'black') was a process of political contestation and struggle,
emerging from shifting relations of exclusion and inequality.

> The fact that only certain physical characteristics are signified to define
> 'races' in specific circumstances indicates that we are investigating not a
> given, natural division of the world's population, but the application of
> historically and culturally specific meanings to the totality of human physio-
> logical variation.
>
> (Miles 1993: 71)

The fluidity of such typifications, and their arbitrary physiological basis, has
led theorists of race to emphasise the distinctions that people draw themselves,
with racialised identities *claimed* and/or *ascribed* identities and affiliations. Racial
divisions provide a clear-cut example of social divisions based on self-conscious
symbolic identities, with overt 'us and them' expressions of difference central to
the experience of racialised groups (Anthias 1998). Because of this, it has sometimes been argued that racial divisions are, in fact, a more likely basis of social
conflict and political mobilisation than economic class and that we should look
to racial groupings for a mobilised 'class-for-itself'.

However, a fundamental tension emerges in accounts of racial divisions,
between 'race' as a form of symbolic and cultural differentiation, and 'race' as a
form of inequality. As Anthias argues:

> Within most approaches to stratification gender and ethnicity are seen to
> pertain primarily to the symbolic or cultural realms, while class is regarded as
> pertaining to material inequality. This constructs gender and ethnic posi-
> tioning as entailing honour, deference, worth, value and differential treatment
> (sometimes expressed through the notion of 'status'), but the social relations
> around these are themselves not seen as constitutive of social stratification.
>
> (Anthias 2001: 367)

Racial divisions – because of their symbolic character – have often been
marginalised in accounts of stratification which focus on material inequality. But,
of course, racial divisions are inextricably bound up with hierarchy, economic

and power inequalities and subordination; so any adequate analysis of race must address how lateral, cultural differentiation relates to vertical, hierarchical inequality. The struggle has been to find the right *balance* between these different elements.

Scientific racism in the nineteenth century presented racial difference as the same as hierarchical inferiority. Early accounts of 'racial' inequality made no clear-cut distinction between racial and class inferiors, and discourses of 'race' arose not just in relation to colonial 'Others' but also to explain class differences within European society (Malik 1996: 81; Pick 1989). However, by the twentieth century, with the incorporation of the working class into political and welfare rights (Bonnett 1998a, b), 'race' came to be seen as increasingly distinct from class:

> Whereas in the past belief in the inferiority of non-European peoples was an extension of the already existing belief in the inferiority of the lower orders at home, now it became a central part of racial discourse. The idea of 'backwardness', which had previously applied to the working class at home, became exclusively associated with the 'native' in the colonies. This reorientation of racial thought helped establish racism as a mass ideology and win popular support for elite ideas of hierarchy. It also helped promote the idea which is so strong today: that racial language was developed in order specifically to describe distinctions between black and white.
>
> (Malik 1996: 119)

This popular distinction between 'class' and 'race' is reflected in academic analysis, and accounts of race/ethnicity and of class/stratification have developed very differently. Research on stratification has included race/ethnicity as an additional explanatory variable, but as an adjunct to more 'central' issues of economic inequality, leading to criticisms that accounts of stratification have marginalised issues of race. Meanwhile, sociological and anthropological accounts of race and ethnicity have developed as distinct research disciplines with their own agenda and frameworks.

This separation is inherited from the classical sociologists, who had relatively little to say on the subject. The classical sociologists saw inequality as socially – and contingently – organised and, in rejecting biological explanations of race, saw race as an 'ideological' construct, based on irrational premises. However, the 'irrational' basis of racial hierarchies does not lessen the social divisions and inequalities that result from them. As Miles argues:

> We live in a world in which the nineteenth century biological conception of 'race', although discredited scientifically, remains an important presence in 'common sense': large numbers of people continue to believe, and to act as if they believe, that the world's population is divided into a number of discrete, biologically distinguishable groups, i.e. 'races'.
>
> (Miles 1999: 138)

The classical sociologists failed to see that 'the foundations of modernity have been dependent on making particular regions and peoples the objects rather than the subjects of international relations. A major goal of racial sociology, in contrast, has been to recover the varied processes by which this objectification and exclusion is accomplished' (Shilling and Mellor 2001: 149). Conventional stratification analysis, drawing so heavily from the classical sociologists, has tended to give primacy to the vertical dimension of material inequalities, marginalising the lateral, and symbolic, aspects of 'race'. What the sociology of race does share with the classical sociologists, however, is a stress on the arbitrary, shifting and essentially 'social' nature of racial divisions, where social differences are *perceived* in 'racial' terms.

From biological hierarchy to cultural diversity

In the early 1900s, distinctively social models of race replaced evolutionary biological accounts of distinct (and unequal) 'races' in favour of models of *cultural* difference. This shift from 'biological hierarchy to cultural diversity' (Malik 1996) saw 'race relations' as social relations between groups which *defined themselves* as 'races', 'rather than biologically determined relations between biologically distinct and discrete "races"' (Miles 1999: 128). The 'primitive races' envisaged by scientific racists were reinterpreted in a more egalitarian and rela- tivist manner, as simply people with distinct cultural practices. What this did was

> effectively to turn the evolutionary ladder of Victorian racial theory on its side, and to conceive of humanity as horizontally rather than vertically segmented. Humanity was not arranged at different points along an ever-rising vertical scale, as the social evolutionists had believed, but at different points along a stationary horizontal axis. Humanity was composed of a multitude of peoples each inhabiting their own symbolic and social worlds. Dispossessed of faith in evolutionary progress, functionalists envisaged society, and social difference in static terms.
>
> (Malik 1996: 156)

However, until the 1960s, social anthropology tended to focus on analysing the societies of the colonised as self-contained entities (rather than looking at their relations to their colonial oppressors), whereas sociological approaches focused on the impact of colonialism and migration on the racial composition of western industrial societies. Here the emphasis was less on racialised cultures as distinct societies, than on 'race relations' within America and Europe.

Assimilationist, or 'race relations', perspectives on race dominated sociolog- ical analysis from the 1940s to the 1960s, and presented racial difference in cultural terms as ethnicity:

> which suggested that race was a *social* category. Race was but one of a number of determinants of ethnic group identity or ethnicity. Ethnicity itself was

understood as the result of a group formation process based on culture and descent. 'Culture' in this formulation included such diverse factors as religion, language, 'customs', nationality, and political identification.

(Omi and Winant 1994: 15)

The work of Robert E. Park exemplifies this approach.

Park was interested in the experience of 'minority' immigrant groups in the socially diverse urban environments of American society. His focus was on 'the subjective dimensions of racial consciousness that help to produce the conditions for the emergence of racial conflict' (Solomos and Back 1999: 101), that is, on those social differences *explicitly recognised* and *acted upon* as 'racial' by the participants of such processes. His concern was with how

> racial differences enter into the consciousness of the individuals and groups so distinguished, and by doing so determine in each case the individual's conception of himself as well as his status in the community. . . . Race consciousness, therefore, is to be regarded as a phenomenon, like class or caste consciousness, that enforces social distances. Race relations, in this sense, are not so much the relations that exist between individuals of different races as between individuals conscious of these differences.

(Park 1999: 104, 105)

Although racial differences were 'the products of migration and conquest' (1999: 107), Park emphasises their cultural aspect and impact on social association, since

> racial differences would not maintain social distances to the extent that they do if they were not symptoms of differences in custom, tradition, and religion, and of sentiments appropriate to them. Differences of race and custom mutually reinforce one another, particularly when they are not broken up by intermarriage. . . . It is the essence of race relations that they are the relations of strangers; of people who are associated primarily for secular and practical purposes; for the exchange of goods and services. They are otherwise the relations of people of diverse races and cultures who have been thrown together by the fortunes of war, and who, for any reason, have not been sufficiently knit together by intermarriage and interbreeding to constitute a single ethnic community, with all that implies.

(Park 1999: 110)

Park argues that migration affects 'culture contact' with immigrant groups going through several stages of contact, conflict, accommodation, before eventually achieving assimilation. The basis of assimilation would, he believed, be the development of 'new relationships' that 'breed new loyalties', but minority groups would have to change their culture to assimilate, since the process entailed 'the more or less complete incorporation of the individual into the moral order' (Park, quoted in Shilling and Mellor 2001: 152).

As critics have pointed out, this means 'the gradual absorption of distinct groups into the mainstream' (Omi and Winant 1994: 11), in which assimilation homogenises cultural diversity. By the 1970s, the notion that migrant groups must abandon any distinct cultural practices seemed both dubious and naive. Critics rejected two central assumptions of the assimilationist approach: 'the European immigrant analogy which suggested that racial minorities could be incorporated into American life in the same way that white ethnic groups had been, and the assumption of a fundamental, underlying American commitment to equality and social justice for racial minorities' (Omi and Winant 1994: 12). Models of assimilation based on the experiences of European immigrants do not apply to black Americans, whose long sojourn in America has not resulted in incorporation. Their experience has been of enduring deliberate exclusion and racial exploitation, rather than mutual separation on the basis of cultural difference.

The problem is that differential association is not simply a process of lateral difference, but is also centrally bound up with inequality and hierarchy. This was, in fact, identified in one of the earliest 'race relations' accounts, Lloyd Warner's theory of 'colour-caste' (Warner and Srole 1959 [1945]). Warner argued that whereas European minorities had moved up the stratification hierarchy over two or three generations and assimilated, this was not the case for black Americans. The emergence of a black middle class had increased stratification within the black community, but rigid social barriers persisted between whites and blacks, and systematic inequalities flowed from these exclusions. Warner argued that a 'caste' barrier split the stratification system in two, and systematic exclusion between castes prevented assimilation. This 'caste' barrier was more impenetrable than class divisions, so that the white middle classes were more likely to associate with poor whites than with the black middle class. Warner's characterisation of American racial divisions in 'caste' terms was simplistic, but his central point is valid. Normal stratification models cannot account for 'racial' divisions, which are a specific form of racialised inequality. Nor, however, can they be understood in terms of 'cultural' difference alone.

The criticisms of the race relations approach shows the limitations of an approach which focuses on 'race' as a dimension of lateral cultural differentiation, without exploring how such difference is bound up with power and inequality. The emphasis on racial division as cultural difference assumes that, with good will and better communication, assimilation will occur. However, the race relations approach said 'nothing about the relations of power which bind the various "ethnic minorities" together and by means of which some groups are subordinated to others' (Lawrence 1982: 135).

Material underpinnings

During the 1980s, the sociological treatment of 'race' – as an account of cultural relations – gave way to the analysis of racism – the ways in which racialised practices are embedded in relations of power, inequality and exploitation.

The rejection of culture was tied up with the notion that one of the inherent dangers of focusing research on the culture of minority communities was the tendency to shift attention from racism to the characteristics of racialised minorities.

(Solomos and Back 1999: 19)

This was a move away from assimilationist emphases on 'race' as contained within the distinctive culture of minority groups (which also erased the 'race' of the majority population), to instead explore 'racism' as relations of domination and subordination.

Marxist-inspired approaches saw racism emerging from capitalist strategies to 'divide and rule' the working class (undermining class solidarity), with *racial* divisions the product of *class* processes (Baran and Sweezy 1966; Castles and Kosack 1973). In such approaches it is the capitalistic profit motive which is seen as the key element to explaining racism, because in the pursuit of profit

'racial otherness' is accepted as a given resource. It is a marker of identity that can serve as a basis for discriminatory actions on the part of the powerful that help produce outcomes conducive to the maintenance of relative economic privilege.

(Shilling and Mellor 2001: 153)

The motivation for racism in such accounts is economic. Racially defined groups are treated differently within the ostensibly impersonal markets of capitalism because this enables greater profit. For many writers, the reason that racially defined groups can be used in this way is because global capitalist development has led to large-scale immigration. The status of workers as *migrants* makes them cheaper and easier to exploit. In Marxist accounts, migrant workers are a 'reserve army' who act as a source of cheap, disposable labour, undercutting the wages of the working class. This pits different fractions of the working classes against each other, as more privileged workers organise against migrants to exclude them from the better jobs, leading to segregation and racist conflict in working and social relations. For some writers the 'cheapness' of the migrant labour system partly arises because the costs of the production of labour power are partly met by the society from which the migrant comes (and may return). The problem is that such accounts reduce processes of racialisation to class processes, with class seen as the more basic explanatory category:

Race, ultimately, is no more than a convenient, pre-existing construct that the economically privileged used to maintain their position. It is capitalism, rather than racism, that is prioritised as elementary to the structuring of social and moral life. Because of this, these approaches have been criticised for reducing the significance of race to economic criteria.

(Omi and Winant 1994: 27)

These disagreements are over whether racialised divisions can be explained by underlying economic structures, or whether race and ethnicity are 'non-reductive' social features which 'have their own specific effects, which cannot be explained away as mere surface forms of appearance of economic relations, nor adequately theorized by reducing them to the economic level of determination' (S. Hall 1980: 306–307). As Hall argues, this division re-hashes general debates on the relations between the 'economic' and the 'social', and between structure and action, but 'the problem here is not whether economic structures are relevant to racial divisions but how the two are theoretically connected' (1980: 308). The problem of theorising their connection, however, has repeatedly led to explanations which *either* stress cultural difference *or* material inequality.

For the Marxist writer Robert Miles, 'race' is an ideology which masks class inequality, so he objects to any notion of the 'autonomy' of racial processes, because

> There are no 'races' and therefore no 'race relations'. There is only the belief that there are such things, a belief which is used by some groups to construct an Other (and therefore the Self) in thought as a prelude to exclusion and domination, and by other groups to define Self (and so to construct an Other) as a means of resisting that exclusion. Hence, if it is used at all, the idea of 'race' should be used to refer descriptively to such uses of the idea of 'race'.
>
> (Miles 1999: 135)

His emphasis is not on 'race' as distinct, cultural formation, but rather how racialisation and racism have emerged as 'ideological forces which, in conjunction with economic and political relations of domination, located certain populations in specific class positions and therefore structured the exploitation of labour power in a particular ideological manner' (Miles 1999: 141). For Miles, 'race' has no autonomous effects, independent of the racist practices which emerge as a product of class regulation and exploitation. Later writers, however, 'have been less concerned with the ontological question of whether race *really* exists and have shifted their focus to examine the *effects* of such truth claims' (Mac an Ghail 1999: 43).

For writers who insist on the 'irreducibility' of 'race', processes of racialisation are affected by class inequalities, but have their own independent dynamic. Rex, for example, in a Weberian analysis, explores how 'race relations' emerge from competitive struggles over distributive resources (such as jobs, but also housing, education, and other valued assets). As a result of being excluded from the housing and employment rights won by white workers through the labour movement, migrant workers occupy a position quite distinct from the location, and processes, governing the white working class: 'instead of identifying with working-class culture, community and politics, they formed their own organisations and became effectively a separate underprivileged class' (Rex and Tomlinson 1979: 275). Although racial divisions are bound up with class, or economic, inequalities, they also operate as an independent force, with their own logic.

An even more complex, and controversial, account of the interconnection between economic and 'racial' factors is offered by William Julius Wilson, who argues that the history of racial discrimination has created a system of racial inequality that lingers on even after racial barriers have come down. Wilson argues that, in American society, the civil rights movement and the dismantling of traditional racial barriers means that there is a 'declining significance of race', in the sense that direct and overt racial oppression is on the wane, and non-racial factors now have a more significant impact on the black community: 'Race relations in America have undergone fundamental changes in recent years, so much so that now the life chances of individual blacks have more to do with their economic class position than with day-to-day encounters with whites' (Wilson 1978: 1).

Wilson does not argue that racial inequality is declining, but says that general processes of economic restructuring explain it. An accumulation of disadvantages associated with previous racial oppression has meant that the most disadvantaged do not have the resources to compete effectively. Economic restructuring has widened the gap between low-scale and higher-scale workers and – because of historic racism – there are a disproportionate number of blacks in the low-scale, poorly educated category. For Wilson this means 'class has become more important than race in determining black access to privilege and power' (1978: 2), and he points to the increasing differentiation of life-chances between the black middle class and an expanding group of underclass blacks, the most 'truly disadvantaged' (1987).

In Wilson's argument, prior to de-industrialisation inner-city neighbourhoods were socially mixed, because racial exclusions meant middle class, working class and poor blacks lived alongside each other. However, with the decline of explicit racial segregation, the middle classes moved out, changing the social composition of black neighbourhoods. The most disadvantaged groups remained in the inner-city areas, but were employed in the sectors hardest hit by de-industrialisation, so that economic restructuring hit black neighbourhoods particularly hard, creating urban ghettoes with few jobs or opportunities, whose inhabitants become locked into poverty. Racial inequalities, in this account, no longer result from racially motivated actions, but rather from processes of economic competition which affect unequal groups unequally, serving to reproduce and deepen racial divisions as a by-product.

Wilson's claims have been attacked, amid arguments that 'direct' racism is still decisive in the situation of the most disadvantaged minorities in America. The notion that black 'middle-class flight' has created extreme concentrations of poverty in black urban neighbourhoods is questioned by critics who instead see it resulting from two factors: generally high levels of poverty in the black population overall, and high levels of racial *segregation*, with most American blacks living in neighbourhoods which are overwhelmingly black (Massey and Denton 1993). Given high poverty levels, the concentration of black populations through segregation also means the concentration of poverty. For Massey and Denton it is enduring *segregation* – organised on racial and not class lines – that explains the situation they describe as 'American apartheid'.

Wilson was not, in fact, arguing that racism had disappeared, but rather had shifted from the economic to the socio-political arena, in struggles between the 'have-nots' over access to decent housing and neighbourhoods, control over public schools, and political control over inner cities (1978: 116). However, quoting Martin Luther King's remark – 'What good is it to be allowed to eat in a restaurant, if you can't afford a hamburger?' (1978: 162) – Wilson argued that the life-chances of blacks depended less on racism than on essentially neutral economic processes. His critics, however, insisted that direct and explicit racism and segregation remain powerful influences on the economic life-chances of American blacks. Massey and Denton pointed out that middle-class blacks experience the *same* high levels of racial segregation as poor blacks, suggesting that economic advancement had not enabled middle-class black Americans to live in integrated communities or to bypass the effects of race in how they were defined. Thus, the furore that surrounded Wilson's claim of the declining significance of race raised another issue: the way in which 'race' and racism remain crucial to how Americans *experience* life, and see themselves and others. That is, 'race' as core component of social experience, cultural communities and identifications.

Here, again, is the ongoing problem of theorising the lateral and hierarchical aspects of 'race' and ethnicity, that is, in understanding 'race' and ethnicity as *both* relations of cultural difference and as relations of inequality and subordination. From the late 1980s, a re-emergence of cultural accounts of 'race' argued that materialists had 'erased the centrality of culture to questions of racial difference' (Mac an Ghail 1999: 22). This led to a substantial shift in research, with new work focusing on racial and ethnic difference as forms of *cultural* experience: as the basis of social identification, community association and political mobilisation.

The cultural (re)turn

This return to cultural analysis has occurred because class approaches have been accused of downplaying cultural difference (seeing 'race' as the ideological 'effect' of class) and of ignoring the use of culture, 'race' and ethnicity as a politics of resistance and claimed identity. Because of this economic reductionism, critics argue, materialist approaches cannot explain the internal dynamics of minority communities, nor the construction of collective identities around race culture and community (Gilroy 1987), resulting in 'the denial of what is a critical, lived category for minorities' (Mac an Ghail 1999: 103). Modood argues that underlying the racist categorisations imposed on ethnic minority groups lie 'real collectivities, common and distinctive forms of thinking and behaviour, of language, custom, religion and so on; not just modes of oppression but modes of being' (Modood 1996: 95).

As Mac an Ghail notes, 'The decoupling of social class and racism needs to be located in the wider sociological arena of the decentring of class' (1999: 32). Despite continuing material inequality, economic divisions have been seen as increasingly less important for political mobilisation or social identity. Other, cultural, forms of division – such as race – are now seen as more significant for how people define themselves and live their lives. As class- or trade union-based politics have declined, for example, there has been a shift to 'new social movements', which organise around issues of gender, sexuality, the environment, and racial and ethnic minority rights. These political mobilisations are – it is argued – loosely, if at all, related to economic divisions. Such social movements represent a shift from the politics of redistribution to a politics of recognition, identity and cultural difference.

Central to these developments have been mobilisations around racial and ethnic cultural identities, which 'take as their starting point the assertion of the rights of racial minorities to equal treatment and justice, and make claims for the empowerment of racially excluded groups' and 'two of the key areas around which sections of racialised minorities are likely to mobilise are culture and religion' (Solomos and Back 1996: 94, 97).

> Ethnic identity, like gender and sexuality, has become politicised and for some people has become a primary focus of their politics. There is an ethnic assertiveness, arising out of the feelings of not being respected or lacking access to public space, consisting of counterposing 'positive' images against traditional or dominant stereotypes. It is a politics of projecting identities in order to challenge existing power relations; of seeking not just toleration for ethnic difference but also public acknowledgement, resources and representation.
>
> (Modood 1997: 290)

Increasingly, attention has turned back to identities formed around religion, culture, claims to a shared homeland, or experience of migration and diaspora. However, this return to a cultural analysis of racial difference is very different from earlier 'race relations' approaches, which focused on the relations between distinct social *groups*. The emphasis is now not on groups, but on cultural *difference* in which 'the living of ethnic and racialized categories and divisions is more contradictory, fragmented, shifting and ambivalent than the dominant public definitions of these categories suggest' (Mac an Ghail 1999: 12). Such work has abandoned the view that cultures are clearly bounded and homogeneous entities, emphasising instead the internal diversity within cultures.

> The features that are taken into account are not the sum of 'objective' differences, but only those which the actors themselves regard as significant ... some cultural features are used by the actors as signals and emblems of difference, others are ignored, and in some relationships radical differences are played down and denied.
>
> (Barth 1969: 14)

Initial approaches focused on 'the ethnic boundary that defines the group rather than the cultural stuff that it encloses' (Barth 1969: 15). Barth emphasises that 'the cultural differences of primary significance for ethnicity are those that people use to mark the distinction, the boundary' (1994: 12), that is, the practices that demarcate a line between 'insiders' from 'outsiders'. Racialised and ethnic cultures are no longer defined by what they have in common, but rather how they organise around a shared notion of who does *not* belong to the group. Subsequent work has moved still further away from the notion of groups, deconstructing Barth's notion of distinct boundaries, and presenting instead the notion of highly fragmented affiliations based on shifting relations of *difference*.

Analysts of post-colonialism, for example, have analysed the way in which diaspora and transnational migration have resulted in cultural dispersal, and the mixing of cultural practices, resulting in shifting 'hybrid' forms of identification which blur the boundaries of traditional categories or groups. In America, for example, the permeable US/Mexican border has produced multiplex transnational identities, 'such as "Chicano", "Latino" and "Hispanic", beyond the more monolithic categories of "Mexicans" and "Americans"'(Lamont and Molnar 2002: 184). Key to recent accounts is the notion that individuals always have a variety of social identities and affiliations, and that these combine in unpredictable and cross-cutting ways.

> In social relations, people occupy certain positions simultaneously. A working-class identity is at the same time a sexual identity and an ethnic identity. We need to think about not the ways in which social categories accumulate but the ways they inflect.
>
> (Mac an Ghail 1999: 47)

As Stuart Hall argues, this means we must recognise 'that all of us are composed of multiple social identities, not one. That we are all complexly constructed through different categories, of different antagonisms, and these may have the effect of locating us socially in multiple positions of marginality and subordination, but which do not operate on us in exactly the same way' (S. Hall 1991: 57). As a result, racial identities, and actions, cannot simply be 'read off' from experience, or class location, since they are always affected by gender, sexuality, nationality, and so on, which act to create cross-cutting allegiances. The highly differentiated and intersecting nature of categories such as 'black', 'white' or 'Asian' means they must be deconstructed, for example, into 'Black British', 'African-Caribbean', 'white gay Scottish middle-class man', 'Tower Hamlets working-class Bengali Muslim woman', and can be deconstructed still further by the addition of additional contextual qualifiers. For many writers, there are no clear-cut social categories, groups, or divisions from which we can predict behaviour and identity, but rather only the unpredictable interplay of multiple dimensions of intersecting difference.

The cultural arbitrary

This shift in focus to 'the making and re-making of culture and ethnic identity formations' (Mac an Ghail 1999: 40) has been accompanied by a much greater stress on the essentially arbitrary nature of such identifications. Materialist writers also referred to the contingent nature of racial difference, but saw such differences as emerging out of underlying *material* divisions. Robert Miles's account of 'race' as ideology, for example, presents shifting racialised divisions as a by-product of class inequality. For Miles:

> it was only after Africans were enslaved that African people were repre-
> sented in negative terms as an Other and that certain of their phenotypical
> characteristics were signified as expressive of their being a different (and
> inferior) type of human being.
>
> (Miles 1999: 140–141)

With the culturalist turn, later writers continue to stress the contingent nature of racialised categories, but reject the idea that class processes underlie them. In doing so, new work focuses on race as a political and cultural *construct*, increasingly shorn of the link to economic relations, as 'questions about race and racism have been refashioned in ways that emphasise cultural difference' (Solomos and Back 1999: 4), and '"Diaspora" and "hybridity" have become important concepts within racial sociology as symbols of the unstable and dynamic features of "racial" identity' (Shilling and Mellor 2001: 158).

The transient and fragile nature of racial identities can be seen in Stuart Hall's account of the shifting meanings of 'black'. In the British context, he argues, a sense of 'Black' identity emerged out of migrants' shared experiences of racism, but was unknown in the Caribbean context from which many migrants came.

> I was brought up in a lower middle class family in Jamaica. I left there in the
> early fifties to go and study in England. Until I left, though I suppose 98 per
> cent of the Jamaican population is either Black or coloured in one way or
> another, I had never heard anybody call themselves, or refer to anybody else
> as 'Black'. Never. I heard a thousand other words. My grandmother could
> differentiate between about fifteen different shades between light brown
> and dark brown. When I left Jamaica, there was a beauty contest in which
> the different shades of women were graded according to different trees, so
> that there was Miss Mahogany, Miss Walnut, etc. People think of Jamaica
> as a simple society. In fact, it had the most complicated colour stratifica-
> tion system in the word. . . . Compared with that, the normal class stratifi-
> cation system is absolute child's play. But the word 'Black' was never uttered.
> Why? No Black people around? Lots of them, thousands and thousands of
> them. Black is not a question of pigmentation . . . it is not because of their
> skins that they are Black in their heads.
>
> (S. Hall 1991: 53)

However, in Britain, during the 1970s, diverse groups 'from the Caribbean, East Africa, the Asian subcontinent, Pakistan, Bangladesh, from different parts of India . . . all identified themselves politically as Black' (S. Hall 1991: 55). The emergence of the term 'black', papering over enormous cultural, religious and social differences, Hall argues, was an essentially fictional identity, but an effective and resonant one because it entailed 'the construction of some defensive collective identity against the practices of racist society. It had to do with the fact that people were being blocked out of and refused an identity and identification within the majority nation, having to find some other roots on which to stand' (S. Hall 1991: 52).

Hall sees political identities as being 'composed of unities within difference' (Solomos and Back 1996: 137). However, such politicised identifications are also transient and unstable, precisely because of the differentiation within them. So the umbrella category of 'black' collapsed in the 1980s, because 'as one advanced to meet the enemy, with a solid front, the differences were raging behind' (S. Hall 1991: 56), and there were increasing perceptions that the term 'black' silenced Asian experiences and essentialised diverse identities. New, hybrid and more pluralistic ethnicities have emerged out of the deconstruction of earlier categories, but are themselves subject to reconstruction because, as Stuart Hall argues, 'we are confronted by a bewildering, fleeting multiplicity of possible identities, any of which we could identify with – at least temporarily' (S. Hall 1992: 277).

Hall's work on 'new ethnicities' presents racial identities as unstable, and underdetermined by material social relations precisely because of the diverse subject positions we all occupy. As Anthias notes, this concern with difference 'has enabled a more adequate theorisation of the multifaceted interactions of social relations' (1998: 508). However, later work has increasingly stressed the *symbolic* nature of racial divisions and 'has not been able to address the issue of social divisions in terms of structured forms of inequality. The issues of class position and indeed gender position and the economic and political relations within which ethnic processes need to be contextualised have been absent from much of the recent debate on "new ethnicities"' (Anthias 1998: 525).

Much recent work has been influenced by the post-structuralist stress on the symbolic and cultural (rather than material) nature of social divisions, which emphasises the discursive construction of difference rather than distinct structural 'categories'. This links up with postmodern influences, to result in accounts which reject general explanatory categories as essentialist, and which focus instead on the contingency, fragility and arbitrariness of human life, and the transient and fragmented nature of subjective identities (Shilling and Mellor 2001).

> Postmodern theory has declared the demise of the metanarrative, the recognition and celebration of difference, diversity and differentiation and the rejection of the unitary notion of the subject which becomes fragmented. A specificity is allocated to the local and particular as opposed to the general and the universal, and analysis needs to focus on concrete instances. One of the assumptions made by the notion of difference is that there is so much cultural diversity that it is impossible to find common threads.
>
> (Anthias 1998: 507)

The material and the symbolic

This stress on the symbolic nature of difference can be seen in work which evokes Benedict Anderson's notion of 'imagined' communities. Emerging out of discussions of nationalism, the nation is *imagined* 'because the members of even the smallest nation will never know most of their fellow-members, meet them, or even hear of them, yet in the minds of each lives the image of their communion' (Anderson 1983: 6). Anderson therefore focuses attention on large-scale collectivities where members are 'linked primarily by common identities but minimally by networks of directly interpersonal relationships – nations, races, classes, genders, Republicans, Muslims and "civilised" people' (1983: 96). Communities are a cultural construction, a way of organising thought into ideas of similarity and difference, rather than a necessary reflection of reality: 'Communities are to be distinguished, not by their falsity/genuineness, but by the style in which they are imagined' (Anderson 1983: 6).

But a stress on the symbolic nature of difference sometimes appears to present racial differences as if they were unattached to material experience and disembedded from substantive social relations altogether. This can be seen in accounts of community identity which stress its symbolic nature. Anthony Cohen's model of the 'symbolic construction' of communal and other collective identities, for example, presents community membership as a symbolic mask of similarity (Jenkins 1996: 105), which is not underpinned by material social relations:

> culture – the community as experienced by its members – does not consist in social structure or in 'the doing' of social behaviour. It inheres, rather, in 'the thinking' about it. It is in this sense that we can speak of the community as a symbolic, rather than a structural, construct.
>
> (Cohen 1985: 98)

However, there is a danger here of making too rigid a distinction between the symbolic, on the one hand, and the material and interactional, on the other (Jenkins 1996).

The recent move to 'cultural' accounts rejects the 'groupism' inherent in taking 'discrete, sharply differentiated, internally homogeneous and externally bounded groups [. . .] as basic constituents of social life, chief protagonists of social conflicts, and fundamental units of social analysis' (Brubaker 2002: 164). This tendency has, rightly, been rejected because it *reifies* ethnic groups; ignoring the apparently arbitrary nature of boundaries that cut across commonalities, and glossing over internal differentiations, treating categories 'as if they were internally homogeneous, externally bounded groups, even unitary collective actors with common purposes' (Brubaker 2002: 164). Brubaker argues that whilst participants themselves often represent racial and ethnic conflict in groupist terms, the categories of 'ethnopolitical practice' should not be uncritically accepted as categories of social analysis (2002: 166).

For analysts like Brubaker, ethnicity and race should not be conceptualised as substantial concrete, bounded and enduring 'groups' 'but rather in relational, processual, dynamic, eventful and disaggregated terms' (2002: 167). That is, we should not think of 'groups', but instead think of 'groupness' as a *process*. 'If we treat groupness as a variable and distinguish between groups and categories, we can attend to the dynamics of group-making as a social, cultural and political project, aimed at transforming categories into groups or increasing level of groupness' (Brubaker 2002: 170–171).

However, for Brubaker, whilst racial and ethnic 'groups' are socially constructed, the *process* of social construction is not entirely symbolic or arbitrary, so instead of simply asserting that they are constructed, we need to specify how this happens, that is, 'how – and when – people identify themselves, perceive others, experience the world and interpret their predicaments in racial, ethnic or national rather than other terms . . . how "groupness" can "crystallise" in some situations while remaining latent and merely potential in others' (Brubaker 2002: 174). For theorists like Brubaker, some arrangements of social relations provide better 'ecological' niches for 'groupness' to crystallise than others.

Within the field of the anthropology of community and ethnicity, theorists such as Vered Amit have been critical of how the notion of imagined community has increasingly led to a view of identity and community that is 'devoid of social content even while it is symbolically marked in terms of opposition between insiders and outsiders' (Amit and Rapport 2002: 165). Yet, as Amit notes, 'some of the most crucial forms of fellowship, of belonging, are barely marked by explicit symbolic icons', and 'some of the most common avenues for forming a sense of fellowship, of belonging and social connection are realized through modest daily practices that are often not strongly marked by symbolic categorical identities', through 'people and relationships known loosely as friends, neighbours, workmates, companions in a variety of leisure, parenting, schooling, political activities' (2002: 64, 165).

> These are forms of community which are conceptualized first and foremost by reference to what is held in common by members rather than in terms of oppositional categories between members and outsiders. That is to say, such consociation and the identities deriving from it are built up through the shared experiences of participation in particular associations and events. What matters most, therefore, is what 'we' have shared, not the boundary dividing 'us' from 'them'. In such circumstances, the identity and sense of community arises in the course of, and is conceptualized in terms of particular forms of social interaction.
>
> (Amit and Rapport 2002: 59–60)

Amit stresses the importance of contextualising symbolic categorical identifications and seeing how they 'are likely to be invoked, by whom, and how these invocations articulate, collide or are bypassed by particular forms of social relations' (2002: 19).

Conclusion

In some perspectives, racial identities appear to be now more 'free floating' of social structure than in the past. But although social location may not *determine* subjective identities (as in the now rejected modernist formulation in which structure gives rise to action), it is clear that substantive social relations and processes of identification are mutually intertwined. The investigation of this relationship is therefore key.

The sociological significance of race has sometimes been seen as primarily *symbolic*, with race conceptualised as a symbol of *(dis)association*:

> individuals construct and reconstruct the symbols they use under the pressure of society: society invests symbols with particular meanings, but these reflect its own divisions, conflicts and patterns of inclusion and exclusion. The meaning of race as a symbol of (dis)association is not naturally given, then, but invokes traditions of social and national belonging that are invented or imagined.
>
> (Shilling and Mellor 2001: 160)

However, there is a danger of neglecting the material dimension of racial inequality, and 'there is a strong tendency in work on "new times" to downplay or erase issues such as that of state power, social class divisions, institutional structures and hegemonic cultural capital' (Mac an Ghail 1999: 15). Because of this weakness, it has been argued that it is now necessary to

> rethink social stratification away from the polarity between the material and the symbolic, and argue that material inequality is informed by claims and struggles over resources of different types, undertaken in terms of gender, ethnicity/race and class. This formulation allows us to include these categorical formations, alongside class, as important elements of social stratification i.e. as determining the allocation of socially valued resources and social places/locations.
>
> (Anthias 2001: 368)

It is important to consider not just how the idea of 'race' affects social relations, but also how social relations give rise to ideas of 'race'. Issues of identity and difference need to be more firmly located within relational accounts of differentiated social *practices*, and in the nature of claims (to recognition and resources) which emerge from different social locations. To do so requires that we analyse difference partly in terms of overt values and claims to identity. However, this must be matched by the analysis of *implicit* assumptions and identities, as they are embedded in social interaction and in practical engagements with the world. The significance of the latter has been under-emphasised, yet is crucial for understanding the processes by which claims to difference take on salience in particular contexts, how they are given voice and mobilised (Bottero and Irwin 2003). The question of how overt constructions of difference both emerge from, and become embedded in, social relationships will be further explored in Chapters 10 and 13.

7 A woman's place

The problem of explaining women's unequal place in society has always run into the difficulty of fitting women into theoretical schemes which seem poorly designed to address the specificity of women's experience. In practice 'we can only make sense of women's and men's social reality when we study them together' (Payne and Abbott 1990: 174), yet stratification theory was slow to realise that its categories were based on men's experience, and neglected gender divisions and inequalities. Yet:

> It is not 'social actors' that are distributed . . . through the places of structure: it is men and women. Their different experiences are interdependent, so that the distribution and situations of men are powerfully influenced by those of women as well as vice versa.
>
> (Marshall *et al.* 1988: 84)

Because of this interdependence, the study of gender divisions has also transformed our understandings of men's place in the world. Gender relations have been based on the asymmetrical, and unequal, interdependence of women and men; with the separation of key aspects of women's and men's lives organised around the assumption of their connection within (heterosexual) family relations. Not all women and men live within such arrangements, but they are all affected by them.

In recent years, however, the impact of family arrangements on women's experience seems to have changed, amid a growing diversity in women's engagements with public life. Conventional theories of gender inequality have struggled to explain this diversity, which for some have led to the collapse of 'gender' as a meaningful category of experience. Because of these difficulties there has been an increasing retreat from structural accounts of gender divisions, with analysts moving instead to explore more fluid relations of gender 'difference' increasingly de-coupled from material social relations. This cultural turn has been matched by an emphasis on the increasing role of choice and reflexivity in social life, with the suggestion that women and men are 'disembedded' from gender constraints. This chapter critically examines these claims, arguing that women's apparent autonomy from men, and from structural constraints, is more apparent than real. Real and dramatic shifts have occurred, but they can only be understood in terms of the patterning of women's and men's practical engagements with the world in material social locations.

Social constructions

In the nineteenth century, gender inequality was seen in terms of *women's* physical embodiment. Women's lives, in such accounts, were expressed through their connection to child-bearing and the household, whilst men's lives depended on their social participation in the public arenas of production and politics. Women's bodies, seen as governed by pregnancy and menstruation, were regarded as too weak and vulnerable for the rigours of public life, so 'the sexual division of labour was said to reflect differences in aptitudes and personality ultimately derived from reproductive function' (Bradley 1996: 83). Take the social psychologist, Gustave Le Bon, writing in 1879 about women's physical, and therefore social, inferiority:

> they are closer to children and savages than to an adult civilised man. They excel in fickleness, inconstancy, absence of thought and logic, and incapacity to reason. Without doubt there exist some distinguished women, very superior to the average man, but they are as exceptional as the birth of any monstrosity, as, for example, of a gorilla with two heads; consequently, we may neglect them entirely. . . . A desire to give them education, and as a consequence, to propose the same goals for them, is a dangerous chimera.
>
> (quoted in Gould 1984: 137)

These views, commonplace in the nineteenth century, accepted the 'fact' of women's physical and mental inferiority and justified their exclusion from citizenship rights and public life. Naturalistic assumptions still exist in contemporary 'common-sense' explanations of gender, and were only challenged within sociological accounts comparatively recently. However (as with the analysis of race), more recent sociological approaches to gender have stressed the social construction of gender, challenging its 'natural' basis. In the 1970s, early feminist accounts distinguished sex from *gender*, seeing the latter as a social construction, exaggerating biological differences, and converting that difference into inequality. Later writers have also suggested that 'biological' sex is as socially constructed as gender (Butler 1998). The distinction between biology and its social construction is undermined because gendered practices do not stay at the level of ideology, since dominant conceptualisations of masculinity and femininity become materially embodied through the different physicality of social practices:

> The physical sense of maleness . . . also derives from the transformation of the body through social practice . . . and includes the greater encouragement boys usually receive in comparison to girls to engage in strenuous physical exercise and 'cults of physicality', such as football and weight training, which

focus on the disciplined management of the body and the occupation of space. . . . So, the different opportunities girls and boys have to engage in muscle-building work and leisure activities can play an important part in developing and transforming their bodies.

(Shilling 1993: 111)

The different activities of women and men mean 'gender' takes real bodily shape, creating different physicalities which can be taken as self-evident 'proof' of different and unequal embodiment. In the same way, the social organisation of 'gender' means that women and men have markedly different routes through life, so they also develop different social interests and capacities. This, of course, is a standard aspect of stratification: lives lived in different locations tend to develop in different ways. So, 'gender' is best understood as the

lived relationships between men and women through which sexual differences and ideas about sexual differences are constructed. Some of these differences, which relate to the sexual division of labour both in and outside the home, are economic: women have lesser access to and control of shares of social wealth. But gender differences are not only rooted in the economy. . . . Gender relations are pervasive and operate at every level of social life. For example, girls and boys have different patterns of play and women's and men's leisure activities are differentiated; women are under-represented, or relegated to specific roles defined as suitable for them, within most areas of the public sphere; sexual practices and orientations take different meanings for women and men; and women and men figure differently in cultural representations of various kinds, from classical paintings to advertisements, from television dramas to the lyrics of rap songs.

(Bradley 1996: 82)

But how do we explain these differences? The formal exclusions of women from public life have now been dismantled, with the removal of legal bars, and the promotion of equal opportunities and full citizenship rights. But substantial differences (and inequalities) in the activities and roles of women and men remain. This persistence of gender differentials, despite the formal freedom of women, has often been taken as a sign of the different *choices* that women and men take with respect to parenting and family life. Women, it is argued, choose to concentrate on family-building, a situation of gender *difference* but not gender *inequality*. In employment, for example, it is argued that women's over-representation in lower-skilled, lower-paid employment is because women concentrate on their familial role, invest less time in education and training, and pursue more intermittent employment careers.

Critics reject the voluntarism of this position, pointing out that the choices that men and women make always occur within a constraining environment, which already contains structured assumptions that the activities of women will be different to those of men. This channels women and men in different directions. If women choose to spend more time in part-time employment, this must be understood in terms of the obligations on their time and child-care costs; since the standard full-time working day is organised on the assumption that, if the worker has children, someone else takes them to school and cares for them afterwards. That 'women choose to work part-time rather than full-time, despite the limited and poor nature of such employment is at least partly due to the limitation of public child care provision in the UK and to the restricted range of occupations in which part-time work is available' (Walby 1997: 14). The gendered assumptions behind the structuring of working arrangements severely constrain the choices of parents, so that women's and men's preferences reflect, rather than create, the gendered division of labour. But how have these asymmetrical, but inter-related, gender routes through social life emerged?

Gender as economic and social

As Chapter 4 shows, classical explanations of stratification said relatively little about divisions such as gender. Their focus was on how *economic* relations produce difference and inequality, but within the assumptions of conventional theories of stratification, gender shouldn't matter as much as it does. Theoretically, the drive for profit should eradicate 'irrational' status distinctions, so the persistence of gender inequality is a substantial theoretical problem.

Until the 1970s, this problem was bracketed because the key areas of sociological investigation – production, class and social status – were curiously 'sex-blind'. Gender went unremarked in theories which accepted gender divisions in an uncritical fashion. When women's social position was discussed, explanations centred on their location within the family, as wives and mothers, and women's overall stratification position was seen to derive from their relations to men. As Giddens put it: 'Given that women still have to await their liberation from the family, it remains the case in the capitalist societies that female workers are largely peripheral to the class system' (1981: 288). Married women were typically given the class position of their husband (even if in waged work themselves), with women's employment seen as secondary to family commitments.

The difficulty is that women generally have different relations to family and employment than men, in ways which cut across class categories. Women are concentrated in the *middle* of the labour market, in intermediate and junior non-manual work and semi-skilled manual and personal service work, 'crowded' into caring, catering and clerical areas. Their greater propensity to work part-time (around half are part-timers) further skews their labour-market distribution, with part-time jobs overwhelmingly concentrated in the semi- and unskilled sectors (such as catering, cleaning, domestic service, child-care). Because women's occupational distribution is so different to that of men, familial relations often cross the manual/non-manual divide. From this, it would appear that 'class' processes work differently for women than men. However, because women's occupational distribution and patterns of work are predicated upon different relations to household labour and resourcing, 'women's employment has often been considered secondary or marginal in social and economic theory' (Walby 1997: 66). Class theorists argued that gender differences in class processes were not significant because men's employment had the decisive influence on family circumstances. The class location of women was derived from their relation to the family, the class location of men from their relations to waged work. Because 'the labour market participation of married women is typically of an intermittent and limited kind' (Goldthorpe 1983: 472), *men's* relations to the class structure were emphasised. It was a mistake to treat 'a typist married to a salaried professional or manager as having the same class position as a typist married to a manual wage-worker' (Goldthorpe 1984: 494), as demonstrated by the fact that a husband's occupation was a better predictor of his wife's voting and health behaviour than her own job.

This division in sociological accounts, with men's lives explained by their labour-market position (a 'job model'), and women's lives analysed in terms of the impact of marriage and parenting (a 'gender model') (Feldberg and Glenn 1984), did not long survive dramatic increases in women's labour-market participation from the 1970s onwards. It became apparent that women's lives were increasingly affected by their own jobs and not just by their relations to men. But if women's stratification position is affected *both* by their labour market *and* their family relations, this also raises the question of how *men's* wider social relations affect their stratification position too.

The increasing interest in gender revealed substantial problems in the 'job model' of inequality. The attempt 'to tuck all other forms of social inequality under that of class' (Walby 1992: 33) was doomed. The problem is that even if capitalism opportunistically exploits status differences such as gender, class theory cannot, by itself, explain how such differences arise in the first place, nor why women fill the most vulnerable positions.

The fact that economic relations cannot fully account for social divisions (or rather that economic relations are narrowly conceived as impersonal) is made clear by the gender debate. Just as class theory pushes gender into an external realm, so gender theorists moved beyond class to explore gender as a distinct system in its own right. In the 1970s, feminists used the term 'patriarchy' to refer to an independent structure: men's control over women. Early accounts located the source of men's power in the private sphere, expressed through men's domination in the household and intimate personal relations, regulated through the threat of male violence and rape. The problem is that it is not just women's and men's unequal situation in the family which affects their labour-market location, but also, conversely, their unequal labour-market situation which affects their location within the family. 'Gender' refers to a set of relations *linking* familial and labour-market positions, in which women and men have asymmetrical, interdependent, and unequal relations to each other. 'Dual systems theory' argued that gender divisions arise out of the *combination* of two systems of inequality, capitalism and patriarchy (Hartmann 1981). In this model, men also organise to monopolise the best jobs in the labour market. However, if gender affects processes of supply and demand, this also means that gender enters into the construction of labour-market positions. As later theorists pointed out, gender does not just affect labour supply, it is also embedded in the social organisation of jobs (Walby 1986). 'The drive to push women from work was backed by the campaign for a "family wage" which would enable a man to maintain a non-employed wife and children at home' (Bradley 1996: 74).

The male monopolisation of better-paid jobs has helped 'package' the hours, pay and gender identity of occupations. The emergence of the 'family wage' system in the mid-nineteenth century is an example of how restricting allocation to jobs also shapes the social organisation of those jobs, embedding gendered claims into work, and maintaining asymmetrical gender roles. The shift to exclude married women from many areas of the labour market was part of skilled workers' campaigns to legitimise male 'breadwinner' pay claims.

> The fact that women and men are employed in jobs highly skewed in their gender composition, and the fact that the highly rewarded jobs are those in which men predominate have led many to argue that 'gender' operates to shape the character of occupations and labour force distributions. The 'gender saturation' of work tasks has been designated a substantial dimension in the social definition of skill and a substantial factor in maintaining the identity of, and inequality between, 'women's work' and 'men's work'.
>
> (Siltanen 1994: 16)

Writers interested in the way in which gender practices are embedded in the labour market have pointed to how, historically, occupations designated as 'women's jobs' have been graded as lower in skill (and thus pay) than men's jobs, in ways which do not reflect the 'technical' requirements of the job. The 'gendered' nature of skill definitions reflects the fact that male workers have been better organised (through trade unions and craft associations), and so better able to assert claims to skilled status and to resist de-skilling through job reorganisation (Walby 1986). Similarly, the predominance of men in certain jobs has also shaped the 'social packaging' of working practices.

> Men can set the rules and norms within the workplace since they occupy top posts. They determine the criteria for acceptable workplace behaviour and the meanings of such key concepts as excellence, leadership potential, a 'good worker', commitment, even 'the working day'. Research into women managers in various industries reveals how work requirements are shaped around male norms. These include the freedom to move around the country to secure promotion; the ability to work long hours, including evenings and weekends; having few restrictions on out of work time; and displaying requisite qualities of competitiveness and toughness.
>
> (Bradley *et al.* 2000: 87)

The analysis of gender inequalities in the labour market identifies social principles operating in the 'economic' – which differentiate between men and women, the old and the young, between parents and the childless – as well as principles based on skill and productivity. It shows that the social identity of incumbents helps construct the 'economic' identity of the jobs they hold, generating the structure of positions. This is more than just a gendered 'constraint' of economic class: it indicates the indivisibility of 'social' and 'economic' processes (Bottero 1998). The difficulty of conventional accounts of stratification is that economic relations are seen as neutral market processes, and are divorced from the social assumptions embedded in them. However, once it becomes apparent that the labour market does 'package' jobs in this fashion then the division between 'economic' and 'social', and 'home' and 'work', breaks down.

Gendered cultures at work

The acknowledgement of the significance of gender has meant a fundamental transformation in how class inequality has been viewed, since 'classes are not only divided by gender: they are "gendered" in the sense that gender is integral to processes of class formation, action and identification' (Bradley 1996: 74). Because women and men have a different pattern of relations to employment, they also often work in settings dominated by one gender, with a marked 'gendering' in workplace cultures:

> segregated workgroups of women and men develop their own highly specific and mutually excluding cultures. Women's cultures centre on their home lives, on families and domesticity: conversations, rituals and symbols are concerned with homes, romance, marriage, children, clothes, food and the feminine lifestyle. . . . By contrast, men's cultures are more work-centred, and also emphasise exaggerated versions of masculinity (sometimes symbolised by aggressive initiation rituals): talk features sport, heavy drinking, sexual bravado, anecdotes stress strength, audacity, resistance to authority, physical exploits of various kinds. . . . Although white-collar and professional workers tend to work in mixed sex groups, studies show that friendship patterns and group relations still emphasise group boundaries.
>
> (Bradley 1989: 70)

As Bradley argues, such 'gendered' work cultures both reflect and enhance segregation, helping to 'preserve conventional views of proper masculine and feminine behaviour both inside and outside work. They "domesticise" or "masculinise" capitalist work conditions' (Bradley 1989: 70). But if the asymmetry of men's and women's relations to the labour market means class experiences are gendered, gendered experiences are also 'classed'.

Waged work, and the independence that such work brings, has been central in the construction of masculinity, and 'masculinity itself is deeply embedded in the social meaning of work' (McDowell 2003: 58). Working-class masculinities, for example, have been strongly shaped by the male-dominated nature of manual labour. The importance of 'heavy' manual work in working-class men's lives has helped shape their masculinities but has also shaped the identity of the 'working class'. In the archetypal manual industries (mining, dockworkers, printers, shipbuilders, etc.) workers were 'overwhelmingly male, worked in individual environments with no supervision . . . or in gangs of closely bonded men where little de facto control was exercised over them . . . and were strongly unionised' (Savage 2000: 128). The shaping of ideas of the 'heroic' nature of (male) working-class identity lay, it is argued, in the (hard-won) collective shop-floor autonomy which helped to form the notion of working-class men as 'autonomous, free and unconstrained by direct supervision' (Savage 2000: 128). So working-class masculinity was shaped not only by breadwinner claims (the sign of a man's ability to support a wife and children), but also by the 'moral' emphasis placed on 'manly' labour, in a quite different manner to the construction of middle-class masculinities.

The 'heroic' nature of working-class masculinity was something denied to working-class women, however, who were constructed as 'dependants' within the family, and marginalised in the same way in their employment status. Historically confined to 'women's work', excluded from trade unions, and working in tightly supervised conditions, working-class women have not been able to construct equivalent 'heroic' or 'rebellious' femininities. Instead, as Skeggs has argued, working-class femininity has emerged as a 'stigmatised' identity, based upon sexualised and pathologised representations of working-class women as 'slags' or 'drudges'. Working-class women have combated such stigmatised identities by emphasising 'respectability' (Skeggs 1997a), but this is parasitic on middle-class notions, and firmly locates working-class femininity in the domestic arena, in the well-kept home, the smartly dressed children, and the clean front step. The traditional working-class collectivism which 'depended on the recognition of the dignity and autonomy of individuals' was based on the independence and autonomy of *men* (Savage 2000: 154).

Differential association

The asymmetry of women's and men's relations is a marked feature of almost all social settings, and leads to considerable separation in women's and men's lives. This is a general feature of stratification. Men and women typically spend much of their lives in different sorts of work and leisure environments, in settings strongly skewed to one gender or the other, and pursue skewed lifestyle tastes and interests. This is a *consequence* of the impact of gender stratification on social arrangements, but it also helps to reproduce gender divisions. Social relationships are strongly patterned by gender, with gendered differential association in friendship and leisure networks affecting the information and opportunities that women and men can access. Take the role of networks in career advancement. It is suggested that, because professional and managerial women are a gender 'minority', they often find themselves excluded from the informal networks which are so crucial for career success. Such networks operate through informal friendship, leisure and sporting activities which are strongly 'homosocial' (sorted by gender):

> Participation in the sporting opportunities and facilities of an organisation, which are frequently male-oriented and dominated, allows for communication about work to occur in an all-male environment such as in the locker room, or on the golf course. . . . Success in the organisation often depends on access to these networks, where the 'real' business goes on . . . many studies indicate that women are largely excluded from old-boy networks, which traditionally are composed of people who hold power in the organisation. . . . While women also have opportunities to talk in men's absence, and have been successful in consciously forming their own networks, both within and between organisations, these networks do not necessarily provide access to the 'old-boy' networks where structural power is held.
>
> (Halford and Leonard 2001: 72–73)

However, there are limits to the differential association, and thus, the social distance of women and men. Gender separation in social networks, and gender segregation and inequality in the labour market, do create different lifestyles for women and men, but this is qualified by the *shared* lifestyles that they make together in (heterosexual) familial relationships. The significance of gender as a dimension of inequality has frequently been discussed in terms of its potential to generate strategic collective activity, or as a focus of group conflict. Yet:

> patterns of social relations have placed severe limits on the kind of collective identity that could convince women to participate in protest. With the exception of radical (and, particularly, lesbian) separatists, women in the West have maintained close social relations with men, whether as fathers, sons, spouses, lovers, brothers, or friends. The continued presence in the lives of most women of strong social connections to males (however asymmetrical or even exploitative these connections might be from the feminist point of view) stands in the way of any collective identity based on a fundamental antagonism between the sexes.
>
> (Gould 1995: 204).

Indeed the inequality, in women's and men's experience, is partly predicated upon the assumption of their interdependence. This intersection creates problems for theories of patriarchy based on the notion of distinct, and opposed, 'male' and 'female' interest groups. The inequality and differential association of class or racial groups creates considerable social separation and marked differences in their life-chances. Gender patterns operate slightly differently. There are also, of course, inequalities in life-chances and social separation *dividing* women from men, but the differential association occurs within particular contexts and is mediated by strong social bonds between women and men, so that the inequalities in life-chances (in access to well-paid jobs, for example) are also mediated by the common standard of living that women and men typically experience by sharing their lives within families.

Women and men routinely experience gender difference in their social relations, but this is very complexly related to patterns of inequality. Women frequently have unequal access to the resources within families (with men taking the lion's share), but the point still holds that asymmetrical gender relations within families occur within the framework of a broad overall standard of living. It has long been noted, for example, that a husband's job is a better predictor of his wife's health chances than her own job (Arber 1991, 1997). It is usually argued that this is because women's more fragmented employment experience does not fully capture their social circumstances. But actually there is a wider point here about how family relations pool resources to create a shared standard of living and lifestyle for *all* family members. This is not to deny the importance of gender divisions in lifestyles and access to opportunities. For example, there are health differences between men and women within class and racial categories, which are a reflection of the different health 'risks' women and men encounter because of differences in the way they lead their daily lives. Yet the asymmetry of gender relations works on the assumption that women and men lead different lives, but together.

Gender inequalities become particularly pressing for women when they stand outside of these standard arrangements of asymmetrical interdependence. For example, lone mothers have a high risk of poverty, and suffer markedly poor health, both because their domestic circumstances make it difficult to work full time, but also because the typical pay associated with 'women's work' falls short of a 'breadwinner's wage' even when they do. But such difficulties arise precisely because women are unequal *within* standard arrangements. That is, the assumptions of asymmetrical gender interdependence which run right through work and family life typically place women in a situation of financial dependence upon men.

Under capitalism, access to waged work – whether directly, or indirectly through social relations – has been of major significance for social position. However, gender inequality cannot be understood solely in 'economic' terms. Gender inequality has been predicated upon social relations of obligation and dependence, in which women and men typically have quite different, and interdependent, access to waged work and family resourcing. The significance of unpaid labour in women's lives, and the financial dependence on men that many women experience, has led some writers to question the centrality of paid occupation in determining the social position of women, and to raise the question of whether a woman's position in a social hierarchy is given directly – by attachment to the labour market – or indirectly – through family relationships. But every member of the household affects the standard of living, lifestyle and outlook of the people they live with. So social position is not just a relationship to the labour market, but a result of the network of close social relationships in which *every* individual is engaged which strongly influences their position in the social hierarchy, and mediates the effect of occupation. How individuals react to the *same* working conditions or level of pay is likely to differ according to their wider social circumstances – their lifecourse stage and social obligations, the family relationships they are engaged in, their social background, past experience and their expectations of the future.

Both family and employment relations have constructed women as men's financial dependants, enshrined through quite different – and gendered – claims for rewards in the labour market. This leads to marked inequalities in the labour market between women and men. Such economic inequalities can only be understood in terms of the social claims and social relations which have shaped them (Holmwood and Stewart 1991; Siltanen 1994; Irwin 1995; Bottero 1998).

Over recent years, however, substantial shifts have occurred which have led to increasing diversity and complexity in gender relations. During the period in which gender has emerged as a 'crucial category for social analysis' the 'lived relationships of gender have been in a state of flux' (Bradley 1996: 81). Indeed, the changes have been so dramatic that some commentators argue that gender asymmetry, and the dependence of women on men, has been dissolved. Because of this growing complexity, analysts have increasingly questioned the significance of 'gender' as an explanatory category, moving instead to explore gender as more fluid relations of 'difference'.

Transformations

Recent decades have indeed seen a revolution in women's patterns of participation in education, employment and in their roles within the family. These changes have been linked to 'reduced discrimination (the result of equal opportunities policies), the declining significance of domestic activities for women's employment; the rise in the educational achievements of women and girls' (Walby 1997: 22). Women have experienced striking increases in employment participation over their working life-times with the trend especially marked amongst mothers of young children. The distinctive 'lifecourse' profile of women's labour-market participation (dipping sharply during the child-bearing phase, then rising again mid-life) has flattened out, paralleling men's labour-market profile, but at a slightly lower rate. Overall, the impact of parenting on women's employment has shifted dramatically since the 1970s, as the majority of women, including mothers, are now employed through most of their working lives. Women have significantly improved their qualification levels, and there is now a strong expectation of being in paid work throughout the lifecourse. Amongst full-time workers there has been a substantial narrowing of the inequalities between women and men, and a major increase in the proportion of women in professional and managerial jobs. Significant sex segregation still remains, but 'Women have made breakthroughs into traditional male higher level jobs at the same time expanding their share of already feminized lower skilled or lower paid occupations' (Rubery *et al.* 1998: 108).

This, for many, indicates a fundamental transformation in gender relations, with women's lives apparently much less centred around the family and dependence upon men. Walby, for example, argues that there has been a shift in gender regime, with women no longer confined to the domestic sphere, as 'step by step women are increasingly participating in the public institutions of education, employment and political decision making' (1997: 64). There are dramatically different opportunities and expectations for *young* women who 'today build their lives around the opportunities and limits of a public gender regime, preparing themselves for a lifetime of paid employment with education and training, delaying or rejecting child birth and marriage' (1997: 12).

The scale (and pace) of change has even led to popular claims that we now live in a 'post-feminist' era of gender equality. Others, however, are more sceptical. Walby, for example, points out that these changes do not involve *all* women, and that women remain segregated into unequal positions within the public sphere. Substantial changes in the working and family patterns of women have also entailed significant continuities in aggregate patterns of gender difference. For although women's employment 'has come to be a key force in the restructuring of work and employment' (Rubery *et al.* 1999: 1), the *form* of this restructuring has meant that significant changes in rates of employment amongst women have occurred alongside major continuities in their disadvantaged position within the labour market. Shifts in gendered employment patterns are part of the recent growth in female-dominated sectors of the economy, in health, retail, catering, education, financial services and clerical work. Long-term shifts in industrial economies have meant that routine non-manual work in the service sector ('women's jobs') has increased. So the changes in gender patterns are substantially qualified by continuing gender inequality. The dramatic increase in female labour-market participation rates has also been marked by increases in low-paid, part-time working; the improvement in women's qualifications and access to higher-level occupations has been paralleled by an increase in women employed in low-level, insecure and poorly paid jobs; the narrowing of the pay gap between male and female workers has only occurred amongst full-time workers; the decline in occupational segregation in the full-time workforce has occurred at the same time as a rise in occupational segregation in the part-time workforce. So whilst a relatively advantaged group of women are in full-time and high-status work with participation maintained throughout the family-building period, the traditional 'female' pattern of discontinuous employment in low-level, low-paid jobs persists.

Research on changing employment participation rates has therefore focused on the polarisation in women's employment opportunities, and the increasing *diversity* of female experience that results:

> women are polarising between those, typically younger, educated and employed, who engage in new patterns of gender relations somewhat convergent with those of men, and those, particularly disadvantaged women, typically older and less educated, who built their life trajectories around patterns of private patriarchy. These new patterns are intertwined with diversities and inequalities generated by social divisions including class, ethnicity and region.
>
> (Walby 1997: 2)

Problems theorising diversity

A number of writers have suggested that this heterogeneity in gender patterns means that no single theoretical explanation can ever be adequate, arguing that a range of explanations must be drawn upon (Hakim 1996; Bradley 1996; Crompton 1989). It has been argued that since other significant social divisions cross-cut gender, the idea of homogeneous 'male' and 'female' interests is problematic (Anthias and Yuval-Davis 1992) and that the stress on opposed 'gender' categories in structural accounts is essentialist and monolithic.

> The fragmentation of macro-analytic concepts in the theorization of 'race', gender and class is a typical part of the post-modernist project. Within each of these fields, there has been a recent move towards arguing that the central category is too internally differentiated to be utilised as a significant unitary concept. Sometimes this has been argued with reference to other categories, for instance, that women are too divided by ethnicity for the concept of 'women' to be useful.
>
> (Walby 1992: 31)

This rejection of the very idea of the unity of the categories of 'women' and 'men', and the stress on the diversity of gendered experience, has led to the increasing rejection of structural theories of gender. Accounts which attempt to explain gender divisions as the outcome of 'systems' of capitalist or patriarchy have been criticised for sidelining other aspects of diversity, such as race and ethnicity. To have to use two social 'structures' to adequately explain behaviour is a little awkward, to have to resort to three structures is just plain embarrassing.

> The social structural models of society that had been organised around the two systems of sex and class found a third axis of inequality hard to accommodate; the already acute difficulties in developing a 'dual systems' analysis were brought to a head with the belated recognition that ethnic difference and disadvantage had been left out. One response to this . . . was the shift to a more micro-level of analysis that lent itself better to the complex interplay of different aspects of inequality. Another was the increasing tendency to theorise the so-called 'triple oppressions' of gender, race and class in a more cultural and symbolic mode.
>
> (Barrett and Phillips 1992: 24)

So the problem of differentiation has raised serious questions about the utility of general explanatory categories, with many accounts turning instead to the specification of the diversity of gender, moving

> from grand theory to local studies, from cross-cultural analyses of patriarchy to the complex and historical interplay of sex, race and class, from notions of female identity or the interests of women towards the instability of female identity and the active creation and recreation of women's needs or concerns.
>
> (Barrett and Phillips 1992: 6–7)

This is an attack on the very idea of structural explanation itself. As Halford and Leonard note, in post-structuralism 'the categories "man" and "woman" are understood as highly specific creations, with no fixity or inherent stability or reality, but rather as fractured and fluid', since with 'such a wide range of alternative constructions of masculinity and femininity, it is seen to be impossible to predict how women and men may behave or identify themselves' (Halford and Leonard 2001: 21). So the 'turn to culture' within gender analysis is also a 'shift away' from a 'determinist model of "social structure" (albeit capitalism, or patriarchy, or a gender-segmented labour market or whatever)', on which 'culture and beliefs, as well as subjectivity and agency, rest' (Barrett 1992: 204, 209). The failure of structural explanations to address the diversity of gender experience has led to a move away from structural accounts altogether, amid the embrace of cultural and discursive constructions of 'difference', and the assertion of the fluid and contingent nature of gender identities. Analysts have instead moved to explore biography and narrative, cultural representations of masculinities and femininities, and the diverse constitution of sexualities.

The dissolution of gender?

This shift has been received with some disquiet by analysts who still wish to explore how 'gender' is bound up with inequality. In particular, there has been concern that the cultural turn effectively abandons the analysis of patterned inequality and material disadvantage.

> While postmodernism has rightly pointed to differences in the experiences of working-class and minority ethnic women, there is an irony here. Current preoccupations with 'sexuality, subjectivity and textuality' may well serve to alienate these newly discovered constituencies further from middle-class feminism, as women lower down the social hierarchy remain concerned with problems of poverty and over-work. Feminism would do well to recover some of its initial zeal in exposing material inequalities rather than retreating too completely into academic theoreticism.
>
> (Bradley 1996: 111–112)

Analysts of gender inequality are inevitably tied to a more materialist understanding, and writers in this area – whilst praising the new insights generated by more discursive interpretations of labour process and organisation – have nonetheless forcefully argued for the need to integrate discursive *and* materialist accounts of gender patterns (Bradley 1996; Walby 1992, 1997). Accounts of the 'gendering' of organisation, for example, now increasingly address how *discourses* of 'masculinity' and 'femininity' are differently embedded in work practices through ideas of the good worker or the good manager (Halford and Leonard 2001; Bradley *et al.* 2000: 86). A series of writers accept some of the postmodern critiques, arguing for more fluid accounts of gender 'relations', but draw back from the larger anti-epistemological claims of postmodernism, acknowledging 'the salience of some of the postmodern criticisms of traditional formulations of social structure, without abandoning the idea of societies as orderly' (Bradley 1996: 44).

As Janet Siltanen notes, however, there is a fundamental tension 'between the use of gender categories in statements of significant differences in experience and the identification of the need to deconstruct gender categories in order to highlight the diversities in experience they mask' (Siltanen 1994: 189).

Theorists of material gender inequality have struggled to cope with the difficulty of interpreting diversity, experiencing particular problems in explaining continuity *and* change in gender relations. This has led, instead, to a split between those writers stressing change and an opposing group stressing continuity (Irwin, forthcoming). Those who insist on the recognition of change, however, are very close to postmodern rejections of the 'orderly' nature of social life, because of their emphasis on the increasing individualisation of gender relations. Within 'materialist' (as opposed to discursive) approaches to gender divisions, a series of influential approaches have argued that there has been a weakening of traditional social structural constraints and codes of behaviour (Irwin and Bottero 2000).

The major explanatory model of gender change, the individualisation thesis, sees gender identities increasingly de-anchored from social structure. Beck, for example, argues that biographical pluralism (the increasing diversity of lifecourse trajectories) means that 'people are being removed from the constraints of gender . . . men and women are *released* from traditional forms and ascribed roles in the search for "a life of their own"' (1992 [1986]: 105). With women's increased employment, and rising divorce rates:

> Women have been cut loose from marital support – the material cornerstone of the traditional housewife's existence. Thus, the entire structure of familial ties and support comes under pressure for individualization. The type of the *negotiated provisional family* emerges.
>
> (Beck 1992 [1986]: 129)

The asymmetry of gender relations is seen to dissolve, and the interdependence of men and women broken, as women acquire increasing financial independence from men and so move beyond constraining family ties. It is suggested that the so-called 'feminization' of the labour market has de-traditionalised gender relations: undermining men's claims to breadwinner status, as manual employment in manufacturing has declined, leading to declining male employment rates, and increased redundancy and unemployment (Bradley *et al.* 2000: 72), whilst at the same time underwriting women's greater financial independence. In the newly dominant service sectors it has been argued that 'many of the skills and qualities sought by employers are those stereotypically associated with women' so that men are disadvantaged in seeking work in these areas (McDowell 2003: 29). McDowell argues employment growth is now in 'jobs, such as cleaning, fast-food and bar work in which the work is often highly routinised, standardised, and subject to control and surveillance, where employees often have to learn and repeat standardised scripts in the interaction with customers' (2003: 31). This has replaced 'locally based manual employment for working class men, which brought with it some dignity and social respect' with 'casualized service employment that is often highly routinized and entirely lacking in discretion' (McDowell 2003: 227).

> Young people on the edge of adulthood can no longer rely on the old moral certainties that constructed men as breadwinners, whose identities were constructed in the main in the workplace, and women as primary carers of dependants in the home. The changes in the institutions of the education system and the workplace have transformed women's opportunities and enhanced their prospects of self-sufficiency and independence. Similarly more diverse and fluid personal relationships have both given women more choice about the circumstances in which they become mothers and less certainty about male support if they do.
>
> (McDowell 2003: 24)

As Irwin notes, in the individualisation perspective 'family ties become increasingly contingent, negotiated by social agents who have a freedom to choose which sets them apart from their forebears' (2000: 6.2). The idea is that women and men have now become 'authors of their own fate', reflexively fashioning their biographies with increasing personal choice; so that the coherence of social divisions and inequalities is undermined as new forms of diversity emerge, along with a growing contingency and unpredictability in family and occupational trajectories. Progressive individualisation has – supposedly – led to increasingly fragmented, fluid and de-anchored social relations.

This emphasis on individualisation and de-materialisation partly arises because conventional explanations of labour-market differences which focused on asymmetrical domestic and parenting relations now seem – in the light of recent changes – inadequate. Most commentators accept, as Walby puts it, that 'there has been an overall massive decline in the impact of domestic responsibilities on the propensity of women to be in paid employment' (Walby 1997: 50). This means that 'there is growing support for the idea that gender processes operate within employment independently of factors associated with the domestic setting' (Siltanen 1994: 3). The idea is that family relations and employment relations have been pulled apart, as men and women become independent economic agents, pursuing their individual career and domestic choices. The deficiencies of structural explanations have therefore led to the perception of a growing division between structure and action, social constraints and individual choices.

These claims of increasing freedom of choice have been treated with considerable scepticism by critics who, as we have seen, point to substantial continuities in gendered inequalities, and stress the continuing importance of structural constraints in women's (and men's) lives. For example, it has been pointed out that childrearing, although taking up less of a woman's lifetime, is still primarily women's work, and that women continue to be more vulnerable to poverty, because their earning power is structured in relation to assumptions of their (at least partial) financial dependence on men.

Such arguments help to rebut assertions of individualisation, and undermine the notion of dissolving gender constraints. However, in this concern to stress *continuity* in women's disadvantaged position, there has been relatively little engagement with very real processes of change in gendered relations. There has been a revolution in gendered patterns of attachment to education, employment and family, with substantial changes in women's and men's relations to household resourcing, and their access to rewards in paid employment. But because the focus is on gender inequality, arguments of continuities in female disadvantage do not fully engage with the nature of the changes.

Siltanen argues that continuities in aggregate patterns of gender inequality should not be mistaken for *no change* in women's relations to childrearing and to male financial support. But the substantial re-working of gender patterns cannot be understood in terms of parenting and the domestic division of labour alone. 'Gender divisions' still bear a strong relation to the practical domestic and material circumstances of women and men. However, to trace out the links 'it is necessary to abandon the use of gender categories as general terms of analysis, and to formulate explanations of social processes that locate and specify gendered experience' (Siltanen 1994: 189).

A more complex understanding of household and employment relations helps to address the explanatory gap, but this entails looking at the 'relations to household financing, and of differentiations between jobs in terms of the social capacities facilitated by wage levels' (Siltanen 1994: 3). For Siltanen, whilst there is no doubt that employment continues to be characterised by a high level of differentiation between women and men, the central issue is whether this pattern is best characterised in terms of a *gender* division. Rather than divide 'women's jobs' from 'men's jobs', Siltanen argues that we can see a division between 'full-wage' and 'component-wage' employment, arguing that perceptions of the appropriateness or otherwise of women and men doing certain *tasks* are less important as an explanation of segregation than issues of hours and pay: the *social packaging* of jobs in relation to household financing. Jobs entail different 'packages' of wages and hours, which allow different social capacities. A component-wage is a wage which cannot support an individual in an independent (one-adult) household at a minimum standard (Siltanen 1994: 115), whereas a full-wage allows an adult to support themselves in an independent household. The division is between 'those who are and those who are not working for wages that cover their own reproduction costs' (Siltanen 1994: 119), that is, whether a wage permits social independence from a reliance on the financial support of others.

The ability of households to 'package' their income to meet minimum household requirements therefore has a direct relation to the ability of household members to command full-wages or component-wages, and to the 'social capacities' that employment permits. The access of women and men (and manual and non-manual workers) to 'full-wage' jobs (and thus to social independence) is severely skewed. There is substantial inequality in the social capacity of wages earned by women and men, and by manual and non-manual workers. Typically, women earn component-wages, manual men earn full-wages for a one adult household, and non-manual men earn full-wages for a two adult, two child household . . . component-wages are a chronic feature of women's employment experience. Even when in full-time employment, many women are routinely earning wages that are not sufficient to support themselves as an independent adult in our society. Increasing inequalities in wages . . . have meant that more men are now earning component-wages. However, men typically earn wages that are at least sufficient to support a one adult household. They do not routinely earn wages sufficient to support a household with dependants, and this capacity has deteriorated for manual men.

(Siltanen 1994: 115, 193–194)

A central feature of the shift in contemporary gender relations is the increased significance of female employment, and the associated modification of male claims to a breadwinner wage, as the earnings of women as well as men become increasingly necessary to the resourcing of households. There has been a decline in the relative sufficiency of male earnings and an increased importance of female earnings across the lifecourse of individuals and families (Irwin 1995). The idea that the male-breadwinner system has collapsed has been met with scepticism by critics who point to continuing female economic vulnerability and social disadvantage. As Irwin notes, however, women's continued positioning as component-wage earners remains consistent with a quite different relationship to household resourcing. The skewed access of women (and the declining access of manual men) to a full-wage means that there has been an increase in the *co-resourcing* of households (Irwin 1995; Irwin and Bottero 2000). With a decline in the availability of 'full-wage' jobs, for a growing proportion of the population the family income package is comprised of two component-wages.

This is not the individualisation of gender relations, nor the weakening of household constraints, but simply a shift in their form. A rise in co-dependency explains the *increase* in female independence and autonomy, and *greater* similarity between women and men's experience, but is still consistent with a continuation in the inequality and interdependence of women and men:

It may be that the increased (but still partial) realisation of claims by women to greater autonomy and independence in respect of forging integration into education and employment have encouraged pronouncements of individualisation yet this is a partial reading of the altered relative social positioning of women and men. The emergent configurations of gender relationships are as much characterised by inter-dependence and mutual claims and obligations as they were in the past, yet they have changed their form.

(Irwin 2000: 6.2)

It is also important to link shifts in gender relations with changes in the claims to independence and obligations between different age groups. The experience of labour-market restructuring has meant that the proportion of men (particularly younger men) earning component-wages has increased since the 1980s, whilst for young women component-wages continue to be a major feature of their employment experience. For young adults the changes of recent decades have witnessed a prolonging of the period of partial dependence upon parents for financial resources, which has variously been seen as causing a 'crisis in masculinity' for young men (as young adults lack access to waged independence), and a weakening of the gender differentials between young men and women. However, this reflects a re-organisation of relations of dependence and obligation rather than the dissolution of social bonds or structural constraints.

> In respect of generations, changes reveal an alteration in their relative position, with young adults now typically partly dependent, and standardly resourced by their parents, for a longer period than ever before. . . . These changes allow young adults to pursue more 'autonomous' paths through this extension of the life course period marked by the relative maturity and necessary social independence of youth and early adulthood and the general absence of familial obligations. Again it seems that a partial reading of this development might engender diagnoses of individualisation.
>
> (Irwin 2000: 6.2)

Recent developments require an understanding of the re-organisation of the relative social positioning of parents and children, and of women and men, because of the way in which generational interdependence is bound up with gender obligations. The increasing employment of married women has helped to *underwrite* the prolonged dependency of young adults. This represents a change in the nature of generational transfers, but is not a dissolution of social bonds, since both sets of arrangements are clearly based on mutual patterns of obligation and dependence reflected in family structure and the relative claims of different groups in employment.

Conclusion

The study of gender in social analysis started off as the problem of how to place women within conventional models of inequality, which made little allowance for gender asymmetry and difference. Grappling with the problem of understanding the particular nature of women's social relations has also entailed rethinking our understanding of the social relations of men. The assumption of gender difference runs through the most everyday of social arrangements, which sets up a different range of options and opportunities for women and men, and is a central feature of gender inequality. But problems in theorising the complexity of gender relations (as both economic and social, as both inequality and difference, as asymmetrical interdependence and differential association, and shot through with other dimensions of intersecting difference) have led to a cultural turn in gender analysis, and the increasing abandonment of any idea of 'gender' as the product of orderly, practical social relations.

But whilst there has been a *shift* in the relative positions of women and men, familial claims and obligations remain key to theorising the changes in gender relations. Changes in household structures, and in the division of labour between women and men, and across generations, have altered these groups' relations to one another in the resourcing of everyday life, changing their identities in important ways. These relational changes are inseparable from shifts in the structure of rewards to employment, which is itself strongly shaped by claims to independence and social obligation. However, this does not represent the dissolution of social constraints, nor the emergence of individualisation, but is simply a move from one set of patterned social arrangements to another.

8 Culture and anarchy

Stratification entails the analysis of structured social inequality in *all* its aspects: economic, social and cultural. However, stratification research has increasingly been dominated by class analysis which focuses on economic inequality. This has led to charges that conventional stratification theory has sidelined the 'social' divisions of race, ethnicity and gender, which have increasingly been characterised in cultural, discursive terms. However, the 'cultural turn' has now been carried to the very heart of class analysis, by critics who suggest that the increasing importance of consumption, status and lifestyle as markers of identity have made structural class analysis irrelevant. But does this cultural turn mean that we have to abandon the very idea of social life as orderly and stratified?

The death of class?

Attacks on the concept of class are almost as old as class analysis itself. From the moment Marx laid down his pen, critics were pointing to flaws in *particular* class models and this has continued to the present day. However, the chorus of disapproval is now increasingly strident, as critics suggest that, in whatever version, class has declining explanatory power. This decline is significant because, for many years, class was seen as the key explanatory variable of social behaviour, and class analysis had a central place within the discipline of sociology. This is no longer the case and, for some, the decline of class theory is partly the result of an exaggerated sense of its importance in the past:

> class analysts may have brought their fate upon themselves by making inflated claims about the importance of class. Investigations into social inequality tended to reduce all social phenomena to divisions of class, denying any independent explanatory power to other sources of social division. Class was all-important. The rejection of class was, perhaps, a natural reaction on the part of those who could produce evidence that gender or ethnicity, say, play a critical role in generating inequalities and exclusions. It was a short step from showing that class did not explain everything, to asserting that it could explain nothing.
>
> (Scott 2001: 127)

Others argue that 'post-industrial' developments (the decline of large-scale heavy manufacturing, the rise of smaller-scale service employment, rising affluence, and the increasing diversity of consumption behaviour) have undermined class divisions. Significantly, a number of writers who were once proponents of class analysis are now amongst its fiercest critics (such as Bauman, Lipset, Pakulski and Waters). They argue that class *once* shaped our lives, but this is now no longer the case.

For example, Clark and Lipset argue that 'class analysis has grown inadequate in recent decades as traditional hierarchies have declined and new social differences have emerged' (1996: 42). Claiming that 'social relations outside the workplace [are] increasingly important for social stratification' (1996: 43), the model they present is one of the breakdown of older workplace divisions and rising affluence, which have led to the emergence of increasingly complex *status* differences on the basis of lifestyle and consumption choices. The importance of consumption differences in social life, and the fact that they lead to more fleeting and fragmented groupings, undermines class as the basis of social association and community. So 'as wealth increases, people take the basics for granted; they grow more concerned with lifestyle and amenities', and this affluence 'weakens hierarchies and collectivism; but it heightens individualism. With more income, the poor depend less on the rich. And all can indulge progressively more elaborate and varied tastes' (1996: 45, 46). This is 'the fragmentation of stratification' caused by 'the weakening of class stratification, especially as shown in distinct class differentiated lifestyles; the decline of economic determinism, and the increased importance of social and cultural factors; politics less organised by class and more by other loyalties; social mobility less family-determined, more ability and education determined' (1996: 48). Quoting Dahrendorf's comment that 'It would take an unusually sharp eye to detect the social class of Saturday morning shoppers in the High Street, whereas to any earlier generation it would have been the most elementary task' (1996: 43), they argue that increasingly differentiated lifestyles make class effects weaker and less visible.

A range of critics present the decline of class as part of a progressive process of individualisation. Beck (1992) argues there has been a decline in the extent to which traditional social ties order people's lives. Increasing labour-market flexibility and mobility, the decline of local class communities, the increasing instability of family life – all these trends mean that individuals are less influenced by external social commitments and instead have to reflexively fashion their own biographies, shaping their lives much more on the basis of individual choice. At the same time, the increasing importance and diversity of consumption choices in people's lives means that there is a much greater array of lifestyles within which individuals must select and identify.

Central to such accounts is the notion that class as a collective, communal phenomenon has been undermined. In the past, Beck argues, class relations were more visible because economic divisions mapped onto status or cultural divisions, creating clear-cut class identities and distinct communities. For Beck, the importance of class derived from its subcultural and community basis. Classes were not simply economic categories with shared life-chances, but also status communities, with workmates living alongside and socialising with each other, sharing a common culture and lifestyle. The mining valley or the steel town would be the classic examples of such occupationally formed, class *communities*. As Pakulski and Waters put it: 'class is most apparent and salient when it occurs in complete and bounded communities based on a few industries' where 'patterns of exploitation and domination can easily be apprehended and class interests can readily become recognised and shared'; however, with the rise of service economies, and more flexible and fragmented labour markets, 'such communities have progressively disappeared from modern societies' (1996: 90).

The increasing importance of skill, qualifications and training in the labour market means that class attachments give way to a more individualised emphasis on individual choice and achievement. In the same way, the rise of more flexible patterns of employment, and the greater choice and diversity offered by modern consumption patterns, lead to a decline in class as the main form of community affiliation. The economic trends of the post-war period have been seen as undermining the conditions which gave rise to class relations in modernity as part of a shift from production to a new era of 'post-modernity' based on consumption (Bauman 1992). As the workplace and economic relations which once defined 'class' societies have been eclipsed by the increasing centrality of consumption, so class allegiances have been replaced by 'hyper-differentiated' consumption differences which produce a shifting kaleidoscope of lifestyles, rather than distinct social class divisions.

Recent trends, therefore, have increasingly divorced class location from status identity:

> as a result of shifts in the standard of living, subcultural class identities have dissipated, class distinctions based on status have lost their traditional support, and processes for the 'diversification' and individualization of lifestyles and ways of life have been set in motion. As a result, the hierarchical model of social classes and stratification has increasingly been subverted.
>
> (Beck 1992: 92–93)

Partly this is the result of the increasing affluence of the working class which has allowed most workers 'access to a complex of status items including home ownership, privatized transportation, electronically mediated mass entertainment, exotic vacations, technologized leisure equipment, high-quality health care, superannuation oriented to income maintenance, tertiary education for children, day care facilities and so on'. This means that the lifestyles of the working class, 'while different from the service class in terms of quantity, are little different in terms of quality' (Crook *et al.* 1992: 121). Once everybody has a TV, computer games and holidays in Ibiza, class inequalities seem less significant. This is not just about affluence, but also the notion that the centrality of consumption in social life allows for the fashioning of a much wider, more fragmented, and more transient array of cultural identities, than lives centred on production ever did.

People with the same income level, or put in the old-fashioned way, within the same 'class', can or even must choose between different lifestyles, subcultures, social ties and identities. From knowing one's 'class' position one can no longer determine one's personal outlook, relations, family position, social and political ideas or identity.

(Beck 1992: 131)

People still occupy class locations but 'the social meaning of inequality has changed' and the 'attachment of people to a "social class" ... has become weaker. It now has much less influence on their actions. They develop ways of life that tend to become individualized' (Beck 1992: 92).

The death of stratification?

As John Scott notes, such claims are not new:

Intimations of the apparent death of class first appeared in reflections on the significance of economic growth, affluence, and embourgeoisement during the 1950s and 1960s. . . . Contemporary societies, it was widely held, were becoming more open, more individualistic, and more meritocratic. The old class identities that were tied to traditional communities and to divisions in the sphere of production were in decay. They were being replaced by new identities that owed more to consumption differences and lifestyles in the fluid suburban neighbourhoods. . . . The traditional working and middle classes were on the wane in the era of high mass consumption.

(Scott 2001: 128)

These earlier attacks must be seen in the context of theories – widely popular in the 1950s – of a 'post-industrial society' (Bell 1973), in which the 'logic of industrialism' (Kerr *et al.* 1973) was producing orderly, affluent societies based on occupational achievement, and high social mobility, with few social barriers. As Chapter 5 shows, such theories were associated with models of stratification which promoted the notion of a seamless status hierarchy, with little sense of social conflict, or of clearly defined social-class groups. But problems with this model of stratification – with its apparent neglect of conflict and social division – led to the re-emergence and increasing dominance of class accounts of stratification. The reappearance of claims of the 'death of class' could, therefore, simply be seen as part of the recycling of sociological fashions. However, there is an important difference. Current attacks on class are not arguing for the revival of gradational, status theories of stratification, instead they are rejecting structural accounts of stratification altogether.

The current attacks on class identify a process which is 'at the heart of the move to a postmodern system of stratification, the abolition of fixed status boundaries' in which 'the whole process of stratification [is] much more fluid and apparently chaotic than it has previously been' (Crook *et al.* 1992: 124). This argument sees social relations as inchoate and shifting, in which identity is not determined in any patterned way by group affiliations, but rather is free-floating and based on individualised lifestyle choices. If true, this would be the end of stratification (as systematically structured inequality).

> Postmodernization is characterized by an unprecedented level of unpre-dictability and apparent chaos. Action is divorced from underlying material constraints (or rather these constraints disappear) and enters the volun-taristic realm of taste, choice and preference. As it does so the boundaries between determined social groups disappear . . . so that the very idea of an independent, purely social structural realm no longer makes sense.
>
> (Crook *et al.* 1992: 35)

Such theorists are not arguing that *material inequality* has declined. For Beck, contemporary society is both highly unequal but also classless: 'it is a capitalism without classes, but individualized social inequality and all the related social and political problems' (Beck 1992: 88). Similarly, Pakulski and Waters insist 'we are not arguing for a decline in inequality and conflict but for a decline in *class* inequality and conflict' (1996: 156). It is the translation of material inequality into social groupings and political action which is questioned. Because society has become individualised and fragmented, the prospects for material inequality giving rise to class communities, solidarity, consciousness and action have receded. Classes are 'crumbling communities of fate' in which 'class communi-ties, neighbourhoods and cultures are eroded and fragmented' (Pakulski and Waters 1996: 90, 66). Material inequality remains high, but is experienced in such highly individualised ways that the social meaning of such inequality is minimal. Class critics claim this 'shifting relationship between class divisions and their social consequences' (Pakulski and Waters 1996: 90) means stratification no longer gives rise to systematic and patterned differences in social identity.

De-classing culture

The postmodern claim is that consumption is increasingly important for how we order our lives and define ourselves, in ways quite independent of economic divisions. Because consumption is 'an order of cultural differentiation which intersects with and challenges the older order of economic differentiation' (Crook *et al.* 1992: 131), consumption identities are more fragmented, floating free of stratification position. This, effectively, is the argument that culture has been de-classed.

It is claimed, for example, that now our cultural interests and affiliations focus on such areas as 'peace or the environment, on such diverse unifying themes as soccer, feminism, *Neighbours*, retirement, sociology, Placido Domingo, being gay, socialism, feminism, monarchism, *Star Trek* and astrology' (Crook *et al.* 1992: 133). However, while these cultural groupings can lead to 'imagined communities' which may 'encourage a sense of fellowship, common interest and shared identity' they 'do not depend on an actuality of shared situation, much less on dense interpersonal networks' (1992: 132). They are subject to more rapid change than the older divisions of class stratification, so this proliferation, and de-materialisation, of social attachments leads to the 'decomposition' and 'decay' of fixed social categories. Class divisions become submerged 'into more fluid cultural patterns of social differentiation in which social membership derives not from underlying material determinants or even from socially constructed groups but rather from symbolically specified associations which are simulated within mass information media' (Crook *et al.* 1992: 111).

> Postmodernization involves a shift in patterns of differentiation from the social to the cultural sphere, from life-chances to lifestyles, from production to consumption. The pattern of inequality will become altogether more fluid than previously and will approximate a mosaic of multiple status identities rather than a small number of enclosed social capsules. Status will not depend on one's location in the society, especially its system of production and reproduction, but on one's status accomplishments in the sphere of consumption, one's access to codes. These will involve the products one uses, the places one goes, the leisure pursuits in which one engages, the clothes one wears. Social membership will be contingent on mass participation, display and profligacy rather than on work and ownership. Interestingly, such attributes cannot be accumulated, reproduced or inherited and while they may give rise to well recognised and sometimes oppressive inequalities they will not give rise to divisive or enduring ones.
>
> (Crook *et al.* 1992: 133)

We can see three aspects to these arguments: the notion that the cultural has detached from economic or social constraints; the notion of the increasing importance of the cultural, as an autonomous source of identity, leading to more fluid lifestyles and multiple identities; and the notion that fixed social groupings 'decompose' because the boundaries between them are blurred by the proliferation of attachments, and cultural affiliations are less enduringly structured.

On the barricades

Allegations of the 'death of class' are controversial, and a spirited defence has been mounted by class theorists. Sceptical about the sweeping assertions of a postmodern transformation, they argue that claims of the death of class are based on sparse and selectively chosen evidence. A crucial issue here is the model of class that class critics and proponents are arguing about (and what sort of evidence is likely to support or reject class analysis). Defenders of class have criticised class critics for operating with an outmoded 'strong' Marxist model of class (and therefore inevitably finding class 'decline'), ignoring the fact that neo-Weberian class analysis makes more limited claims about the links between class position and social behaviour. Class stalwarts argue that the wealth of empirical evidence shows class remains an excellent predictor of people's behaviour across a range of issues (voting, marriage, health, social mobility, etc.), supporting this more limited class model.

Hout and colleagues (1996) argue that claims of the 'fragmentation of stratification' ignore empirical evidence which shows the continuing importance of class inequalities in people's lives. Clark and Lipset 'ignore the remarkable persistence in the high levels of wealth controlled by the bourgeoisie' and their capacity to influence political processes (1996: 52). Moreover, the growth of the middle classes has not eradicated income inequality and has not influenced the proportion of the population living in extreme poverty.

> In the US . . . it is becoming increasingly common for privileged professionals and managers to live in secluded enclaves and suburbs (often behind locked gates) . . . while marginalised sectors of the populations are crowded into increasingly dangerous inner-city areas. As long as such conditions prevail, we are sceptical that sociologists should abandon the concept of class.
>
> (Hout *et al.* 1996: 53)

So whilst 'class structures have undergone important changes . . . the birth of new sources of inequality does not imply the death of the old ones' (Hout *et al.* 1996: 58). Rejecting the argument that class matters less in political matters, they argue 'class was always only one source of political identity and action alongside race, religion, nationality, gender and others. To say that class matters less now than it used to requires that one exaggerate its importance in the past and understate its importance at present' (Hout *et al.* 1996: 55).

Goldthorpe and Marshall (1992) argue that class critics have set up a 'straw person' model of class analysis. They distinguish between Marxist class theory – which makes strong theoretical claims that class position affects consciousness and action – and their own class *analysis*, which argues that the worth of class must be decided by the results it produces. Their own research programme is a 'far more limited project', which amounts to an extended empirical test in which 'the reality of "class" is demonstrated by the persistence of an empirical association between "classes" (i.e. those aggregates generated by the application of the Goldthorpe class scheme) and "class effects"' (Crompton 1996: 62). In this defence 'class' is important as long as it remains a good predictor of social behaviour. For Goldthorpe, the evidence that 'class' continues to be well associated statistically with a range of social behaviours vindicates class analysis.

The evidence of continuing structured social inequality in life-chances *is* impressive, and raises fundamental objections to claims of the supposedly 'fragmented', 'inchoate' or shifting nature of stratification.

> There remain sharp inequalities of life chances around the distribution of property and employment opportunities. These inequalities of income and assets are reflected in a wide range of material life chances: birth weight, infant mortality, life expectancy, disability, serious illness, housing, education,

victimisation in crime, and many other areas are shaped, overwhelmingly, by class situation. These are not simply economic inequalities, they are socially structured differences in life chances that often have their effects 'behind the backs' of the people involved and that may not be reflected in their social awareness or the cultural meanings that they give to their lives. Class relations have a causal effect on people's lives, despite the fact that they may not articulate this in class terms.

(Scott 2001: 141)

Class analysts demonstrate that structured inequalities in life-chances affect almost every aspect of our lives, and show remarkable persistence over time – regardless of our consciousness of them. This, they argue, is incontrovertible evidence of the enduring, systematically patterned, and socially divisive nature of stratification. However, class critics have never denied the persistence of structured inequality, instead it is the *relevance* of this inequality – for the formation of subjective consciousness and cultural identity – which is in question. Pointing to structured inequality in life-chances will not address this claim, which entails a quite different level of 'class' process.

This point is made by Scott, who distinguishes five different questions when assessing the relevance of class (2001: 135):

- Are class situations the most significant influence on life-chances?
- Can class situations be clustered into economically homogeneous categories?
- Do classes show distinct patterns of association and mobility?
- Do the members of social classes have a shared awareness of their social position?
- Is class the basis of political and social movements?

He argues that class critics have focused on the last two issues – seeing 'class' processes only in conscious awareness and cultural identity – and ignored the structured social inequality of the first three questions, which are central to the defence made by class analysts. Scott insists that although 'the changes highlighted by the critics of class analysis reveal a weakening of the cultural and political aspects of class formation', 'it is a fundamental error to assume that the absence of a strong consciousness of class means that there is no material reality to social classes and class situations' (2001: 142, 139).

De-culturing class

In their differing interpretations of what 'class' means, class critics and class defenders disagree about the centrality of the *link* between structured class inequality and cultural identity. Critics claim that without consciousness and cultural identity 'class' does not exist. Defenders argue that 'class' *stratification* continues to be relevant and important, even when class *consciousness* is not in evidence. This raises a fundamental question of the place of cultural identity within class theory. In Marxist class theory, economic relations give rise to cultural identity, as structure *determines* consciousness and action. The Weberian modification of this allows for a more contingent relationship, with class location only one, potential, basis for cultural identity and consciousness. In defending the relevance of 'class' as structured social inequality, however, contemporary class defenders have downplayed the significance of cultural identity still further. They have effectively *de-cultured* class analysis, retaining the causal model of class location and cultural 'effects', but now seeing those effects as precariously contingent, redefining the core of class analysis quite independently of cultural identity.

This can be seen in the Nuffield conception of 'class': which rejects the idea that political action 'follows directly and "objectively" from class position' (Goldthorpe and Marshall 1992: 383–384):

> the version of class analysis that we endorse takes in no theory of class-based collective action, according to which individuals holding similar positions within the class structure will thereby automatically develop a shared consciousness of their situation and will, in turn, be prompted to act together in the pursuit of their common class interests . . . the occupancy of class positions is seen as creating only potential interests, such as may also rise from various other structural locations.
>
> (Goldthorpe and Marshall 1992: 383–384)

These increasingly cautious claims arose in rebuttal of sweeping charges in the 'death of class' debate, but are also prompted by a very real problem: that there is precious little evidence of class identities. For many commentators there is an increasing divide between class conditions and the subjective perceptions and reactions to those conditions. There seems to be little connection between class inequalities and class identities, and the link between class location and cultural identity appears to have unravelled.

> Class differences persist and have, in many respects, become sharper. However, these are far less directly reflected in distinct differences of social status, and so they are less directly reflected in sharp differences in attitude and outlook. Class consciousness – at least as conventionally understood – is no longer a central feature of contemporary class relations. Traditional status values, that for so long defined the character of British class relations, have decayed. This has undermined the everyday use of the language of class which [. . .] rests, in fact, on 'status' differences in accent, dress and background. [. . .] Class, as defined by Marx and Weber, remains the crucial determinant of life chances, and it shapes the opportunities that people have for pursuing particular lifestyles, but *it is less visible to people, who tend to define their positions in status terms.*
>
> (Scott 2000: 38–39)

Savage, reviewing the evidence of the relation between class position and social attitudes and beliefs, concludes that most studies have found severe limits to class consciousness. For 'although people can identify as members of classes, this identification seems contextual and of limited significance, rather than being a major source of their identity and group belonging'; and so 'people's social attitudes and views are too ambivalent to be seen as part of a consistent class-related world view', because 'class location shapes only some of their views, and even then, in highly mediated and complex ways' (Savage 2000: 40).

A series of qualitative studies of class identity have indicated that people are reluctant to claim class identities, and adopt a 'defensive', 'hesitant', 'ambivalent' or 'ambiguous' attitude to class labels or groupings (Savage *et al.* 2001; Reay 1998a, b; Skeggs 1997a). Whilst people recognise the continuing salience of economic and social inequality, and are willing to talk about class as a political issue (Savage *et al.* 2001; Devine 1992), they refuse to place themselves 'within' classes, often explicitly dis-avowing class identities (Skeggs 1997a; Reay 1998a). When confronted with questions about class issues, the respondents in such studies are often concerned to establish their own 'ordinariness' (Devine 1992; Savage *et al.* 2001). Savage suggests that such responses 'refuse' class identities and deny class discourses (Savage 2000: 35).

Conventional class analysis has retreated in the face of these difficulties. 'Class' – constructed as employment aggregates – might give rise to distinct cultural beliefs and identities, and class analysis merely investigates whether it does so or not. This is a considerable retrenchment from earlier accounts which made stronger theoretical claims about the links between economic and social behaviour. This retrenchment has itself been taken by critics as a sign of the theoretical exhaustion of class theory (Pahl 1993), and even those sympathetic to class analysis have become alarmed at its rapidly narrowing focus. What causes most concern is the way in which the boundaries of class analysis have been redrawn to exclude cultural identity.

Traditional class analysts are increasingly cautious about the extent to which class relations generate class identities (Goldthorpe and Marshall 1992; Hout *et al.* 1996). Some have re-worked class theory to dispense with the need for class identities at all. Goldthorpe (1996), for example, has increasingly adopted 'rational action theory' to explain the motives and strategies of individuals operating within class structures. Rational action theory (a form of rational choice theory) adopts a minimalist explanation of strategic action, arguing that when faced with different options, people do what they believe will have the best available outcome: that is the most rational choice. Goldthorpe's use of rational action theory allows him to argue that the *same* attitudes and beliefs have quite different consequences for those in differing class locations. So middle-class and working-class individuals may make very different choices about, for example, whether or not to go to university, not because they have different cultural attitudes or values about university education, but because the costs and risks of going to university are very much greater for working-class individuals. The same rational calculation of options will – for individuals in different class locations – lead to very different choices. It is the opportunities (and risks) presented by the different class locations of rationally acting individuals which constrain their behaviour, rather than variations in class cultures or attitudes.

As Savage notes, 'Goldthorpe's account is designed specifically to avoid appealing to . . . cultural frames of reference, since he knows that people's class identities are actually rather weak' (2000: 87). The use of rational action theory 'is a defensive attempt to shore up' class analysis in the absence of clear-cut class identities, because it allows Goldthorpe 'to explain how individuals act in class ways even when they lack developed class awareness' (Savage 2000: 85). This is de-cultured class analysis.

The problem of class identities has created a curious symmetry. Just as postmodern writers have abandoned economic relations in their attempt to explain cultural identity, so class traditionalists have jettisoned cultural identity as a key component of class analysis. In both camps, the theoretical links between class location and cultural identity have been unpicked. However, even supporters of class theory have recoiled from this theoretical retrenchment, seeing such 'attenuation' (Morris and Scott 1996) and 'minimalism' (Devine 1998), that they argue that class analysis has become increasingly less relevant to the broader concerns of social analysis (Crompton and Scott 2000: 4). For a newer generation of class theorists, the response of conventional class analysis to the problem of class identity and culture is simply too restrictive. Class analysis has 'presided over the marginalization of the study of the cultural and subjective dimensions of class at the same time that issues of identity and culture have taken on a higher profile in the social sciences as a whole' (Savage 2000: 1). For such critics, conventional class theory has ceded issues of cultural analysis to other sub-disciplines, in the process becoming ever more narrow and remote in appeal.

The use of rational action theory has been criticised on the grounds that cultural identity cannot be excluded from our explanations of decision-making processes: 'it is simply not possible to ignore the cultural frameworks which people use to make sense of their social location and which will thus condition the kinds of rational responses that they will make' (Savage 2000: 87). Devine argues that the rational action approach is only possible because of the minimal way in which Goldthorpe defines class in terms of employment relations, rather than as 'collectivities of people who share identities and practices' (Devine 1998: 23). She criticises Goldthorpe for focusing on the mobilisation of economic resources in class reproduction, ignoring the influence of cultural and social resources on the 'micro processes by which classes are created and sustained over time and space' (1998: 33). She points to the importance of 'social resources – defined as social networks and other less structured contacts which act as channels of both information and influence – in the reproduction of advantage' (1998: 32).

New class theorists are unwilling to abandon issues of cultural identity, but are put in an interesting situation, since 'the starting point for studies of class and culture should be the weakness of class consciousness' (Savage 2000: 34). This new generation of class theorists attacks both postmodern arguments that individualisation undermines class identities, as well as the class defence which reformulates class analysis without class identities. Instead, they want to reinstate issues of cultural identity to the heart of class theory. However, they recognise that such issues cannot be theorised from within traditional class analysis. Theorists such as Devine and Savage insist on a third alternative, a 'culturalist class analysis', which requires a focus on how 'in various settings of social life, processes of inequality are produced and reproduced routinely and how this involves both economic and cultural practices' (Devine and Savage 2000: 196). This entails rejecting the older analytical model in which economic class structure gives rise to status (or cultural) differences:

> Rather than seeking to isolate the two so that the interaction between separate spheres can be determined, we might instead focus on how cultural processes are embedded within specific kinds of socio-economic practices. [. . .] It is not especially useful to isolate the economic from the cultural but to show their embeddedness within specific kinds of social contexts. [. . .] It is not the case that given economic relations lead to particular kinds of cultural dispositions, but rather that certain modes of cultural deportment may be crucial to the smooth working of 'economic' relationships.
>
> (Devine and Savage 2000: 194–195)

Recent approaches define class in cultural and lifestyle terms, in effect fusing economic and status elements. This stress on the indivisibly social, cultural and economic nature of stratification draws inspiration from the work of the French sociologist, Pierre Bourdieu (Bourdieu 1984 [1979], 1985, 1987). Bourdieu's reconceptualisation of stratification will be discussed in greater detail in the next chapter; however, I will briefly introduce his most significant contribution to recent debates: the placing of cultural processes at the heart of class analysis.

Culturalist class analysis

'Culturalist' class approaches re-centre culture, lifestyle and taste at the heart of the reproduction of hierarchy and inequality. This is an acknowledgement of the increasing centrality of cultural lifestyle in social life, and echoes postmodern claims. The crucial difference is that culturalist class theorists argue that cultural and economic relations are embedded in each other in processes of stratification. Bourdieu's most famous work, the ground-breaking book *Distinction* (1984 [1979]: 581), explicitly rejects Daniel Bell's (1973) earlier 'death of class' claims that distinct class cultures have declined in post-industrial societies, but also rebuts similar postmodern claims about the increasingly 'free-floating' nature of cultural lifestyles.

Using French data, Bourdieu shows that cultural tastes are systematically and enduringly related to class position. But the relationship between the economic and the cultural is far more complicated than the 'economic-cause leading to social-effects' model of conventional class theory. Culture is not an *effect* of class location but rather a central mechanism by which class positions are *constituted*.

Conventional class theory has always maintained that there is a good association between (economic) class location and cultural tastes and lifestyles, but Bourdieu's approach

> goes beyond the mere demonstration of their association, to explore the ways in which taste may be seen to be a resource which is deployed by groups within the stratification system in order to establish or enhance their location within the social order.
>
> (Crompton 1998: 147)

Bourdieu argues that cultural knowledge and educational credentials are valued assets in the competitive struggle for advantage, and therefore should be seen as a form of *cultural capital*: with cultural resources playing an equivalent role to economic resources in generating stratification position. Bourdieu argues that cultural capital is increasingly important to stratification in western societies. This is connected to the rise in consumer-oriented economies:

> whose functioning depends as much on the production of needs and consensus as on the production of goods [. . .] a social world which judges people by their capacity for consumption, their 'standard of living', their life-style, as much as by their capacity for production.
>
> (Bourdieu 1984 [1979]: 310)

Consumption-based economies have resulted in new occupations based on cultural production, in which the possession of cultural capital is a marketable commodity. This includes jobs

> involving representation and presentation (sales, marketing, advertising, public relations, fashion, decoration and so forth) and in all the institutions providing symbolic goods and services. These include the various jobs in medical and social assistance (marriage guidance, sex therapy, dietetics, vocational guidance, paediatric advice etc.) and in cultural production and organization (youth leaders, play leaders, tutors and monitors, radio and TV producers and presenters, magazine journalists) which have expanded considerably in recent years.
>
> (Bourdieu 1984 [1979]: 359)

Social advancement in such jobs depends less on economic resources than on cultural competences and social connections. More generally, educational credentials have become increasingly important in modern societies, and this has 'precipitated a shift in upper-class inheritance practices from one of direct transfer of property to reliance upon the cultural transmission of economic privilege: investment in education gives upper-class offspring the chance to appropriate family privilege and wealth through access to the more powerful and remunerative institutional positions' (Swartz 1997: 181). A central claim of culturalist class analysis is that access to educational credentials is increasingly vital to maintaining position in the social hierarchy, and investment in education and cultural knowledge is a key strategy in class competition (Bourdieu 1984 [1979]; Savage 2000; Reay 1998b; Lareau 2000).

Bourdieu examines how access to different *types* of capital positions individuals and groups differently within the stratification order. Bourdieu argues 'that people actively invest cultural capital to realise economic capital – and vice versa. The complex interplay between these two forms of capital give rise to the emergence of a number of different social groups' (Savage *et al.* 1992: 100). Bourdieu's work is important because he shows that processes of lateral differentiation are centrally bound up with hierarchical class distinctions, as groups *within* the middle classes 'are engaging in endless though reasonably genteel battles to assert their own identities, social positions and worth' (Savage *et al.* 1992: 100). That is, cultural differentiation within the middle classes is part of their lateral competition with each other.

Bourdieu identifies a 'dominant' class who have a high overall level of capital, but within this grouping he distinguishes several sub-groupings: the *bourgeoisie* (business owners and financiers) have high economic capital but lower cultural capital, and thus limited contact with *intellectuals* (writers, artists, university professors) whose high social position is the result of high levels of cultural capital, but who have relatively lower economic capital; a third group of *professionals and senior managers* have more balanced levels of cultural and economic capital. Bourdieu sees the same divisions with the middle class (who have more modest overall levels of capital), distinguishing such groups as primary teachers (more cultural capital than economic capital) from shopkeepers (more economic capital than cultural capital), or technicians (balanced levels of cultural and economic capital). The working class is defined by their relative lack of either cultural or economic assets, compared to the groups above them, and Bourdieu argues that the greater economic constraints they face severely limit their ability to accumulate cultural capital. So differences in the *amount* and *type* of capital give rise to different 'class' positions in social space; and people in these positions exhibit systematic differences of lifestyle and taste, which serve as both *markers* of class difference, but also as *resources* in the competitive differentiation of class fractions, since they can act as barriers in processes of inclusion and exclusion.

Bourdieu's model sees hierarchical inequality reproduced in such simple actions as the (differentiated) choice of friends and marriage partners, or cultural tastes and preferences. Whether people like Country and Western or jazz, prefer sushi to hot dogs, or would rather watch a monster truck rally than go to the opera is not just a simple matter of individual taste, but also an *expression of class relationships*. For Bourdieu, taste is both a product of our class backgrounds, a marker identifying our class difference from others, and also a mechanism which helps to maintain social divisions between and within classes. Such distinctions of preference act to place individuals, and construct not class identities, but rather *classed identifications*, since 'taste classifies, and it classifies the classifier' (1984 [1979]: 6).

By liking the things and people that we like, we – often quite inadvertently – 'place' ourselves and others. For Savage, Bourdieu's arguments

> lead not to an emphasis on class as heroic collective agency, but towards class as implicit, as encoded in people's sense of self-worth and in their attitudes to and awareness of others – on how they carry themselves as individuals. [. . .] It is hence the very salience of class struggles over distinction which explains why it is so difficult for them to be explicitly named and identified by their protagonists, and to be tied down into a neat model specifying the relationship between social location and culture.
>
> (Savage 2000: 107)

Class dis-identification

By fusing economic and cultural elements within class analysis, this new form of class theory no longer requires class identities to form in a distinct and explicit manner.

> What establishes the relationship between class and culture (i.e., what establishes the classed nature of cultural dispositions) is not the existence of class consciousness, or the coherence or uniformity of a distinct set of cultural dispositions. Rather, the relationship is to be found in the way in which cultural outlooks are implicated in modes of exclusion and/or domination.
>
> (Devine and Savage 2000: 195)

The focus of new class theory is on how specific cultural practices are bound up with the reproduction of hierarchy. People do not have to explicitly recognise class issues or identify with discrete class groupings for class processes to operate. The emphasis is not on the development (or not) of class consciousness, but rather on the classed nature of particular social and cultural practices. Class cultures are viewed as modes of differentiation rather than as types of collectivity, and 'class' processes operate through individualised distinction rather than in social groupings (Savage 2000: 102). For the newer generation of class theorists this helps tackle the paradox that class remains structurally important in shaping people's lives but that this does not translate into consciously 'claimed' cultural identities.

Savage is not suggesting that we focus on structural inequality and abandon ideas of class as a form of social identity, but insists that we do need to rethink how class affects social identity. Savage argues that individualisation does not involve the death of class, but represents a *shift in how class operates*. Conventional class models which 'focus on class as a collective process [have] neglected how class identities and class processes are bound up with individualised processes' and so have missed social changes which has led to 'the reforming of class cultures around individualized axes' (Savage 2000: xii).

So class still shapes social identity, even if it is experienced and perceived in highly individualised ways:

> rather than evoking a sense of belonging to a collective group, it invokes a sense of differentiation from others. In most cases it means that they are not one of the privileged who have it easy, nor are they one of those at the bottom who are morally suspect. People's sense of self-identity is linked to a claim of 'ordinariness' or 'normality' which operates as a double reaction against both above and below.
>
> (Savage 2000: 115)

Rather than abandon ideas of class as a form of cultural identity, such authors have instead abandoned the old model of class, fundamentally rethinking how class location is bound up with cultural identity. Individualisation does not involve the death of class, but rather a shift in how class operates: for 'while collective class identities are indeed weak, people continue to define their own individual identities in ways which inevitably involve relational comparisons with members of various social classes': this represents the reorganisation of class cultures around 'individualized axes' (Savage 2000: xii).

The newer generation of class theorists recognise that the failure of class identities is a problem for class analysis, but refuse to see in lay denials of class the failure of class processes. Rather, the *absence* of class identities is re-characterised as *evidence* of class, albeit 'class' in a transformed state. Dis-identification does not undermine class theory, because such dis-identifications are seen as the *result* of class processes. Skeggs, for example, notes that in her sample of working-class women class identifications were rare, but that whilst the women 'dissimulate from class, their dissimulations are produced from it' (Skeggs 1997a: 94).

> These women are highly sensitive to issues of class and difference but they have no discourses available for them to articulate it as a positive identity. Their class struggle is waged on a daily basis to overcome the denigration and delegitimising associated with their class positioning.
>
> (Skeggs 1997a: 95)

Skeggs argues that class identities and cultures are relational, in which middle-class constructions of 'respectability' are partly organised around *not* being 'working class', with aspects of working-class culture consequently being devalued and stigmatised. As a result, Skeggs argues that the 'pathologisation' of working-class women (as 'dirty, dangerous and without value' (1997a: 74)) means that women shrink from claiming working-class identity. A similar account is offered by Reay (1997, 1998a), and such studies relate *female* working-class dis-identification to the fact that working-class identity is a 'spoiled identity' for women. Whilst recognising that, historically, male working-class identity has had more positive associations, Savage argues there has also been a 'dissolution of the working-class as a salient cultural identifier' (2000: 148), because recent organisational shifts mean that manual labour is now no longer associated with 'manly independence' but, instead, has increasingly been identified as a 'form of subordinate and dependent labour' for men as well as women (Savage 2000: 134).

In such accounts, class dis-identification is *itself* a class process, because the values which shape people's willingness to identify with class (or not) are themselves class differentiated and arise out of class oppositions and struggles. Further: 'despite a pervasive denial of class status, there are emotional intimacies of class which continue to shape individuals' everyday understandings, attitudes and actions' (Reay 1998b: 267). The absence of direct reference to class in everyday discourse is taken as a *sign* of class in action, since 'class' is now encoded in implicit ways.

It is clear that arguments about class operating through processes of individualisation and dis-identification entail a very different understanding of what 'class' means. Such accounts fuse status and class elements, and 'class' identity has been redefined from explicit attachment to a collectivity, to a sense of relational social distance within a hierarchy: 'Although a majority of mothers did not mention social class until I asked them to self-identify in class terms, they continually drew on distinctions of "people like us" and "people unlike us" in order to differentiate themselves and others' (Reay 1998b: 269). Such statements imply much more implicit and unselfconscious 'class identities', but legitimately argue that 'class' continues to shape people's social identity (even if experienced and perceived in highly individualised ways) because class cultures are now viewed as 'modes of differentiation rather than as types of collectivity' (Savage 2000: 102). So whilst 'collective class consciousness may be dying away, class remains both a social filter and a key mechanism individuals utilise in placing themselves and others' (Reay 1997: 226).

Conclusion

The crisis of class identities has resulted in a new focus in class analysis: on class as an individualised process of hierarchical distinction. It is argued that 'class' processes have become more implicit and less visible, but that the effects of class are no less pervasive in people's lives. This amounts to a radical shift in how class is seen to operate. In rejecting both arguments of the 'death of class', and the increasingly minimalist positions of class traditionalists, a newer generation of stratification theorists have transformed the scope and analytical framework of class analysis: inflating 'class' to include social and cultural formations, reconfiguring the causal model that has underpinned class analysis, and abandoning the notion of distinct class identities or groups, focusing instead on individualised hierarchical differentiation. Rather than the polar terms of 'class-in-itself' giving rise to 'class-for-itself' in which inequality triggered consciousness and action, this new model sets out a reverse process, in which explicit class identification and awareness dissolve, leaving behind a hierarchical version of 'class' implicitly encoded in identity through practice. Such accounts draw inspiration from the work of Bourdieu, and his notion that 'class' inequalities are, in part, reproduced through the hierarchically differentiated nature of tastes and dispositions.

Bourdieu's work emphasises the stratification ordering as a 'space of relation-ships'. Part 3 of this book, 'Re-orderings', looks in further detail at the work of Bourdieu as well as other, relational, models of 'social space'; showing how these very different approaches to stratification help illuminate a range of social rela-tions, rebutting postmodern claims of chaotic disorder in social experience, and demonstrating how ordinary, everyday social experiences are an essential aspect reproducing the stratification order.

Part 3

Re-orderings

9   Social space

As an alternative to both conventional stratification and 'postmodern' frameworks, this chapter explores approaches which emphasise the fused cultural and social aspects of hierarchy, using a model of social distance and social interaction within a social space. Founded on the idea that economic and social relations are embedded within each other, these approaches theorise stratification as a social space of relationships. Exploring the nature of social space involves mapping the network of social interaction – patterns of friendship, partnership and cultural similarity – which gives rise to relations of social closeness and distance. Differential association is therefore used to define distance within a social space, using close social networks and shared cultural tastes and lifestyles to identify social similarity.

Such approaches abandon the causal model that has underpinned class analysis, in which economic structures give rise to social and cultural formations, instead seeing stratification position constituted through the clustering of economic, social and cultural relations. They place less emphasis on the notion of distinct class identities or groups, focusing instead on stratification as a highly differentiated space of relationships. However, such approaches also emphasise the highly ordered and constraining nature of patterned social relations, and so reject postmodern claims of chaotic disorder in social experience, to argue instead that the routine choices and decisions of ordinary, everyday life are key in the (unintentional) reproduction of hierarchical social distance. Later chapters will look in greater detail at stratified social relations – in patterns of friendship, sexual partnership – and their consequences for access to resources and social opportunities. However, it is first necessary to explore the meaning of stratification understood as a patterning of social relationships.

The social space of relationships

In *Distinction* (1984 [1979]) Bourdieu found different occupational groups had consistently different cultural tastes in music, food, art and entertainment. Using statistical analysis, Bourdieu used the relationship between occupational groups and lifestyle items to establish a three-dimensional social space – a space of relations – placing groups with similar tastes close to each other in the space, whilst groups with very different tastes were placed as more distant. The theoretical assumption is that people sharing a similar social position have similar social and lifestyle practices.

> On the basis of the knowledge of the space of positions, one can separate out classes, in the logical sense of the word, i.e., sets of agents who occupy similar positions and who, being placed in similar conditions and subjected to similar conditionings, have every likelihood of having similar positions and interests and therefore of producing similar practices and adopting similar stances.
>
> (Bourdieu 1985: 725)

So by identifying patterned differences in the lifestyles of occupational groups Bourdieu mapped their distance and proximity within an overall social space. Although he uses cultural items to identify the stratification order, he argues this is simply the study of 'social relations objectified in familiar objects' (1984 [1979]: 77).

Bourdieu describes his approach as the study of class relations, but this is slightly misleading as his concept of the 'class' order is really an overall description of 'stratification':

> The conceptual space within which Bourdieu defines class is not that of production, but that of social relationships in general. Class relations are not defined by relations to the means of production, but by differing conditions of existence, differing systems of dispositions produced by differential conditioning, and differing endowments of power or capital.
>
> (Brubaker 1985: 761)

Bourdieu sees the stratification order emerging out of struggles for power, with the location of groups within the social order generated by different sorts of capital:

- economic capital (material resources: wealth, income, property);
- cultural capital (cultural knowledge, educational credentials);
- social capital (social connections, networks, patronage);
- symbolic capital (symbolic legitimation, respect, reputation).

The 'social space', which Bourdieu describes as a 'space of relationships' (1985: 725), is made up of various economic, social and cultural, and symbolic elements, with the two most important being *economic* and *cultural* capital, as Bourdieu believes people 'tend to draw disproportionately from either cultural or economic resources in their struggle to maintain and enhance their positions in the social order' (Swartz 1997: 137). His empirical work explores how access to these different sorts of resources positions individuals and groups differently within this space.

Bourdieu extends 'the idea of capital to all forms of power, whether they be material, cultural, social or symbolic', and such resources are seen as *capital* 'when they function as a "social relation of *power*," that is when they become objects of struggle as valued resources' (Swartz 1997: 73–74). These different capitals have different principles of operation and value, but are strongly linked in practical social relations, because 'reconversion strategies' can translate one set of resources into another. Cultural resources can be converted into economic capital (educational credentials can be used to get high-paying jobs), and vice versa (high income can be used to gain access to elite educational institutions). Our social position depends on the *combination* of the capital available to us; as we draw on not just our economic resources, but also on the social networks we have contacts with, and the symbolic and cultural resources we can take advantage of (using insider cultural knowledge, educational credentials, social honour and respectability) to maintain and advance our social position.

> Thus the social world can be represented as a space (with several dimensions) constructed on the basis of principles of differentiation or distribution constituted by the properties active within the social universe in question, ie., capable of conferring strength, power within that universe, on their holder. Agents and groups of agents are thus defined by their relative positions within that space.
>
> (Bourdieu 1985: 723–724)

Figure 9.1 shows this patterning of lifestyles (distinctive cultural tastes). There are three dimensions to the space of relationships: Bourdieu interprets these as the total *volume* of capital, the *composition* of capital (the relative degree of economic and cultural capital) and social *trajectory* (shifts in the amount or type of capital that groups acquire over time). Bourdieu 'argues that individuals who share similar positions on all three dimensions also share similar conditions of existence or class condition. Where they do, one can anticipate observing corresponding similarities in all forms of cultural and social practices' (Swartz 1997: 162–163).

So people with the same total amount of capital, but with different combinations of economic as opposed to cultural capital, also have distinct lifestyles. The 'high-brow' tastes of university teachers (whose overall position depends more on their high cultural capital than their lower economic capital) are very different from the 'low-brow', but expensive, tastes of industrialists (whose overall position depends less on their cultural capital than on their high economic capital). Bourdieu's argument is that everyday tastes in things ranging from the types of food and clothing we like to our preferences in music, art, decoration, gardening, or sports, and even our intellectual attitudes, act as both a reflection and reinforcement of 'class' differences, but class is interpreted very broadly in terms of location within an economic and cultural space.

Bourdieu sees lifestyle differences as 'perhaps the strongest barriers between the classes', since 'every sort of taste . . . unites and separates' (1984 [1979]: 185, 57). So: 'aesthetic stances adopted in matters like cosmetics, clothing or home decoration are opportunities to experience or assert one's position in social space, as rank to be upheld or a distance to be kept' (1984 [1979]: 57).

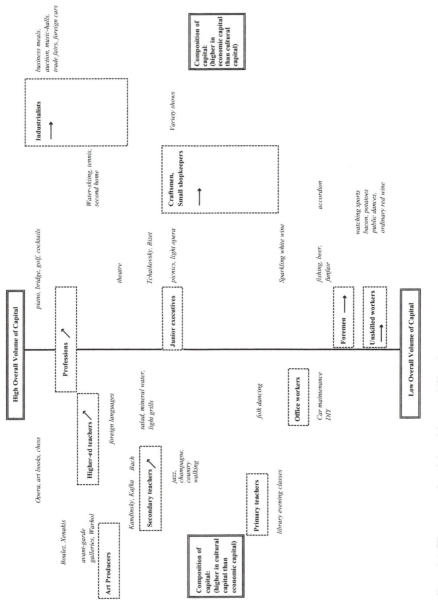

Figure 9.1 The space of social positions and lifestyles

Source: Adapted from Bourdieu 1984 [1979]: 128–129

Note: Space of positions indicated by bold type; space of lifestyles indicated by italic type.

For Bourdieu 'these lifestyle characteristics are *not* intrinsic features of each class. Rather, they obtain analytical significance *only* in relation to and by way of contrast with each other. Thus a dominated culture like a dominated social class is always defined in relation to a dominant culture and a dominant class, and vice versa' (Swartz 1997: 63). So, Bourdieu argues that working-class tastes 'make a virtue of necessity' (for example, favouring food that is 'good value', 'nourishing', 'filling', 'no-nonsense') whilst dominant class tastes, which celebrate 'freedom from necessity', can only be fully understood by the *oppositions* they mark to working-class tastes (favouring the 'light', 'refined' or the 'lean' and rejecting 'heavy', 'fatty' or 'coarse' foods). 'It matters little whether professionals prefer tennis, hockey, rugby, boxing, or cricket. What matters is that their preferences express systematic opposition to those of other classes' (Swartz 1997: 163).

Bourdieu believes that inequalities are, in part, reproduced through the hierarchically differentiated nature of tastes and disposition, and that these subtle forms of distinction are part of the competitive struggles over resources (and the symbolic legitimation of claims to resources) which position groups in social space. However, Bourdieu emphasises that these should not be seen as *deliberate* or *conscious* strategies of exclusion. Such processes 'owe their special efficacy to the fact that they function below the level of consciousness and language, beyond the reach of introspective scrutiny or control by the will' (Bourdieu 1984 [1979]: 467).

Disguised and legitimated power

Bourdieu believes that, as we grow up, our emerging tastes, preferences, and ambitions are shaped by the people and social conditions around us. Because social conditions shape our tastes and ambitions, this means that the choices we make in the future are also likely to be class-differentiated; so that our choices (of friends, lifestyle, career plans) tend to *reproduce* our position in the social order. Bourdieu therefore sees a process by which external structures are internalised, leading to (largely unconscious) tastes and aspirations which maintain class distinctions. Bourdieu calls this *habitus*:

> habitus, which is akin to the idea of class subculture, refers to a set of relatively permanent and largely unconscious ideas about one's chances of success and how society works that are common to members of a social class or status group. These ideas or, more precisely, dispositions, lead individuals to act in such a way as to reproduce the prevailing structure of life chances and status distinctions.
>
> (Swartz 1997: 197)

So we do not have to *consciously* pursue class strategies of differentiation, because simply by preferring our own tastes over those of others (whom we may see as 'snobby', 'vulgar', 'ostentatious', etc.) we unconsciously align ourselves with people who have the same class position (and tastes) and distance ourselves from class unequals.

'Taste', for Bourdieu, reflects internalised class dispositions. Taste

> functions as a sort of social orientation, a 'sense of one's place', guides the
> occupants of a given place in social space towards the social positions
> adjusted to their properties, and towards the practices of goods which befit
> the occupants of that position.
>
> (Bourdieu 1984 [1979]: 466–467)

So research on access to higher education shows that, because working-class
applicants fear social discomfort and the prospect of feeling 'out of place'
in overwhelmingly middle-class elite institutions, they often apply to lower-
level institutions where they feel they are more likely to get in and to encounter
'people like us' (Ball *et al.* 2002). Here habitus – operating at the level of
taken-for-granted assumptions, and preferences for social familiarity – guides
individuals to *self-select* class-differentiated routes and rewards, with the most
disadvantaged adjusting their aspirations to what they feel is 'realistic'. But by
developing a sense of what is appropriate and possible for people in their social
situation, the disadvantaged – quite unconsciously and implicitly – pursue class-
differentiated choices which help to reproduce their position in social space:

> objective limits become a sense of limits, a practical anticipation of objec-
> tive limits acquired by experience of objective limits, a 'sense of one's place'
> which leads one to exclude oneself from the goods, persons, place and so
> forth from which one is excluded.
>
> (Bourdieu 1984 [1979]: 471)

Bourdieu thinks power requires symbolic legitimation that creates '*misrecognition*' of its arbitrary nature. Misrecognition occurs when inequalities are not
recognised as a power relation but are instead seen as 'legitimate demands for
recognition, deference, obedience, or the service of others' (Swartz 1997: 42).
Inequality is reproduced through 'innocent' cultural and symbolic practices,
which do not appear to be about economic power, and which people accept in a
'taken-for-granted' manner. This means that inequality can persist for generations without people resisting it or even being aware of the true nature of power
relations.

Take the educational credentials which act as a key mechanism for access
to good jobs. Underlying such credentials is a powerful symbolic assumption:
that rewards accrue to those displaying talent and effort. This acts to legitimate inequality, with unequal rewards seen as merited or deserved. However,
Bourdieu argues that success in examinations is not just a feature of ability, but is
also dependent on pre-existing *cultural capital*, which is unequally distributed
amongst classes. Middle-class children, by virtue of their upbringing, already
have reserves of the knowledge (of 'high' culture) and competences (abstract
reasoning) which are rewarded in examinations, and so are always likely to do
better than equally bright, hard-working working-class children. Therefore,

Bourdieu sees educational credentials as a form of 'symbolic violence', because they conceal the way in which class advantage is embedded in the reward system. Because the symbolic legitimation of education as meritocratic is widely accepted, the working-class internalise failure, seeing it as the result of their individual lack of ability. For all concerned, the emphasis on *ability* in the education system leads to the misrecognition of the fact that it is mainly *middle-class* knowledge and competences which are valued and rewarded. Ironically, those who uphold 'fair competition' fail to see how their stress on 'rewards based on merit' itself helps to reproduce class inequalities.

Cultural consensus and reproduction

Bourdieu's account is a *reproductionist* one: emphasising how everyday practices that occur within a hierarchical social space themselves – quite unintentionally – help to reproduce that hierarchy. In emphasising orderly social relations, Bourdieu is attempting to by-pass the structure/action merry-go-round of conventional class analysis. However, Bourdieu has still been accused of structural determinism: 'The analytical emphasis falls upon causes rather than reasons. Structures produce the habitus, which generates practice, which reproduces the structures, and so on' (Jenkins 2000 [1982]: 152). This is an overstatement, but there is some truth in the charge. As Swartz notes:

> While Bourdieu is not rigidly deterministic, as some critics charge, his conceptual framework is clearly more attentive to patterns of continuity than to change. The concepts of habitus, cultural capital, and field stress the tendency to perpetuate structures inherited from the past. The propensity of habitus is clearly to address new situations in habituated ways, it takes capital to accumulate more capital, and field permits an impressive mapping of social positions and their continuity over time.
>
> (Swartz 1997: 290)

The problem is not simply that Bourdieu neglects processes of change, but that he also tends to over-state the amount of reproduction that actually occurs. Bourdieu has been criticised (Goldthorpe 1996) for underestimating social mobility in western societies – which all exhibit substantial patterns of movement in which people travel beyond their class origins, following ambitions which take them to quite different positions (and lifestyles). Bourdieu has also been accused of placing too much emphasis on how early social location shapes subsequent tastes and aspirations, ignoring the way in which tastes continue to shift and develop; and neglecting evidence that ambitions are never as 'realistically' adjusted as his model suggests. Bourdieu's model has therefore been accused of being overly reproductionist. A recurring problem within this model is the role of shared values and consensus in the reproduction of disadvantage.

The problem can be seen in Bourdieu's account of cultural difference. In Bourdieu's model, cultural distinction operates as a hierarchy of culture in which the values of the dominant class are the only ones regarded as legitimate. Bourdieu argues that class-differentiated cultural tastes are not just *different*, they are also *unequal*. That is, there is a general perception that the tastes of lower social groups are less tasteful, civilised and cultivated: in effect, less *cultured*. Bourdieu, for example, would argue that classical music (the music of elite taste) is generally regarded as a *higher* cultural form than, say, heavy metal, even by people who do not like classical music. Bourdieu argues that a consensus on 'good' taste emerges out of power relations – dominant social groups are able to impose *their* values as morally and culturally superior. The tastes of higher-level groups become seen as higher tastes.

On this view, the cultural tastes of working-class people are not merely *different* from the middle class, they are inevitably constructed as *inferior*. This assumption derives from Bourdieu's relational logic:

> Bourdieu suggests that a legitimate and a 'dominated' culture exist because the value of cultural preferences and behaviours are defined relationally around structuring binary oppositions such as high/low, pure/impure, distinguished/vulgar, and aesthetic/useful.
>
> (Lamont and Lareau 1988: 157)

In Bourdieu's account, working-class or 'popular' culture is *defined in terms of its deficiencies in relation to 'high' culture* (i.e. lacking refinement, elegance, sophistication, etc.). And Bourdieu insists that this is not just what higher-level groups believe, their social subordinates, he argues, also – however grudgingly – agree. The domination of middle-class values in society means that subordinate groups (implicitly) *accept* the legitimacy of middle-class culture but can only develop an impoverished, deficit version of it. 'Popular' culture is actually *dominated* culture, defined by a lack of cultural capital rather than an authentic, alternative version of culture:

> Adapting to a dominated position implies a form of acceptance of domin-ation. [. . .] It would be easy to enumerate the features of the lifestyle of the dominated classes which, through a sense of incompetence, failure or cul-tural unworthiness, imply a form of recognition of the dominant values. [. . .] As much as by the absence of luxury goods, whisky or paintings, champagne or concerts, cruises or art exhibitions, caviar or antiques, the working-class lifestyle is characterized by numerous cheap substitutes for these rare goods, 'sparkling white wine' for champagne, imitation leather for real leather, reproductions for paintings, indices of a dispossession at the second power, which accepts the definition of the goods worthy of being possessed.
>
> (Bourdieu 1984 [1979]: 386)

For Bourdieu, then, the correspondence between class hierarchies and cultural hierarchies means that higher social groups are able to use cultural prac-tices in processes of status competition, with 'cultured' lifestyles a means of asserting social superiority and social exclusion. However, whilst Bourdieu's account is highly influential, widespread doubts have emerged about whether there is a hierarchy of 'high' and 'low' culture, a field of class conflict, within which cultural taste emerges as a form of symbolic violence against other forms of cultural choice. Claims that elite cultural distinctions are less apparent in American society (Lamont 1992) have been linked to postmodern arguments of cultural pluralism which suggest that the hierarchical ranking of 'elite' and 'popular' culture has broken down.

Bourdieu's account is a 'top down' view of cultural values in which popular culture is defined in terms of what it lacks. Critics argue that this dismisses the pleasures that people take in cultural items for their own sake. It has been suggested that popular cultural practices have their own logic, quite independent of 'high culture' referents, and sociologists of culture have questioned whether there is still a clearly established 'class' hierarchy in which everyone wishes to imitate higher social classes.

The extent to which there is a hierarchical ordering of lifestyle practice remains an important empirical question, since it is suggested that cultural specialisation and diversity have made the signs of distinction increasingly hard to recognise, and so less well related to stratification processes. It is argued that 'mass cultures' aimed at the widest possible audience are weakly differentiated 'and because non-differentiated, relatively non-hierarchical' (DiMaggio 1987: 442). Postmodern critics argue that we no longer have 'a hierarchically organised, symbolically consensual prestige structure in society, one in which all groups, classes and coteries looked in the same direction for cues for what was to be thought beautiful, accept-able, and fashionable' (Davis, quoted in S. Miles 1998: 171). If the distinction between 'high' and 'low' culture has collapsed, and people have increasingly diverse cultural tastes, then there are no longer clear cultural hierarchies through which processes of social distinction can operate. Does the cultural eclecticism of (post-)modern tastes mean that individuals are unlikely to privilege a taste for Debussy over a taste for *The Simpsons*, and so taste cannot be so easily used to mark out social superiority and inferiority?

There is some empirical evidence of this. Peterson (1992, 1996) argues that a rise in cultural *omnivorousness* undermines cultural rankings (and so the extent to which culture can be used in status competition). Cultural omnivorousness can be seen in high-status groups who no longer confine their tastes to 'elite' art forms, but eclectically draw on both 'high' and 'popular' forms in their cultural practice. So, in America, although high-status individuals are much more likely to prefer classical music than other social groups, still only a minority of them (29 per cent) choose to listen to this type of music; they are more likely to prefer country music (normally seen as a low-brow genre) to opera, and in general have very wide-ranging tastes (Peterson and Simkus 1992). This undermines the clear-cut ranking of cultural forms which Bourdieu's model assumes. Peterson and Simkus suggest there is increasingly less *consensus* about the rankings of different cultural forms with a 'large number of alternative forms having more or less equal taste value' so that 'the taste hierarchy represents not so much a slim column of taste genres one on top of the other as a pyramid with one elite taste at the top and more alternative forms about the same level as one moves down the pyramid . . . as one approaches the bottom, musical taste serves to mark not only status levels but also the status boundaries between groups defined by age, gender, race, region, religion, life-style, etc. at roughly the same stratum level' (1992: 168–169).

One suggestion is that Bourdieu's stress on a singular cultural hierarchy emerges from the particularities of the French, who have always placed great stress on 'high culture'. It is argued that the value of cultural capital depends on a broad *consensus* on cultural values, so culture may play less of a role in stratification in societies with greater cultural diversity, or where 'high' culture is less well developed (Lamont and Lareau 1988; Swartz 1997). Comparative research by Lamont (1992) found that American upper-middle-class men were less likely to draw boundaries on the basis of cultural sophistication than their French counterparts. In America, there was far less agreement on what constituted 'acceptable' cultural behaviour, a broader cultural repertoire, and greater tolerance of cultural difference, so perceptions of difference were less easily translated into cultural hierarchies (in which different tastes are characterised as 'good/bad', 'right/wrong', 'refined/vulgar', etc.). As a result, cultural boundaries and hierarchies were weaker than in France and less likely to map on to socio-economic inequalities (Lamont 1992: 90). For Lamont, this means that we cannot assume that 'differentiation necessarily leads to hierarchalization' (1992: 118) since this process depends on the level of agreement over cultural values and the sharpness of cultural boundaries.

Such arguments raise important questions about the need to look at the links between lifestyle *practice*, cultural *evaluation* as it is embedded in social relations, and discursive claims and *perceptions* about cultural items. In fact, there is no reason why a hierarchical ordering of cultural *practices* should be dependent on any *consensual evaluation* of the 'superiority' of 'high' over 'low' culture, or middle-class choices over working-class choices, since mutually distinct values – about partners, friends, or cultural items – may still produce a hierarchical ordering of practices (in which different groups in a hierarchy have consistently different preferences). That is, 'a plurality of practices need not necessarily stand in relationships of superiority and inferiority' (Warde *et al.* 1999: 123). All that is required for the cultural reproduction of inequality is for the various groups in a hierarchy to value things and people *differently*. To the extent that they do so *consistently*, social practices will be hierarchically differentiated in an orderly manner, even though discursive evaluations may be chaotically discordant.

In fact, there is considerable evidence that 'cultural consumption continues to reflect social inequalities and, if it symbolises refinement, is a potential mechanism for social exclusion' (Warde *et al.* 1999: 124). Most studies demonstrate consistent differences in the cultural practices of unequally placed social groups (McMeekin and Tomlinson 1998; Tomlinson 1994; Warde *et al.* 1999; Bennett *et al.* 1999). Although there are some 'mass' activities in which almost everybody participates (swimming, for example, or going to the cinema) there are many others in which participation is much more unevenly distributed, showing a clear stratification gradient; with higher-level groups much more likely to go to the theatre and restaurants, to play squash or ski, to watch public service television channels rather than commercial ones, to read broadsheets rather than tabloids, for example.

Omnivorousness does mean that there is often considerable *overlap* in the sorts of activities that different social groups engage in (so that we cannot see discrete social groups with distinct and mutually exclusive cultural tastes). However, just because we can't distinguish 'snobs' from 'slobs' doesn't mean that culture is unrelated to stratification. Studies of cultural omnivorousness show this pattern is itself *class differentiated*. Omnivores tend to come from higher, more educated social classes. Higher-level, better-educated groups participate more often not only in high art forms, but also in *most* kinds of leisure activities (and have higher levels of participation in all formal voluntary associations (Bennett *et al.* 1999; Hall 1999; Parry *et al.* 1992; Johnston and Jowell 2001; Li *et al.* 2002, 2003a, b; Warde *et al.* 2003)). Peterson (1992) distinguishes the activities of high-status groups from the practice of lower-level groups which exhibit what he calls 'univore' tastes, engaging in less cultural activities, and exhibiting strong likes for just a few cultural forms. This distinction, between 'inclusive' and 'restricted' cultural participation, shows up in other research in Australia and Britain (Bennett *et al.* 1999; Warde *et al.* 1999): higher-level groups (managers and employers) have higher levels of activity and greater variety in their cultural activities, whilst lower-level groups have lower levels of activity with fewer cultural preferences.

Because cultural omnivorousness is hierarchically differentiated it can also be used to express social superiority since, as Bryson argues, 'tolerance itself may separate high-status culture from other group cultures' and the variety of tastes valued by upper-level groups can be used as a form of '*multicultural capital* – the social prestige afforded by familiarity with a range of cultural styles that is both broad and predictably exclusive' (1996: 897, 888). 'It may carry just as much kudos at a dinner party to show that you know the current line-up of the Spice Girls as to know the name of Philip Glass' latest composition' (Bennett *et al.* 1999: 200). Erickson (1996) argues that the valuing of cultural variety also emerges from instrumental stratification processes. Managers and employers have the most diverse cultural knowledge because they use this knowledge to smooth social encounters with their social subordinates at work because 'Those who interact with a wider variety of people must respond to a wider variety of culture shown by others and, hence, develop a wider repertoire of culture themselves' (Erickson 1996: 220–221). The ability to talk about sports, for example, is a social leveller, enabling people at different social levels to communicate effectively:

> the most powerful single teacher of cultural variety is contact with people in many different locations: network variety builds cultural variety. Advantaged people, including higher-class people, will certainly have better cultural resources, but this is not because of their class as such but because of the diverse networks that advantaged people have.

(Erickson 1996: 224)

So the link is between (stratified) social networks and cultural lifestyles. In Erickson's research it was the *network variety* of individuals (the extent to which they had to interact with people at different social levels) which was the best predictor of cultural variety. However, as Chapter 10 shows, higher-level groups also have the most diverse networks. This reiterates the links between cultural and social capital outlined by Bourdieu. However, as we now see, the importance of social networks in stratification means that we can use social interaction to identify the stratification ordering – literally as a social space of relationships.

Social interaction distance approaches

Bourdieu sees similarities of lifestyle as being inseparable from processes of social interaction. He says, for example, that 'the surest guarantor of homogamy and, thereby, of social reproduction, is the spontaneous affinity . . . which brings together the agents endowed with dispositions or tastes that are similar' (Bourdieu 1990: 71). The implication is that 'those who are similar in terms of lifestyle prefer to interact socially and those who choose to interact socially tend to be similar in terms of lifestyle' (Prandy 1999a: 229). However, Bourdieu's theoretical claim is not empirically addressed. Indeed, whilst Bourdieu includes social capital (social connections and networks as a set of resources) as one of his three key elements of the social space, his theoretical account of it is much less well developed than his account of economic and cultural capital (Erickson 1996), and levels of social capital are seldom measured in his work (Swartz 1997; Warde and Tampubolon 2002). However, there is a set of approaches – social interaction distance approaches – which map social space by looking directly at social networks and patterns of differential association. It is to these approaches that we now turn.

Even amongst authors who stress the continuing importance of culture as an arena of class differentiation, it has been suggested that the ability of individuals to discriminate between cultural items does not indicate the *significance* of such items in the everyday life of subjects (Longhurst and Savage 1996). However, interaction approaches to stratification directly address this issue by focusing on people's most important social relations, and so are better placed to identify lifestyle preferences which are significant in social practice.

Differential association – the fact that who we associate with is affected by our social location – has long been seen as a key aspect of stratification, and the impact of hierarchical position on our choice of friends and partners, and on our cultural tastes and activities, is well known. Differential association, in which 'similarity breeds connection', refers to the powerful relationship between social *association* and social *similarity* (McPherson *et al.* 2001: 416). A wealth of evidence shows that marriage and friendship exhibit clear patterns of homophily (marriage and friendship between those with the same or very similar social characteristics), and that 'birds of a feather flock together' along lines of education, class or socio-economic status position, and by religion and ethnicity (Kalmijn 1991, 1998; McPherson *et al.* 2001). This will be the focus of the next chapter.

But because people tend to befriend and marry individuals who are from roughly similar social positions to themselves we can use this information to map the social space within which the relationships occur.

> Differential association can be seen as a way of defining distances within a social space: social interaction will occur most frequently between persons who are socially close to one another and relatively infrequently between those that are socially distant. It is possible to reconstruct this social space from the information about the set of distances. The social space determined in this way will reflect and represent the structure of stratification arrangements. The space is inherently social structural, not an aggregation of individual or group characteristics; it does not deal with each occupational group taken separately, but with each in relation to all of the others.
>
> (Prandy 1999a: 215)

Social interaction distance approaches theorise a social space – composed out of social interaction – which can be seen as a structure of social distance. Partners, friends and acquaintances tend to be chosen from amongst those who share a similar lifestyle, which is in turn dependent on the resources and rewards that are available to groups of people. All close social relationships, such as marriage/partnership and friendship, are therefore closely bound up with processes of hierarchy and differentiation. Because we tend to form close social relationships with individuals near to us in the social order, we thus – intentionally or unintentionally – help to confirm and reproduce that social order.

This does not assume a simple model of in-group association, since some close relationships inevitably occur across social divides. The assumption is simply that close social ties such as friendship and marriage/partnership are *more likely* between people in those occupations that are similarly placed in the social order; through contiguity, through similar standards of lifestyle, through routine social interactions – at work, in the community and so on – which bring them and their families into contact with each other (Prandy and Bottero 1998: 1.3).

So rather than defining a stratification structure (composed of a set of class or status groups) and then looking for the extent of interaction within and across the boundaries of such groupings, social interaction distance approaches *reverse* the conventional approach, using patterns of interaction to *determine the nature of the stratification order itself*.

The pioneering work on differential association, by Laumann (Laumann and Guttman 1966) emerged out of the Warner tradition of research on community association (Warner *et al.* 1949). As we have seen, this approach attempted to look at how economic resources, cultural activities, networks and social cliques *combine* to form stratified social 'clusters', but ran into difficulties through relying on participants' subjective perceptions of these clusters. Instead of relying on *perceptions* of 'evaluated participation' in small communities, Laumann looked directly at actual social relations. Having defined a stratified social structure as 'one in which there is a tendency for people to confine their intimate social relationships with others of approximately equal rank or status' (Laumann and Guttman 1966: 170), Laumann measured the relative distances between occupations in terms of how often their members associated with each other (as friends, neighbours or in-laws). This was a revolutionary procedure since occupations were ordered not by production relations, economic criteria, or perceptions of social standing, but rather by how the occupations were embedded in patterns of social association. However, this methodological innovation was not matched by a corresponding re-evaluation of the theoretical meaning of the stratification order (Bottero and Prandy 2003).

However, the theoretical significance of social interaction distance in understandings of stratification has been explored by Sandy Stewart, Bob Blackburn and Ken Prandy, of the Cambridge Stratification Group. They have developed a series of *interaction scales* which use friendship and marriage choices to map the social ordering of occupations (Stewart *et al.* 1980; Prandy 1990; Prandy and Bottero 1998, 2000a; Prandy and Lambert 2003; Prandy and Jones 2001), and give a very different *theoretical* account of stratification processes from that contained in conventional accounts.

The social interaction space

The Cambridge approach uses patterns of social interaction to determine the relative distances between occupational groups (as indicated by higher or lower levels of interaction) and from these the nature of the social space in which the occupations are located. Originally, friendship was used, but more recent work has focused on marriage (including cohabitation). Using these different types of social association the group has developed a hierarchical scale of stratification arrangements: an 'ordering of occupations on the basis of social similarity as defined by the extent of social interaction' (Prandy 1999a: 231). This, they argue, is a scale of 'shared experience', measuring material and social advantage which are 'indivisible concepts' (Stewart *et al.* 1980: 28).

The argument is that social interaction, lifestyle and the hierarchy of advantage that constitutes social stratification are intimately interlinked, the conception is 'of stratification arrangements that involve differences in generalised advantage (and disadvantage) and hence in lifestyle and in social interaction related to level of advantage and lifestyle' (Prandy 1990: 635). This is the same approach as Bourdieu, the only difference being that instead of tracing the distance between social groups and *lifestyle* items the social space is identified by empirically mapping *social interactions* (Bottero and Prandy 2003). The logic is simple: by investigating social relationships of social *closeness* – patterns of friendship and partnership, social similarity and contiguity – we can identify which groups interact at a *distance* or in terms of dissimilarity. This provides a hierarchical ordering of the occupations, given solely by the patterns of marriage or friendship between the occupational groups (Prandy and Bottero 1998). Once the nature of the distances between groups has been identified, this is treated as a *measure* of social distance and used to investigate other aspects of stratification.

The approach rejects the division between class and status that has informed most conventional accounts of stratification, arguing for

> an integrated conceptualisation of stratification which allows for both those resources associated with work and employment that typically figure in class schemas and for those associated with social interaction and evaluation that inform ideas of status. The two are simply aspects of a unified social reality. [. . .] The theoretical model underlying the Cambridge Scale is one of distributed social resources and associated differential advantage. The scale itself is derived from the social interaction that derives from the common life styles of those with equivalent levels of resources.
>
> (Prandy 1998: 361–362)

The social distance method 'puts social relationships at the heart of stratification analysis' (Bottero and Prandy 1998), using 'information about real social choices, telling us about the frequency of relatively high, relatively low and all intermediate levels of social interaction' (Prandy 1999a: 230). It examines social hierarchy and differentiation by focusing on choices that are *socially meaningful to the people concerned*. This is similar to Bourdieu's method, using lifestyle items, but sidesteps the problem of interpreting how important such choices are in people's lives, by instead focusing on close and intimate social relationships – such as friendship and marriage – which, by definition, are significant and meaningful in people's lives.

Occupation is the *tag* by which the method locates an individual's place in the social hierarchy, but occupations are not seen as aspects of a prior economic structure which determines social identity and behaviour, but rather are viewed as integral elements of a space of relationships. The hierarchy of occupations is thus not given in their typical pay, skill or employment conditions but instead derives from the typical patterns of social relationships within which such occupations are located and take their *social meaning*. Social interaction measures use finely disaggregated occupational units, but if differences in the pay, skill or employment status of occupations are not reflected in typical patterns of social interaction then they will receive the same position in the social ordering, which measures general (rather than just labour-market) advantage. Within this method, the distinction between a skilled and a semi-skilled fitter only counts if it makes a difference in the important social relationships of the people involved.

The approach orders occupations in terms of the differences regarded as socially meaningful by the participants of stratification processes (as these emerge in interaction). This is a departure from *objectivist* approaches which impose observer's categories and ordering criteria. However, neither is the method *subjectivist*, since it does not directly access subjects' perceptions of the worth, prestige or social location of different occupations. Distance scales map actual social relations of intimacy and similarity, and therefore they tap the social ordering of occupations as it is *concretely embedded in social practice*.

This is a multi-dimensional approach to stratification, in that there are many, overlapping, influences on an individual's location in the social order. However, the first, major dimension of the space is taken in social distance approaches as a generalised social ordering, giving a one-dimensional scale of stratification position. Again, this is similar to Bourdieu, who identifies the social distance of occupational groups based on their lifestyle preferences. The major dimension of his space is what Bourdieu calls the 'global volume of capital', which can be interpreted as essentially the same as the 'generalised advantage' (encompassing material, cultural and social resources) measured by social interaction scales. Bourdieu insisted on a disaggregated two-dimensional model of the social space, in order to be able to identify differences in the level of different types of capital (1984 [1979]: 125). However, as we have seen, Bourdieu's model does not encompass levels of social capital and, whilst useful for *mapping* levels of economic and cultural capital, is not sufficiently empirically rigorous to function as a *measure* of social position that can be used to explore other aspects of stratification. Social interaction scales, by contrast, are *measures* of interaction distance which emphasise the overall social position which results from access to multiple social resources.

> Advantage is conferred by command over resources of various kinds, including those that would conventionally come under the heading of class; some of these can be converted into other resources and many of them are strongly inter-related. In this sense, stratification is 'multi-dimensional', but this should not be confused with the more strictly defined, orthogonal, independent dimensions of statistical analysis. What the space and the distances within it reveal is the way in which combinations of particular resources are socially aggregated into generalized advantage.
>
> (Bottero and Prandy 2003: 190)

As a measure of 'generalized advantage of lifestyle', interaction scales have been used to look at the impact of social distance on educational outcomes (Blackburn and Jarman 1993; Blackburn and Marsh 1991), ethnic inequality (Blackburn *et al.* 1997), health and lifestyle (Bartley *et al.* 1999a, b; Chandola 1998; Prandy 1999b; Sacker *et al.* 2001), occupational segregation by gender (Blackburn *et al.* 1999), party and class identification (Prandy 2000) and social mobility (Prandy 1998; Prandy and Bottero 1998; Prandy and Bottero 2000a, b).

Clearly, differential association is affected by *perceptions* of the relative prestige or status of the individuals involved, but close social relationships are governed by factors that go beyond prestige judgements. Distance measures also tap into the social resources that underpin such interactions, since association is affected by the various economic and material resources to which individuals have access. But social distance is not a measure of labour-market advantage as such, since relationships of intimacy are affected not just by economic resources but also by cultural background, social networks, contiguity and opportunity of access, and so forth.

Interaction distance is governed by a variety of social, cultural and economic processes and so interaction distance measures can be regarded as a reflection of the generalised advantage and disadvantage which underpin such interactions (Bottero and Prandy 2003):

> spouses, friends and acquaintances tend to be chosen from amongst those who share a similar lifestyle, which is dependent on the resources and rewards that are available to groups of people. Resources and rewards constitute a hierarchy – of inequalities, of relative advantage or disadvantage, which will be reflected in a (complex) hierarchy of lifestyles. The social space of social interaction will, in turn, reflect this hierarchy, simplifying it through a process by which different inequalities come to be evaluated relative to one another, through everyday practice.
>
> (Prandy 1999a: 215–216)

This notion of social space rejects conventional theories that locate the structuring principle underlying processes of inequality in the economic sphere since 'The analysis of stratification cannot be seen in terms of a social reflection of an economic base; rather it has to be seen in terms of a process of social reproduction' (Prandy 1999a: 230). Rather than seeing social relations as the effects of an economic structure, instead they theorise a hierarchically differentiated *social space*, which is reproduced in the social relations which constitute it:

> one must look to the nature of the social itself; that is, to those features of society that give it a degree of permanence despite a constantly changing personnel, a degree of coherence resulting from the actions of a multitude of members, and a meaningful context within which those members can act out their lives. In other words, we must realise that there is a reality to the social that is as detectable as any reality of the economic, and which in fact has to be seen as embracing the economic. At the same time we must recognise that the dynamism provides in the very processes of reproducing the structure, the relationships which are producing change. Thus it is a defining feature of any stratification order that it will be reproduced through the circumstances and actions of those involved in it; and, in turn, that these processes of reproduction themselves constitute an aspect of the order that is being reproduced.
>
> (Blackburn and Prandy 1997: 502)

The *process* of reproduction, however, does not have to be conscious or intended, because of the way in which hierarchy is embedded and reproduced in everyday social actions.

> The theoretical basis of interaction measures is . . . an emphasis on the reproduction of inequality; that is, that those with greater advantage will act in such a way as to maintain their position. They can do so by associating with

others at a similar level, by engaging in cultural practices that are symbolic of their position and by seeking to pass on their position to their offspring.

(Bottero and Prandy 2003: 190)

Conclusion

This chapter has explored relational accounts of 'social space', which reverse the method of conventional approaches to stratification. Rather than seeing 'structure' as an influence on patterns of association, differential association and lifestyle are taken as *constituting* the stratification order. So stratification emerges from the routine daily activities of people's lives, in the patterned choices that we all make.

Bourdieu sees distinctions in lifestyle as a means of asserting social superiority, whereas the Cambridge group argue that differences in social interaction emerge out of situations where individuals feel more socially comfortable with, and more akin to, some kinds of people than others (rather than there necessarily being a competitive struggle to secure high-status friends or partners). It has been argued that difference (preferences for different people or things) can only lead to hierarchical inequality if there is *agreement* over what is valued (and thus those who only have access to poorly valued items are lowly ranked). Lamont, in criticising Bourdieu's assumption of consensus about cultural values, argues that it is: 'Only when boundaries are widely agreed upon, i.e., only when people agree that some traits are better than others, can symbolic boundaries take on a widely constraining (or structural) character and pattern social interaction in an important way' (Lamont 1992: 178). However, there doesn't necessarily have to be value agreement, only some level of mutual consistency in the disagreements over what is preferred (in tastes, friends, partners).

Preferences necessarily entail value judgements (of the 'my tastes are better than yours' variety), but there need not be general *agreement* about which choices are *best* for such preferences to be bound up with hierarchy. All that is required is for lower-class individuals consistently to have different tastes to those of higher-class individuals (and vice versa). People can agree to disagree about what, or who, they value; but as long as those preferences are mutually inconsistent, they can still be associated with hierarchy. That is, there can be a coherent hierarchical differentiation of practices without a coherent or shared value structure.

Relational approaches emphasise the finely graded basis of the social space of relationships, and give a similar 'reproductionist' account of how stratified social relations are generated (Bottero and Prandy 2003). Rather than identifying a particular set of criteria, such as work and market situation or employment relations, and deriving a stratification structure from them, they concentrate on the way in which stratified social relations persist over time. They emphasise social distance as a continuum of relations, in which the 'clusters' of lifestyle, economic and social relations are better understood as regions in social space rather than as sharply demarcated groupings, with well-defined boundaries.

Bourdieu insisted that 'the social classes that can be separated out in social space ... do not exist as real groups' (1985: 724, 725). They can only be very loosely regarded as 'groups' because their boundaries are like 'a flame whose edges are in constant movement, oscillating around a line or surface' (1987: 13). Bourdieu believes that 'in the reality of the social world, there are no clear-cut boundaries, no more absolute breaks, than there are in the physical world' and that 'classes on paper' only become 'classes-in-reality' through symbolic and political mobilisation over the 'legitimate vision of the social world and of its divisions' (1987: 3). As Swartz notes (1997: 148), 'it is this political reality of symbolic struggle over the very identities of classes as social groups that Bourdieu defines as the proper object for stratification research'. Of course, however, as Bourdieu himself notes, there are many ways of dividing up the stratified social order, and actors' struggles over the definition and formation of 'groups' out of differentiated social relations do not always take a 'class' form.

Bourdieu's work (and that of the Cambridge Stratification Group) focuses on how occupations are embedded in cultural and social association, and so have sometimes been seen in narrowly 'economic' or 'class' terms. In fact, both approaches attempt to locate economic relations within wider stratification processes, but it is also true that neither set of approaches has said much about the formation of gender, racial or ethnic relations. However, the notion of differential association and stratified social networks which underlie conventional stratification processes are also a central aspect of 'gendered' and 'racialised' relations. So a more unified approach to stratification is possible.

> Individuals located at different points in that space – that is socially close or distant from each other – will be engaged in a great variety of social relations. The space is highly differentiated, and we need not expect there to be clear cut-off points in experience (that is distinct and homogenous groups). Yet it is also clear that, at certain points in the space, clear lines of demarcation are drawn by the individuals involved. People do identify as being part of a distinct group, but on either side these boundaries the difference in experience may be quite small, whilst within the group the range of experience may be quite wide, so such identifications may be flexible and shifting.
>
> (Bottero 1998: 482)

That is, we need to think of the differentiated social order, the networks of social interaction, and cultural similarity and dissimilarity which give 'rise to relations of social closeness and distance and to *ideas* of gender, class, ethnicity and so on' (Bottero 1998: 483).

10 Someone like me

Why is the social background of friends so strongly related? And why is falling in love affected by our social position? Although we feel that we freely choose our friends and lovers, in fact our most personal and intimate choices are constrained by patterns of social similarity and differential association. This chapter looks at the effects of hierarchy and social distance on where we live, whom we associate with, our tastes and leisure-time activities, and whom we choose (and hang on to) as our friends and partners. The pattern of *homophily* (the principle that similarity breeds connection) has a major impact on social networks. Social similarity (not just in terms of occupational status, but also along dimensions of race, ethnicity, education, age, religion, attitudes, tastes and beliefs) strongly structures a range of network relations (from long-lasting intense relations such as marriage/part-nership and friendship, to shorter and more circumscribed ties, such as providing career support, to 'knowing someone', or appearing together in a public place) (Kalmijn 1991, 1998; McPherson *et al.* 2001). A range of studies indicates a powerful relationship between 'association and similarity' so that, as the old phrase has it, 'birds of a feather flock together' (McPherson *et al.* 2001: 416). This *social sorting* process means that the people with whom we interact tend to be similar to ourselves in education, social class background, race/ethnicity, religion, and attitudes.

Whilst we all have very complex *networks* of relations to a range of different people, social characteristics (class, gender, race, etc.) are systematically embed-ded in these social networks, and the people closest to us also tend to be socially similar to us, along many dimensions of difference and inequality. So personal networks are highly differentiated, yet at the same time also highly ordered. In relational approaches, stratification is seen to reside in these networks, which structure differential access to resources, information, people and places in ways which help to organise unequal class and status relations. So the ordinary routines of social life – going to work, spending time with our friends, pursuing hobbies and interests, socialising with our family – both reflect and help to repro-duce differences in social position and resources. The separation in people's intimate contacts has sometimes been seen as a sign of group boundaries and social closure. However, whilst group boundaries and social exclusion are an important aspect of differential association, patterns of social distance also occur in much less 'bounded' social networks, and through people following stratified social routes and routines through life.

Birds of a feather

A social sorting process can be seen in our choice of our friends and sexual partners, the most intimate and personal decisions of our life. Take (heterosexual) sexual partnership. Bozon and Heran's classic analysis of 'finding a spouse' in France looked at the social origins of couples, by comparing their *fathers'* occupations, and showed that 'Cupid's arrows do not strike the social chess-board at random, but form a diagonal line, perfectly visible in the cross-tabulation of social origin of spouses' (1989: 117). *Homogamy* (marriage between individuals with similar social characteristics) is frequent, with individuals more likely to marry those nearer in status to themselves than those more distant. The effect extends well beyond class: 'Disproportionate numbers of spouses are members of the same group or stratum. Catholics tend to marry Catholics; whites, whites; persons of Greek descent, other Greek-Americans; and members of the upper-middle class, others in the same class' (Blau *et al.* 1984: 600). The 'socially embedded' nature of partnership also holds for more fleeting sexual contacts with short-term sexual encounters also exhibiting homogamy on racial/ethnic, educational and religious characteristics (Laumann *et al.* 1994: 268). We think of friendship as the most *voluntary* of our social relations, unconstrained by wider social pressures, yet such choices are also socially patterned, by gender, race and ethnicity, age, and, as Figure 10.1 shows, by social class, where the 'friendship structure closely mirrors that of the respondents' (Li *et al.* 2003a: 4.1).

One reason is that friendships and partnerships typically emerge out of organisational settings and activities (neighbourhoods, work-places, families,

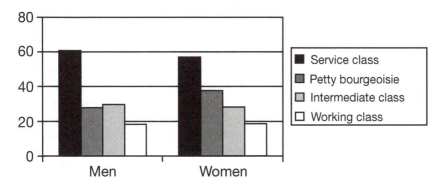

Figure 10.1 Percentage of individuals from different social classes with 'service-class friends' (1998, England and Wales)

Source: Adapted from Li *et al.* 2003a: 4.1

schools, teams and clubs) which bring together 'people who are similar to one another' in repeated interactions (Feld and Carter 1998: 137). Schools sort people by age, education and neighbourhood characteristics; universities sort by education and class; work-places by gender, occupation or skill-level, and class. Because the *social settings* in which we meet people are already socially sorted, our pool of potential friends and partners is likely to be similar to us.

Australian research (Bennett *et al.* 1999) found a major division between those whose friendships are formed away from home (at work, among school friends, or from sport or leisure groups), and those whose friends are chosen from among their neighbours. This division – between 'inclusive' and 'restricted' forms of association – was class-differentiated, in which an 'older, less-educated, less urban, lower-income group forms its friendships from among the resources to hand, perhaps valuing the local and the familiar over the wider world of strangers' whilst higher-income, better-educated, more urban groups were more likely to look outwards for their friends, at work, school and 'in the sporting and leisure groups to which they belong' (1999: 94–95). Similarly, in Britain, middle-class sociability is more segmented, tends to be drawn from a more diverse range of sources (voluntary associations, work, etc.) with friends who are not closely connected to each other (Allan 1991; Goldthorpe *et al.* 1987). However, whilst higher-class friendships are formed in wider social settings and thus more 'inclusive', these settings are still strongly socially differentiated and pre-selected (on education, age, etc.). This reflects the class-differentiated nature of leisure activities. The middle-class tendency to make more friends through voluntary associations is partly because these organisations are dominated by the middle classes. Professionals, managers, the more highly educated, are more likely to participate in *all* forms of voluntary associations (sports clubs, religious groups, political parties, parent–teacher groups, neighbourhood watch schemes) than the working classes who have low levels of participation (Bennett *et al.* 1999; P. Hall 1999; Parry *et al.* 1992; Johnston and Jowell 2001).

Of course, friendship also involves people with shared cultural tastes and interests, which, at first sight, might seem more personal and individual. Cultural tastes and interests tend, as we have seen, to be rather diffuse and varied and, as Chapter 9 shows, cultural 'omnivorism' (amongst middle-class fractions) means that the tastes of different social groups overlap. But the middle classes are more active in *all* forms of cultural activity and there is still a stratification gradient to many cultural tastes, so the settings for activities are often substantially segregated. Whilst less than a third of the upper class goes to classical music concerts on a regular basis, the working-class take-up is much lower, so the audience for these events is still overwhelmingly middle class (DiMaggio and Useem 1978; Peterson 1996). Anyone making friends through a shared interest in classical music is likely to be making *upper-middle-class* friends. Cultural tastes and activities also vary by age, race and ethnicity, region and gender. The audience for classical concerts is predominantly white, and older, so other features of social similarity also come into play. In the same way, in America, those liking country and western music tend to be older, white and working class, whilst those liking rap music tend to be younger, black, male and working class (Mark 1998). Of course, these are just average tendencies: there are plenty of white, middle-class rap fans, and black classical music lovers. Average tendencies cannot be translated into stereotypical 'groups' who share the same likes and dislikes. However, given the way in which cultural tastes map onto socio-demographic characteristics, the clubs which play different sorts of music also tend to have different sorts of clientele. Once we factor in the neighbourhoods in which gigs and clubs are located, then a fairly strong process of social sorting can be seen. The same is true of other leisure activities. In Britain, a love of football cuts across social classes, race and ethnicity (though not across gender). However, Asian and black supporters are less likely to be seen on the predominantly white terraces (partly through fear of racism), and amateur football clubs are drawn from local neighbourhoods, friendship networks, or pubs, and so tend to be socially sorted by class, race and ethnicity. In the same way, African-Americans avoid racist social slurs and unpleasant incidents by adopting 'protective practices', selectively frequenting places 'where other blacks were likely to be found' (Landry, quoted in DiMaggio and Ostrower 1990: 758).

So the 'choice of partners for personal relationships is constrained by the opportunities people have to meet and interact with others. Our opportunities to interact are structured, and are an important reason why people generally form relationships with persons who are socially or culturally similar to themselves' (Kalmijn and Flap 2001: 1289). In America, around two-thirds of married couples were introduced by family and friends, co-workers, classmates, or neighbours; and another third introduced themselves, but still via social networks, at parties given by mutual friends or through social organisations or clubs (Laumann *et al.* 1994). We typically meet sexual partners through intimate social networks of people who are similar to us. The choice of sexual partners is

> directly mediated by an individual's social network and the particular events in which he or she participates. This means that the pool of eligible people from which one identifies potential sex partners is not a random subset of the population but rather a highly constrained subset. For this reason, it is a bit misleading to speak of a person *choosing* a partner on the basis of specific racial/ethnic, educational, or religious characteristics. Rather, we argue that the concept of *differential association* more accurately describes the process by which sexual networks become organised according to these social attributes. It is unlikely, however, that people are immediately aware of this phenomenon since, from the individual's point of view, he or she is simply responding to the opportunities for partnering that appear to be available.
>
> (Laumann *et al.* 1994: 266–267)

Bozon and Heran argue that 'the spatial segregation of the different social classes leads to a parallel segregation in their meeting places, which in turn favours homogamy' (1989: 91). Because the networks and activities of groups differ, they are less likely to run into each other, and so less likely to form friendship or partnerships.

> 'Opportunity makes the thief.' If upper-level professionals tend to marry a fellow student and manual workers a dancing partner, is this not simply because the former more frequently pursue their studies and the latter more often go dancing? Is it surprising that people become acquainted with their future spouse in their familiar social circle?
>
> (Bozon and Heran 1989: 112)

It is the way in which our everyday lives are affected by our location in social space which produces patterns of homophily and homogamy. It is assortative *meeting* which leads to assortative *mating* (Kalmijn and Flap 2001).

> Three basic mechanisms ensure that the social situations (or events) in which people participate are composed of socially similar individuals. The first is that certain settings, such as regional high schools, community colleges, churches and neighbourhood bars, primarily draw participants who live nearby. Thus, since geographic areas are segregated by attributes such as race (Massey and Denton 1993), income, and in some cases age, they will be primarily composed of individuals who are similar with respect to these attributes. A second mechanism has to do with the nature of the situations themselves. Schools, for instance, bring together people who have attained the same level of education; dance clubs bring together people who like the same type of music; and jobs often bring together people who have similar interests and ability. Yet a third mechanism results from the link between participants in specific events and the structure of social networks. [. . .] The point is that the locations in which people meet their sex partners reflect boundaries on the types of partners which they are likely to encounter.
>
> (Laumann *et al.* 1994: 229, 257)

The comfort zone

But what are the consequences of homophily on how we live our lives?

> The result is that people's personal networks are homogenous with regard to many sociodemographic, behavioural, and intrapersonal characteristics. Homophily limits people's social worlds in a way that has powerful implications for the information they receive, the attitudes they form, and the interactions they experience.
>
> (McPherson *et al.* 2001: 415)

Of course, the extent of homophily should not be overstated. The influence of social similarity on social networks does not mean entirely homogeneous *groups*.

The principle of social similarity is only an aggregate tendency – we sit at the centre of associates from a *range* of social locations, more or less similar to ourselves. We belong to various different social groups and possess many different social characteristics, which intersect to varying degrees. Whilst our associates may be very similar on some dimensions, they may be mixed on others. Some contexts are more homophilous on certain characteristics than others: workplaces tend to be sorted by skill, education, occupation and gender (promoting friendships within these categories) but less differentiated by race and ethnicity (promoting friendships across these categories). Neighbourhoods are sorted by race and class but not by age or gender. To the extent that different social circles intersect (for example bringing work-friends and neighbours together) then some degree of heterophily (social mixing) will result.

However, because social settings, and associates, are socially sorted – to a greater or lesser degree – people's experience of unfamiliar (or socially distant) locations can be unsettling. The extensive body of research on differential association has been used to investigate *social boundaries*, using social ties to establish the extent of social closure between groups. The lack of social ties between groups has often been seen as the result of boundary maintenance, in which one group deliberately excludes another. However, quite routine processes of differential association create very uneven opportunities for various groups to meet, let alone form social relationships. But because many social settings are already socially sorted this can create feelings of isolation and discomfort in social interaction, which can prevent the formation of close relationships between socially distant individuals.

Within this model, no barriers need exist in the social order, yet social contact can still be limited by social and cultural dissimilarity. Differences in taste and manners, and lack of ease in interaction, may help to reproduce patterns of social distance. Of course, such differences are partly the result of pre-existing social distance and are often employed in strategies of exclusion and in the erection of social barriers, but it is also important to recognise the way in which social distance is also routinely and unintentionally reproduced, through the search for social familiarity and comfort (Bottero and Prandy 2003).

Processes of social sorting, for example, can result from *self-selection*. Take going to university. In British universities, working-class and ethnic-minority students are dramatically outnumbered by those from white, middle-class backgrounds. It has been argued that this creates problems of isolation for 'non-traditional' students (those who do not fit the typical 'white, middle-class' pattern of university entrance) and can deter such students from applying. Conceptions of the 'good university' are 'racialised and classed', so that ethnic-minority and working-class students 'often allude to the problems inherent in going places "where there are few people like me"' (Reay *et al.* 2001: 865). Working-class and ethnic-minority students are over-concentrated in the post-1992 'New Universities', which are of lower status, but this is partly the result of self-selection, with students choosing to go to institutions where they are likely to find people like themselves:

> Most of the students are applying to low risk universities where if they are from an ethnic minority there is an ethnic mix, if they are privileged they will find intellectual and social peers, and if they are mature students there is a high percentage of mature students.
>
> (Reay *et al.* 2001: 865)

Working-class students (with a relative lack of family and friends who have gone to university, and differences between their 'home' culture and the predominantly middle-class university culture) often see higher education as 'remote and alien from the lives of their families', and know very little about college life (Lynch and O'Riordan 1998: 461). Similarly, for ethnic-minority students fearing potential racism and social isolation (Archer and Hutchings 2000: 563), the ethnic composition of universities is often a key issue.

These processes illustrate Bourdieu's theories of how differences in initial cultural and social capital are reproduced in educational systems, in part by processes of *self-exclusion*. It is argued that lower-class and ethnic-minority students often rule out high-status choices, because they believe they will lead to unfamiliar and socially uncomfortable territory. Ball *et al.* report the unease felt by Ong, a Chinese student, on attending an interview at Cambridge University:

> It was a complete shock, it was different from anywhere else I have ever been, it was too traditional, too old-fashioned, from another time altogether. I didn't like it at all. It was like going through a medieval castle when you were going down the corridors. The dining room was giant long tables, pictures, it was like a proper castle, and I was thinking – where's the moat, where's the armour? Save me from this. You know, you expect little pictures with eyes moving around, watching you all the time. And I just didn't like the atmosphere, not one bit. . . . All typical private school, posh people . . . posh and white.
>
> (Ball *et al.* 2002: 68)

For 'non-traditional students' choosing to go to a 'good' university is often associated with leaving behind 'people like us', and fears about high-status universities are part of 'a pattern of "class aversion" among state-school students, in which there is an aspect of social-class self-reproduction and the maintenance of class demarcations by "self-exclusion"' (Ball *et al.* 2002: 68). Middle-class students 'choosing high-status universities are also making a choice that ensures they will be with others "like them" in terms of culture and ethnicity, but this is an implicit rather than explicit aspect of choice and the "classed" nature of particular institutions' (Ball *et al.* 2002: 60).

However, we should again be careful of overstating such processes. It has been suggested that theories of self-exclusion are *overly* reproductionist and exaggerate the extent to which aspirations are class (and ethnicity) 'adjusted'. As Chapter 12 shows, there is widespread social mobility in Britain, which leads people into new, unfamiliar and socially distant social positions. Of course, there are potential difficulties in such transitions. It has been suggested that the socially mobile are 'caught between two worlds': 'out of tune with others both in their new and original strata in the occupational hierarchy' (Blau 1956: 290). A classic example is provided in Jackson and Marsden's (1966) study of 88 working-class children who experienced mobility into the middle class, by winning grammar school places. They had experienced tensions between home and school, feeling too 'working class' at school, yet perceived as too 'uppish' in their neighbourhoods. One described how her school uniform and violin marked her out from her working-class peers: 'I used to dread carrying that violin case. I used to plot my way from the yard at home to the teachers, but that violin case seemed to stand out – that brought more bashings than anything else' (Jackson and Marsden 1966: 96).

However, other research on the impact of mobility on personal ties shows that the experience does not lead to social marginality because the mobile rapidly become 'effectively assimilated' (Goldthorpe *et al.* 1980: 207), acquiring the friendship patterns of their new class rather than the patterns of the class they have left behind (Goldthorpe *et al.* 1980; Li *et al.* 2003a, b). Friendship patterns amongst the socially mobile are strongly homophilous, with 'highly differential association, on class lines . . . a dominant feature of the structure of sociability' (Goldthorpe *et al.* 1980: 180). The socially mobile do not 'drop' their kin, but there is a segregation of social networks, with interaction with colleagues and friends kept distinct from family relations. Upwardly mobile respondents were less likely to draw on kin or old schoolmates for associates, drawing more heavily on work colleagues and people they met at voluntary associations, so that the majority of their friends came from the middle class (Goldthorpe *et al.* 1980). Longitudinal research on partnership also reveals a similar sorting pattern, since marriage generally occurs between two partners of similar occupational class and education, who are on similar class trajectories (Jones 1990: 118). People with stable careers tend to marry one another, while those who are socially mobile continue their pattern of upward or downward mobility in their marriages.

What is striking about such processes is how people's social relations appear to 'adjust' as their social location changes, and the principle of social similarity reasserts itself. There is apparently an ongoing process of accommodation to the social sorting process, in which people effectively 'fit in' to their new surroundings.

Choice and opportunity

There are two, complementary, ways of looking at the 'similarity principle' in social relationships. 'Supply-side perspectives' argue that the *social contexts* in which people participate mould their networks by shaping the pool from which they draw their contacts, whereas 'demand-side theories' emphasise the *preferences* people have to meet and select a specific type of partner. We choose our friends and partners, but our choices are constrained by context and opportunity.

Since marriage and friendship patterns result from *both* preference and opportunity, we cannot assume that low levels of friendship or partnership between
social groups reflect their antipathy or prejudice.

> Opportunity to marry within the group depends on many factors, such as resi-
> dential segregation, the composition of local marriage markets, group size, and
> so on. As a result, endogamy does not necessarily point to a personally felt
> social distance toward a certain outgroup. Such preferences play a role, but to
> what extent they determine the actual choices people make is an empirical
> question. Marriage patterns simply tell us which groups interact with whom,
> and while this is an important piece of information, they do not tell us why.
>
> (Kalmijn 1998: 397)

The pattern of interaction between different social groups is affected by their
relative sizes (which affects their opportunities for interaction regardless of preferences), since 'when differences in group size are very great, most members of
the majority have no social contact with the minority' (Blau 1977: 35), and the
smaller a minority group is, the more likely it is to have networks dominated by
the majority group (McPherson *et al.* 2001: 420). Similarly, highly segregated
groups are more likely to form in-group ties because they have less chance to
interact with others from outside the group.

Group size and segregation intersect, as 'members of large groups can
construct segregated lives more easily than members of small groups because
large groups have the numbers to dominate neighbourhoods, schools, work-
places' (Model and Fisher 2002: 730). Differences in intermarriage relate to the
geographic concentration of different groups. Asian-Americans 'marry out' less
often in California, where they are more concentrated, African-Americans
'marry out' less in states where the percentage of African-Americans in the
population is large, whilst the regional distribution of religious groups (Baptists
and Methodists in the American South, Catholics in the North-east) affects the
extent of religious homogamy in different areas (Kalmijn 1998).

It is therefore important to recognise 'the influences of population distributions
on social life', which means that we cannot assume that 'individual preferences
determine behaviour or that social patterns must ultimately be explained in terms
of psychological dispositions.... For social conditions set limits on human
options' and 'structural conditions can influence social life even in disregard of
prevailing preferences' (Blau *et al.* 1984: 591). Most research distinguishes between
baseline homophily (that is, the level of homophily we would expect simply on the
basis of the proportion of groups in the population) and *inbreeding homophily* (the
bias that leads similar people to associate more often than they would be expected
to, given their relative numbers in the opportunity pool) (McPherson *et al.* 2001:
419). However, the *structural* opportunity to meet different groups is also related to
the *preferences* people have for in-group associations, because the probabilities of
meeting different groups in various areas partly depends on the prior *choices* that
people have made about which neighbourhoods (and neighbours) they prefer.

The 'proclivity for living in the same neighbourhoods as co-ethnics' is assessed by Lieberson's P* index 'which measures the probability of the next person one meets in the street being of that ethnic group' (Peach 1998: 1674). These probabilities are affected by the *size* of different groups and are asymmetric: members of a big group have a low chance of meeting the members of a small group. The expectation of a white person in Greater London meeting someone from 'Caribbean' origin (using 1991 Census categories) in their home area is 3.6 per cent, whilst the probability of a Caribbean person meeting a white person in their home area is 66.5 per cent (Peach 1999). However, this is affected by the 'clustering' of groups into different neighbourhoods. The probability of someone of Caribbean origin meeting someone from their *own* ethnic group in their neighbourhood is about 11.6 per cent, but this is higher than we would expect simply on the basis of the size of this group, and indicates ethnic clustering. Comparing P* with group size allows us to control for 'baseline' residential homophily (which arises solely from group size) and instead look at 'inbreeding' residential homophily (in which people 'over-select' people of their own group for co-residence).

> Although Caribbeans form 4.4% of the population of London, their P* is 11.6. Thus they are about two and a half times more clustered than the random expectation might expect. However, the Indians, who form 5.5% of the London population, have a P* of 20.5, so that they are four times more clustered than random. Their isolation index is twice as high as for the Caribbeans. However, the most dramatically isolated group is the Bangladeshis, with a P* of 23.7. This is over 18 times the 1.2% that they form of the London population.
>
> (Peach 1999: 338)

People with different social attributes are less likely to interact and form social relationships because there is *already* social distance between them, in that they are less likely to be connected by the social networks and locations through which opportunities for interaction occur. Simply by going about their daily lives people's routine actions serve to reinforce and maintain social distance. Standard social routines – going to college or to work, hanging out in bars and clubs with friends, visiting family – provide the socially differentiated contexts within which we make new relationships with people very similar in social attributes to those we already know. This helps maintain social network distance between different social groups. However, not all such effects are unforeseen or unintended. People also actively strive to maintain and reinforce social distance in the face of opportunities for greater contacts with socially dissimilar others. This can be seen in patterns of neighbourhood residence.

Not in my backyard?

We all know of 'richer' and 'poorer' neighbourhoods in our local area, as well as areas with very uneven racial or ethnic distributions. Such neighbourhoods are rarely homogeneous in social class, or racial and ethnic, composition; but there are limits to both the ability and desire of different groups to live in such areas. There is considerable (geographical) spatial sorting on both class and racial/ethnic lines. This occurs partly in relation to the uneven distribution of *structural opportunities* (such as work and travel facilities, the price of property and private rents, and the availability of social housing, all influenced by welfare policy and local governance) but also through *preferences for differential association*.

Geographical sorting occurs because people act on preferences: to live in 'desirable' areas and to avoid 'rough' ones, to stay in their 'local' neighbourhoods or with their 'own' community, to avoid high crime areas or harassment, or to live in an area with the 'right' facilities, a 'good atmosphere', or the 'right' social mix. However, there are always constraints on the exercise of preferences. Housing preferences are routinely coded by class, status, race and ethnicity, but groups vary in their *ability* to live where they want to. An important influence on spatial segregation is the way in which certain groups (the affluent, the members of racial majorities) have greater choice and control over where they live, and who they associate with.

In London, in the 1970s, council housing was concentrated in run-down inner-city areas, limiting the opportunities for poorer Londoners to live in the leafier middle-class suburbs (Lawson and Wilson 1995). The bars, schools, clubs and associations in these neighbourhoods reflected their different populations, affecting the opportunities for contact between different social classes, a form of unintended social distance. Social distance also arises out of processes of unequal competition for the best resources. Middle-class families often move house when their children reach secondary-school age, strategically re-locating to better school catchment areas (Butler and Robson 2001). As a result, a system of 'post-code apartheid' has emerged with the middle classes congregated in areas with good schools, so that 'good schools cause house prices to rise in their "catchment areas" by between 15–19 per cent' (Butler and Robson 2003: 9).

Since the 1970s, the selling-off of council homes, increases in home ownership and rising property prices have meant poorer inner-city areas have been re-developed for the better-off. The renovation of delapidated housing, and the growth of luxury condominia, gated 'villages' and warehouse conversions have 'gentrified' the inner city, pricing the working class out of their old neighbourhoods, and displacing them to cheaper owner-occupation elsewhere (Foster 1998; Lyons 2003). However, social housing still exists in the inner city 'cheek by jowl' with smaller gentrified enclaves (Butler and Robson 2003). But as the more affluent working class have left, those who cannot move – the very poorest – have been concentrated into the worst remaining council housing. In gentrified areas like Battersea, Brixton and Islington, the most affluent live as a minority alongside the most deprived, but 'have managed the classic manoeuvre of gentrification: coupling a necessary spatial proximity to other urban groups while strategically maintaining and protecting their material and cultural distance from them' (Butler and Robson 2003: 24). Butler and Robson call this a 'tectonic' pattern of informal, voluntary segregation, in which 'relations between different social and ethnic groups in the area tend to be of a parallel rather than integrative nature; people keep, by and large, to themselves' (2001: 2157). Social distance is maintained by distinct patterns of association within the (white) middle class, who opt out of local schools, educate their children privately, and maintain distinct consumption patterns, eating out in the high-priced restaurants and bistros which have sprung up locally to accommodate them. These are options not open to their poorer neighbours, so, even in the patterns of move-ment which bring different social classes into 'cheek by jowl' contact, we can see patterns of social distance, with more advantaged groups better able to take control of ongoing processes of spatial re-sorting.

Similarly, in America, 'the persistence of the near-total residential segregation of blacks and the deliberate stacking of public housing in the poorest black areas of large cities, [amount] to a system of *de facto* urban apartheid' (Wacquant 1994: 250) in which many poorer blacks have no choice but to live in highly deprived ghetto areas. This is partly the result of agitation by predominantly white suburban communities to ensure that social housing (and poor blacks) were not sited in their neighbourhoods. Both structural differentiation of opportunities and preferences for social similarity are helping to shape a sorting process giving rise to socio-spatial divisions and segregation in housing neighbourhoods.

Social sorting along racial lines is entwined with class sorting. In America, processes of counter-urbanisation (the movement of populations out of cities into the suburbs) are class *and* racially selective, with large-scale movement of ethnic minorities into cities, accompanied by a growing suburbanisation of the white middle class. This division along racial/ethnic lines is also between poorer and richer groups, with cities like Detroit comprising a poor black inner city surrounded by a predominantly white middle-class suburban ring. And racial segregation in American cities has helped to concentrate poverty in inner-city black neighbourhoods (Massey and Denton 1993). The overall proportion of ethnic minorities in European cities is smaller than in America (ethnic minorities comprised 29 per cent of the population of London [ONS 2001], compared to 64 per cent in New York City in 1990 or 61 per cent in Los Angeles [Hamnett 1999: 251]), with nothing approaching the levels of urban concentration of minorities that is seen in the USA. However, within the context of smaller ethnic-minority populations, we can still see racial and ethnic clustering, often in the most disadvantaged inner-city neighbourhoods.

But does the *economic* disadvantage of migrant groups explain their spatial concentration? One argument is that poor migrant groups are forced to take the worst jobs and cheapest housing, becoming concentrated in deprived inner-city areas. Structural assimilation models assume that as migrant groups acquire better education and jobs they will experience spatial dispersal, becoming spatially sorted by class rather than race or ethnicity. For small minority groups, of course, this means their incorporation into the wider majority population. Structural-assimila-tion has occurred for some migrants: historically for white European migrants to America – where Polish, Italian or Irish groups have dissolved into the 'melting pot'; whilst currently in the USA, some Asian and Hispanic groups also seem to be experiencing spatial dispersion with economic advancement (Charles 2003).

Certainly, migrants experience skewed economic opportunities which force spatial clustering. The ethnic-minority populations that migrated to Britain in the post-Second World War period were often directly recruited by employers in specific locations, 'filling the gaps caused by the occupational upward mobility of the white population and by the white population's geographical decentralisation from major cities' (Peach 1998: 1658). However, whilst some minority groups have experienced dispersal over time, others have not, and this is not related to economic advancement. Black Britons show relatively high levels of spatial dispersion, despite continuing economic marginalisation, whilst British Asian groups – whose average economic profile is better – exhibit higher levels of segregation and 'Asian encapsulation continues whether the group is economically upward mobile or economically marginalised' (Peach 1998: 1677). Racial sorting exists on top of class sorting, for 'working-class ethnic minorities live in working-class areas, but not in all working-class areas. Wealthy minorities live in wealthy areas, but not in all wealthy areas' (Peach 1999: 342).

In America, middle-class blacks live in neighbourhoods almost as racially segregated as their poor counterparts, in predominantly 'black' middle-class suburbs (Massey and Denton 1993; Charles 2003). Persistent segregation presents another model of spatial sorting – *pluralism* – in which groups experiencing economic integration maintain social distinctiveness and spatial segregation. This separation may be either enforced or voluntary (Peach 1999). It is usually argued that the uniquely high segregation of African-Americans is *enforced*, reflecting the power of white Americans to prevent racially integrated communities. Research on housing movement shows African-Americans have moved into predominantly white neighbourhoods 'at a pace sufficient to increase their numbers there, but neighbourhoods with increasing black populations tend to lose white populations rapidly', both through 'white flight' and a reduction in whites moving into 'mixed' neighbourhoods (Quillian 1991: 1). White communities have erected direct barriers against integration, with explicitly discriminatory housing practices aimed at maintaining existing levels of segregation in neighbourhoods, and racist violence and harassment aimed at black incomers.

Segregation can occur through 'voluntaristic and protective' (Peach 1996b: 385) processes, as migrants 'are also attracted to live in neighbourhoods with members of their own ethnic group for reasons of cultural security and self-help, alongside the same people who effectively sponsored their migration in many cases through the chain migration process' (Johnston *et al.* 2002: 592–593). Of course, this is not entirely voluntary, since white racism acts as a 'double whammy', influencing not only where whites choose to live, but also affecting minority group preferences, since 'areas perceived as hostile toward particular minority groups are . . . less attractive' (Charles 2003: 191). However, the fact that the various ethnic minorities in Britain also experience segregation from *each other* is seen as evidence of internal 'cultural' pressures for the maintenance of ethnic and religious identity (Peach 1998: 1668). Black Caribbeans are as segregated from British Asians as they are from whites, and Bangladeshis show high levels of segregation with all groups (Peach 1999). For Peach ethnic 'clustering' has positive aspects, since 'concentration allows the group to maintain its social cohesion. It maintains cultural values, it strengthens social networks, it allows the passing of critical thresholds for the support of institutions and shops' (1996b: 386). However, concerns about 'social isolation' resulting in 'parallel lives' have raised doubts about the impact of self-imposed voluntary segregation on social integration and community cohesion (Cantle 2001), about 'the fragmentation and polarisation of communities – on economic, geographical, racial and cultural lines – on a scale which amounts to segregation, albeit to an extent by choice' (Denham 2002: 11). The process of different ethnic groups 'segregating themselves from each other and retreating into "comfort zones" made up of people like themselves' (Ouselely, quoted in Denham 2002: 12) is seen as a problem.

However, there is a danger of reducing complex processes of social marginalisation, exclusion and tension to a simple paradigm of 'cultural' difference, and of over-emphasising 'cultural' separation in accounts of racial and ethnic minorities (Alexander 2000). Although research indicates that British South Asians do endorse homophily for social and cultural reasons, reasons for wanting to live within ethnic clusters 'go well beyond the cultural, with over one-quarter stressing the importance of clustering for reasons of safety as well. The fear of racial attack remains a pervasive force' (Phillips 1998: 1684). Cultural separation can be a response to racialised conflict, not simply a cause of it. In discussing ethnic-minority patterns of affiliation and association there has been a tendency to emphasise the 'racialised' aspects of homophily, which clearly occur for a variety of reasons, arising from 'defensive minoritisation' (McGhee forthcoming), skewed economic opportunities, chain-migration, and network mobilisation. The focus on these processes as 'cultural' difference (as ethnicised community, tradition and religion) raises serious questions as to why certain aspects of differential association are seen as more important, and troubling, than others. Given that ethnic minority communities also experience marked differential association along lines of age, class, gender, lifestyle and leisure pursuits, the question is why certain forms of division are more clearly marked than others.

In fact, the 'cultural isolation' of British ethnic minorities needs to be put into some kind of context. Whilst there are areas with high concentrations of ethnic minorities, minorities comprise a majority of the population in only a very small number of areas (Peach 1998) with 'little evidence of much ethnic group concentration into polarised enclaves and ghettos in English cities' (Johnston *et al.* 2002: 601):

> Most members of England's ethnic minorities live in parts of the country's cities . . . where members of their host society [sic] form a substantial, if not a majority, component of the local population and are thus daily exposed to their cultural norms and practices – although the reverse is clearly not the case; most members of the host society live in relative isolation from members of the ethnic minorities and have little contact with their cultural norms and practices.
>
> (Johnston *et al.* 2002: 610)

Britain also has relatively high levels of 'interracial' partnership, but the partnership rates, and the social impact, are necessarily much greater for ethnic minority populations (less than 7.9 per cent of the British population in 2001) than for the white majority. This asymmetry can be seen clearly in the fact that around half of all (British-born) black men in a relationship have a white partner, as do a third of black women, one-fifth of Asian men and 10 per cent of Asian women. Yet, partly reflecting the relatively small size of the ethnic minority population, white Britons are much less likely to have a black or Asian partner, and 'mixed-race' partnerships make up less than 1 per cent of partnerships in the British population as a whole (Berthoud and Beishon 1997). Of course, despite the relatively high levels of out-marriage shown by certain ethnic minority groups, given the small *size* of ethnic minority populations in Britain, these partnership patterns, paradoxically, are still evidence for quite strong preferences for in-group association. But if ethnic minorities did not show preferences for in-group association their networks would be dominated by members of the white majority.

Similar concerns of 'cultural separation' have been raised about the enforced 'social isolation' of Black Americans (Wilson 1991), but this is based on much higher levels of racial segregation than occurs in British cities. We have already seen that, in London, the probability of someone of Caribbean origin meeting someone from their *own* ethnic group in their neighbourhood is about 11.6 per cent. In New York, the probability of an African-American meeting someone of the same racial group in their neighbourhood is 62.7 per cent, whilst in Chicago the probability is 82.8 per cent (Massey and Denton 1989). US metropolitan areas are 'composed largely of neighbourhoods that are predominantly [80 per cent or more] white or black' (Krivo and Kaufman 1999: 94), and levels of racial segregation are so high in America, they take the form of racial ghettos, in which 'nearly all African-Americans are located in the ghetto; nearly all those in the ghetto are African-American' (Peach 1999: 320). These uniquely high levels of black/white residential segregation are characterised as *hyper-segregation* (Massey and Denton 1989) in which blacks have virtually no contact with whites in their own or neighbouring communities. This is not a form of 'cultural' separation, but the deliberate exclusion of African-Americans.

In thinking about the 'social separation' of ethnic minorities, it is worth remembering that processes of social sorting occur amongst all social groups, along a variety of socio-demographic characteristics. Yet it is striking that the 'comfort zones' of more affluent groups (such as middle-class gated communities) are rarely seen as social problems in the same way as the supposed 'cultural' separation of poor ethnic minorities. It is important to recognise that patterns of social distance and social sorting are affected not simply by distinct 'cultural patterns', but also by social exclusion, by the structure of opportunities (economic, social and spatial), and by group numbers. Social sorting occurs along multiple dimensions of difference and inequality at every level of the social hierarchy. Everybody engages in homophily (to a greater or lesser degree), but from different positions of power, honour and social resources. The key issue is how differential association is bound up with economic, cultural and social disadvantage. The next section explores how the patterning of social similarity in networks is an important factor in the concentration of social and economic resources, unevenly affecting the access of groups to opportunities and rewards.

Capitalising on connections

Whatever the reasons for homophily, the consequences of social similarity in our everyday lives have important effects on the social information we receive, our access to resources, and – unintentionally – the reproduction of patterns of social inequality. The similarity principle is a feature of the organisation and patterning of social networks, and – to a lesser degree – of neighbourhoods. However, one feature of social networks is the way in which they generate *social capital*. Social capital refers to the resources that are drawn upon by the use of social connections, the idea being that such networks open up resources to which we would not normally have access. There is evidence, for example, that finding a job, or obtaining promotion once we have got a job, depends a great deal on the quality of the social networks that we can tap into (Granovetter 1995; Lin 2001).

Part of the value of social capital is also said to lie in the norms of obligation and trust that are anchored in social networks and which help coordinate joint activities. The idea is that the more people are embedded in networks of 'civic engagement' (neighbourhood associations and clubs) the more likely it is that members of a community will cooperate for mutual benefit. One set of approaches, made famous by the work of Robert Putnam (2000), explores the advantages of high levels of social capital on communities, in which dense and extensive social ties (arising out of kin and friendship networks, and participation in leisure clubs and civic associations) are said to generate community cohesion, 'neighbourliness' and encourage norms of reciprocity and trust. Dense social networks, in this model, are a community *resource* which enable more effective local coordination, and are said to produce lower crime rates, better health outcomes, and greater economic growth. Here homophily – which generates solidarity on the basis of social similarity – would be seen to increase levels of social capital in communities.

However, other approaches emphasise social capital as a *hierarchical* resource used in competitive processes of status attainment (Lin 2001; Bourdieu 1984 [1979]). Bourdieu argues social networks reflect and reinforce social stratification, because there is uneven access to social networks and resources are unequally embedded in them. For Bourdieu 'social capital is not a means of encouraging generalised trust, but a means for particular social groups to maintain their social exclusiveness by forming tight bonds with others similar to themselves' (Li *et al.* 2003b: 500). In this version, social capital is a 'weapon' which allows its possessors to wield power (Bourdieu and Wacquant 1992), and the bonding effect of homophilous social networks is bound up with social exclusion.

> If social capital is a resource available through social networks, the resources that some individuals claim come at the expense of others. . . . The same strong ties that help members of a group often enable it to exclude outsiders. Consider how ethnic groups dominate certain occupations or industries . . . for example, the tight control exercised by white ethnics – descendants of Italian, Irish, and Polish immigrants – over the construction trades and the fire and police unions in New York.
>
> (Portes and Landolt 1996: 18)

For authors like Putnam, *bonding social capital* (which arises out of the strong ties and dense personal networks between family and friends) is valuable because it 'bolsters our inner selves', mobilises in-group solidarity and generates reciprocity (2000: 23). Putnam recognises that bonding capital is also inward looking, can reinforce 'exclusive identities and homogenous groups' and 'by creating strong in-group loyalty, may also create strong out-group antagonism' (2000: 22, 23), but he fails to explore the stratification implications of social capital and still tends to see social capital as a general community 'good'. Putnam's approach has been criticised for showing little interest in how membership of social networks might affect the opportunities of individual members, and only a 'passing concern' about the distribution of social capital among different social groups (Bridgen 2003).

The implication is that communities with low levels of social capital have higher levels of social problems. However, it is the most disadvantaged groups who draw most heavily on (bonding) social capital (Portes 1998; Lin 1999). The real problem is that they draw upon networks with very few resources. In a community with high unemployment, for example, connections will not help you get a job, if few people in your network have a job themselves.

> It is not the lack of social capital, but the lack of objective economic resources – beginning with decent jobs – that underlies the plight of impoverished urban groups. . . . Undoubtedly, individuals and communities can benefit greatly from social participation and mutual trust, but the outcomes will vary depending on what resources are obtained, who is excluded from them, and what is demanded in exchange.
>
> (Portes and Landolt 1996: 20)

Social similarity in networks tends to reinforce and concentrate existing inequalities in the levels of resources between groups. For network theorists of stratification, the value of the social capital that any individual possesses depends not only on the size and density of their networks but also on the *level of resources* that such contacts can access. Because of the impact of social similarity on networks, social capital tends to act as a conservative force, reproducing inequalities.

Putnam recognises that some forms of capital are better than others, and argues that *bridging social capital*, arising from weaker social ties (between acquaintances in clubs or associations, or work colleagues), which are 'outward looking and encompass people across diverse social cleavages', are also 'better for linkage to external assets and information diffusion' (2000: 22):

> the 'weak' ties that link me to distant acquaintances who move in different circles from mine are actually more valuable than the 'strong' ties that link me to relatives and friends whose sociological niche is very like my own. Bonding social capital is . . . good for 'getting by', but bridging social capital is crucial for 'getting ahead'.
>
> (Putnam 2000: 22–23)

The reason for the competitive advantage of weaker social ties is that they tend to be less homophilous than strong social ties. Weaker social ties bridge more distant social positions and allow access to resources beyond the immediate social milieu. However, research into the impact of networks on information flows shows that the real value of 'weak ties' is that they access higher-level contacts. 'Small world' studies (which attempt to get parcels passed – by hand through social contacts – to named, but distant, strangers in a local community) show that the best 'contact' chains are those that reach *upwards* to people holding higher socio-economic positions (Lin 1999). Such chains are more successful because they can access people with superior social resources and information. However, homophily means that it is usually higher-level individuals who can access high-level contacts. Success in drawing on social networks depends both on the initial status position of the person seeking to capitalise on the network, and on the overall status and resources of the people in the network (Lin 2001).

The patterning of weak social networks is class-differentiated. Surveys of 'weaker ties' indicate that most formal associational activity (particularly membership in clubs, sporting, leisure and civic associations, etc.) is undertaken by the *middle classes* and those with *more education* (Bennett *et al.* 1999; P. Hall 1999; Li *et al.* 2003a, b), whilst working-class groups have lower levels of bridging social capital. In Britain, the picture is of 'a nation divided between a well-connected and highly active group of citizens with generally prosperous lives and another set of citizens whose associational life and involvement in politics are very limited', essentially a gap between the 'connected' (middle class, middle-aged) and the 'disconnected' (working class, young) (P. Hall 1999: 455). It is also the middle class who have the highest turnover in associational membership (Li *et al.* 2003a, b), again increasing their range of instrumentally valuable 'weak' ties. And social class distinctions in patterns of association have hardened over time. In Britain in the 1970s, civic association membership showed a strong class division (with distinctive working-class associations such as trade unions and working-men's clubs), but a decline in working-class membership since that time has led to the middle classes dominating all forms of (formal) associational activity (Li *et al.* 2002, 2003a, b; Warde *et al.* 2003).

Since associational membership not only increases political participation, and hence political influence . . . but also delivers benefits of sociability including instrumental networks, we have ... evidence of polarisation in British society where the most advantaged class is consolidating its privileges relative to the rest.

(Li *et al.* 2002: 4.15)

Conclusion

Differential association is the social sorting of people's intimate and everyday social networks, patterning who we meet, and how we meet them. This separation in people's intimate contacts has sometimes been seen as a sign of social closure, in which distinct social groups reinforce their internal solidarity by drawing distinct boundaries (in intimate interaction and lifestyle) between those who fall inside and outside the group. However, as Barnes (1992: 262) points out, one of the faults of sociological theory is that it 'sometimes takes for granted the existence of ... groups as part of a "given" social order'. As Barnes notes, 'boundary maintenance takes work'. In this chapter, it has been argued that whilst differential association is clearly bound up with attempts at boundary construction, and with exclusion and segregation between symbolically defined 'groups', there are also other, more general, processes at work.

The analysis of differential association shows that the intimate choices we make in life (of friends and partners) are constrained by the social sorting that already occurs in the clubs, schools, workplaces, and neighbourhoods in which we live our lives. This is a key feature of stratification – it leads to social distance in our personal relations. Since differential association is routinely embedded in social arrangements, social distance can occur without any requirement for strategies limiting contact or denying access to privileged circles. People differently located in social space experience different routes through life, and so often develop differences in taste and manners. The opportunities for different people to meet are very uneven, and when they do meet, they may not have much in common. The processes that generate differential association are, at least in part, determined by preference and habituation, rather than by exclusion alone. Within this model, no barriers need exist in the social order, yet social contact or movement can still be limited by social and cultural dissimilarity. Such differences are very often employed in strategies of exclusion and in the erection of social barriers, but it is also important to recognise the way in which social distance is routinely and unintentionally reproduced, through the most everyday of social actions. Whether we wish to or not, we all routinely reproduce hierarchy and social distance 'behind our backs'.

What this means is that differential association in practical social relations does not always have to relate to the social relations in our heads. That is, social distance is not always based upon the perception of 'difference' (or the drawing of symbolic boundaries) because it occurs through people in different areas of social space having different routes through life. However, the drawing of symbolic boundaries is intimately bound up with people's location in (patterned) social networks, because just as differential association can reinforce difference (shaping different opportunities and interests), so perceptions of difference can reinforce differential association. Later chapters will explore in more detail how the drawing of symbolic boundaries affects processes of stratification.

11 Hierarchy makes you sick

What are the effects of hierarchy and social distance on well-being, and how do rank and subordination influence our health? Social position continues to be important for health even when a society's living standards are high, and there are health inequalities between every level of the social hierarchy, not just between top and bottom. This chapter explores how living within a hierarchy can itself cause ill health, even controlling for factors associated with inequality (such as poverty, bad nutrition, etc.). Because of this it has been argued that it is not just the absolute level of our material situation that affects our health, but also our position relative to others. 'Psychosocial' arguments suggest that high levels of hierarchy influence social cohesion and feelings of empowerment and self-worth, and it is this which affects our health.

Written on the body

Social inequalities are written on the body. In the past, the poor and the working classes were not only more short-lived than their richer counterparts, their poorer health meant that for contemporaries they were, literally, inferior physical specimens. In 1840, it was said of handloom weavers that they were 'decayed in their bodies, the whole race of them is rapidly descending to the size of Lilliputians' (quoted in Floud and Harris 1997: 96). Eugenicists believed the biological inferiority of the urban poor explained their physical weaknesses and their lower social position. It was easy for the rich to look down on the poor, because social superiority was mirrored by physical differences: the poor *were* smaller in stature and more sickly (Porter 1991: 211). In the 1800s, upper-class boys attending the Royal Military Academy at Sandhurst were nearly six inches taller than poor boys attending the Marine Society, and there were still sharp differences in height by the beginning of the twentieth century (Floud *et al.* 1990). However, modern interpretations of such patterns argue that it is social inequalities which explain biological differences. Height is a good measure of the 'biological standard of living' so that if the poor are smaller and more sickly it is because inequalities in their levels of nutrition, living standards and environmental conditions affect their growth and subsequent health.

Inequalities in health reflect power relations, and the way groups are valued differently, affecting their access to resources. The children of slaves in the USA, for example, had much lower birthweights and higher mortality rates than free workers (more than a third of slave infants died before their first birthday), reflecting the low value that slave-owners placed on their lives (Harris 1994). Health inequalities reflect the impact of disadvantage, social exclusion, and discrimination on people's lives, an embodied index of hierarchy and inequality. As modern industrial societies have raised living standards, the physical condition of populations has also improved. But whilst physical differences are less visible than they were in the past, important inequalities in health remain. Hierarchy continues to be written on the body. Social class differences in health and mortality have stayed constant and – at certain points – have even widened. The health 'gap' between social classes has endured the shift from absolute to relative inequality.

Enduring health inequalities

These points need to be understood in relationship to the 'epidemiological transition'. Greater economic development leads to a shift in the nature of diseases that affect societies. In economically less-developed countries, populations are primarily affected by infectious diseases (cholera, diphtheria, influenza, etc.). These diseases are associated with poverty, because malnutrition reduces the body's ability to fight off infectious diseases which proliferate in overcrowded, insanitary conditions. Overall health is strongly related to the wealth of the country (associated with higher standards of living). In Britain, improvements in life expectancy were mainly achieved by the increased prosperity and better nutrition of the population, rather than by advances in medical care (Fogel 1994). However, rich societies become affected by degenerative diseases (cancers, heart disease, strokes, etc.), which are associated with more affluent standards of living (that is, with smoking, obesity, high cholesterol levels, inactive lifestyles, etc.).

So when countries reach a certain level of development, gains in prosperity have only a modest effect in improving levels of health. America is one of the wealthiest countries in the world, yet has mortality rates higher than many poorer countries; Greece has a GDP per capita half that of America, yet has higher life expectancy (Wilkinson 1999a). However, the affluent Americans also have the highest rates of obesity in the world, and high rates of heart disease, and so on. The diseases of affluence complicate the relationship between the wealth of nations and their health, raising the central question of why some wealthy countries have better health than others.

Within affluent societies, the relationship between health and inequality is straightforward – the poorest individuals have the worst health. The solution seems obvious: to improve the situation of the poor. However, health inequalities have proved remarkably persistent, even in the face of improving standards of living. The fundamental question is: 'if health inequalities were due to poverty, why have they got bigger in countries such as Britain during the last fifty years, despite huge rises in the standard of living?' (Wilkinson 1996: 3). The persistence of health inequalities is a paradox, since in western industrialised societies the diseases which make us sick are the diseases of affluence rather than diseases of poverty, yet it is the disadvantaged who are hit the hardest. Indeed, 'some of the most important causes of death reversed their social distribution during the course of the twentieth century' (Wilkinson 1996: 62) so that killers like coronary heart disease, stroke, hypertension, obesity, duodenal ulcers, suicide and lung cancer which once used to afflict the rich are now more common amongst the poor.

Rising standards of living do not eradicate health inequalities, even though in western societies, the absolute level of health has improved for all. Average life expectancy for boys and girls born in 2002 was 76 and 81 respectively, compared to 45 and 49 for those born in 1901 (Government Actuary's Department 2003, http://www.ons.gov.uk). Yet class differentials in health have persisted even in countries like Britain, where the welfare state has eradicated absolute poverty, guaranteed a minimum standard of living for all citizens, and provided universal access to free health care. In most developed economies there is a mean difference in life expectancy between those at the top and at the bottom of a society's social structure of between 4 to 10 years, and there has been a 'widening of social inequalities in health during the final quarter of the last century despite considerable progress in medical science and an increase in health care spending' (Siegrist and Marmot 2003: 1464). Between 1972 and 1999, in England and Wales, the life expectancy of unskilled manual workers increased (from 67 to 71 for men, and from 74 to 77 for women); but the life expectancy of professional workers also increased (from 72 to 79 for men, and from 79 to 83 for women) (*Social Trends* 2003: 130). The health of the poor improved, but so did the health of the wealthier, and at a faster rate, so the class gap in life expectancy actually widened. Babies born to professional fathers have levels of infant mortality half that of babies born in the unskilled manual class (3.6 deaths per 1,000 live births compared to 7.2, of children born inside marriage) (*Social Trends* 2003: 131) and death rates in the lowest social class are over double that of the highest class. There is a strong socio-economic gradient to almost all patterns of disease and ill-health. The lower your socio-economic position the greater your risk of low birthweight, infections, cancer, coronary heart disease, respiratory disease, stroke, accidents, nervous and mental illnesses. Such differences are 'preventable' inequalities, because 'if it is possible for some people to have death rates as low as those in upper social groups, then it should be possible to achieve equally low death rates in all groups' (Wilkinson 1996: 59).

Most of this association reflects the influence of socio-economic status on illness, rather than of illness on socio-economic status (Adler *et al.* 1994: 17), as longitudinal research indicates that 'selection' (in which the healthy rise up, and the ill sink down the occupational structure) plays little part in the socio-economic health gradient (Bartley and Plewis 1997). There are many aspects to this effect of hierarchy on health. There are specific occupational hazards, with certain manual jobs having greater risks of accidental injury, working with toxic materials, noise and vibration hazards, and pollution. Poorer people are more likely to live in areas which have higher material hazards, such as pollution and traffic volume. Poor children are more likely to die from accidents – particularly from being hit by cars – because they have fewer 'safe spaces' in which to play. Similarly, poor areas 'are less well-resourced in terms of shops, recreational facilities, public transport and primary healthcare services' (Bartley *et al.* 1998). The poor are more likely to live in damp, poorly heated or overcrowded homes, to have poor diets, and are less likely to be able to exercise. There are also inequalities in poor people's access to good quality health care and take-up of such services. However, whilst social differences in access to medical care may explain some of the heath gradients in countries like the USA, this does not explain the gradient in countries like the UK, where there is universal access to nationalised health care. It is argued that the *incidence* of disease has the greatest impact on death rates, since health services simply 'pick up the pieces' of prior class inequalities in health (Wilkinson 1996: 67). The key issue is why poorer people get sicker in the first place. This is not an issue of deprivation alone, because health differences run right across society with every rung in the social hierarchy having worse health than the one just above it.

> Health inequalities are not only found between rich and poor, or between 'the deprived' and everyone else. We use the term 'fine grain' to refer to the fine level of social differentiation in health risks. Life expectancy is greater in those who own their own homes and two cars than in home-owners with only one car ... in those with a car and a garden than in those with only a car.
>
> (Bartley *et al.* 1998: 3)

Health inequalities are not just a function of poverty or material deprivation, since health differences occur between groups who are clearly not deprived. The 'challenge' of the health gradient (Adler *et al.* 1994) is to explain why at every level in the hierarchy – including the highest echelons – there are health differences associated with social position.

The health gradient

The gradient in health inequalities – right the way up the social hierarchy – has led health analysts to think about the different ways in which hierarchical social location influences our social and work relations, lifestyle and psychological reactions, in ways which are likely to affect health outcomes.

The most famous study of the health gradient, the Whitehall study (Marmot *et al.* 1984), which examined mortality amongst British civil servants, found health inequalities between every grade of employment. Compared to the mortality risk of the top administrators (and controlling for age) the relative risk of mortality was 1.6 for the professional-executive grades, 2.2 for the clerical grades, and 2.7 for the lowest grades (messengers).

These were all non-industrial civil servants in office-based jobs. At that time their jobs were stable, with high security of employment, and presumably free from chemical and physical industrial hazards. We were surprised, therefore, to discover that the nearly threefold difference in mortality between bottom and top grades of the civil service was larger than the difference between the top and bottom social classes in mortality. . . . This presumably reflects the precise hierarchical classification of occupations within the civil service. [. . .] The task for explanation here is not why there is a link between poverty and ill health, but why there is a social gradient that runs across the whole of society. In the higher grades of the civil service there is no poverty, yet those who are near the top have worse health than those at the top, and the gradient continues all the way down.

(Marmot 1996: 43, 47–48)

The Whitehall workers were all white-collar staff, but there were substantial behavioural differences, with higher grades engaging in healthier lifestyles. The 'risk' lifestyle factors associated with the main cause of death, heart failure (being a smoker, being inactive, consuming saturated fats, obesity), were higher amongst the lower grades. But these risk factors explained less than a quarter of the gradient in heart disease deaths; even when controlling for the risk factors, there were still substantial differences in health by level in the hierarchy.

The study concluded that what was affecting the health of those lower in the hierarchy was precisely that – being lower in the hierarchy. Those low in the hierarchy had lower control over their working environment, greater stress, and lower feelings of self-worth. These factors are called *psychosocial* effects, because psychological reactions to social conditions can have adverse health conse-quences. Psychosocial factors raise health risks *indirectly* by affecting health-related behaviours such as diet, inactivity and smoking (the more stressed a person is the more likely they are to drink and smoke), but the stress of lower social posi-tion also has *direct* effects, by causing physiological or metabolic changes which increase the risk of disease and death. So 'chronic anxiety, insecurity, low self-esteem, social isolation, and lack of control over work appear to undermine mental and physical health' because 'if the biological stress response is activated too often and for too long, there may be multiple health costs. These include depression, increased susceptibility to infection, diabetes, high blood pressure, and accumulation of cholesterol in blood vessel walls, with the attendant risks of heart attack and stroke' (Brunner and Marmot 1999: 41). High stress levels can affect the endocrine and immunology systems (which affect our ability to fight off disease), and high levels of stress are associated with a range of diseases.

A follow-up study, looking at male and female civil servants (Whitehall II), directly tested this hypothesis, confirming that, for major killers like coronary heart disease, low job control accounts for much of the grade difference in CHD frequency (Marmot *et al.* 1997: 238). The authors also pointed to broader psychosocial factors: 'Work conditions are not the only way to activate these neuroendocrine pathways: low control in other areas of life, a self-image of low efficiency, and hostility may be other social or psychological factors that activate these pathways' (Marmot *et al.* 1997: 239). So psychosocial aspects of hierarchy, extending right through a society, can influence health inequalities. Being relatively unequal (less prestigious, less in control over our lives, less valued or esteemed than others) can affect health over and above the material conditions of our life, because of the way in which our relative position affects our psychosocial reactions.

Unhealthy societies?

For wealthy societies, there is only a weak relationship between GDP and health. The health of populations is related less to how wealthy a society is than to how *equally* that wealth is distributed amongst the population. The healthiest societies are those with the smallest income differences between rich and poor. A series of studies has found that more egalitarian societies – with narrower income distributions and smaller proportions of the population in relative poverty – have better health than countries with more relative inequality. Egalitarian Japan has better health than inegalitarian Britain and America, and trends in income confirm this effect. Since the 1960s, Britain and America have experienced increasing income inequality and widening health inequalities; whilst Japan, by contrast, has experienced both dramatic improvements in health and a marked reduction in income inequality. It is argued that these improvements in Japanese life expectancy cannot be explained in terms of changes in nutrition, health care, or preventative health policies (Marmot and Davey-Smith 1989) and that the Japanese example demonstrates the health importance of narrowing income differentials. For some, this suggests that it is not just the absolute level of material situation that affects health, but position relative to others that is important. The link between relative inequality and rates of disease and death has led to the analysis of how *relative* differences and inequalities affect the health of everybody in a society. It is suggested that hierarchy can *itself* cause ill health, even controlling for material factors associated with inequality (such as poverty, poor housing, bad nutrition, etc.).

In the light of correlations between mortality rates and national measures of income inequality (such as the percentage share of income received by the least well-off 70 per cent of the population), it has been argued that relative inequality affects population health by disrupting social cohesion (undermining trust, co-operation and civic participation, and increasing hostility and stress). The most famous exponent of such claims, Richard Wilkinson, argues that relative social location affects the quality of social relationships and psychological reactions to unequal situations:

> greater income inequality is one of the major influences on the proportion of the population who find themselves in situations that deny them a sense of dignity, situations that increase the insecurity they feel about their personal worth and competence, and that carry connotations of inferiority in which few can feel respected, valued and confident.
>
> (Wilkinson 1999a: 267)

Here feelings of self-worth and supportive social integration are the medi-ating element between equality and health. In Wilkinson's account, a sense of relative deprivation (having less income, honour or esteem than others) is trans-lated 'inside' the body into poorer health (through stress-induced risk behaviours and psychopathological reactions), and is also translated 'outside' the individual into anti-social behaviour, and reduced social cohesion, so that 'perceptions of relative income thus link individual and social pathology' (Lynch *et al.* 2000: 1201). The main thrust of psychosocial theories is that

> social inequalities, i.e. not only income inequalities, but also power inequalities (for instance, authoritarian hierarchies and non-democratic social organisa-tions) and status inequalities (for instance, as between the two genders, or between ethnic groups), have a fundamental influence on the content of social relationships and interactions. The greater the social inequalities (longer distances from top to bottom of the income scale, more authoritarian patterns in families, schools, etc.), the more will the quality of social relations suffer. Inequalities will tend to produce anger, frustration, hostility, fear, insecurity, and other negative emotions. Material inequalities will often go together with fear of, or the actual distressing experiences of, failures to secure a socially accept-able standard of living. Authoritarian power patterns engender feelings of hostility and anger. Differences in status produce contempt from those above and fright and insecurity from those below. Thus, an overall association is assumed to exist between the amount of inequalities in society and the amount of negative feelings and emotions signifying psychological stress.
>
> (Elstad 1998: 50)

So inequality affects health not only through the impact of living standards, but also because relative social position affects psychosocial reactions:

> To feel depressed, cheated, bitter, desperate, vulnerable, frightened, angry, worried about debts or job and housing insecurity; to feel devalued, useless, helpless, uncared for, hopeless, isolated, anxious and a failure; these feelings can dominate people's whole experience of life, colouring their experience of everything else. It is the chronic stress arising from feelings like these which does the damage. It is the social feelings which matter, not exposure to a supposedly toxic material environment. The material environment is merely the indelible mark and constant reminder of the oppressive fact of one's failure, of the atrophy of any sense of having a place in the community, and of one's social exclusion and devaluation as a human being.
>
> (Wilkinson 1996: 215)

Material and cultural inequality

Arguments about the psychosocial consequences of hierarchy suggest that *cultural responses* to relative social position may be more important than the material resources of social location. Wilkinson suggests high relative inequality creates 'symptoms of disintegration' in which there is 'a culture of inequality which is less supportive, more aggressive, and usually more macho or "laddish"' (Wilkinson 1999a: 266).

> The unrelenting processes of social differentiation which reflect and amplify social hierarchy are fundamentally important in any analysis of social integration and community. It is these processes which create social exclusion, which stigmatise the most deprived and establish social distances throughout society. . . . Because processes of social differentiation feed on these inequalities and destroy social cohesion . . . a society that is divided, dominated by status, prejudice and social exclusion, which give rise to aggressive subgroups antagonistic to the rest of society, and the stigmatisation of the most disadvantaged, will be closely related to the extent of income inequality.
>
> (Wilkinson 1996: 172)

This is an attempt to explain the association between aggregate income inequality and health. However, there is considerable disagreement about how these associations should be interpreted, and whether the relationship is a causal one. Some writers argue that the aggregate relationship between the health and relative inequality of nations is a by-product of the *individual* level association between income and health. If so, the relationship between relative inequality and health is an artefact of how individual health is affected by individual income (and so not caused by psychosocial reactions).

To explain this it must be understood that the relationship between individual health and income distribution is curved. For poorer individuals there are sharp improvements in health for each unit increase in income, but this curve flattens out for richer individuals, with diminishing returns to health for the same amount of increasing income. This makes sense, since an extra £1,000 of income will have a bigger impact on the standard of living (and thus the health) of someone living on £12,000 a year than on someone earning £60,000 a year. However, this curved relationship means that any *redistribution* of income, from rich to poor, will improve the health of the poor by a larger amount than it reduces the health of the wealthy. So, for populations with the *same* average level of income, societies with a more egalitarian distribution of income will have the better health (simply because a given amount of extra income has a greater health impact at the lower levels of a society than at the top).

So the apparent relationship between a country's income distribution and its health is *partly* explained by the impact of the *absolute* level of material living standards on individual health. There is disagreement, however, as to how much of the relationship between income distribution and health is explained by this (Judge *et al.* 1998; Wilkinson 1996; Kawachi and Kennedy 2002). The policy implication – for Wilkinson and his critics – is that the health of a society will be improved by reducing income inequalities. They disagree, however, as to *why* this should be the case. For Wilkinson's critics, reductions in income inequality improve the material living standards of the poor. For Wilkinson, there are additional effects of relative inequality on health, over and above the impact of absolute living standards.

> The powerful influence which relative income seems to have suggests that it is not so much a matter of what your circumstances are in themselves, but of their standing in relation to others: of where they place you in the overall scale of things, and of the impact which this has on your psychological, emotional and social life.
>
> (Wilkinson 1996: 113)

Reviewing the research, Lynch and colleagues found that 'contextual health effects of income distribution have remained after adjustment for individual income in most studies – but not all' (2000: 1201, but see Wagstaff and van Doorslaer 2000). However, this still does not mean that relative inequality *causally* affects health outcomes since 'income inequality is accompanied by many differences in conditions of life at the individual and population levels, which may adversely influence health' (Lynch *et al.* 2000: 1200). Lynch and colleagues argue, instead, for a *neo-materialist* interpretation of health inequalities (Muntaner and Lynch 1999; Muntaner *et al.* 1999; Lynch *et al.* 2000). They suggest that societies with high levels of relative inequality also have great differences in material resources and poorer investment in social services, and it is these latter factors, rather than reactions to relative inequality, which causally affect health:

> the effect of income inequality on health reflects a combination of negative exposures and lack of resources held by individuals, along with systematic underinvestments across a wide range of human, physical, health, and social infrastructure. An unequal income distribution is one result of historical, cultural, and political-economic processes. These processes influence the private resources available to individuals and shape the nature of public infrastructure – education, health services, transportation, environmental controls, availability of food, quality of housing, occupational health regulations – that form the 'neo-material' matrix of contemporary life.
>
> (Lynch *et al.* 2000: 1202)

Psychosocial theories are criticised for their emphasis on psychological *perceptions* and *cultures* of inequality at the expense of material inequalities. This, it is argued, unnecessarily 'psychopathologises' the relatively deprived, ignoring environmental and occupational hazards which influence health regardless of perceptions of them (Muntaner *et al.* 1999: 699). The difference between neo-materialist and psychosocial positions is explained using the metaphor of airline travel:

> First class passengers get, among other advantages such as better food and service, more space and a wider, more comfortable seat that reclines into a bed. First class passengers arrive refreshed and rested, while many in economy

arrive feeling a bit rough. Under a psychosocial interpretation, these health inequalities are due to negative emotions engendered by perceptions of relative disadvantage. Under a neo-material interpretation, people in economy have worse health because they sat in a cramped space and an uncomfortable seat, and they were not able to sleep. The fact that they can see the bigger seats as they walk off the plane is not the cause of their poorer health. Under a psychosocial interpretation, these health inequalities would be reduced by abolishing first class, or perhaps by mass psychotherapy to alter perceptions of relative disadvantage. From the neo-material viewpoint, health inequalities can be reduced by upgrading conditions in economy class.

(Lynch *et al.* 2000: 1202–1203)

In particular, neo-materialists attack the emphasis on the role of social capital and social cohesion in psychosocial theories. This emphasis arises out of the observation that countries with lower levels of relative inequality have not only better overall health but also higher levels of social capital (as measured by civic associational activity, social ties, and so on).

Looking at a number of different examples of healthy egalitarian societies, an important characteristic they all seem to share is their social cohesion. They have a strong community life. [. . .] People are more likely to be involved in social and voluntary activities outside the home. There are fewer signs of anti-social aggressiveness, and society appears more caring. [. . .] What this means is that the quality of the social life of a society is one of the most powerful determinants of health and that this, in turn, is very closely related to the degree of income inequality.

(Wilkinson 1996: 4, 5)

The implication is that high social capital (or social cohesion) is the mediating factor *explaining* the better health in societies with low relative inequality. Wider income differences are seen as socially divisive, creating societies in which people show less concern for the welfare of others; with the impact of low cohesion seen in the fact that less egalitarian societies not only have worse health, but also higher rates of crime, homicide, deaths by injury, traffic accidents, and alcohol and drug mis-use (Wilkinson *et al.* 1998).

At the aggregate level, US states with high income inequality have low levels of 'trust' and group membership, and high mortality and self-reported illness (Kawachi *et al.* 1999). And a series of studies indicates that more 'integrated' individuals (those with stronger and more extensive social networks) tend to have reduced mortality risks, better mental health, and better recovery rates from illness, even when controlling for other socio-demographic characteristics – although the *quality* of ties also plays a part (conflict-ridden ties may not have the same benefits) (Seeman 1996: 442; Berkman *et al.* 2000: 849–850). The health inequalities of individuals can be related to the nature of their networks and limited social integration, just as the poorer health of unequal societies can be related to their lower social cohesion.

However, just as there is a danger of focusing on the psychological reactions to social location, rather than on unequal social locations themselves, so there is also a danger of thinking that health inequalities can be improved by raising levels of social capital rather than by tackling social inequalities directly. Putnam, the populariser of the social capital concept, appears to fall into just this error, advocating strengthening social networks to improve health.

> Social networks help you stay healthy. . . . For example, stroke victims who had strong support networks functioned better after the stroke, and re-covered more physical capacities, than did stroke networks with thin social networks. Older people who are involved with clubs, volunteer work, and local politics consider themselves to be in better general health than do uninvolved people, even after accounting for socioeconomic status, demo-graphics, level of medical care use, and years of retirement. The bottom line from this multitude of studies: As a rough rule of thumb, if you belong to no groups but decide to join one, you cut your risk of dying over the next year *in half.*
>
> (Putnam 2000: 331)

For Putnam and, it is argued, many health researchers using the concept of social capital (Lynch *et al.* 2000), there is less interest in health *inequalities* than overall population health. Putnam's approach directs attention away from inequality to instead emphasise the connection between social capital and health, advocating improving overall health by increasing general levels of civic engagement (Bridgen 2003).

Beyond the material/cultural divide

But the distribution of social capital is hierarchically differentiated: lower-class individuals and poorer communities tend to have lower levels of (associational) social capital. Social affiliations cannot be presented uncritically as an influence on well-being, since

> groups are powerful social institutions which often act to reinforce social distinctions rather than promote social cohesion. . . . Groups, therefore, can also be seen as instruments through which social inequalities are perpetuated, and the higher incidence of group membership in affluent communities could equally be explained by the desire of those communities to define themselves as being separate from those deemed to be of lower status, thereby maintaining their position in the social order . . . middle-class communities are better at organising themselves to resist potentially problematic develop-ments in their communities, such as power stations, refugee placements or bail hostels, with the result that the burden of such environmental and social stressors has become more concentrated in already-deprived areas.
>
> (Forbes and Wainwright 2001: 802–803)

The role of social networks in health is connected to how they reflect and reinforce inequalities of power and resources. However:

> Surprisingly little research has sought to examine differential access to material goods, resources and services as a mechanism through which social networks might operate. This, in our view, is unfortunate given the work of sociologists showing that social networks operate by regulating an individual's access to life-opportunities by virtue of the extent to which networks overlap with other networks. In this way networks operate to provide access or to restrict opportunities much the same way that social status works.
>
> (Berkman *et al.* 2000: 849–850)

Rather than seeing psychosocial mechanisms as an alternative to materialist explanations, they should more properly be seen as an interface between structural divisions and cultural and lifestyle differences. In thinking about 'social capital', for example, 'it is critical to maintain a view of social networks as lodged within ... larger social and cultural contexts which shape the structure of networks' (Berkman *et al.* 2000: 846).

> While social support is the mechanism most commonly invoked, social networks also influence health through additional behavioural mechanisms including: (1) forces of social influence; (2) levels of social engagement and participation; (3) the regulation of contact with infectious disease; and (4) access to material goods and resources. These mechanisms are not mutually exclusive. In fact, it is most likely that in many cases they operate simultaneously.
>
> (Berkman *et al.* 2000: 850)

Within the Putnamesque approach to social capital, differential access to social capital is not seen in terms of power and resource inequalities, but rather in terms of community deficits (that some communities are more socially integrated than others). Indeed, the need for increasing community social cohesion has sometimes been seen as an *alternative* to reductions in income inequality (Muntaner and Lynch 1999: 70), with the concomitant danger of arguing that 'the problems of poor and minority communities are really a result of deficits of strong social networks; and that local communities must solve their own problems', which, it is argued, is 'akin to victim blaming at the community level' (Lynch *et al.* 2000: 1202).

Neo-materialists see the stress on community social cohesion as a 'culture of poverty' theory. Such theories have been attacked for suggesting that 'poor communities bring poverty upon themselves because of a dearth of community ties and community heritage (i.e., social capital). Perceptions and subjectivity are all important, because it is not objective inequalities that ultimately determine the well-being of populations but the subjective response to those inequalities – which affected individuals and groups can control' (Muntaner *et al.* 2001: 225). So, cultural explanations lead to an emphasis on self-help and changing the culture of poor communities, rather than addressing their material inequalities.

This opposition – between 'materialist' and 'cultural' explanations, structure and agency – is long standing in the health inequalities literature. However, as Smaje notes:

> Debate has become ensnared in a largely political opposition between, on the one hand, a (radical) emphasis on the material or structural determinants of health, and, on the other, a (conservative) privileging of cultural explanations embedded in the notion of unhealthy individual lifestyles ... with 'cultural' explanations which appear to 'blame the victim' counterposed to material ones which 'blame society'.
>
> (Smaje 1996: 154)

It would be unfair to characterise Wilkinson's approach as a 'cultural' approach, since his whole approach is predicated on the centrality of *stratification* to processes of community cohesion and health. Wilkinson does sometimes downplay the effects of material conditions, but his argument still places inequality at the heart of health inequalities, since it is inequality which fuels the processes of social differentiation which stigmatise and exclude the most disadvantaged (Bridgen 2003). Wilkinson is not simply arguing that the relatively disadvantaged have different (unhealthier) cultural lifestyles, but rather that cultural difference is centrally entangled in hierarchical processes by which different groups are placed not only in unequal locations but are also presented as being of differential worth. Indeed, it could be argued that what Wilkinson is attempting is the fusion of cultural and material explanations, rather than advocating one over the other.

It is well known, for example, that the lower your class the more likely you are to take up smoking, and the less likely to give up. But there are no class differences in the wish to give up, so the question is 'why those in the most socially disadvantaged positions seem least able to adopt healthier lifestyles' since 'studies show that they are equally willing to do so' (Bartley *et al.* 1998: 6). As Sacker *et al.* (2001: 764) note, there are central unasked questions in the literature on health lifestyles: for why should people with lower incomes smoke more, and why should people with more routine work tend to have poorer diets and take less exercise? The issue is how health-related lifestyle behaviours are bound up with unequal social location. For Wilkinson, such lifestyle differences are a feature of hierarchy: of lives lived in unequal locations with limited prospects, and the feelings of shame, hopelessness and low self-worth which result. So, of 'the many ways people respond to stress, unhappiness and unmet emotional needs, one is to increase their consumption of various comforting foods – which usually have high sugar and fat content – and of various drugs, including alcohol and of course tobacco' (Wilkinson 1996: 186). Furthermore, 'giving up smoking is easier when your self-esteem is high, you feel optimistic about life and you feel in control. But when things are going badly and prospects look pretty hopeless, you are ... more likely to regard smoking as your only relaxation and luxury' (Wilkinson 1996: 185).

Social interaction, cultural differentiation and health

The link between hierarchical position and health shows up in studies using diverse indicators – ranging from economic status, measured by income, social status, measured by education, and work status and control, measured by occupation – which 'suggests that a broader underlying dimension of social stratification or social ordering is the potent factor' (Adler *et al.* 1994: 15). Studies comparing different stratification measures have found that interaction-based measures (the Cambridge scale) explain more of the variation in health inequalities than class-based measures (Nuffield scheme) (Bartley *et al.* 2000; Chandola 1998). However, measures of material deprivation remain the best predictor, with the total effect of material deprivation on ill-health fives times greater than that of class, and three times greater than interaction-based measures (Bartley *et al.* 2000). The fact that material deprivation is such a powerful predictor of health inequalities is significant but to be expected, given that the relationship between health and inequality is curved. The steepest end of the health inequalities curve (and thus the greatest variation in health) is at the *bottom* of the social scale, where we would expect material deprivation to be the most severe and to have the greatest impact on health. However, interaction-based measures continue to be significantly related to health, even when controlling for material deprivation, which indicates that associational lifestyle also affects health (Chandola 1998). Interaction-based measures of stratification are based on the assumption that those with similar lifestyles and resources tend to interact more with one another in close social relationships, so that the social interaction distance between occupations reflects dissimilarities in lifestyles.

> It is possible that people who are social equals or who often interact socially (friends engaging in leisure activities, for example), have similar lifestyles in terms of health behaviours as well as similar resources which enable them to pursue these health resources. There is evidence showing that people's smoking behaviour is influenced by their friends' smoking . . . [and] their parents' and partner's smoking. . . . Wives of physically active men tend to be physically active themselves. . . . [and] wives of coronary high risk men were more likely to be smokers and have unhealthier dietary habits.
>
> (Chandola 1998: 526)

We have already seen that people's location in social networks structures their access to material and cultural resources, limits their association with unequal and culturally distinct others, and helps shape differentiated lifestyles and leisure activities. All of this is likely to affect health outcomes. It is important therefore not to counterpose 'material' and 'cultural' explanations, but rather to explore their interrelationship. Rather than trying to explore whether apparently 'class', 'ethnic' or 'gender' differences in health can be explained by reference to other, usually material, factors, the burden of explanation is to explore just how 'class', 'ethnicity' and 'gender' are implicated in processes of *both* material disadvantage *and* social differentiation. The health differences between different class, racial and gender groups are often discussed in terms of their supposed 'cultural' difference, by reference to the 'lifestyle' differences between groups, and their relative propensity of engaging in health 'risk' behaviours. However, the role of hierarchical and cultural differentiation on health is about more than the propensity to smoke, drink or take exercise. Such differences have to be understood more generally in terms of the way in which inequality is simultaneously bound up with cultural differentiation, as inequality entails people following different routes through life, and sharing their lives with groups with very different memberships.

Take the links between race and health. It has often been noted, for example, that adjustment for socio-economic position substantially reduces but does not eliminate racial and ethnic disparities in health (Williams and Collins 1995: 364). So, although the health of some ethnic minorities is affected by more disadvantaged socio-economic profiles, ethnic inequalities in health persist within each class grouping. In the gap left by socio-economic position 'explanations tend to fall to unmeasured genetic and cultural factors based on stereotypes, because such meanings are easily imposed on ethnic categorisations' (Nazroo 1998: 155). There is a genetic component to disease, which may vary between ethnic groups, but this only accounts for a small percentage of the 'ethnic penalty' (Williams and Collins 1995: 364), and environmental factors are more important (Smaje 1996: 156). Attention has instead focused on how the 'cultural heritage' of ethnic minorities leads to unhealthier lifestyles.

For writers critical of such culturalist approaches this 'leads to a form of victim blaming, where the *inherent* characteristics of the ethnic (minority) group are seen to be at fault and in need of rectifying' (Nazroo 1998: 156). An example of this can be found in the discussion of how 'South Asians' in Britain have an elevated risk of coronary heart disease (CHD). It is suggested that 'cultural' factors (such as the use of ghee in cooking and a lack of physical exercise) explain the difference, and that 'South Asians' should be encouraged to take up healthier lifestyles. However, as Nazroo has pointed out, only certain groups within this category have higher risk of CHD. Nazroo therefore argues that ethnic classifications are not natural and fixed divisions between groups, and that it is necessary to explore just *how* such classifications tap into different aspects of social position, such as culture, lifestyle, the consequences of racialisation, socio-economic location, and so on (1998: 157).

Studies which see cultural difference as the explanation of racial health inequalities 'overemphasise cultural differences between groups and neglect socio-material explanations . . . while the existence of socio-economic differences within ethnic minority populations may be ignored' (Davey-Smith *et al.* 2000: 26). Take the complex links between race, socio-economic position and health. Minorities often experience additional 'racial' penalties in the labour and housing markets which means that conventional socio-economic classifications (using employment status, housing tenure, or occupational class) may not fully represent their material social location. Many ethnic minority groups have poorer-quality housing than whites regardless of tenure, are concentrated at the bottom of occupational grades, have lower income than white people in the same class, are more likely to work unsociable hours, and suffer poorer job security, and greater stress (Davey-Smith *et al.* 2000; Nazroo 1998). Ethnic minorities are also more concentrated in inner cities with worse transport, retail and leisure facilities and environmental pollution, which may have an additional 'ecological' effect on their health. The material disadvantages of such groups may therefore be imperfectly captured by normal socio-economic classifications, giving rise to the appearance of additional 'cultural' factors. Nazroo found that controlling for *standard of living* (using a more direct measurement of the material circumstances of respondents than 'class' or housing tenure) dramatically reduced the health differences by ethnicity, so a more sophisticated measurement of social position shows that 'socio-economic differences, in fact, make a large and key contribution to ethnic inequalities in health' (1998: 160).

However, socio-economic differences do not 'explain' away the influence of ethnicity on health. There is a danger that by adjusting for socio-economic position (and thus treating it as a 'confounding variable') attention is directed away from how socio-economic status is produced and reproduced in different ethnic groups, obscuring the relationship *between* socio-economic position, ethnicity and health (Nazroo 1998; Smaje 1996: 158–159). Smaje argues much analysis of the ethnic patterning of health has failed to examine 'the social meaning of ethnicity, while too often becoming enmeshed in unhelpful dualities which counterpose material to cultural explanation' (1996: 139). Drawing on Bourdieu, Smaje argues that what is required are theoretical approaches which can explain ethnicity both 'as a mode of identity (an affective claim by which we identify a human collectivity to which we feel a belonging, thus distinguishing an "us" from a "them"), and as a principle of social structuring (by which ethnic collectivities enjoy differential access to variety of social resources)' (1996: 140).

The same issues arise in relation to gender (and in relation to hierarchical divisions more generally). In discussions of gender and health it has usually been argued that health differences between women and men (women live longer, but experience higher levels of illness throughout their lives, so that 'women get sicker but men die quicker') are largely a reflection of the different health 'risks' women and men encounter because of gender divisions in the way they lead their daily lives. Differences in the structural location and lifestyles of women and men (at home, in the family, in leisure pursuits, and at work) play out in different stressors and risk lifestyles, different patterns of disease, and different rates of morbidity and mortality. As with race, gender differences in health cut across class categories. So, whilst the 'class' effect still holds for women (women's health worsens at lower levels of socio-economic position), the class gradient appears to be shallower for women. There is little difference in the health of female skilled, semi- and unskilled manual workers, compared to sharp differences in the health of male manual workers by skill level (Arber 1991, 1997). Sara Arber, for example, has noted that married women's health is better predicted by their husband's occupation than their own, indicating the role of wider household circumstances in shaping individual social circumstances and lifestyles. However, we should be careful of assuming that gender *mediates* class effects because women experience work differently, or because paid work is of less significance in women's lives. Rather, as Arber notes, there is (again) an issue of how well the categories of analysis are capturing the wider social circumstances of women's experience.

Conclusion

It is clear that there are many components to the relationship between stratification and health: flowing through material, cultural, social and psychological pathways. This chapter shows that the pursuit of 'healthy' or 'unhealthy' lifestyles is not just about material resources, or occupational location, but rather is better seen as part of broader cultural differences which are markers of, and strategies in, the membership of different and unequal social groups.

> Income per se is important for access to certain types of cultural pursuit. However, it costs no more to listen to classical music than other forms on the radio or in recorded form, and costs nothing to follow a diet and exercise regime at home, suggesting that income alone will not explain social differences in leisure differences. These practices seem to be undertaken in part as a way of expressing or seeking membership of certain social groups and social distance or differentiation from others (Bourdieu 1984 [1979]). It is this which may enable us to understand better the link between inequalities of prestige and inequalities in health.
>
> (Bartley *et al.* 2000: 61)

It is important not to see lifestyle differences as simply flowing from structural location, for lifestyles are themselves resources used by participants in processes of hierarchical differentiation and distinction. It is not that occupation gives rise to lifestyle, but rather that occupation and lifestyle are mutually implicated, both emerging out of processes of hierarchical distinction and differentiation.

Take class-differentiated patterns of 'healthy' living. Savage *et al.* (1992) argue that the middle-class adoption of 'healthy lifestyles' relates to broader social and cultural distinctions and manoeuvres over social identity. Amongst the British middle classes, Savage *et al.* identify three distinct segments with different cultural assets and lifestyles:

- those living a 'postmodern' lifestyle, with no coherent single organising principle, instead combining high extravagance and excess (in terms of diet and alcohol consumption), with a 'culture of the body' (diets and gym membership), who were as likely to appreciate opera as disco dancing (1992: 108–109);
- an 'ascetic' group of intellectuals, people with cultural assets but not much money, such as teachers, welfare and medical workers, pursuing lifestyles based on healthy diet and exercise: yoga, jogging, and outdoor activities, such as climbing and mountain holidays; but also an interest in the arts, attending plays and concerts;

- and an 'undistinguished' or conventional group, of 'organisational' bureaucrats and government workers, did not have a distinctive lifestyle.

Savage *et al.* note the strong link between high levels of educational attainment and high incomes, and an engagement with a new culture of health and body maintenance, associated with keeping fit. They see a version of the ascetics' 'healthy lifestyle' now being rapidly adopted by more prosperous sections of the middle classes, particularly by professional workers in law, financial services, personnel, marketing, advertising, and so on, who adopt a postmodern 'health with champagne' approach (1992: 115–116). This spread, it is argued, reflects the middle classes' 'investment in the self', part and parcel of the accumulation of cultural capital, where 'the body is of crucial importance as the actual vehicle in which cultural assets are stored' (1992: 111). So among the middle classes 'a "healthy lifestyle" is in effect becoming instrumentally converted into health for increased earning capacity and the accumulation of economic assets' (1992: 114–115).

Bodily lifestyles are not simply a reflection of social location, and the material circumstances which contextualise people's lives, shaping what is available to them; they also reflect *habitus*, the deeply engrained habits, tastes and predispositions, which are shaped in childhood and are moulded by our affiliations and intimate relationships. As Bourdieu notes:

> The inclination of the privileged classes towards a 'stylised' way of life [in which] the body is treated as an end in itself which ... inclines them towards a cult of health-consciousness and the appearance of the body: the body as a thing displayed to others. ... this concern for the cultivation of the body results in a high value being placed on moderate drinking, and careful diet in the middle classes.
>
> (quoted in Bartley *et al.* 2000: 60–61)

For Bourdieu, people's relation to the body, their way 'of treating it, caring for it, feeding it, maintaining it ... reveals the deepest dispositions of the habitus' (1984 [1979]: 190), so that social relations are *expressed through* bodily dispositions and demeanour, in 'the most automatic gestures or the apparently most insignificant techniques of the body – ways of talking or blowing one's nose, ways of eating or talking – and engage the most fundamental principles of construction and evaluation of the social world' (Bourdieu 1984 [1979]: 466).

It is apparent that hierarchy is a process of both distance and differentiation in social relations. Those distant in the hierarchy are also distant from each other in terms of social relations, and so are socially dissimilar, lead different lives in different places, have different friends and different interests, and all this bound up with different levels of resources, respect and social control. It is not that hierarchy gives rise to lifestyle differences but rather that lifestyle differences are one of the many ways in which hierarchical lives are lived. All of this, of course, fundamentally impacts on the health of unequally placed groups.

A person's past social experiences become written into the physiology and pathology of their body. The social is, literally, embodied; and the body records the past, whether as an ex-officer's duelling scars or an ex-miner's emphysema. The duelling scar as mark of social distinction, in turn, predisposes to future advancement and social advantage, while the emphysema robs the employee of their labour power and predisposes to future deprivation and social disadvantage . . . the social distribution of health and disease results from these processes of accumulating advantage or disadvantage.

(Blane 1999: 64)

12 Movements in space

Previous chapters have explored how hierarchy is embedded in our most intimate social relationships, and shown that such unequal social relations help to reproduce inequalities in health, access to resources, and social prospects, over time. But if stratification is concerned with the relatively stable nature of inequalities in social relationships – the extent to which unequal social position endures over time – the study of social mobility explores the extent of movement between unequal positions. For many theorists, the extent of social mobility is a crucial test of the persistence of inequality. The more mobility there is – between generations or over the lifecourse – the less durable inequality seems. The study of 'social mobility' has been a corner-stone of class analysis because of the evidence it presents on the potential formation of classes and the openness of society – the idea being that groups who experience continuity of inequality are more likely to perceive that inequality and to act on it. Yet it is difficult to assess the reproduction of inequality over time because of the extensive and rapid social change undergone by all western industrial societies. As we shall see, partly because of extensive social transformation, total levels of social mobility in most western industrial societies are strikingly high, and liberal theorists have concluded that more mobility means less enduring inequality, and that industrial societies are increasingly more 'open'. This is rejected by class theorists, who argue that relative inequality persists between generations even in the face of large amounts of movement, and who thus stress continuity of inequality.

There is an important question, however, as to how long-run social change can be accommodated in accounts of inequality, given that such change alters the *social meaning* of unequal social locations. The pioneer of mobility analysis, Pitirim Sorokin (1927), defined it as the shifting of people in social space. His interest was in its consequences on 'social metabolism' – how movement affects the relations of social groups differently located in the social structure. But our understanding of social movement partly depends on how we view the 'social space' within which movement occurs. Furthermore, information on the *amount* of social movement needs to be balanced by an account of the meaning of such movements for the individuals concerned. In fact, movement is so widespread, that any view of stratification as the straightforward inheritance of social location must be questioned. But if the persistence of inequality resides in unequal patterns of *movement* we have to ask what this means for how inequality is experienced and perceived.

Movement within a structure

The conventional way of measuring mobility first defines a structure of inequality and then explores patterns of movement within it. The class tradition, for example, analyses movements between fixed class categories to explore how this influences the formation of distinct social groups. Low levels of mobility between categories are thought to give rise to fixed social groups, with low social mixing, and high inter-generational stability; high levels of mobility are said to blur such divisions. The alternative, status-attainment tradition looks at the various factors influencing how high an individual rises in the (finely graded) social scale. Here the emphasis is on the relative importance of social background versus individual achievement as determinants of individual success. This is a concern with social *equity*, since 'it is one of the postulates of a democratic and egalitarian society, that ability, whatever its social background, shall not be denied the chance to fulfil itself' (Glass 1954: 25). If social success is based on what people can *do*, not who they *are* (or their social connections, or inherited privilege), there should be a weakening link between origins and destinations, structure and action. Class theorists see this from the viewpoint of class formation, arguing that equity (societies based on achievement) reduces social resentment, limiting the possibility of distinct class groups. A genuinely open society would imply 'the serious attenuation of classes in the sense of aggregates of individuals, or families, identifiable in the extent to which they occupy similar locations in the social division of labour over time' (Goldthorpe *et al.* 1980: 28).

Yet both approaches are concerned with the transmission and reproduction of patterns of advantage over time. There are two components to this: inter-generational mobility (the extent to which family social position is handed on to subsequent generations); and intra-generational mobility (the extent to which individuals experience a change in their social situation over the course of their lives). For both approaches, the extent of movement indicates the continuity of structural inequality. If, during their lives, people do not move far from their social origins, then the importance of structural factors is confirmed. Status-attainment approaches are looking to find mobility, class approaches, immobility, but the extent of social movement is taken as crucial evidence of the significance of structural inequality.

Social formation

From a class perspective, limited social movement implies continuity of inequality, and the formation of social groups. In this approach mobility flows between classes have two aspects, flip-sides of the same coin: *outflow mobility* from an origin class (for example, to what extent do working-class children get jobs outside the working class?); and *inflow mobility* into a destination class (for example, how diverse are the class backgrounds of people currently in middle-class jobs?). The *combination* of different class patterns of outflow and inflow mobility is considered a key factor in 'the degree to which they have formed as collectivities of individuals and households through the continuity of their association with particular sets of class positions over time' (Erikson and Goldthorpe 1992: 226). If most of the children born into the working class themselves got working-class jobs, then the working class would show inter-generational continuity over time. A potential consequence of this low outflow mobility might be a strong sense of social similarity and solidarity. Since family connections to the middle class would be limited, social distance between classes would be strong. However, the formation of distinct 'demographic' classes depends on more than the extent of attachment to class of origin, since this must be measured against inflow mobility, as the amount of movement *into* destination classes also affects solidarity. Even if many middle-class people stayed in their class, if large numbers from lower classes moved into it, this would make it heterogeneous, composed of individuals with diverse social backgrounds and mobility experiences. Because of these internal differences, such a class is less likely to develop a shared class outlook or identity. So:

> The crucial test of whether a class is a demographic entity is not whether those who are born into it tend to remain, but whether they have characteristic life-chances, that is, chances of mobility and immobility that set them apart from other classes.
>
> (Roberts 2001: 196)

The classic study of British (male) social mobility, the Oxford Mobility Study, found different classes had very different patterns of inflow and outflow mobility (Goldthorpe *et al.* 1980). The service class (professional and managerial workers) had low homogeneity, but high 'holding power' (large numbers of individuals from lower social classes moved into the class, but children born into the service class tend to stay there: high 'inflow', but low 'outflow'). The working class (unskilled and semi-skilled manual workers) had lower retentiveness, but high homogeneity (large numbers of working-class children moved out of the class, but very few moved into it from higher-class backgrounds: high 'outflow' but low 'inflow'). The working class is essentially self-recruiting, with considerable movement out but little movement in, so Goldthorpe concluded that it was only the working class that had a clear 'demographic identity' over time that could result in socio-political action.

The conventional class model therefore identifies class formation in the inter-generational continuity of the working class. But these conclusions have been questioned. Research by Egerton and Savage (2000) indicates that since the 1970s manual work has increasingly been undertaken by *young* men, who then move into other kinds of jobs. High *work-life mobility* out of the working class means that a snap-shot picture of the working class at a given point in time captures many 'young people destined to work only for a short time in manual work. Hence, there is no demographically coherent working class' (Savage 2000: 93). It is also argued that high outflow mobility undermines class coherence. In the original Oxford Mobility Study, 43 per cent of the sons of working-class fathers were mobile out of the working class, and this figure has risen in recent years.

> Most working-class adults who became parents in the second half of the twentieth century would have seen one of their children ascend at least into the intermediate classes . . . upward mobility has been quite a common experience, nothing exceptional. Those who have remained immobile will have seen others getting ahead: people who they knew at school, in their neighbourhoods, and sometimes from their own families. Cross-class family links and friendships will mitigate against any tendency for people to see other classes as enemies.
>
> (Roberts 2001: 201)

Because of these very high levels of social movement, conventional class approaches have placed increasingly less emphasis on the formation of distinct class 'groups'. Instead, attention has moved to the consideration of how individuals from different classes have unequal chances of success in life. But first it is necessary to understand just how much social movement there is.

How much movement?

Total levels of social mobility in most western industrial societies are strikingly high, with mobility 'the norm, not the exception, for both women and men' (Savage 2000: 80). Cross-national class research (Erikson and Goldthorpe 1992) shows vertical social mobility in a range of industrialised societies. In England and Wales, fully 50 per cent of sons were in a different class to their fathers, with 32 per cent upwardly mobile. Even Ireland, the country exhibiting least mobility in the study, saw 39 per cent of sons vertically mobile. More recent studies indicate that male mobility has increased over time (Marshall *et al.* 1997; Heath and Payne 2000), with similar amounts of mobility amongst women (Heath and Payne 2000).

Female mobility is under-researched, partly because of difficulties incorporating women's different employment profiles into the assumptions of 'male' mobility models (Payne and Abbott 1990). The pattern of female mobility is different since, as Savage notes, 'women tend to be employed in exclusively female forms of work (notably routine white-collar employment) . . . this entails daughters being more mobile than sons in relation to their fathers' (2000: 80). The standard father–son comparisons of mobility analysis are made more problematic when we compare fathers and daughters. Because women's employment distribution is so different from that of men 'what passes for upward mobility must also necessarily be different' (Payne *et al.* 1990: 59). The daughters of professional fathers are more likely to be downwardly mobile than their brothers, and working-class women are more likely to end up in non-manual occupations than their brothers (Heath 1981; Abbott and Sapsford 1987), but there is a serious question as to whether such transitions constitute 'mobility' in the same way that they would for men. Women show a lot of mobility from all classes alike into lower white-collar work, reflecting the concentration of women in this type of work. Fewer women than men follow their father's footsteps into the service class, and into the petty bourgeoisie, but women are also less likely to inherit positions in manual work, with more movement into the middle of the class structure (Heath and Payne 2000). Heath and Payne argue this is because of differential shifts over time in the opportunity structure for women: with less room at the top for women, but more room in the middle, with the feminisation of routine non-manual work.

Overall, a series of cross-national studies indicate that over the course of the twentieth century, for both women and men, there have been large amounts of social mobility, and total levels of mobility have increased (Erikson and Goldthorpe 1992; Marshall *et al.* 1997). Such high levels of mobility have implications for the fairness of society. In western industrial societies, between a third and a half of individuals will wind up in a different social class to their parents. For some, this indicates that western industrial societies have become more open and fair over time. This was famously argued in Blau and Duncan's (1967) analysis of American mobility patterns. As Chapter 5 shows, the focus of this study was on the various factors which influence *individual* occupational success or failure. It found ascribed factors (such as social background) were less important than achieved factors (such as educational qualifications) in explaining an individual's occupational position; concluding that American society was increasingly meritocratic, with relatively little systematic class inequality. A similar conclusion was drawn by Saunders, investigating the relationship between ability, social background and mobility in Britain (1990, 1996). He found individual ability and motivation, not parental background, were the best predictors of people's destinations, concluding that 'in the end what matters most is whether you are bright, and whether you work hard' (Saunders 1996: 72). The implication is that structural inequality is increasingly less important in shaping people's lives.

However, studies which focus on the determinants of individual success find it hard to adequately account for the structural factors which constrain individual achievement. Yet one reason for the declining link between origins and destinations in western societies is the massive shift in the structure of opportunities. 'In one sense, individual achievement is a basis for occupational movement, and the extent of this will vary across societies. However, in another sense, all "achievement" is entirely dependent on socially defined structures and opportunities' (Blackburn and Prandy 1997: 493).

In all industrial societies, there has been an expansion of middle-level jobs, and a contraction of manual jobs, with the shift from agricultural to industrial, to service economies. In Britain, between 1901 and 1991, the proportion of the working population employed as manual workers fell from 75 per cent to 38 per cent, whilst the proportion of professionals and managers rose from 8 per cent to 34 per cent (Gallie 2000: 288). From one generation to the next a sea-change in the opportunity structure meant that many of the children of manual workers *had* to experience upward mobility. Even if most of the children of professionals and managers got similar work themselves, solely on the basis of nepotism, there would still have to be inflow mobility into service-class occupations, because the expansion of such jobs meant there were many more places to fill.

These structural changes 'force' increased rates of mobility, because children face a very different opportunity structure to their parents, and large numbers must end up in different (and better) social positions. We would therefore expect a loosening relationship between origins and destinations, with ability and qualifications strongly affecting individual success. But this does not mean that individual ability has triumphed over structural constraints:

> Structural variables cannot be simply counterposed to individual ones and their relative importance empirically adjudicated. It is not surprising to report that 'able' young people from disadvantaged backgrounds will tend to do better than their less 'able' peers. However, in a society where there are growing numbers of middle-class jobs it is likely that working-class children will be drawn in to fill these new positions. It is quite plausible – indeed likely – that those who fill these jobs will be deemed to be 'brighter' than those who do not. However, in this case 'brightness' does not *cause* mobility, it is simply the filter that distinguishes those who are upwardly mobile from those who are not. The apparent correlation between an individual's ability and their upward mobility can be consistent with the power of social class.
>
> (Savage 2000: 77)

Class analysts believe trends in absolute mobility offer a misleading picture of how fair a society is because increases in mobility can result from either the increasing significance of achievement in allocation processes or from an improvement in the general opportunities available. Mobility out of the working class may have increased because the working class have taken a *bigger share* of the pie, or because they have taken the *same share* of a bigger pie. Absolute mobility rates cannot distinguish between these two outcomes, which have quite different implications for fairness. Mobility is so heavily affected by structural change, that it tells us little about meritocracy. All we see is that opportunities as a whole have improved. But one of the main reasons for looking at social mobility is to consider how unequally placed groups fare over time *in relation to each other*.

Class analysts attempt to control for shifts in the opportunity structure over time, by comparing the *relative chances* of children from different backgrounds in gaining access to the opportunities available at any given point. For example, what are the chances of working-class children getting a professional job compared to the chances of service-class children? In the original Oxford Mobility Study the chances of service-class sons gaining access to professional and managerial jobs compared to working-class sons were 4 to1. The chances of service-class sons *avoiding* working-class jobs compared to those from manual origins showed the same ratio (Goldthorpe *et al.* 1987: 50). Looking at relative mobility chances allows us to compare how the relative advantage of one group against another changes over time, independent of structural shifts. A number of studies indicate that the relative chances of success of service-class children compared to working-class children have not changed much over time:

more 'room at the top' has not been accompanied by greater equality in the opportunities to get there. . . . In sum, the growth of skilled white-collar work has increased opportunities for mobility generally, but the distribution of those opportunities across the classes has stayed the same.

(Marshall 1997: 5)

Despite considerable upward mobility throughout the twentieth century, the relative chances of children from different class backgrounds gaining access to high-level positions *remained* very unequal, with little change in social fluidity (or relative mobility chances) in the post-war period. Working-class individuals took advantage of expanding opportunities to improve their social position; however, the middle class has also seized the advantage, *and at about the same rate*, so relative differences between the groups stayed the same. Over time, the middle class has taken the same share of a bigger pie. Goldthorpe describes this as 'the constant flux' – the continuity of relative disadvantage in the midst of continual social movement (Erikson and Goldthorpe 1992). Comparative class research shows a similar pattern in most countries studied (Erikson and Goldthorpe 1992; Marshall *et al.* 1997). As we shall see later, these findings have been disputed. However, because of this apparent continuity in the inequality of relative mobility chances, most mobility analysts have argued that the societies studied have not become more 'open' over time.

The brightest and the best?

We can see a similar pattern if we look at what happened to class differentials in the face of the expansion of educational opportunities. Over the last 100 years, a dramatic increase in educational opportunities has meant the *average* level of educational attainment has risen substantially in all western industrial societies. However, 'greater access to education is not necessarily reflected in a reduction in class-based inequalities' (Blossfeld and Shavit 1993: 61). The absolute chances of attending university in Britain, for example, increased for all in the post-war period, but the relative chances of entry for different classes remained the same (Heath and Clifford 1990; Blackburn and Jarman 1993). The expansion in university places meant an increased number of working-class university students, but there was also an increase in the *middle-class* take-up of places. As a result, the relative proportion of working-class to middle-class university students remained largely unchanged.

Of course, this partly reflects class differences in educational *achievement*, as working-class children perform much worse in school. But whilst 'family background has remained an important determinant for educational attainment throughout this century' (Furlong 1997: 59), it is usually argued that working-class children face greater obstacles to academic success, ranging from material deprivation (leading to poorer health and nutrition, overcrowding at home, no money for books or special coaching, and over-crowded, poorly resourced schools) to poorer cultural capital (with success in school subjects reflecting middle-class knowledge and values). A range of research indicates middle-class parents are both more strategic and more successful in negotiating their children through the school system. Saunders however argues that 'to show that a society is unequal is by no means the same as showing that it is unfair' because differences in *ability* may explain unequal class outcomes (1990: 51). Higher-class individuals perform better in all forms of educational testing, and achieve much higher qualifications. However, class theorists counter that the poorer performance of lower-class individuals is the *result* of their class disadvantages, not the cause of it. Indeed, they suggest that the stress on ability serves to legitimate inequality, since people come to 'see as natural inability things which are only the result of an inferior social status' (Bourdieu, quoted in Furlong 1997: 58).

Marshall and Swift (1996) found that children from service-class backgrounds are more likely to arrive at service-class destinations than working-class children even when they have attained similar qualifications. At the highest level of educational achievement (degree level), they found little class influence. However, those with lower-level qualifications are affected by class background: service-class children with only 'low' or 'medium' educational qualifications are much more likely to get jobs in the service class than lower-class individuals with the same qualifications. So being born in a higher class can 'insure' against poor educational achievement: 'there is still a substantial direct effect of class background on class destinations which is not mediated by educational achievement', which means that 'equals are being treated unequally' (Marshall and Swift 1993: 206).

A similar point is made by Savage and Egerton, who are less interested in whether ability is related to mobility (clearly it is) than in how 'ability' is related to processes of competition between classes.

> When bright middle-class children are in competition with bright working-class children, who is it that tends to come off better? Or, perhaps more interestingly, when bright working-class children are in competition with less intelligent middle-class children, who comes off better?
>
> (Savage and Egerton 1997: 649–650)

For Savage and Egerton, whilst 'there are dramatic class differences in the numbers of respondents who score well or badly in ability tests', the crucial issue is 'whether ability appears to "wipe out" class advantage' (1997: 655, 657). They found that it did not. Around three-quarters of the 'high-ability' sons of service-class fathers stayed in the service class, but less than half of the 'high-ability' boys from working-class origins were mobile into the service class. Similarly, amongst 'low-ability' boys, those from working-class origins were very likely to stay in the working class (76%), but most 'low-ability' boys from the service class (65%) were able to avoid a fall into manual work. 'High-ability' working-class boys had roughly the same prospects of moving into the service class as the 'low-ability' service-class boys: 'This is a considerable dent for those arguing the meritocratic case. The more privileged social classes are able to find ways of preventing even their less "able" sons from moving down the social spectrum' (Savage and Egerton 1997: 657).

For men, parental social class affected mobility, over and above measured ability. However, the implications for women were rather different. Controlling for ability did not wipe out class differences in women's mobility chances, but class differences were less marked than amongst men. However, a 'major reason for this is that intermediate white-collar work is the largest single destination point for daughters from every social class (except professionals)' (Savage and Egerton 1997: 659). The conclusion Savage and Egerton drew was that for women, class effects operated mainly through class differences in attainment, whereas men 'seemed to have more potential to tap into other resources than those based on ability alone' (1997: 659) (through perhaps direct inheritance or social contacts). So:

> some of the advantages of middle-class children rest in their ability to score higher in ability tests and thereby go on to do better in the educational system. However, it is also clearly the case that middle-class advantages are also apparent even controlling for level of ability, and therefore that there are other mechanisms at work which tend to reproduce class inequalities.
>
> (Savage and Egerton 1997: 666)

Absolute mobility or social fluidity?

An emphasis on the relative access to opportunities suggests 'constant social fluidity' with class differentials persisting in the face of improving prospects for all. The conclusion is that society has not become more open, and that structural inequalities still dominate people's lives. This conclusion has not gone unchallenged, however. Saunders argues that the emphasis on relative chances ignores the impact of absolute mobility on people's lives, because we cannot assume that 'if everybody has gained, nothing really has changed' (1995: 25). Saunders argues that conventional mobility research grossly underestimates the impact of increasing absolute mobility on how people *experience* class inequality. For 'whether we are interested in people's objective life chances or in their subjective lived experiences, what matters is precisely that there is now "more room at the top"' (Saunders 1995: 25). So absolute rates of mobility are significant in their own right, not only in their influence on class formation, but also for their effect on how people perceive their social position and how they judge fairness in social life.

Geoff Payne spells out the impact of rising affluence:

> Manual workers in this country now expect to own a car, and a television, to occupy a dwelling of several rooms in good physical condition, to take a holiday abroad, to have several sets of clothing. Such a lifestyle (even if still not available to more than, say, three-quarters of households) would in 1950 have been associated with the middle or upper classes, who made up about one quarter of society. In less than a single lifetime, manual workers have in consumption terms been upwardly mobile, 'even while we're standing still' ... If one compares 1921 with 1991, the contrast is even greater. Because

we have continued to think of mobility as class movement in a monolithic way across a single dimensional social divide, we have ignored the very real change in material experience for the working class, a change which however imperfectly also extends to improved health, access to education and political rights.

(Payne 1992: 220)

The reason sociologists have looked at the *amount* of mobility is to see how mobility flows affect the fairness of society, and whether the patterning of mobility gives rise to distinct social groups. But both these issues crucially depend on how people perceive social movement. Yet 'how people feel about or experience changes in their class standing is an issue that has been almost entirely overlooked' (Marshall and Firth 1999: 29). So how important are the different sorts of social movement for the subjective experience of inequality?

Saunders believes it is absolute mobility that counts, and gives an unusual illustration of his argument comparing the mobility experiences of the working and middle classes to that of a dwarf and a giant in a hot air balloon:

As they rise above the ground, both clearly benefit from an enhanced view, but the dwarf never gets his or her head to the level enjoyed by the giant. If we insist on measuring their ascent purely in relative terms (i.e. relative to each other), we shall conclude that nothing significant has changed. [. . .] The fact that both of them are now many times higher than they were before they entered the balloon is dismissed as unimportant or uninteresting, yet it is their joint ascent which is in reality far more crucial in determining the quality of the view which they can each now achieve. Like the dwarf and the giant, the working-class and the middle-class have shared equally in a marked improvement in their chances of achieving a high position, and it is this which has arguably had the major impact on our lives.

(Saunders 1996: 16)

In response to Saunders, class analysts acknowledge that the increase in overall mobility has improved most people's chances in life. However, they insist that the key issue

is the distribution of opportunities, rather than the fact that people have got more opportunities now than in the past. [. . .] [T]he concept of equality is inherently comparative: it necessarily invites us to examine the advantages of different groups or different individuals and to assess these advantages relative to one another.

(Marshall and Swift 1996: 376)

This is an important point, but it raises an under-researched question, namely to what extent are people actually aware of relative inequalities of opportunity between classes? For many sociologists the relative odds of success bear 'little relevance to the experiential worlds in which most people live. The simple figures describing the proportion of working-class children who are upwardly mobile, for example, bear a closer resemblance to the worlds that lay people inhabit' (Roberts 2001: 195). Roberts argues that the perception of relative inequality may be more common *within* classes than *across* them, and that it is levels of abso-lute mobility which loom largest in people's minds:

> Very few if any people live in neighbourhoods which are microcosms of the national structure. Very few children attend schools where children from different social class backgrounds are present in the same proportions as in the national population. The classes tend to live, and to have their children educated, separately, not necessarily consciously and deliberately, but because primary schools in particular tend to have local catchment areas, certainly in towns and cities. People are better able to compare, and are more likely to be conscious of, the differences between how they themselves have fared in life and the achievements of others from the same neighbour-hoods and schools, than how their entire classes' achievements compare with those of other classes.
>
> (Roberts 2001: 199)

The problem is that the study of what people think about mobility is much less developed than the analysis of the volume and rate of mobility flows. Conventional approaches to mobility make 'a strong analytical distinction between social mobility processes and what people themselves actually think about mobility. The implication is that mobility processes can be analysed without consideration of how people reflect on or think about mobility' (Savage 1997: 318). For critics like Savage, this is an untenable separation, since mobility is as much about what people think about their mobility as it is about their objective prospects (Savage 2000: 73).

The little research that does exist on subjective perceptions of mobility indi-cates that the subjects of social movement do not always see their experience in the same way as mobility analysts. The Oxford Mobility Study investigated subjective perceptions amongst a sub-sample and found 'a very wide awareness of having been socially mobile in one way or another, including among those men whom we would categorise as being stable in class position' (Goldthorpe *et al.* 1980: 247). Men in the same class category as their fathers still felt that they had been mobile, and even those who did not feel that they had moved occupational level, felt 'mobile in an intergenerational perspective: that is, in enjoying, relative to their fathers, greatly improved pay and conditions of employ-ment and in general a much higher standard of living' (1980: 225). There was no distinction between mobility 'within a class' from mobility 'across classes', and 'the distinction between inter- and intra-occupational movement was largely obliterated within a "career" perspective' (1980: 228).

Since individuals tend to conflate general improvements in living standards, career mobility and intergenerational mobility, the perception of movement is much greater than the objective measurements of class analysis. A further issue is that the total *amount* of mobility in a society affects the *meaning* of any individual movement. Experiencing social movement when large numbers of people are moving alongside you is very different from experiencing social movement as an isolated individual. Goldthorpe makes this point in relation to the easy way in which the upwardly mobile assimilated into their new class (discussed in Chapter 10). He argues that one of the reasons for this easy transition was that, because so many people had moved into the class, their experience was the majority one. Over two-thirds of the service class had started off in lower classes so, even if the established middle class were standoffish, the upwardly mobile could 'provide *each other* with ample possibilities for relations of sociability' (Goldthorpe *et al.* 1980: 200). In a mobile society

> the problem of assimilation facing the mobile person is far less severe than in societies in which such rates are low. It is not, or not necessarily, a problem of gaining acceptance, as a conspicuous outsider, into established social circles but rather, one may suppose, a problem not essentially different from that facing the stable individual – that is to say, one of forming relationships with, so to speak, his own kind, whom he can find about him in some number.
>
> (Goldthorpe *et al.* 1980: 200)

However, large amounts of social movement – through routine work-life career trajectories, absolute upward mobility or the expansion of opportunities – are a *standard feature* of modern societies. Immobility, rather than mobility, is the more unusual experience in modern life, and large numbers of people believe that they have experienced social movement of some kind. In the face of such movement class analysts have increasingly turned to relative mobility as evidence of the continuity of structural disadvantage. However, if participants cannot tell the difference between absolute and relative inequality, and feel that they themselves have experienced some form of mobility, then there is a serious question as to whether relative disadvantage is perceived or experienced as inequality. The sheer amount of social movement creates difficulty for class analysis, and has led to a declining emphasis on class formation in class theory because, in the conventional approach, class formation is only seen to emerge out of 'stasis and continuity'. The problem, as Savage notes, is that

> mobility and class formation are defined in terms of opposition. Rather than class formation being itself a dynamic process, involving a particular way of linking pasts, present and futures, it is posited as being based on a static attachment to fixed positions.
>
> (Savage 2000: 83–84)

Movement as structure?

Movement is so widespread, that any view of stratification as the straightforward inheritance of social location must be rejected. Large numbers of individuals have seen their positions improve in relation to their parents. In addition, this movement has occurred within the context of rising standards of living, and more affluent consumption-based lifestyles. But whilst differential patterns of movement clearly do amount to substantial and enduring inequality, because this consists of unequal patterns of movement (rather than in attachment to fixed and unequal positions), there is a question of how such inequalities are perceived by the people concerned. Because the ubiquity of movement inevitably changes the meaning of mobility, some commentators argue that rather than focusing on *movement within* a structure of inequality, we should instead look at how standard patterns of movement constitute the structure of inequality.

Savage, for example, argues that class identities are formed by common patterns of movement, rather than through continuity of position, suggesting that, in particular, middle-class formation 'involves a dynamic relation to time, in which middle-class people expect prospective rewards, and in which work lives are embedded around ideas of individual progress, and advancement in the longer term (often . . . around the narrative of "career")' (2000: 83–84). However, there is a broader question of work-life trajectories, because standard routes of work-life movement occur at *every level* of the labour market:

> usually short-range, and along a limited number of main routes. People who start their working lives as apprentices become skilled workers. Others who are not formally trained become informally recognised as skilled. Some manual workers are promoted to supervisory and even management posts. [. . .] Another common career is from lower-level office and sales jobs into the middle class proper. Another is from the lower to the higher grades within the middle class. A further type of movement is from all other kinds of occupations into self-employment.
>
> (Roberts 2001: 208)

Work-life movement is very common, and often shifts individuals into slightly better occupations, even if the movement is only short-range. These patterns are complicated by gender, since women's working patterns do not always follow the male 'linear' career of continuous, rising labour-market position, and even in female professions low-status truncated career 'niches' have developed which show continuity of occupational position rather than progression (Crompton and Sanderson 1990). However, lifecourse shifts mean that it is common for women to experience 'both upward and downward mobility, and . . . continuity of status, let alone monotonic career progression, is *not* the typical experience of women. *Our fundamental conception of mobility should therefore be not a move from one origin to one destination, but a profile*' (Payne and Abbott 1990: 165).

Work-life movement, of some kind, is so frequent that we need to take this into account when we consider people's overall occupational position. Such movements affect the meaning of 'snap-shot' occupational locations, since people at very different career stages are frequently found in the same jobs. But, of course, individuals travelling on different work-life trajectories are likely to react to the *same* labour-market conditions in very different ways. A student doing temporary work in a factory is likely to see the pay and conditions in a different light to someone working there for 20 years. How individuals react to the *same* working conditions or level of pay is likely to differ according to their wider social circumstances – their lifecourse stage and social obligations, the family relationships they are engaged in, their social background, past experience and their expectations of the future. But this means we need to see how jobs fit into an overall sequence: 'People's social location does not simply reflect their current experience. Their past, and even their anticipated future, experience also plays a critical part' (Prandy and Bottero 2000a: 271).

In comparing the social positions of parents and children it is better to compare entire career *trajectories* rather than taking snap-shots at single moments in time (which may come at different points in the employment routes of parent and child). This approach recognises the way in which standard patterns of movement *within* generations need to be taken account of when we compare movement *across* generations. However:

> In comparing the occupations of two individuals at different points in time, therefore, we also have to consider the network of social relationships – the influence of past history and future prospects – in which occupations are embedded and which give them influence and meaning. Focussing on work life trajectory is one aspect of a *social interaction* approach to stratification. Social class categorisations, which tend to abstract the individual from his or her social relationships and to classify them solely in terms of current economic location, cannot readily accommodate such an approach.
>
> (Prandy and Bottero 2000a: 266)

Savage argues 'the high degree of mobility should be at the heart of our understanding of class identities and class formation' (2000: 82). However, movement is so common that we have to recognise that it shapes not only class identities, but also the structure of inequality itself. Indeed one argument is that the pattern of (unequal) social movement *is* the structure of inequality.

Conventionally, the structure of inequality has been understood as the (unequal) relations between static labour-market positions, with mobility conceived as movement *within* the structure. But as a number of commentators have noted (Blackburn and Prandy 1997; Savage 2000) there is a problem in making a sharp distinction between the class structure and the individuals who move (or stay still) within it.

> It is necessary to recognise that occupational careers are not simply mobility between fixed points; they are part of a self-reproducing structure. In order for a social structure to survive there must be constant movement to replace people as they move on. [. . .] Thus careers are intra-generational mobility *and* they are part of the reproduction of occupationally based inequality.
>
> (Blackburn and Prandy 1997: 499)

Movement does not just occur within a structure: it helps to shape and define the locations within the structure, so that movement needs to be understood 'as an aspect of structure' (Blackburn and Prandy 1997: 501). But if the structure of inequality is itself composed of (patterned) social movement, how can we measure or assess movement within it?

This certainly makes the analysis of movement more difficult. Indeed, it raises a fundamental question about what *sorts* of movement constitute 'mobility'. What does it actually mean to be 'socially mobile'? The notion of upward mobility contains the idea that it represents the triumph of individual achievement over structural constraints. Liberal, status-attainment approaches see high levels of mobility as the ability of individuals to escape their social origins, but class approaches also see mobility across class categories as a significant shift in social location. Yet as soon as we acknowledge that certain sorts of movement are built into the labour market we have to recognise that not all movement is 'mobility' in this sense.

Take career mobility, which is not just movement *within* the labour market, as upward movement is a structured feature *of the labour-market itself.* The term 'career' refers to both an individual employment trajectory, but also to a sequence of linked jobs in the labour market. In one sense, to have a career is to experience individual success. But, in another sense, movement is structured into occupations themselves. It is routine and typical for junior doctors, for example, to advance to consultancy positions or their own practices. Many junior management jobs carry the expectation that the incumbents not only can, but *should*, rise to more senior positions. Certain sorts of clerical and sales jobs are widely seen as the first rung on the ladder of managerial careers. Not everyone will progress along these common routes, but – depending on the typicality of the route – it is the people who *do not progress* who stand out (as 'under-achievers'), whereas the people who do progress are simply seen as following the path laid out for them. On such routes, movement up is unremarkable and expected, and amounts to a continuation of social position rather than a shift in circumstances.

Take an individual whose work-life progresses from a start as an apprentice bricklayer to becoming a builder, owning a business employing several workers. This route – to self-employment and small-business ownership – is quite a common transition in craft trades, although in conventional class categorisations it is seen as mobility (from the manual to the intermediate class). It is also common for such transitions to be related to family firms, so that the father of our bricklayer may have made the same transition – from bricky to builder – himself. In that case, of course, our individual will have experienced upward work-life *mobility* but will have stayed intergenerationally *immobile*, having the same work-life trajectory as his father. Similar transitions occur in family shops, where children inheriting the family business transit from shop assistant to shop owner, in the same way as their parents. In such examples, parent and child occupy essentially the same social position, but to correctly identify this we have to compare their whole work-life trajectories, in which both follow the same route. So work-life movement may represent a very real improvement in labour-market conditions, but it could be argued that this work-life mobility is more apparent than real. If work-life mobility brings about the *inheritance* of the parents' social position, then social movement is entirely consistent with the *reproduction* of position in a structure of social inequality. In the same way, it is very common for working mothers to experience a period of downward occupational mobility mid-career; however, this period may not fully represent their social location:

> It is important to remember that women employed over their family formation period, or shortly after returning to work, are likely to be in jobs which under-represent their potential and their lifetime career preferences. That they may have experienced temporary downward social mobility will be important in studies concerned with current household income, poverty, lifestyle and consumption patterns. However, such mobility will probably not be important in the socialization process, as operated through the family, or its property transmission over generations etc.
>
> (Dex 1990: 136)

So 'any adequate conception of structure must also include the processes of movement, which have to be seen as part of the reproduction of the structure of inequality' (Blackburn and Prandy 1997: 491).

Relative position versus absolute location

It is also important to remember that social movement affects the meaning of structural locations, because shifts in the pattern of movement between occupation positions changes the individual *experience of occupying those positions* (regardless of whether or not the occupants are mobile).

> If we follow the usual practice of defining classes by constant sets of occupations we are faced with a steady drift upwards in the class structure; the top class has been growing and the bottom one shrinking. [. . .] However, it is questionable whether treating class as fixed sets of occupations is theoretically meaningful. At the very least the social meaning of membership of a greatly enlarged top class must be different. More fundamentally, with the general upward movement of class membership there cannot be a corresponding rise in the relative social advantage bestowed by higher class membership.
>
> (Blackburn and Jarman 1993: 203–204)

As occupations at the top of the hierarchy expand in numbers they also lose their exclusiveness, and as those at the bottom of the hierarchy contract, they become relatively more disadvantaged. To be a manual worker at the beginning of the twentieth century was to hold a position shared by three-quarters of the population, by the end of the century, manual workers were in a minority, with nearly two-thirds of workers in more privileged jobs. The reverse holds for professional and managerial jobs. There are important differences, therefore, in being in the 'working class' or 'service class', between then and now, because the *relative (dis)advantage* of the positions has changed. This has important consequences for how we measure social mobility over time.

> The idea of indexing a person's origin and destination by occupation is weakened if the *meaning* of being, say, a manual worker is not the same at origin and destination. Historical comparisons become unreliable. Second, the significance of lack of upward mobility is lessened: to remain in the same relative position is still to experience improvements in the quality of life. Arguments about class formation and the growth of class consciousness based on a sense of disadvantage . . . seem to be less powerful.
>
> (Payne 1992: 220)

The children of manual workers may be in a very different social position to their parents, even if they are in manual work themselves, because proportional shifts in occupational distributions (the upward movement of *other people*) affect the social meaning of staying still. It is not enough to identify that someone has stayed in the same class 'box', because the meaning of the box itself is not fixed, and depends upon movement within the overall structure.

A related point is made by Bourdieu, who stresses that occupational mobility does not necessarily imply social mobility. For:

> the reproduction of the social structure may, in certain conditions, demand very little 'occupational heredity'. This is true whenever agents can only maintain their position in the social structure by means of a shift into a new condition (e.g. the shift from small landowner to junior civil servant, or from small craftsman to office worker or commercial employee).
>
> (Bourdieu 1984 [1979]: 131)

Groups can increase their standard of living yet remain in the same relative position within the social hierarchy, so that 'the pecking order . . . remains unchanged' (Swartz 1997: 183). However, as Swartz notes:

> It is one thing to dismiss the uncritical use of occupational categories in mobility tables and to counsel caution in determining the proper sociological significance in changing occupational titles, but quite another to offer a plausible empirical test of just what change in social structure might look like.
>
> (Swartz 1997: 184)

Because large amounts of intergenerational mobility change the meaning of labour-market categories, any comparison of the social position of different generations is potentially misleading if we focus on labour-market criteria alone. Conventional mobility analysis recognises the problem posed by the general expansion of opportunities but attempts to factor it out by focusing on social fluidity (in effect holding structural change constant). However, another way around this is to look at relative advantage more directly.

The social interaction scales of the Cambridge Stratification Group produce a hierarchical ordering of occupations through their relations of social distance. They look at the social location of the typical friends or marriage connections of the people in a job, and so order occupations by their relative social position. This means that social interaction scales should be more sensitive to shifts in the social meaning of occupations (through composition changes, or expanding opportunities) than schemes which class occupations on labour-market criteria alone. If the relative advantage of an occupation changes, we would expect this to be reflected in the typical social relationships of the people in the occupation. For example, if we think the social meaning of being a 'clerk' changed from the nineteenth to the twentieth century (because so many more people became clerks), we would expect the social associates of 'clerks' also to have changed. In fact, social interaction scales do show 'clerks' slipping slightly down the social order over the course of the nineteenth century (Prandy and Bottero 2000a; Bottero and Prandy 2001), which corresponds well with the declining exclusivity of the job.

Social interaction distance scales are continuous measures of the relative advantage of finely differentiated occupations. Instead of analysing mobility flows between class categories they instead look at the extent to which relative social position within a hierarchy of advantage is passed on (or not) from generation to generation.

What do social interaction scales (which measure relative social position) tell us about the inheritance of social position over time? The study which looks at the longest time period is Ken Prandy's research on the social reproduction of advantage, comparing (male) birth cohorts from 1790 to 1909 (Prandy and Bottero 2000a, b). This study found quite a high degree of stability in relative social position throughout the period, so that despite major changes in the opportunity structure (the decline in the importance of agriculture, landed property and 'family' firms; the rise of education, bureaucratic careers, white-collar employment and credentialism), 'family influence on social position has remained remarkably buoyant in the face of these changes' (Prandy and Bottero 2000a: 276). However, there was 'an extremely slow shift towards a weakening of family influence. This process appears to have accelerated for those born in the last quarter of the nineteenth century, a period of both educational reform and major change in Britain's industrial organisation' (Prandy and Bottero 2000a: 265). How do these findings of very slow decline in family influence on social position square with the findings of conventional class analysis?

As we have seen, studies of relative class mobility rates have usually argued for 'constant social fluidity', that is, continuity in the relative chances of success. There have been studies which disagreed with this view, which have pointed to 'a world wide secular trend towards increased social openness' (Ganzeboom *et al.* 1989: 44). However, it is usually argued that the rate of change is extremely slow, showing 'a negligible amount in the short run (and therefore difficult to estimate over short periods)' (Ganzeboom *et al.* 1989: 45). So the diagnosis of constant social fluidity partly arises from the *time-scale* used to study the process of change (Prandy *et al.* 2003a). Snap-shot surveys reveal little change because the process of change is so slow. Therefore it is necessary to use a longer-time frame to explore the process. However, because of long-term shifts in the meaning of occupational categories, to compare social location over the long term, it is necessary to focus on social reproduction (the inheritance, or not, of relative position within the social hierarchy) rather than social mobility (the movement between fixed categories). Pooling their historical data with large-scale, contemporary data sets, Prandy and colleagues (2003a, b) analysed inheritance of (relative) social position in Britain over a two-century period and found a trend of substantially decreasing social reproduction, but at such a 'glacial' rate that the full extent of change only becomes apparent by taking a very long-term perspective (Prandy *et al.* 2003a). They concluded that there has been a significant long-term reduction in the extent to which children's social position is influenced by that of their family; however, from generation to generation, the rate of change has been funereal (Prandy *et al.* 2003a, b).

Conclusion

Since stratification analysis is concerned with the relatively stable nature of inequalities in social relationships, the study of social mobility – the movement between unequal social positions – has been taken as a crucial test of the enduring nature of inequality. The more mobility there is, the less durable inequality seems. Yet western industrial societies have been characterised by extensive social change, forcing very high levels of absolute social mobility. The conclusion of liberal theorists is that society has become more mobile, and so more open. For them, more absolute mobility means less persistent inequality. This argument has been rejected by class theorists, who point out that inequality persists between generations even in the face of large amounts of movement. In insisting on the stability of inequality, class theorists have increasingly factored out structural change, and moved towards the analysis of differential rates of access to opportunities, rather than the consideration of movement itself. But this ignores one of the more interesting aspects of enduring inequality, namely how it is bound up in change and movement, since it is clear that inequality is as much reproduced through routine (and unequal) patterns of movement, as it is through stasis.

There have been questions as to whether these trends in movement will continue, with the suggestion that a slowing in the expansion of professional and managerial jobs has resulted in lower levels of absolute mobility (Payne and Roberts 2002). This may lead to greater intergenerational continuity in the future (Noble 2000). However, studies of very long-term social change indicate that family influences on social position show a steadily weakening influence over time (Prandy *et al.* 2003).

Since the long-term evidence is that social movement is a common and typical feature of social experience in modern society, we must ask how this relates to how we conceive inequality. The problem is that conventional theories of inequality are rather poorly placed to address social movement on this scale. The crux of the problem of social mobility is that large amounts of social movement appear to be a stable feature of the structure of inequality, with routine patterns of movement an important element in how patterns of inequality are reproduced over time. Because social movement is so common it has meant that large numbers of individuals have seen their positions improve in relation to their parents, amid rising standards of living. Class differentials are still in evidence, but this is rather complexly manifested in *relative* access to opportunities.

This suggests that there are no clear-cut social boundaries in the stratification order. For although differential patterns of movement do amount to substantial inequality, because this consists of unequal patterns of movement (rather than in attachment to fixed and unequal positions), there is a question of how such inequalities are perceived by the people concerned. Once stratification is conceived as a structuring of movement (rather than movement within a structure), there are major questions about how social distance creates boundaries between groups, and why people draw the lines that they do, in some places and not others.

13 'Us' and 'them'

Stratification researchers have long sought to discover material social gulfs – the gaps in people's social relations and experience – which might explain the fissures in people's perceptions of each other. As Chapters 10 and 12 show, the problem is that there do not seem to be *sharp breaks* in the relations, lifestyles, or even in the social prospects of unequal groups. What we find instead are relative *degrees* of inequality: differential, but overlapping, patterns of association; uneven chances of success; different rates of *relative* mobility. The inequality of lower-level groups consists not in their exclusion from the better educational and labour-market positions, but rather in lower rates of movement *into* them, amid generally high patterns of overall mobility. And although differential patterns of movement clearly do amount to substantial and enduring inequality, because they consist of unequal patterns of *movement* (rather than in attachment to fixed and unequal positions), there is a question of how such inequalities are perceived by the people concerned. Of course, finely shaded differences and relative inequalities, when summed up, amount to a massive gap in the opportunities, experiences and social relations of those at the top and the bottom of stratification hierarchies. But such distinctions are blurred by the finely graded nature of difference and inequality, and the substantial amount of movement in between.

Yet in their subjective identifications, people do draw sharp lines of demarcation – between insiders and outsiders, between 'us' and 'them'. How do such subjective boundaries relate to social experience? The search for social gulfs has often focused on the very rich or the poor, to see if living at the extremes of the stratification hierarchy creates different kinds of people, leading parallel lives disconnected from the rest of society. In such discussions, however, there has been a constant problem of establishing whether such groups are really different, or merely *perceived* to be different. The first section of the chapter, 'Looking for social gulfs', looks at the attempt to discover material social gulfs in this way, and the problems which have emerged in such accounts. The third section of the chapter, 'Drawing lines in the sand', explores how symbolic boundaries emerge across relatively fine difference in social experience. The overall question, therefore, is how well *perceptions* of difference map onto the *experience* of social differentiation.

Looking for social gulfs

The idea that the very poorest groups in society lie outside 'normal' social life is a clear attempt to discover a social gulf at the bottom of society. It arises from the perception of social 'disorganisation' in deprived neighbourhoods, which exhibit high rates of illegitimacy, broken families, disorder and crime, and was originally discussed in relationship to African-American ghettoisation. Here racial residential segregation was said to create such high spatial concentrations of poverty that 'a significant share of black America is condemned to experience a social environment where poverty and joblessness are the norm, where most families are on welfare, where educational failure prevails, and where social and physical deterioration abound' (Massey and Denton 1993: 2).

The notion that the poor behave differently from the rest of society draws upon an axiom of stratification analysis, the idea that unequally placed individuals also have different cultural behaviours. But is this a cause or consequence of poverty? One controversial position argues that poverty results from dysfunctional values (including poor commitment to paid work, a willingness to be dependent on welfare, criminality, 'broken' and fatherless families, illegitimacy and teenage pregnancy) (Murray 1984). This is a classic 'us' and 'them' dichotomy, in which the behaviour of the 'underclass' sets it apart from the rest of 'respectable', hard-working society.

Others are sceptical of the very idea of a distinct underclass, because of the lack of permanence, inter-generational continuity and homogeneity amongst those who experience deprivation (Bagguley and Mann 1992; Morris 1994). In Britain, groups falling into poverty include the long-term unemployed, the elderly, 'unwed' teenage mothers, divorced and separated mothers; with situations so disparate that the notion of a distinct 'underclass' is difficult to sustain. Many fall into poverty as part of lifecourse changes (retirement, unemployment, divorce), and are groups who, at earlier stages of their lives, would have been part of 'mainstream' society. For writers within the class tradition, the key issue is the way in which capitalist economies create large numbers of low-wage, poorly skilled, insecure workers who are in danger of falling into poverty, depending on the ebb and flow of wider economic conditions. In highly unequal labour markets there is always someone at the bottom, but this does not mean that the lowest brick is any different from the other bricks in the pile. The 'underclass' are simply elements of the working class who have been hit by adverse lifecourse events or economic recession. For some writers, the so-called cultural distinctiveness of the 'underclass' is irrelevant because, as past experience of 'outsider' groups shows, such 'outcasts' have been easily reabsorbed when labour-market conditions have improved (Bagguley and Mann 1992).

However, whilst many are critical of the general claim that the poor are a distinct *group* set apart from the rest of society, others suggest that highly deprived conditions in particular localities can create social gulfs for certain *sections* of the poor. These accounts argue that the so-called 'disorganised' social relations of the 'ghetto poor' *result* from structural inequality, from the way economic restructuring and middle-class flight, or racist exclusion and segrega-tion, create neighbourhoods with few resources or opportunities (Wilson 1991; Massey and Denton 1993). However, such accounts also contain the idea that cultural adaptations to poverty may themselves become a constraint on prospects, creating social conditions which limit the chances of successive generations. Wilson, for example, argues that high-poverty neighbourhoods can adversely shape the aspirations of 'youngsters who grow up in households without a steady breadwinner and in neighbourhoods that are not organised around work – in other words a milieu in which one is more exposed to the less disciplined habits associated with casual or less frequent work' (Wilson 1991: 10). However, authors are also careful to claim that such differences that *do* arise are simply the result of ordinary individuals responding to intolerable circumstances:

> Ghetto dwellers are not a distinctive breed of men and women in need of a special denomination; they are ordinary people trying to make a living and to improve their lot as best they can under the unusually oppressive and depressed circumstances imposed upon them . . . not part of a separate group somehow severed from the rest of society, as many advocates of the 'underclass' thesis would have us believe. They belong, rather, to unskilled and socially disqualified fractions of the black working class, if only by virtue of the multifarious kinship and marital links, social ties, cultural connections, and institutional processes that cut across the alleged divide between them and the rest of the Afro-American community.
>
> (Wacquant 1994: 237)

These are analyses of *social exclusion*, which place a greater emphasis on the processes by which particular groups are disadvantaged and excluded by the society in which they live.

Social exclusion and neighbourhood effects

The notion of social exclusion originated with Townsend's demonstration that relative poverty affects social participation. The poor are socially excluded if they cannot obtain

> the conditions of life – that is, the diets, amenities, standards and services – which allow them to play the roles, participate in the relationships and follow customary behaviour which is expected of them by virtue of their membership of society.
>
> (Townsend 1993: 36)

The advantage of such a perspective is the way it links material inequality to social and cultural participation and citizenship. However, it has been argued that more recent approaches have shifted 'the conceptualisation of poverty from ex-treme class inequality and lack of resources in the Townsendian tradition . . . to a broader insider-outsider problematique' (Andersen 1999: 376–377). So the concept of social exclusion 'may become a euphemism for stigmatized, isolated or scapegoated groups' (Silver 1994: 572), again shifting the emphasis from the *processes* of inclusion/exclusion to focus on the characteristics of the excluded.

Social-exclusion analysis has increasingly focused on excluded neighbourhoods, because 'spatial exclusion is the most visible and evident form of exclusion' (Byrne 1999: 110). But this directs attention back to cultural differences because

> Spatial concentration of levels in the social hierarchy generates spatially distinctive cultural forms, especially when spatial concentration means that there is little social contact among the levels of the social order. If 'cultures of poverty' do exist, spatial concentration is a key element in their generation.
>
> (Byrne 1999: 111)

For writers like Wilson 'The issue is not simply that the . . . ghetto poor have a marginal position in the labour market similar to that of other disadvantaged groups, it is also that their economic position is uniquely reinforced by their social milieu' (Wilson 1991: 12). He rejects 'simplistic either/or notions of culture and social structure' (Wilson 1992: 652), in explanations of poverty, arguing that structure and culture must be seen as inter-linked.

For Wilson, living in highly segregated neighbourhoods with dense concentrations of poverty (over 40 per cent of the area poor) results in *social isolation* for the most deprived African-Americans, not only from white America, but also from middle- and working-class black households, who once operated as a 'social buffer' for the poor (Wilson 1992: 641).

> Social isolation deprives residents of inner-city neighbourhoods, not only of resources and conventional job models, whose former presence buffered the effects of neighbourhood joblessness, but also of the kind of cultural learning from mainstream social networks that facilitates social and economic advancement in modern industrial society. The lack of neighbourhood material resources, the relative absence of conventional role models, and the circumscribed cultural learning produce outcomes, or concentrate effects, that restrict social mobility. Some of these outcomes are structural (lack of labor force attachment and access to informal job networks), and some are social-psychological (negative social dispositions, limited aspirations, and casual work habits).
>
> (Wilson 1992: 642)

The suggestion is that ghetto residents become trapped in poverty, because neighbourhood concentration reinforces social exclusion. This perspective suggests that there are additional disadvantages to the spatial concentration of poverty – *neighbourhood effects* – which disadvantage people living in high-poverty neighbourhoods over and above their individual economic situation. But does being poor in an area where most of your neighbours are *also* poor have a worse effect on your prospects than being poor in a more mixed-income neighbourhood?

The idea of 'neighbourhood effects' is supported by a number of empirical studies, although exactly how such effects work is still imperfectly understood (Bauder 2002; Corcoran 1995), with both cultural and instrumental mechanisms suggested (Small and Newman 2001). Socialisation models argue that the concentration of poverty affects residents through peer-group influences spreading anti-social behaviour and through the lack of positive neighbourhood role-models. The idea is that 'neighbourhood effects will be small until the neighbourhood has tipped past the critical point for an epidemic' (Corcoran 1995: 247). Instrumental models focus on how poor neighbourhoods lack key community resources, which affects individual agency. In the USA, for example, decentralised service provision hits high-poverty neighbourhoods particularly hard, because the local tax-base in such areas is too small to adequately support the area schools and community welfare facilities, and the demand for such services is particularly high. Similarly, the network isolation model 'argues that being in poor, or extensively unemployed, neighbourhoods will disconnect individuals from social networks of employed people, making it difficult for them to obtain information about job opportunities' (Small and Newman 2001: 33).

However, it is often suggested that network isolation also limits access to moral or cultural examples, so cultural and material factors intertwine. Dilapidated physical infrastructure is said to further destabilise the cohesion of deprived communities. The 'broken windows' hypothesis argues accumulating physical neglect can 'tip' a community into lower social controls:

> vandalism can occur anywhere once communal barriers – the sense of mutual regard and the obligations of civility – are lowered by actions that seem to signal that 'no one cares'. [. . .] A piece of property is abandoned, weeds grow up, a window is smashed. Adults stop scolding rowdy children; the children, emboldened, become more rowdy. Families move out, unattached adults move in. Teenagers gather in front of the corner store. The merchant asks them to move; they refuse. Fights occur. Litter accumulates. People start drinking in front of the grocery; in time, an inebriate slumps to the sidewalk and is allowed to sleep it off. [. . .] Though it is not inevitable, it is more likely that here, rather than in places where people are confident they can regulate public behaviour by informal controls, drugs will change hands, prostitutes will solicit, and cars will be stripped.
>
> (Wilson and Kelling 1982: 31, 32)

The idea is that deprived communities have low social cohesion, because high concentrations of poverty erode social capital, making it harder to combat community problems as they arise. Furthermore, this is said to affect the individual's sense of empowerment:

> Residents who lack a sense of control over their living environment and day-to-day security, and who lose trust in others also often lack confidence in their ability to control other aspects of their lives, such as job prospects or housing choices. . . . A sense of powerlessness and alienation can develop, and is evidenced by high levels of depression, low levels of take-up of support services, and the need for confidence building and support for people who do follow education or training programmes.
>
> (Lupton and Power 2002: 135)

These models suggest that poor neighbourhoods 'lack the necessary qualities of self-help, mutuality and trust which could assist in their regeneration – and this, in part, explains, and is a cumulative product of, their decline' (Forrest and Kearns 2001: 2139).

However, a note of caution is required. During the high US unemployment of the 1980s, it was argued that a culture of low 'self-efficacy' amongst the black poor made it harder for them to seize labour-market opportunities (Wilson 1991). But the employment rate of black men dramatically improved in the 1990s when labour-market conditions shifted, casting doubt on the role of low self-efficacy and neighbourhood 'cultural traits' in the reproduction of disadvantage (Small and Newman 2001: 38). Furthermore, simply 'to show that there are area or neighbourhood differences is not the same as showing that there are neighbourhood effects' (Buck 2001: 2252) since critics suggest that neighbourhood effects are 'mostly the result of the "sum of individual differences" among residents, rather than unique neighbourhood-based norms, group behaviour and local "emergent properties"' (Bauder 2002: 87).

The evidence is mixed. Housing relocation programmes (such as the Gatreaux programme in the USA, which offers vouchers for housing relocation) appear to show that moving children into low-poverty areas means they are less likely to display 'problem' behaviours (Sampson *et al.* 2002). However:

> the most one can conclude . . . is that growing up in 'bad' neighbourhoods is bad for children, but we don't know what it is about bad neighbourhoods that matters. It could be neighbourhood poverty, neighbourhood welfare use, an inadequate tax base, poor public services, neighbourhood family structure, absence of middle-class role models, or a host of other possibilities.
>
> (Corcoran 1995: 258)

In the UK, there is evidence that people living in deprived areas have less chance of getting a job, of leaving poverty (and a greater risk of re-entering poverty) than people in non-deprived areas, even when controlling for individual characteristics. However, none of the effects are very large, and individual characteristics are more important (Buck 2001: 2272).

We therefore need to distinguish between excluded neighbourhoods and the people who live within them:

It is much easier to identify 'excluded (and excluding) spaces', the consequences of the transition of cities to a post-industrial status . . . a sharp and
clear divide which corresponds exactly with popular conceptions. However,
we have to remember that people move in space as well as time. Those who
live in the peripheral estates of the Red Belt of Paris or the outer estates of
Glasgow or Sunderland in the UK are clearly living in excluded spaces, but
the degree of movement into and out of these places is very considerable.

(Byrne 1999: 127–128)

As Byrne notes, there is high residential turnover in deprived areas, and 'if
people can get on they will get out' (1999: 8), partly because of the stigmatisation
of the people who live in such areas.

In Britain, the analysis of multiple dimensions of social inclusion (social
participation across the spheres of consumption, production, political engagement and social integration) indicates that the evidence

> does not fit easily with the idea of an underclass, cut off from mainstream
> society. Rather, inclusion and exclusion are found to be on a continuum, both
> across dimensions of exclusion and by duration. If anything, the results draw
> attention to the possibility of an 'overclass' – those who never dip below an
> exclusion threshold . . . and their role in protecting a privileged position.
>
> (Burchardt et al. 2002: 42)

> Social exclusion is often equated with permanent unemployment, but the
> reality is that permanent unemployment is a relatively uncommon condition
> in contrast with the phenomenon of chômage d'exclusion, the cycling from un-
> employment to poorly paid work, whether within the regular economy or the
> irregular economy, and back, with an equal cycling between full dependency
> on state benefits and dependency on . . . supplements to low incomes.
>
> (Byrne 1999: 127)

The same pattern emerges in relation to poverty. Longitudinal data-sets,
tracing people's fate over the lifecourse, indicate more persistent poverty than
'snapshots' of cross-sectional data (Corcoran 1995). Rather than 'a picture of a
mass of people permanently poor, there is both considerable movement in and
out of the population in poverty'; however, 'while for many this is a once-off
event, many who escape do not move far from poverty, and among those who
are poor, there is a group who experience repeated and persistent poverty'
(Burgess and Popper 2002: 51, 61). The picture is one of accumulating disadvantage over the lifecourse, so that the experience of inequality and exclusion
becomes harder to shake off. The fate of the poor is not fixed, however, even
amongst the most disadvantaged. Corcoran (1995) examined the intergenerational consequences of growing up poor in the USA and found considerable
continuity of disadvantage: black children raised in poor families were 2.5 times
more likely to be poor in early adulthood than black children raised in non-poor

families, and white children raised in poor families were 7.5 times more likely to be poor as adults than white children raised in non-poor families. But there was also considerable mobility – less than one in four black children and one in ten white children remained poor in early adulthood (Corcoran 1995: 249–250).

Even looking at the situation of the very poorest, although we can see patterns of social exclusion and isolation, and the accumulation of disadvantage, this still does not amount to a culturally or socially distinct 'underclass'. There are substantial social and cultural links between the poor and more 'respectable' groups above them in the hierarchy, because 'the poor' are, in fact, individuals who move between these situations. The 'poor' are not a permanent 'underclass', but rather those who – over their lifetimes – are more likely to fall into poverty. Poverty is an isolating experience of accumulating disadvantage, but 'the poor' are still not a distinct group. Rather the disadvantage of the poor consists of greater risks of poverty over the lifetime, in which those who experience poverty as children are more likely to cycle in and out of poverty as adults, and between poorly paid employment and unemployment. Again, it is the higher relative risk of experiencing spells of poverty which is the nature of the disadvantage, rather than fixed attachment to an excluded group or location.

Drawing lines in the sand

Yet in their subjective identifications, people do draw sharp lines of demarcation – between insiders and outsiders, 'us' and 'them' – often across minor differences in social experience, so that such subjective boundaries and divisions often appear arbitrary. Indeed, in looking at subjective identifications many analysts have stressed the arbitrary, shifting and fluid nature of constructions of identity and difference, arguing that such distinctions are primarily symbolic, detached from 'structure', and unanchored to material social relations. However, the question then arises that – if we cannot easily map subjective 'groups' onto distinct breaks in social relations and experience – how is it that perceptions and discourses of polarised divisions and social gulfs emerge?

Certainly the consequences of such sharp symbolic demarcations are highly significant. For example, a key issue of poverty is not necessarily any inherent cultural difference in the inhabitants of deprived neighbourhoods, but rather that they are *perceived* to be different. As Harold Bauder argues, 'Negative stereotypes of poor neighbourhoods have existed long before neighbourhood effects studies emerged' (2002: 88) and stereotypical perceptions of the difference and deficiencies of deprived communities may be as much of a factor in constraining residents as any inherent cultural differences of the neighbourhood. Living in the 'wrong' area can disadvantage job seekers ('postcode discrimination') but this is often because of employers' cultural discrimination against stigmatised residential areas. Similarly, the success of relocation programmes in changing the behavioural, education and labour-market outcomes of children from deprived neighbourhoods may be because they 'experience less cultural discrimination in the school system, the labour market and other institutions' (Bauder 2002: 89).

It has been argued that there has been an undue focus on the supposed cultural difference of deprived communities, which are only analysed in terms of their deficiencies as 'disorganised' formations. As a result, there is a *'tendency to exoticize the ghetto* and its residents, that is, to highlight the most extreme and unusual aspects of ghetto life as seen from outside and above' (Wacquant 1997: 342). However, such stereotypical, stigmatising depictions are widespread in the *public perception* of deprived neighbourhoods, and are an important part of the everyday processes by which the urban poor are excluded and disadvantaged. As Lawson and Wilson note:

> the most significant welfare state backlash in this period has occurred, not where social spending is highest, but in countries like the United States where there has been a more marked 'us/them' divide in social policy between programs for the broad middle mass in society and programs for the poor. . . . To many middle Americans, the nation's poorest citizens had come to be virtually synonymous with a 'welfare class' posing a growing threat to the public peace and to dominant American norms.
>
> (Lawson and Wilson 1995: 702, 703)

In fact, *fears* of underclass crime and urban anarchy have led to a different sort of spatial separation, in which the rich(er) barricade themselves off from the disorderly 'others' of popular perception, so that 'the other, often overlooked side in the socio-spatial polarisation process is the affluent, gated communities' (Andersen 1999: 376). In America a growth in gated communities – housing developments which are highly socially selective by income (and, in practice, by race) – offer high security, walled residential environments protected by security staff, electronic surveillance and 'rapid response' units. In such environments 'the predominantly white upper middle-class residents can turn their backs on the growing social and economic problems of the ethnically diverse central cities and retreat behind the walls' (Hamnett 1999 : 251). This is a highly symbolic boundary dividing 'us' from 'them':

> Neighbourhoods have always been able to exclude some potential residents through discrimination and housing costs. With gates and walls, they can exclude not only undesirable new residents, but casual passers-by and the people from the neighbourhood next door. Gates are a visible sign of exclusion, an even stronger signal to those who already see themselves as excluded from the larger mainstream milieu.
>
> (Blakely and Snyder 1997: 153)

As Blakely and Snyder, note, gated communities do not in fact have lower crime levels, but the fear of crime and retreat from social 'others' is a significant form of symbolic separation, which has wider political and social consequences:

The significance of social isolation in all this is simply that the lack of empathy between the majority and socially isolated minorities makes it easier for ambitious politicians to advance their careers by demonising and ultimately dehumanising these minorities. . . . The social isolation of any group makes the incorporation of its interests into political programmes more problematic.

(Barry 2002: 25)

Symbolic demarcations between 'us' and 'them' therefore have important consequences for the fate of people who become assigned to such categories. But how do these sharp symbolic divisions, often drawn across fine differences in practical social relations, come about?

The social and the symbolic

Lamont and Molnar argue that we need to understand the role of symbolic resources 'in creating and maintaining, contesting, or even dissolving institution-alised social difference (e.g., class, gender, race, territorial inequality)' (2002: 169). They make a distinction between symbolic and social boundaries:

Symbolic boundaries are conceptual distinctions made by social actors to categorise objects, people, practices, and even time and space. They are tools by which individuals and groups struggle over and come to agree upon definitions of reality. . . . Symbolic boundaries also separate people into groups and generate feelings of similarity and group membership. . . . They are an essential medium through which people acquire status and monopol-ize resources. Social boundaries are objectified forms of social differences manifested in unequal access to and unequal distribution of resources (mater-ial and non-material) and social opportunities. They are also revealed in stable behavioural patterns of association, as manifested in connubiality and commensality.

(Lamont and Molnar 2002: 169)

This, of course, is another attempt to rethink the relationship between struc-ture and action, social relations and social identity, or the objective and subjective. In understanding symbolic boundaries ('us and them'), however, we need, as Bourdieu puts it, to establish the relations 'between the points occupied within that space and the points of view on that very space, which play a part in the reality and evolution of that space' (1985: 734). The older, now much derided, version of this relationship argued that social location *determined* subjec-tive identity, that symbolic boundaries followed on from social boundaries. However, as we have seen throughout this book, this model of the formation of subjective and symbolic divisions has increasingly been rejected by theorists who have pointed to the arbitrary and indeterminate nature of the relationship.

Take the problem of class identities. Despite widening material inequalities, class is no longer 'a major source of . . . identity and group belonging' (Savage

2000: 40). As Chapter 8 shows, people refuse to place themselves 'within' classes, disavow class identities, and are concerned to establish their own 'ordinariness'. The decline of explicit class identities has led to a curious situation where class relations express differentiation but not 'difference'. This has raised questions of whether social values have come 'unstuck' from material relations, leading some theorists to conclude that individualisation has resulted in the increasing free-floating nature of cultural identity. Similar claims have been made in relation to race and ethnicity, where racialised categories and identities have been seen as being based on essentially arbitrary and shifting lines of division.

A series of theorists have been uneasy with the notion that identities are unanchored to practical social relations, and have attempted to rethink the relations between differentiation and 'difference', between structure and action. For example, a newer generation of class theorists insists that class is still significant, but argues that it is *implicit* in social relations rather than in explicit self-identifications. Following Bourdieu's account of cultural distinction, it is argued that hierarchical position acts as a constraint on aspirations and tastes, social networks and resources, and that hierarchy is therefore an important element shaping social identity, in which the recognition of social divisions – or rather social distance – is embedded in *practice.*

However, in rebutting the notion that culture has become detached from material relations, such accounts raise another problem: namely, what is the *relationship* between hierarchical differentiation (as an ordering of social relations in which cultural values are implicit and normative) and 'class' (as a set of explicit and politicised claims)? Or to put it another way – what is the relationship between spoken and unspoken identities? If hierarchy is so decisive in shaping our opportunities, lifestyles, and our sense of ourselves and others, then why is there not a more reflexive awareness of it? Part of the reason lies in the nature of hierarchical differentiation itself. The line between 'us' and 'them' is a notoriously shifting marker, and 'generic categorisations' are often undermined by the perception of more differentiated distinctions *within* categories. But explicit identities do emerge in very particular contexts. The question then is why, and under what circumstances, hierarchically differentiated groups *adopt* explicit class or race discourses and identities.

Take, for example, the 'working class'. The evidence of collective working-class identities in the past is comparatively thin. As Savage notes, research into class consciousness in a supposedly more collectivist past, the 1970s, found that 'no clear patterns of class consciousness existed, but rather that different kinds of views were "wheeled on" in different situations' (2000: 27). Even further back, historians argue that signs of collectivism in the nineteenth century are better characterised as 'populist' rather than 'class' activities (Calhoun 1981; Stedman Jones 1984; Joyce 1990). As Cannadine suggests, 'the connection between social vocabularies and social identities is more complex and contingent than is generally recognised', since different models of society ('us and them', hierarchical and tripartite) have dominated discursive constructions of 'class' in Britain, and 'for much of the time they have easily co-existed in people's minds and imaginations'

(1998: 166). It is the hierarchical vision of society ('strongly individualist') which has been 'the most pervasive and persuasive, with collective and more adversarial ways of seeing ("us and them") only emerging at particular times and contexts, often with the explicit politicisation of social description' (1998: 167).

As Bourdieu notes, 'the same experience of the social may be uttered in very different expressions' and the social world can be 'constructed in different ways' (1985: 730, 726). For Bourdieu, the emergence of 'groups' out of complexly differentiated relations of social space, is an 'act of social magic which consists in trying to bring into existence the thing named' (1991: 223) and only occurs through 'struggles over classifications, struggles over the monopoly of the power to make people see and believe, to get them to know and recognise, to impose the legitimate definition of the divisions of the social world and, thereby, to *make and unmake groups*' (1991: 221). How does this act of 'magic' happen? For Bourdieu, the working class as a subjective *group* has its '*existence in thought*, an existence in the thinking of a large proportion of those whom the taxonomies designate as workers, but also in the thinking of the occupants of the positions remotest from the workers in the social space' (1985: 741). However:

> This almost universally recognised existence is itself based on the existence of a *working class in representation*, i.e., of political and trade-union apparatuses and professional spokespersons vitally interested in believing that it exists and in having this believed both by those who identify with it and those who exclude themselves from it, and capable of making the 'working class' *speak*, and with one voice, of invoking it, as one invokes gods or patron saints, even of symbolically manifesting it through *demonstration*, a sort of theatrical deployment of the class-in-representation, with on the one hand the corps of professional representatives and all the symbolism constitutive of its existence, and on the other hand the most convinced fraction of the believers who, through their presence, enable their representatives to manifest their representativeness.
>
> (Bourdieu 1985: 741–742)

The 'groupness' of the working class is a *symbolic enterprise*, in which the 'working class' is a 'mystical body', a 'class in representation' emerging from the activities of 'mandated representatives who give it material speech and visible presence' and who develop a more widespread 'belief in its existence' (1985: 742), both among those who are made to feel that they belong to the 'working class', but also among those who come to believe that they stand outside 'it'.

To put it another way, as long as trade unions, political parties, activists and analysts continue to invoke the 'working class' as a distinct group with identifiable communal interests, and can mobilise demonstrations, actions, and events in support of those interests, then the 'working class' exists, through the power of *imposing* symbolic divisions on the social world which 'establish meaning and a consensus about meaning, and in particular about the identity and unity of the group, which creates the reality of the unity and the identity of the group' (Bourdieu 1991: 221).

Symbolic representation helps to actively constitute 'classes' out of relations of differentiation, and social relations can be symbolically divided in a variety of ways. This symbolic constitution of groups also occurs within the complex differentiations of ethnicity, regionality, and so on:

> The act of categorisation, when it manages to achieve recognition or when it is exercised by a recognised authority, exercises by itself a certain power: 'ethnic' or 'regional' categories, like categories of kinship, institute a reality by using the power of *revelation* and *construction* exercised by *objectification in discourse*.
>
> (Bourdieu 1991: 223)

However, this is not an arbitrary process. Not just anyone can do it. The symbolic capital which gives individuals the ability to impose their categorisations as 'real' or legitimate is unevenly distributed, and partly depends on prior power or position. Governments, for example, can impose their classifications on people, making their categories real through the uneven allocation of resources and recognition. However, this is also a contested process, and the role of representatives and spokespersons is particularly important. Rogers Brubaker (in relation to ethnic 'groupness') refers to the role of 'ethnopolitical entrepreneurs' who:

> By *invoking* groups ... seek to evoke them, summon them, call them into being. Their categories are *for doing* – designed to stir, summon, justify, mobilise, kindle and energise. By reifing groups, by treating them as substantial things-in-the-world, ethnopolitical entrepreneurs may, as Bourdieu notes, 'contribute to producing what they apparently describe or designate' (1991: 220).
>
> (Brubaker 2002: 166)

For Brubaker, such symbolic constitutions mean that 'groupness' is a *process*, rather than an end-state, so that we must attend 'to the dynamics of group-making as a social, cultural and political project, aimed at transforming categories into groups or increasing level of groupness' (2002: 170–171). This

> allows us to take account of – and potentially, to account for – phases of extraordinary cohesion and moments of intensely felt collective solidarity, without implicitly treating high levels of groupness as constant, enduring or definitionally present. It allows us to treat groupness as an *event*, as something that 'happens', as E. P. Thompson famously said about class. At the same time it keeps us analytically attuned to the possibility that groupness may not happen, that high levels of groupness may *fail* to crystallise, despite the group-making efforts of ethnopolitical entrepreneurs and even in situations of intense elite-level ethnopolitical conflict.
>
> (Brubaker 2002: 168)

Spoken and unspoken identities

The complex, and uneven, differentiation of social relations provides a fertile playing ground for the symbolic imposition of boundaries (and this differentiation is always a force for the potential re-drawing or dissolution of such boundaries). However, this is not a cake that can be cut up in any way we please. The symbolic demarcation of complex social differentiation into 'groups' is not random or arbitrary, since the probability of assembling people into groups 'is greater when they are closer together in the social space and belong to a more restricted and therefore more homogenous constructed class' (Bourdieu 1985: 726). Relations of social similarity and interaction closeness (being located within the same region in social space) gives 'political entrepreneurs' a greater chance of galvanising 'groupness':

> alliance between those who are closest is never *necessary*, inevitable (because the effects of immediate competition may act as a screen), and alliance between those most distant from each other is never *impossible*. . . . But groupings grounded in the struggle of the space constructed in terms of capital distribution are more likely to be stable and durable, while other forms of grouping will always be threatened by splits and oppositions linked to distances in social space. To speak of a social space means that one cannot group just *anyone* with *anyone* else while ignoring the fundamental differences, particularly economic and cultural differences.
>
> (Bourdieu 1985: 726)

As we see here, Bourdieu sees the 'social space' primarily in terms of economic and cultural capital (i.e. in terms of cultural class), but his model of an associational space contains the possibility of theorising race and ethnic 'groupness' because of the way in which difference and inequality are embedded in the interaction order.

By exploring people's location in social networks, and the role of differential association in structuring and reproducing both material inequality and cultural difference, we can trace out in more detail the links between social identities and practical social relations. In particular, this helps to explore how it is that unspoken, implicit, or background social 'identities' – as expressed through patterned differential association, resources and lifestyles – can suddenly be galvanised into spoken, explicit or foreground symbolic 'identities' – as expressed through symbolic boundaries and collectivised activities. Class relations, as we have seen, have increasingly been characterised as an unspoken, implicit identity, embedded within differentiated social relations, whilst racial and ethnic identities have been seen as spoken identities, explicit and symbolic. However, class too has its 'symbolically' explicit moments, just as certain racialised identities are unspoken and implicit. To explain how symbolic identities rise and fall, we have to relate *both* spoken *and* unspoken identities to the lived experience of practical social relations.

Class(ed) identities

Gould argues that 'meaningful group boundaries are predicated on the presence (and perception) of common patterns of durable ties' (1995: 19) and explains changes in the salience of class in collective mobilisation in France in the nineteenth century by the emergence of strongly residential neighbourhoods, which made the local community more central in mobilising individuals (1995: 28). In this model, people's location within different types of networks affects the extent to which different types of identity can be mobilised. In particular, Gould sees collective identities arising from *spatially* concentrated networks, because

> spatially bounded relationships have a significant property not shared by most social ties with nonspatial bases: an intrinsic tendency toward intransitivity. If I associate primarily with my neighbours and most of those with whom I associate do the same, then my friends' friends are necessarily (at least) my neighbours. This simple fact means that social networks founded on spatial proximity provide fertile ground for the emergence of plausible collective identities: individuals with ties to neighbours can readily observe numerous others whose patterns of social interaction match their own. In contrast, when social ties are based not on joint residence but on diverse interests (shared schooling, athletics, amateur pursuits), people are likely to see their associates' social networks as distinct from their own, discouraging the formation of broad collective identities.
>
> (Gould 1995: 205–206)

Other theorists have focused on workplace networks to explain the mobilisation of class identities. Savage, for example, argues that we can relate explicit 'class' identities to forms of boundary erection and maintenance embedded in organisational cultures (such as shopfloor versus management). Once, organisational culture clearly demarcated a collar divide, feeding into wider perceptions of 'class' as oppositional and bounded. So, explicit 'us and them' class identities were partly related to organisational boundaries demarcating

> a set of management structures distant from the world of manual employment, which defined themselves as resting 'above' the dirty world of manual work … a peculiarly English determination to symbolically mark off manual from non-manual work and to emphasise the distance between the two forms of employment.
>
> (Savage 2000: 132)

However, explaining why symbolic identities coalesce in certain places and times is important, but does not address a more pressing problem: that is, why do processes of hierarchical differentiation so rarely give rise to collectivised 'class' identities, or indeed explicit 'class' identities of any kind? We have to reject the notion that inequality is automatically recognised by the people who experience it.

Whilst hierarchy may be decisive in shaping our experience, key aspects of *the way* in which it affects our lives often serve to obscure the nature of inequality and to prevent explicit class identities from forming. If the fine grading of hierarchical distinction provides an uncertain and shifting basis for collectivity (as opposed to categorisation) this is linked to another reason for the 'invisibility' of hierarchy. It is *precisely because* the activities which serve to reproduce hierarchy are so ubiquitous and mundane that they are often not intended or *experienced* as conflict or struggle. It is legitimate for 'new' class analysis to downgrade the search for self-conscious class awareness or identity, because social interaction and lifestyle have an orderly and consistent pattern strongly constrained by hierarchy. As this book shows, not merely cultural tastes, but also our most intimate and important social relationships, are strongly influenced by hierarchical position. Kinship, friendship and partnership all exhibit a strong patterning by social class and status, and the strength of this pattern has endured over very long periods of time. However, since such processes are also a crucial component reproducing hierarchy this must affect how we view the rise and fall of identities.

Take the evidence that people shrug off class labels, locating themselves as 'ordinary' or 'middling'. Savage argues that 'people seem keen to invoke a distinction between their personal lives – in which class is rarely seen as a salient issue – and the world "out there", the world of politics, the economy, the media' (2000: 37, 117). As Savage notes, when they speak in personal terms 'people want to belong to a group of ordinary, average types' (2000: 116). Savage seeks 'to ground this populist, anti-elitist culture more fully in work and employment relations, in order to show it has distinctive roots in class relationships' (118), arguing that newly individualised organisational relations have de-coupled class from the 'visible public anchorage' (141) of shopfloor versus management. Distinct class identities dissipate because of changes in the workplace. For Savage, the remaking of the culture of individualisation (related to shifts in workplace organisation) has dissolved symbolic class boundaries, creating 'a society that routinely reproduces social inequality at the same time as deflecting the attention of its key agents sideways rather than upwards and downwards, so making the issue of social inequality largely "invisible" and somehow "uninteresting"' (2000: 159).

However, class *dis-identification* goes beyond organisational structures. Claims to being 'ordinary' or 'middling' are strongly related to the hierarchical nature of general social networks, over and above workplace relations. In a six-nation study of class identification, Kelley and Evans found a 'middling' self-image 'holds at all levels of the objective stratification hierarchy. Rich and poor, well-educated and poorly educated, high-status and low status, all see themselves near the middle of the class system, rarely at the top or bottom' (1995: 166). Their conclusion: 'in all societies . . . people's subjective class identification is with the middle classes or just below, with very few people identifying with the top or bottom classes'. The reason is that 'reference-group forces restrict the subjective arena to a narrow range in the middle of the class hierarchy' (166). Because our personal world is largely filled with people just like us, we tend to think of our social situation as normal and unexceptional, and we therefore see our hierarchical position as 'average' or 'middling'.

People draw their images of class, particularly the less visible aspects of class, from their experiences among family, friends, and coworkers. Peer groups are mainly homogenous in social status, so people see themselves in the middle of the class hierarchy – this is true of rich and poor, educated and illiterate, worker and boss in all six nations. So strong are these intimate images that they attenuate the objective facts of the social hierarchy.

(Kelley and Evans 1995: 174)

Many of the processes of everyday life lived within an unequal structure *themselves* help to undermine a sense of class or, at least, fray the edges in such a manner that clear-cut identities fail to emerge. It is *because* personal life (friendship, marriage, the people who surround us) is hierarchically ordered that people tend to see themselves as 'ordinary', and thus downplay the significance of hierarchy in their lives. Of course, this is only an *aggregate* tendency – we sit at the centre of associates from a range of social locations, more or less similar to ourselves. Whilst this allows us to make relational comparisons, it is within a limited range, and only serves to normalise our own situation as 'middling', so people are likely to feel that 'class' and class conflict are less significant as a feature of *personal* identity.

Skeggs notes that it is the 'intimate positioning of myself with "others" that enables me to see differences and feel inequality' (1997b: 132–133). But, ironically, because of the deep-seated way in which hierarchy is embedded in personal relationships such differences are likely to be perceived in *public* rather than personal contexts. 'Class' exists 'out there' in the public domain, the arena of politics, the media, the workplace, in our encounters with those socially distant from ourselves (again, normally, in various public contexts, or through stereotyped representations of 'them').

The rise (and fall) of oppositional class cultures and explicit identities is related to the nature of 'class' in public life, particularly to politicised claims and discourses or ideologies of hierarchy and inequality. It is not inequality or hierarchy per se which generates explicit, collective class identities, but rather how, at particular times and with varying success, collective 'class' has been mobilised as an organising (and dividing) principle: at work and in political life. Such mobilisations are contextual and often fleeting, in part because of the way in which other, general, processes of hierarchy work counter to 'class' processes (in the explicit, collective sense). Particular organisational cultures can throw up sharp breaks in the social contacts, lifestyle, and opportunities of different workers, creating discourses and identifications of an explicitly 'economic' or 'class' kind. Yet, recent history demonstrates such identifications can also dissolve. This is partly because of shifts in organisational cultures, and in politicised discourses; however, it also relates to the way in which normal processes of hierarchical differentiation work to obscure the significance of inequality, and limit the application of 'class' discourses in our personal lives.

Racial(ised) identities

New theoretical accounts of 'class' have shown how hierarchy is implicit and deeply embedded in social practice. In a parallel vein, Reay argues this is also true of constructions of 'whiteness', because 'despite whiteness remaining an unspoken taken-for-granted for white women, it powerfully influences actions and attitudes' (1998: 265). The implicit nature of 'whiteness' is such that

> in Western representation whites are overwhelmingly and disproportionately dominant, have the central and elaborated roles, and above all are placed as the norm, the ordinary, the standard. Whites are everywhere in representation. Yet precisely because of this and their placing as the norm they seem not to be represented to themselves *as* whites but as people who are variously gendered, classed, sexualised and abled. At the level of racial representation, in other words, whites are not of a certain race, they're just the human race.
> (Dyer 2000: 541)

Noting the 'apparent emptiness of "white" as a cultural identity' (2000: 448), Frankenberg argues that, nonetheless, 'racism shapes white people's lives and identities in a way that is inseparable from other facets of daily life' (Frankenberg 2000: 451). For Frankenberg, whiteness is a location of structural advantage, but 'refers to a set of cultural practices that are usually unmarked and unnamed' (2000: 447). The implicit and taken-for-granted nature of 'whiteness' means that white experience becomes naturalised and normative, and is represented as 'individual, multifarious and graded' (Dyer 2000: 534), concealed behind class, age, gender, etc., differences rather than as 'whiteness' *per se*.

But how do processes which generate 'whiteness' as invisible and taken-for-granted relate to other racialised or ethnic identities, which are framed in terms of explicit symbolic boundaries? How are we to reconcile accounts of 'whiteness' as implicit with more 'up front' identifications of ethnic belonging and difference? As we have seen, the effect of hierarchy on social networks means that we tend to associate with people from broadly similar backgrounds, meaning that processes shaping inequality can become less 'visible'. Because individuals overestimate the number of persons similar to themselves and their intimates, we think of our social situation as normal and unexceptional, and project our own hierarchical position as 'average' or 'middling'. Of course, close social networks (of friendship, marriage and partnership) are additionally constrained by ethnicity, and people thus also tend to associate with those from broadly similar ethnic identities (Kalmijn 1994, 1998).

However, social distance effects work very differently for majority ethnic and minority ethnic groups. Whiteness takes on the status of 'seeming normativity ... structured invisibility' because of the link between 'where one stands in society and what one perceives' (Frankenberg 2000: 451, 452). For white people in a majority white society, the effects of social distance and reference group processes mean that white people will typically associate with other white people, and will tend to normalise that experience:

White people have power and believe that they think, feel and act like and for all other people; white people, unable to see their particularity, cannot take account of other people's; white people create the dominant images of the world and don't quite see that they thus construct the world in their own image

(Dyer 1997: 9)

Where similar reference group effects operate within minority ethnic groups they are forcefully confronted with majoritarian constructions of the same thing. Thus reference group effects for minority groups work to *reinforce* the experience of differentiation and being positioned as different.

Of course reference group effects cannot be separated out from the values and claims which help shape the nature of such reference groups. Reference group effects, along with group boundaries, are strengthened, and re-worked, in the wake of ethno-political manoeuvring, and cultural recognition claims. These claims have fed into an altered landscape which puts racism more firmly on policy agendas and alters the cultural context by more effectively challenging the normativity of white 'majority' assumptions (Bottero and Irwin 2003).

Brubaker stresses the cognitive dimension of ethnicity, as 'a way of seeing and interpreting the world [which] works in and through categories and category-based common sense knowledge' (Brubaker 2002: 184). Such cognitive perspectives 'include systems of classification, categorization and identification, formal and informal. And they include the tacit, taken-for-granted background knowledge, embodied in persons and embedded in institutionalised routines and practices, through which people recognise and experience objects, places, persons, actions or situations as ethnically, racially or nationally marked or meaningful' (Brubaker 2002: 174). It is important to identify *how* ethnicity, race and nationhood are constructed, to specify

how – and when – people identify themselves, perceive others, experience the world and interpret their predicaments in racial, ethnic or national rather than other terms . . . how 'groupness' can 'crystallise' in some situations while remaining latent and merely potential in others.

(Brubaker 2002: 174)

Brubaker takes the example of ethnic Hungarians in Romania, whose position in Transylvanian cities shows varying degrees of 'groupness'. Brubaker relates this varying groupness to two processes. On the one hand, there is social distance and differential association which helps provide the categories of distinction and difference which are essential background factors for groupness to emerge. For ethnic Hungarians in Transylvanian cities this is related to such institutional factors as the separate Hungarian-language school system which parallels the mainstream system. On the other hand, there are more specific processes of ethnic-mobilisation, which target and work within these broader processes of social differentiation. Symbolic mobilisation into 'us and them' categories (the process of generating 'groupness') thus works within wider (and more 'inert') processes of multiplex social differentiation:

> Categories need ecological niches in which to survive and flourish; the parallel school system provides such a niche for 'Hungarian' as an ethnonational category. Hungarian schools not only provide a legitimate institutional home and a protected public space for the category. They also generate the social structural conditions for a small Hungarian world within the larger Romanian one. . . . Since the schools shape opportunity structures and contact probabilities and thereby influence friendship patterns (and, at the high school and university level, influence marriage patterns as well), this world is to a certain extent a self-reproducing one. Note that the (partial) reproduction of this social world – this interlocking set of social relationships linking school, friendship circles and family – does not require strong nationalist commitments or group loyalties. Ethnic networks can be reproduced without high degrees of groupness, largely through the logic of contact probabilities and opportunity structures and the resulting moderately high degrees of ethnic endogamy.
>
> (Brubaker 2002: 185)

Conclusion

For Bourdieu, people similarly located in social space are more likely to be seen as 'the same', and so social proximity (of conditions, and therefore of dispositions) is more likely to be translated into durable social groupings. However, he also argues that 'socially known and recognised differences only exist for a subject capable not only of perceiving differences but of recognising them as significant' (1985: 730). This has sometimes been taken to mean that social differentiation presupposes symbolic divisions, that symbolic division is prior to social distance. Lamont and Molnar, for example, argue that 'Only when symbolic boundaries are widely agreed upon can they take on a constraining character and pattern social interaction in important ways. Moreover, only then can they become social boundaries' (2002: 169).

However, as we have seen in earlier chapters, social distance occurs for a variety of reasons, not all of which are based on strong symbolic divisions, or on the clear-cut exclusion of 'others'. That is, systematic differential association occurs long before, and quite independent of, any sense of 'groupness'. Differential association occurs in quite routine ways, as stratified social relations mean that people follow different routes through life, unintentionally sharing their lives with some but not others, and developing shared interests and activities with the socially similar others they encounter en route. Many of these processes arise through the structured opportunities for association that stratification generates, and do not directly arise from the perception of difference, or from symbolic demarcation. As Amit and Rapport note:

some of the most crucial forms of fellowship, of belonging, are barely marked by explicit symbolic icons. They arise when students in a Montreal high school extol the sense of 'family' they come to feel with each other. They are formed when parents of community athletes get to know each other over the course of rainy mornings spent together while their children compete, of long bus trips to competition fields, of endless waits together for competition to start. . . . These forms of fellowship and belonging are intrinsically contextual and therefore often ephemeral. . . . But some of the personal links that arise through these experiences carry on.

(Amit and Rapport 2002: 64)

However, this means that such social distance can be the basis on which situational identities, boundary drawing, and the perception of difference can emerge and harden.

So if symbolic identities cannot be 'read off' from social relations, because of the complex nature of networks of differential association and affiliation, this does not mean that the mobilisation and formation of such identities is somehow random, arbitrary, or detached from the underlying orderliness of patterned social relations. For whilst social relations are too complex to determine symbolic identities, it is still the case that the ordered nature of stratified differential association shapes the success of attempts to 'read on' symbolic demarcations to practical social relations. Social relations and social identities have a complex relationship, but they are related nonetheless, and the investigation of the links between the social and the symbolic has much to tell us about the shaping of individual lives.

14 Reproducing hierarchy

Stratification remains a powerful influence in the late modern world. Throughout, this book has critically examined claims that social divisions are increasingly 'free-floating' of structural relations, and that agency is now dominant in social affairs, with a weakening of social structural constraints. Yet whilst culture and consumption have become key arenas of social life, it is apparent that economic divisions and inequalities are still bound up in the formation of cultural lifestyles, and that the hierarchical differentiation of lifestyles remains a key feature of stratification processes. In recent times it has become commonplace to associate stratification with structural determinism, and to see an emphasis on material inequality as the last gasp of a now outmoded commitment to 'grand theory'. Postmodern accounts of 'difference' have stressed the hyper-differentiated nature of social relations, arguing that the complex nature of our social ties means that social identities can never be 'read off' from social location. The limitations of structural categories in explaining behaviour, and the increasing awareness of diversity in social arrangements, have been taken as evidence that 'action' has been increasingly de-coupled from 'structure'. Because of their complexity, social relations are presented as fragmented, as liquid flows and shifting attachments, so that the formation of identities appears regulated by ideas and meanings, rather than by material structures. This, as we have seen, amounts to the abandonment of the very idea of stratification and inequality, in favour of accounts of the discursive construction of difference. Other arguments focus on the increasing role of choice and reflexivity in social life, so that whilst inequalities persist, the 'objective' and 'subjective' dimensions of social life are increasingly divorced. Individuals are 'disembedded' from social constraints: 'Individuals become actors, builders, jugglers, stage managers of their own biographies and identities and also of their social links and networks' (Beck and Beck-Gernsheim 2002: 23). In this argument there is a new indeterminacy between structure and agency, between social conditions and values, so that individuals are now increasingly obliged to reflexively fashion their own biographies. As Giddens puts it, in this brave new world, 'we are, not what we are but what we make ourselves' (1991: 75).

We should be highly sceptical of these claims, which some have seen as an unacknowledged 'middle-class' standpoint on social arrangements (Savage 2003).

It is frequently noted that the less advantaged still live lives encumbered by structural constraints, and that inequality continues to mean that some have more freedom and choice than others:

> For the educated middle class with potentially high-earning capacities . . . the arguments about the growing individualisation of advanced industrial societies in which personal biographies are increasingly a matter for reflexive choice . . . may have some resonance. . . . But for 'generic labourers' with few skills and little social capital, especially the type of social capital that is valued in a service-dominated economy, notions of increased agency in the constitution and reconstitution of their lives and the growing ability to construct an employment career that is based on reflexive choice have never had much resonance. Older patterns in which class position and geographical location broadly determine the shape of their future lives for working class young people still have a persistent hold.
>
> (McDowell 2003: 221)

And despite the increasingly cosmopolitan, mobile and rapidly changing nature of the world: 'Most people live in narrow gemeinschaftlich worlds of neighbourhood and kin. Cosmopolitan intellectuals seem all too ready to forget or to deny the small-scale domesticity of most people's lives' (Pahl 1991: 346).

These are important points. But we cannot simply counterpose the agentic freedom of the privileged few with the structural constraint of the disadvantaged. The structural should not be opposed to 'choice' (in which increasing choice means the demise of structure), rather 'structure' is better understood as consisting of the (patterned) choices that people do in fact make. As we have seen, at every level of the social scale, people's choices continue to be highly patterned, so that any rejection of the ordered nature of social life is unwarranted. Social location continues to be an important factor in the construction of cultural identities and social difference, and inequality remains as relevant as ever in shaping destinies, and in providing the materials for social and cultural differentiation, for rich and poor, excluded and included alike. The more privileged do have greater freedom and choice, but this is as an *aspect of their social position*, rather than the negation of it.

Persistent inequality

Despite enormous changes in modern society, there are remarkable continuities in patterns of inequality. These continuities are not manifested in the *fixed attachment* to unequal positions, nor in the *denial* of opportunities to the disadvantaged, but rather emerge in *unequal patterns of movement* to new social positions. Even as the less disadvantaged have taken up bright new opportunities they still receive an unequal share of them, maintaining their position relative to others. The world has changed, but relative inequality persists within the very fabric of that change. So, despite a dramatic improvement in general standards of living, and the provision of health care in all western societies, marked inequalities in health remain, surviving the jump from absolute to relative inequality. The same pattern is evident in the expansion of educational and labour-market opportunities and rising affluence which have been a key feature of late modernity. The less advantaged have benefited enormously from these changes, which have helped transform their lives; but so too have the advantaged, and at about the same rate. Even as the disadvantaged have stepped forward to better lives, others have stayed in front of them. Of course, these are aggregate tendencies. Western societies have been characterised by dramatic upward social mobility, with more 'room at the top', so that many children from disadvantaged backgrounds have travelled to the most privileged social positions. The inequality lies in the fact that privileged children remain much more likely to achieve such positions. So the patterning of inequality *within* social change makes the fact of inequality much less visible for the people who experience it. But it persists nonetheless.

This continuity of inequality in the face of dramatic change for all is a remarkable feature of social life, and takes some explaining. Take the intergenerational inheritance of relative social position. As we have seen, if we look over the long term we can see a significant loosening of the impact of parental position on where a child ends up. But to identify this we have to take a very long-term view indeed. From generation to generation there has been only the most imperceptible change, with the decline in relative inequality occurring 'by slow degrees' (Prandy *et al.* 2003a). The ability of parents to hand down social advantages to their children obviously depends on the changing nature of the 'currency' of advantage and position, and the last two hundred years have seen some truly amazing shifts in the opportunity structure: the decline in the importance of agriculture, landed property and 'family' firms; the rise of education, bureaucratic careers, white-collar employment and credentialism; and the emergence of consumer society and cultural careers. Yet family influence on social position has proved 'remarkably buoyant' in the face of these changes (Prandy and Bottero 2000a: 276).

Social advantage – in whatever form – gives those who possess it a considerable head start in weathering the social changes and upheaval that confront successive generations. If you start ahead you tend to stay ahead – whatever life throws at you. This provides support for Bourdieu's contention that the various sources of advantage are readily convertible into each other. Indeed, the persistence of relative inequality has only been possible because of the relative ease with which the more privileged have been able to convert economic holdings into educational and cultural success. It is still the case that economic position can 'insure' against poor educational performance, and numerous studies show that low-achieving children from more privileged backgrounds have much better careers than their less-advantaged peers. So if advantaged children do not do well academically, alternative resources are used to ensure their success. But the link between social background and educational attainment has also strengthened over time. The more advantaged are dramatically more successful in educational terms, and this is true even when we hold measured 'ability' constant. If there has been a loosening of the impact of family background on social position it has not been 'by degrees' – the educational route – since family background has been increasingly significant for educational success (Prandy *et al.* 2003b). Whether it is through living in better areas (with better schools), through the hiring of private tutors, through the choice of private schooling, through the possession of cultural capital, through the more strategic and confident negotiation of the school system, through the mobilisation of well-placed social contacts, or through the higher aspirations that privileged parents have for their children, or indeed through all of these factors – the fact remains that it is harder for privileged children to fail than it is for disadvantaged children to succeed. Education has not contributed to increased social mobility, but rather has served as a mechanism for social reproduction. But how is it that advantage reproduces itself?

Reproduction

It is a central tenet of stratification analysis that, by their nature, unequal social relations are

> highly resistant to change: those groupings who enjoy positions of superior advantage and disadvantage cannot be expected to yield them up without a struggle, but will rather typically seek to exploit the resources they can command in order to preserve their superiority.
>
> (Goldthorpe *et al.* 1980: 28)

Those with advantages are better placed to capitalise on them, and to seize new opportunities as they arise, than those with fewer resources. In this way, inequality is reproduced. However, opinions differ as to whether this is a process of primarily economic or cultural reproduction.

As we have seen, the central question of Bourdieu's work is 'how stratified social systems of hierarchy and domination persist and reproduce intergenerationally without powerful resistance and without the conscious recognition of their members' (Swartz 1997: 6). Bourdieu wishes to avoid determinism, insisting that actors are not simply following internalised rules, but rather are pursuing practical engagements and responding creatively to new situations (albeit in ways shaped by class predispositions). However, 'agents bring the properties of their location in a hierarchically structured social order into each and every situation and interaction' (Bourdieu 1984 [1979]: 44). Because individuals occupy specific locations their view of the social space is always partial. And the impact of social location on perception often occurs in implicit, taken-for-granted ways in which 'the cognitive structures which social agents implement in their practical knowledge of the world are internalized, "embodied" social structures' (Bourdieu 1984 [1979]: 468).

> The categories of perception of the social world are, as regards their most essential features, the product of the internalization, the incorporation, of

the objective structures of social space. Consequently, they incline agents to accept the social world as it is, to take it for granted, rather than to rebel against it, to counterpose to it different, even antagonistic, possibilities. The sense of one's place, as a sense of what one can or cannot 'permit oneself', implies a tacit acceptance of one's place, a sense of limits ('that's not for the likes of us') or, which amounts to the same thing – a sense of distances, to be marked and kept, respected or expected.

(Bourdieu 1985: 728)

As we have seen, Bourdieu's work emphasises the way in which the dominated in a structure of inequality accept their fate, and adjust their aspirations according to their position and thus, however unintentionally, help to reproduce their inequality by 'self-selecting' class-differentiated routes through life. But whilst hierarchy and inequality do create very different social contexts for social unequals, and thus shape lives with different tastes and interests, throughout the book I have shown that there is also a danger that cultural accounts of inequality can slip into 'culture of poverty' explanations. 'Culture of poverty' explanations characterise the disadvantaged as hopeless and helpless victims of circumstance, complicit in their own fate. There are twin dangers here, of both determinism and voluntarism: of on the one hand characterising the disadvantaged as simple reflections of their structural position, with little control over their own fates; and, on the other hand, of seeing inequality as the product of the choices that the disadvantaged themselves make, the result of their impoverished cultural life and contacts, and their 'poverty of aspiration'. The implication is that the disadvantaged condemn themselves.

A series of writers has questioned the implication of such arguments: that the adaptations that the less advantaged must – inevitably – make to their social location somehow mean that they cannot take up new and better social positions. For whilst it is important to recognise that unequal social relations do provide fewer opportunities and resources, and thus relatively less agency and control, for the disadvantaged, the fact remains that when opportunities have opened up they have been as quick to seize them as their social superiors. A 'sense of one's place' and limited cultural capital have not stopped increasing numbers of working-class children from seizing their chances in the expanding opportunities of the educational system and labour market in the second half of the twentieth century, for example.

The standard criticism of theories of the cultural reproduction of inequality, then, is that they explain too much. For the inequality of less advantaged groups in late modern societies consists not in their lack of access to opportunities, but in their differential rates of access. Take going to university. For critics like John Goldthorpe, the problem is not why working-class children do not go to university (they clearly do, and their numbers have dramatically increased over time), but rather why their rates of entry have kept pace with the expanding numbers from middle-class backgrounds. This, he suggests, depends not on cultural reproduction (which would lead to working-class exclusion), but on the *differential economic risks* that unequally placed groups face in considering their options. Goldthorpe rejects Bourdieu's emphasis on the 'poverty of aspiration' amongst the working class, which he sees as a form of 'blaming the victim':

> it need not be supposed that the tendency of children from working-class families to pursue in general less ambitious educational careers than children from service-class families derives from a 'poverty' of aspirations: the patterns of choice made could be more or less equivalent ones. It is simpler to assume that there is no systematic variation in levels of aspiration, or related values, among classes, and that variations in the courses of action that are actually taken arise from the fact that, in pursuing any given goal from different class origins, different 'social distances' will have to be traversed – or, as Boudon . . . more usefully puts it, differential opportunities and constraints, and thus the evaluation of differential sets of probable costs and benefits, will be involved.
>
> (Goldthorpe 1996: 489–490)

Goldthorpe's argument is that going to university entails more risks for working-class children. Quite rationally, therefore, working-class individuals are less likely to choose such routes than middle-class individuals, not because of any difference in aspirations, or cultural know-how between them, but rather because the economic costs of failure are so much greater. The same choice – going to university – is more costly for lower-class individuals than it is for the more privileged, since the expenses are proportionally larger against lower-class incomes, and the risks of failure are greater compared to the sacrifices that will have to be undergone. Goldthorpe distinguishes 'strategies from above', in which the advantaged seek to maintain their position with ample resources, from 'strategies from below', in which the less advantaged face a more difficult route of advancement with limited resources (Goldthorpe 2000). Goldthorpe's argument is that 'cultural' differences are not necessary in the explanation of why expanding opportunities have not changed class differentials in access. The expansion of opportunities has not changed the relative risks, because social-class differences in family income remain, and it is these economic differences which are central to how actors make their choices (Scott 1996: 509).

Goldthorpe's argument insists on the primacy of economic resources in the reproduction of class differentials. The less advantaged always have a greater relative distance to travel to achieve the same goals. In aiming for the same goals the disadvantaged have to be *more ambitious* than the advantaged, who are simply aiming to maintain their social position. For Goldthorpe, it is the distance in structural location which explains the different choices made. However, the question is whether such 'distances' can be seen in purely economic terms, since the less advantaged also have to travel further in social and cultural terms to achieve 'middle-class' goals. As we have seen in Chapter 8, Goldthorpe's approach has been criticised by those advocating culturalist class analysis, because it ignores the way in which 'decision making depends on specific kinds of cultural framework' (Savage 2000: 86).

Culturalist theorists suggest the rather bloodless rational decision-making of Goldthorpe's theory needs to be put into broader social and cultural perspective. For example, research into education choices amongst young people suggests that 'cultural and social capital, material constraints . . . social perceptions and distinctions, and forms of self-exclusion . . . are all at work in the processes of choice' (Ball *et al.* 2002: 54):

> decisions were pragmatic, rather than systematic. They were based on partial information located in the familiar and the known. The decision-making was context-related, and could not be separated from the family background, culture and life-histories of the [young people]. The decisions were opportunistic, being based on fortuitous contacts and experiences. [. . .] Decisions were only partially rational, being also influenced by feelings and emotions. Finally, decisions often involved accepting one option rather than choosing between many.
>
> (Hodgkinson and Sparkes, quoted in Ball *et al.* 2002: 55)

There is considerable evidence that middle-class parents exhibit great anxiety over their children's futures, perceive the competition to be tough, and have little sense of the relatively straightforward 'reproduction of advantage' which objective middle-class mobility chances suggest (Power *et al.* 2003; Devine 2004; Ball *et al.* 2002). This suggests that aspirations and decision-making depend on local frameworks of reference and comparison. Middle-class children following advantaged routes still often feel like relative failures (for example, for going to a non-Oxbridge university) compared to their more successful peers (Power *et al.* 2003). So the very strategic educational interventions of the middle classes relate to fears of relative failure, and to the way in which aspirations emerge from social context.

There is a fundamental question, however, of the precise role that cultural differentiation plays in the reproduction of inequality; since cultural differences should not be seen solely in terms of social *values*, but rather as an aspect of how different social locations entail different practical engagements with the world. Culture should not be counterposed to material location, since cultural differentiation is part and parcel of the structured nature of social life.

Culture, social networks and reproduction

Bourdieu's central contribution has been to show that processes of lateral, 'cultural' differentiation are, in fact, bound up with vertical, hierarchical differentiation. Because the 'cultural' differences of people at the same level of the hierarchy are part of struggles over social and cultural distinction by which groups establish a position in the hierarchy. These processes of competition and differentiation occur as individuals try to mobilise various social, cultural and economic resources to maintain or improve their position. And – as Bourdieu notes – processes of competition are often at their most fierce between those at the same level of the hierarchy; that is, not between unequals, but rather between broadly equivalent individuals who seek to find a competitive advantage through pursuing different social or cultural avenues.

One criticism of Bourdieu's relational approach is that it leads to a 'zero-sum' view of power in social hierarchies, in which one person's gain is inevitably another person's loss; where the respect or value of some (the middle classes) must be based on the denigration or devaluing of others (the working classes). Bourdieu's approach to social analysis is *relational*, and he rejects seeing social location in terms of the *content* of social positions or cultural practices, arguing that the meaning of any particular practice emerges out of the relations of opposition and proximity to other practices. Because Bourdieu believes that meaning is defined *relationally*, *all* cultural practices are 'automatically classified and classifying, rank-ordered and rank-ordering' (1984 [1979]: 223). As Lamont has noted, this implies that 'distinct preferences necessarily negate one another', that 'cultural differences automatically translate into domination . . . [and] by the mere fact of being defined in opposition to one another, generate hierarchies of meaning as well as discipline and repression' (Lamont 1992: 182, 177). Certainly, those at the bottom of hierarchies are often stigmatised, and seen not merely as subordinate but also of lower worth, but it is not clear that cultural differentiation can be seen quite so simply as the product of a dominant class imposing their values on the rest.

Social and cultural relations cannot be so neatly coupled into equations of gain or loss, and there is a danger of downplaying 'the possible significance of popular cultural resources, by only dealing with working-class identities as stigmatised ones' (Savage 2003: 541). For: 'In Bourdieu's frequently reductive account of social interests, the primary (often, it seems, the exclusive) function of possession of cultural capital is that of maintaining and extending social status' (Bennett *et al.* 1999: 263–264).

Critics point out that social and cultural practices have their own logic, independent of status competition. Not all forms of differentiation are strategies in hierarchical activities and forms of cultural difference can be pursued for their own sake, for the love of the thing itself. A love of opera, for example, is not always about indicating cultural distance from the unwashed masses. In the same way differential association can occur through restricted opportunities to meet unlike others, and through the comfort and familiarity of associating with those who are socially similar to us, not just through hierarchical competition.

> Bourdieu's relational method . . . seems to presuppose a tightly coupled social order where contrastive practices are continuously operative and always hierarchical. It tends to downplay processes of imitation or cooperation that can also be formative of social identity as are processes of distinction.
>
> (Swartz 1997: 64)

Forms of difference have their own dynamic, independent of processes of hierarchy. Differentiation occurs independently of hierarchical processes. For example, if we think of cultural 'taste':

Rather than displaying a singular structure of value running from the legitimate and prestigious to the illegitimate and valueless . . . cultural practices in all their heterogeneity are organised by different and often incommensurable scales. Watching the football on Saturday, playing beach cricket, growing giant pumpkins for the show, driving a stock car, walking a bush trail, doing voluntary work for a service club, playing bridge, gardening, working out, going to the movies or to a dance club. . . . each of these is diversely configured and specially valued in ways that do not sustain generalisation. . . . This is not to deny the importance of cultural capital in the formation and differentiation of social classes: clearly 'high'-cultural preferences and practices are important in the formation of the class of professionals, just as rock music is important in the definition of the working classes. All we want to argue is that these processes do not take place along a singular scale of cultural value, and that it is not possible to extrapolate effects of dominance from them. They have effects of cohesion in relation to any one class, but they do not necessarily have effects beyond that nexus of class and culture.

(Bennett *et al.* 1999: 263, 268)

The implication of this is that cultural tastes and preferences are primarily bound up with stratification, not through the imposition of a dominant group's values, but rather through their role in processes of differential association in which groups have *different* tastes and values. So that

cultural judgement has its primary effect through its capacity to solidify and entrench social networks. It is by achieving communicative competence with others in a similar social position that the possibility of exchanging or transforming cultural capital into economic capital or social power is realised.

(Warde *et al.* 1999: 124)

Erickson (1996), who has pointed to Bourdieu's relative neglect of the role of social capital in the formation and differentiation of social groups, argues that social networks play a stronger role in the maintenance of social position than does the possession of cultural capital. Because cultural differentiation is a feature of differential association, it is part and parcel of the wider role social networks play in maintaining and reproducing stratification.

As this book has demonstrated, a series of relational approaches to stratification has shown that differential association is crucial as both an effect and also a cause of stratification. The reproduction of hierarchy is about more than the intergenerational transmission of advantage, since it is also bound up in how people in different social locations with different social and cultural resources also tend to make very different marriage and friendship choices. Whom we fall in love and settle down with, and the friends and social contacts that we make throughout our life, are all affected by our hierarchical position. We connect to a range of different sorts of people, directly and indirectly, through complex *networks* of relations. Since social characteristics (class, gender, race, etc.) are systematically embedded in these social networks, the people closest to us also tend to be socially similar to us, along a range of characteristics.

Our social networks are therefore patterned in a hierarchical manner (along lines of class and status, but also along lines of race, ethnicity, and so on). But what this means is that people's disagreements (about who and what they value) can – if they disagree consistently – be the basis of a hierarchy of practices, and of differentiated social networks, without there being a common hierarchy of values. But the network of social relationships and affiliations within which each individual sits affects their access to resources, opportunities, and so on. Since networks are strongly affected by differential association and social similarity, overall they create a pattern of highly unequal social relations which structure differential access to resources, information, people and places. But since the most ordinary and everyday of social activities reflect people's location in unequal social relations, this also means that – *simply by going about their everyday social routines* – people's practical social activities help to reproduce those unequal relations.

It is apparent that hierarchy is a process of both distance and differentiation in social relations. Those distant in the hierarchy lead different lives in different locations, with different friends and interests, and this social dissimilarity is bound up with unequal levels of resources, respect and social control. So the mundane, everyday activities of all our social lives – going to work, spending time with our friends, pursuing hobbies and interests, socialising with our family – both reflect and help to reproduce differences in social position and resources.

> The continuity of social structure is itself produced by myriad individual decisions and actions. Most people who decide whether or not to take a school exam or aim for promotion for work are not consciously reproducing the class system: they are doing what seems best to them at the time. Similarly most people lighting up a cigarette or going out jogging are not aiming to reproduce the pattern of health inequality.
>
> (Bartley *et al.* 1998: 6)

The separation in people's intimate contacts has sometimes been seen as a sign of group boundaries and social closure. However, whilst group boundaries and social exclusion are an important aspect of differential association, patterns of social distance also occur in much less 'bounded' social networks, and through people following stratified social routes and routines through life. The analysis of differential association shows that the intimate choices we make in life (of friends and partners) are constrained by the social sorting that already occurs in the clubs, schools, workplaces, and neighbourhoods in which we live our lives. This is a key feature of stratification – it leads to social distance in our personal relations. Since differential association is routinely embedded in social arrangements, social distance can occur without any requirement for strategies limiting contact or denying access to privileged circles. People differently located in social space experience different routes through life, and so often develop differences in taste and manners. Such differences are very often employed in strategies of exclusion and in the erection of social barriers, but it is also important to recognise the way in which social distance is routinely and unintentionally reproduced, through the most everyday of social actions. Whether we wish to or not, we all routinely reproduce hierarchy and social distance 'behind our backs'.

However, no form of differentiation is innocent of hierarchical implications. Cultural and social differences can be, and frequently are, used opportunistically in strategies of exclusion, ranking and subordination. Relations of difference can become ascribed as forms of superiority and inferiority and, although this is always a contested process, the conversion of markers of difference into markers of hierarchy is commonplace. Therefore differential association can be the basis on which boundary drawing, and perceptions of difference, can emerge and harden. And vice versa, perceptions of difference, however stereotypical, can reinforce social distances, reproduce inequalities, enforce social isolation, and thus produce differential association.

Stratification, therefore, is a practical accomplishment of everyday life, whether we intend it or not. Inequality, for Bourdieu, exists in its most fundamental form in implicit, common-sense ways of seeing the world, generating a 'matrix of perception' (Lamont 1992: 187) which extends well beyond conscious reflection or identity. It is one of his central insights that inequality and social distance are reproduced in everyday, routine activities, in which knowledge of or attitudes towards inequality or the stratification order are entirely irrelevant. People – simply by liking the things and people they like – cannot help but reproduce the stratification order, regardless of what they know or think about inequality.

However, Bourdieu also slips into a more voluntaristic account, in which the reproduction of inequality is based on false consciousness and shared cultural values. Here people are ignorant of the 'true' nature of power and share the values that condemn them to social inferiority. Bourdieu's work is important for showing that social control does not have to depend upon overt conflict or physical coercion, and that taken-for-granted social relations help to reproduce hierarchy and inequality. But a concern for critics has been the way in which Bourdieu sees the stability of inequality in processes of misrecognition and 'symbolic violence' in which the dominated come to *accept* the conditions of their own inequality as fair and just. This neglects the importance of sheer economic clout and the role of coercion and collective or organised class struggle as features of *contested* power relations (Jenkins 2000; Swartz 1997), and overestimates the importance of symbolic legitimation in maintaining the stability of power inequalities. Bourdieu argues that 'genuine scientific research embodies a threat to the "social order"' (Bourdieu and Hahn, quoted in Swartz 1997: 260) because of the way in which it unmasks hidden power relations. This implies that if people saw their true social position then inequality could not persist. Yet, as Swartz argues, this 'overstates the role that false consciousness has in maintaining groups in subordinate positions' since 'individuals and groups often see clearly the arbitrary character of power relations but lack the requisite resources to change them' (Swartz 1997: 289).

There is a danger of voluntarism, of assuming that the stability of inequality rests on the consent and acceptance of those involved. In voluntaristic accounts it is assumed that 'the lack of agitation for change on the part of the deprived has to be based upon either a moral consensus or upon some form of ignorance of true social processes. Their consciousness has been characterised as either limited or fragmented or false' (Stewart *et al.* 1980: 143–144). However:

> All these approaches separate the individual from the social system and argue as if the free consideration of social arrangements and consequent moral judgements of them was a significant human problem. We believe, on the contrary, that most aspects of social life are, generally, seen to lie beyond the competence of any identifiable social group or individual to change. They are, for most people, facts of existence determined by an impersonal social system.
>
> (Stewart and Blackburn 1975: 481–482)

The coherence and stability of the stratification order need not reside in shared values, nor in ignorance of inequality or power relations. For,

> whether or not there is a true level of analysis concerned with the 'social' as a world distinct from the 'individual', the social is experienced as if it occupied a separate realm. . . . There are important consequences for individual consciousness when society in certain of its aspects is confronted as 'natural', as residing in the operation of general principles external to individuals and therefore descriptively known, rather than in norms or values which are prescriptive or contingent. Attitudes to social arrangements then become questions of knowledge rather than of evaluation.
>
> (Stewart *et al.* 1980: 7)

The Cambridge school emphasise that 'Individual actions are not usually oriented towards the reproduction of the stratification order, and their effects on its reproduction are not necessarily foreseeable' (Blackburn and Prandy 1997: 503). Because the hierarchical social order is reproduced through routine, everyday actions, people may not intend, or even be consciously aware of, the consequences of their actions: social distance is *reproduced* in such simple actions as our choice of friends and marriage partners, or our cultural tastes and preferences. The reproduction of hierarchy is carried out every day, by every one of us, simply by going about our daily lives (Bottero and Prandy 2003). In this way, power and inequality are reproduced through daily routine activities:

> Social advantage is maintained, not by the personal competence of individuals in conscious control of decision-making processes, but rather by the exercise of ordinary rights and privileges which accrue to positions in the social structure. Within relatively stable systems individuals will usually experience power in situations where they can successfully resist attempts to

erode their customary privileges – to change the nature of social arrangements. To a large extent this power becomes visible only when challenged. Their ability to initiate change in the social structure is a great deal more limited. They are not free to determine the nature of the system. The differential distribution of power in a society is, then, integral to the everyday experience of its members. For the majority of the population this is essentially a structure of external constraint, both in terms of the quality of their social relationships and their relationships with the material world. The nature and extent of the constraints varies with position in this structure, and on this depends the quality of life. Though they cannot determine the nature of the structure, the privileged have greater freedom to choose their position within the structure.

(Stewart and Blackburn 1975: 483–484)

Conclusion

It is certainly the case that patterns of inequality are very complexly structured, and that unequal social relations are fluid, and highly differentiated. What we find are relative *degrees* of inequality, differential but overlapping and multiplex *patterns* of association, uneven *chances* of success; different *rates* of movement. Of course, the persistence of inequality in unequal patterns of access to opportunities even as those opportunities expand is a form of inequality that is sometimes hard to see. It has been noted that relative inequality often appears 'counter-intuitive' to the people who experience it (Devine 2004); certainly it is beyond the intuition of those eminent commentators who have pronounced the death of stratification. But differential association and movement still amount to substantial and enduring inequality, in which people's social relations continue to order their chances in life, and thus provide the basis for patterned choices. Fluid change may be a characteristic of late modern societies, so that 'all that is solid melts into air', yet within these restless movements patterned inequality endures. The complexity of stratification does not mean that the coherence of social divisions and inequalities has been undermined or that progressive individualisation has led to chaotic, unstructured social relations. Choice cannot be counterposed to social location, movement cannot be counterposed to structure, and hyper-differentiation cannot be counterposed to the orderly and patterned nature of social relations, since choice, movement, and complex differentiation are essential aspects of stratification.

The complex and uneven differentiation of social relations does mean that the relation between social relations and social identities is not straightforward. But if symbolic identities cannot be 'read off' from social relations, because of the complex nature of networks of differential association and affiliation, this does not mean that the mobilisation of identities is disconnected from the underlying orderliness of patterned social relations. Differential association occurs in diverse ways, as stratified social relations mean that people follow different routes through life. Many of these processes arise through the structured opportunities for association that stratification generates, and do not directly arise from the perception of difference, or from symbolic demarcation. However, differential association – and the different social worlds this gives rise to – shape and are shaped by unspoken, implicit, or background social 'identities', expressed through the patterning of our practical social relations, resources and lifestyles. And such differences help to explain how symbolic boundaries and collectivised identities rise, and fall. But above all, stratification resides in the everyday practices of lives lived in unequal locations, in which social difference and social distance intertwine.

Bibliography

Abbott, P. and Sapsford, R. (1987) *Women and Social Class*, London: Tavistock.

Adler, N., Boyce, T., Chesney, M., Cohen, S., Folkman, S., Kahn, R. and Syme, L. S. (1994) 'Socioeconomic Status and Health: The Challenge of the Gradient', *American Psychologist*, 49 (1): 15–24.

Alexander, C. (2000) *The Asian Gang*, Oxford: Berg.

Allan, G. (1991) *Friendship*, London: Perseus.

Amit, V. and Rapport, N. (2002) *The Trouble With Community*, London: Pluto Press.

Andersen, J. (1999) 'Post-industrial Solidarity or Meritocracy?', *Acta Sociologica*, 42: 375–385.

Anderson, B. (1983) *Imagined Communities*, London: Verso.

Anthias, F. (1998) 'Rethinking Social Divisions: Some Notes towards a Theoretical Framework', *The Sociological Review*, 46 (3): 505–535.

Anthias, F. (2001) 'The Material and the Symbolic in Theorizing Social Stratification', *British Journal of Sociology*, 52 (3): 367–390.

Anthias, F. and Yuval-Davis, N. (1992) *Racialised Boundaries*, London: Routledge.

Arber, S. (1991) 'Class, Paid Employment and Family Roles', *Social Science Medicine*, 32 (4): 425–436.

Arber, S. (1997) 'Comparing Health Inequalities in Women's and Men's Health: Britain in the 1990s', *Social Science Medicine*, 44 (6): 773–787.

Archer, L. and Hutchings, M. (2000) '"Bettering Yourself"? Discourses of Risk, Cost and Benefit in Ethnically Diverse, Young Working-class Non-participants' Constructions of Higher Education', *British Journal of Sociology of Education*, 21 (4): 555–574.

Bagguley, P. and Mann, K. (1992) 'Idle Thieving Bastards? Scholarly Representations of the "Underclass"', *Work, Employment and Society*, 6 (1): 113–126.

Ball, S., Davies, J., David, M. and Reay, D. (2002) '"Classification" and "Judgement": Social Class and the "Cognitive Structures" of Choice of Higher Education', *British Journal of Sociology of Education*, 23 (1): 51–72.

Baran, P. and Sweezy, P. (1966) *Monopoly Capital*, Harmondsworth: Penguin.

Barber, B. (1957) *Social Stratification*, New York: Harcourt, Brace & World.

Barnes, B. (1992) 'Status Groups and Collective Action', *Sociology*, 26 (2): 259–270.

Barrett, M. (1992) 'Words and Things: Materialism and Method in Contemporary Feminist Analysis', in M. Barrett and A. Phillips (eds) *Destabilizing Theory*, Cambridge: Polity.

Barrett, M. and Phillips, A. (1992) *Destabilizing Theory*, Cambridge: Polity.

Barry, B. (2002) 'Social Exclusion, Social Isolation and the Distribution of Income', in J. Hills, J. Le Grand and D. Piachaud (eds) *Understanding Social Exclusion*, Oxford: Oxford University Press.

Barth, F. (ed.) (1969) *Ethnic Groups and Boundaries*, Oslo: Oslo University Press.

Barth, F. (1994) 'Enduring and Emerging Issues in the Analysis of Ethnicity', in H. Vermeulen and C. Grovers (eds) *The Anthropology of Ethnicity: Beyond Ethnic Groups and Boundaries*, The Hague: Het Spinhuis.

Bartley, M. and Plewis, I. (1997) 'Does Health-selective Mobility Account for Socioeconomic Differences in Health? Evidence from England and Wales, 1971 to 1991', *Journal of Health and Social Behaviour*, 38 (4): 376–386.

Bartley, M., Blane, D. and Davey-Smith, G. (1998) 'Introduction: Beyond the Black Report', in M. Bartley, D. Blane and G. Davey-Smith (eds) *The Sociology of Health Inequalities*, Oxford: Blackwell.

Bartley, M., Sacker, A., Firth, D. and Fitzpatrick, R. (1999a) 'Social Position, Social Roles and Women's Health in England: Changing Relationships 1984–1993', *Social Science and Medicine*, 48 (1): 99–115.

Bartley, M., Sacker, A., Firth, D. and Fitzpatrick, R. (1999b) 'Understanding Social Variation in Cardiovascular Risk Factors in Women and Men: The Advantages of Theoretically Based Measures', *Social Science and Medicine* 49 (6): 831–846.

Bartley, M., Sacker, A., Firth, D. and Fitzpatrick, R. (2000) 'Dimensions of Inequality and the Health of Women', in H. Graham (ed.) *Understanding Health Inequalities*, Buckingham: Open University Press.

Bauder, H. (2002) 'Neighbourhood Effects and Cultural Exclusion', *Urban Studies*, 39 (1): 85–93.

Bauman, Z. (1992) *Intimations of Postmodernity*, London: Routledge.

Beck, U. (1992) [1986] *Risk Society*, London: Sage.

Beck, U. and Beck-Gernsheim, E. (2002) *Individualization*, London: Sage.

Bell, C. and Newby, H. (1971) *Community Studies*, London: George Allen & Unwin.

Bell, D. (1973) *The Coming of Post-Industrial Society*, London: Heinemann.

Bennett, T., Emmison, M. and Frow, J. (1999) *Accounting for Taste*, Cambridge: Cambridge University Press.

Berkman, L., Glass, T., Brissette, I. and Seeman, T. (2000) 'From Social Integration to Health: Durkheim in the New Millennium', *Social Science and Medicine*, 51 (5): 843–857.

Berthoud, R. and Beishon, S. (1997) 'People, Families and Households', in T. Modood, R. Berthoud and J. Lakey (eds) *Ethnic Minorities in Britain: Diversity and Disadvantage*, London: Policy Studies Institute.

Blackburn, R., Brooks, B. and Jarman, J. (1999) *Gender Inequality in the Labour Market: The Vertical Dimension of Occupational Segregation*, Cambridge Studies in Social Research.

Blackburn, R. M., Dale, A. and Jarman, J. (1997) 'Ethnic Differences in Attainment in Education, Occupation and Life-style', in V. Karn (ed.) *Ethnicity in the 1991 Census: Volume Four*, London: ONS/Stationery Office.

Blackburn, R. M. and Jarman, J. (1993) 'Changing Inequalities in Access to British Universities', in *Oxford Review of Education*, 19 (2): 197–215.

Blackburn, R. M. and Marsh, C. (1991) 'Education and Social Class: Revisiting the 1944 Education Act with Fixed Marginals', *British Journal of Sociology*, 42 (4): 507–536.

Blackburn, R. M. and Prandy, K. (1997) 'The Reproduction of Social Inequality', *Sociology*, 31 (3): 491–509.

Blakely, E. and Snyder, M. (1997) *Fortress America*, Washington, DC: Brookings Institute.

Blane, D. (1999) 'The Life Course, the Social Gradient and Health', in M. Marmot and R. Wilkinson (eds) *Social Determinants of Health*, Oxford: Oxford University Press.

Blau, P. (1956) 'Social Mobility and Interpersonal Relations', *American Sociological Review*, 21 (3): 290–295.

Blau, P. (1977) 'A Macrosociological Theory of Social Structure', *American Journal of Sociology*, 83 (1): 26–54.

Blau, P. and Duncan, O. (1967) *The American Occupational Structure*, New York: John Wiley.

Blau, P., Beeker, C. and Fitzpatrick, K. (1984) 'Intersecting Social Affiliations and Intermarriage', *Social Forces*, 62 (3): 585–606.

Blossfeld, H.-P. and Shavit, Y. (1993) 'Persisting Barriers: Changes in Educational Opportunities in Thirteen Countries', in Y. Shavit and H.-P. Blossfeld (eds) *Persistent Inequality*, Boulder, CO: Westview Press.

Bogardus, E. (1925) 'Measuring Social Distance', *Journal of Applied Sociology*, 9: 299–308.

Bonnett, A. (1998a) 'How the British Working Class Became White: The Symbolic (Re)formation of Racialized Capitalism', *Journal of Historical Sociology*, 11 (3): 316–340.

Bonnett, A. (1998b) 'Who Was White? The Disappearance of Non-European White Identities and the Formation of European Racial Whiteness', *Ethnic and Racial Studies*, 21 (6): 1029–1055.

Bottero, W. (1998) 'Clinging to the Wreckage? Gender and the Legacy of Class', *Sociology*, 32 (3): 469–490.

Bottero, W. and Irwin, S. (2003) 'Locating Difference: Class, "Race" and Gender and the Shaping of Social Inequalities', *Sociological Review*, 51 (4): 463–483.

Bottero, W. and Prandy, K. (2001) 'Women's Occupations and the Social Order in Nineteenth Century Britain', *Sociological Research Online*, 6 (2): www.socresonline.org.uk/6/2/bottero.html

Bottero, W. and Prandy, K. (2003) 'Social Interaction Distance and Stratification', *British Journal of Sociology*, 54 (2): 177–197.

Bourdieu, P. (1984) [1979] *Distinction: A Social Critique of the Judgement of Taste*, London: Routledge & Kegan Paul.

Bourdieu, P. (1985) 'Social Space and the Genesis of Groups', *Theory and Society*, 14 (6): 723–744.

Bourdieu, P. (1987) 'What Makes a Social Class? On the Theoretical and Practical Existence of Groups', *Berkeley Journal of Sociology*, 32: 1–18.

Bourdieu, P. (1990) *In Other Words: Essays Towards a Reflexive Sociology*, Cambridge: Polity.

Bourdieu, P. (1991) [1980] 'Identity and Representation', in *Language and Symbolic Power*, Cambridge: Polity.

Bourdieu, P. and Wacquant, L. (1992) *An Invitation to Reflexive Sociology*, Cambridge: Polity.

Bozon, M. and Heran, F. (1989) 'Finding a Spouse: A Survey of How French Couples Meet', *Population*, 44 (1): 91–121.

Bradley, H. (1989) *Men's Work, Women's Work*, Cambridge: Polity.

Bradley, H. (1996) *Fractured Identities*, Cambridge: Polity.

Bradley, H., Erickson, M., Stephenson, C. and Williams, S. (2000) *Myths at Work*, Cambridge: Polity.

Bridgen, P. (2003) 'Social Capital, Community Empowerment and Public Health: Policy Developments in the United Kingdom since 1997', unpublished paper.

Brubaker, R. (1985) 'Rethinking Classical Theory: The Sociological Vision of Pierre Bourdieu', *Theory and Society*, 14 (6): 745–775.

Brubaker, R. (2002) 'Ethnicity Without Groups', *European Journal of Sociology*, XLIII (2): 163–189.

Brunner, E. and Marmot, M. (1999) 'Social Organization, Stress and Health', in M. Marmot and R. Wilkinson (eds) *Social Determinants of Health*, Oxford: Oxford University Press.

Bryson, B. (1996) '"Anything but Heavy Metal": Symbolic Exclusion and Musical Dislikes', *American Sociological Review*, 61 (5): 884–899.

Buck, N. (2001) 'Identifying Neighbourhood Effects on Social Exclusion', *Urban Studies*, 38 (12): 2251–2275.

Burchardt, T., Le Grand, J. and Piachaud, D. (2002) 'Degrees of Exclusion', in J. Hills, J. Le Grand and D. Piachaud (eds) *Understanding Social Exclusion*, Oxford: Oxford University Press.

Burgess, S. and Popper, C. (2002) 'The Dynamics of Poverty in Britain', in J. Hills, J. Le Grand and D. Piachaud (eds) *Understanding Social Exclusion*, Oxford: Oxford University Press.

Butler, J. (1998) *Gender Trouble*, London: Routledge.

Butler, T. and Robson, G. (2001) 'Social Capital, Gentrification and Neighbourhood Change in London: A Comparison of Three South London Neighbourhoods', *Urban Studies*, 38 (12): 2145–2162.

Butler, T. and Robson, G. (2003) 'Plotting the Middle Classes: Gentrification and Circuits of Education in London', *Housing Studies*, 18 (1): 5–28.

Byrne, D. (1999) *Social Exclusion*, Buckingham: Open University Press.

Calhoun, C. (1981) *The Question of Class Struggle*, Chicago: University of Chicago Press.

Cameron, S. and Field, A. (2000) 'Community, Ethnicity and Neighbourhood', *Housing Studies*, 15 (6): 827–843.

Cannadine, D. (1998) *Class in Britain*, London: Yale University Press.

Cantle, T. (2001) *Community Cohesion*, London: HMSO.

Castles, S. and Kosack, G. (1973) *Immigrant Workers and Class Structure in Western Europe*, London: Oxford University Press.

Chandola, T. (1998) 'Social Inequality in Coronary Heart Disease: A Comparison of Occupational Classifications', *Social Science Medicine*, 47 (4): 525–533.

Charles, C. Z. (2003) 'The Dynamics of Racial Residential Segregation', *Annual Review of Sociology*, 29: 167–207.

Clark, T. and Lipset, S. (1996) 'Are Social Classes Dying?', in D. Lee and B. Turner (eds) *Conflicts about Class*, Harlow: Longman.

Cohen, A. (1985) *The Symbolic Construction of Community*, Chichester: Ellis Horwood.

Corcoran, M. (1995) 'Rags to Rags: Poverty and Mobility in the United States', *Annual Sociological Review*, 21: 237–267.

Corfield, P. J. (1991) 'Class by Name and Number in Eighteenth-Century Britain', in P. J. Corfield (ed.) *Language, History and Class*, Oxford: Basil Blackwell.

Coser, L. (1977) *Masters of Sociological Thought*, New York: Harcourt Brace.

Coxon, A. and Jones, C. (1978) *The Images of Occupational Prestige*, London: Macmillan.

Coxon, A. and Davies, P. with Jones, C. (1986) *Images of Social Stratification*, London: Sage.

Craib, I. (1997) *Classical Social Theory*, Oxford: Oxford University Press.

Crompton, R. (1989) 'Class Theory and Gender', *British Journal of Sociology*, 40 (4): 56–67.

Crompton, R. (1996) 'The Fragmentation of Class Analysis', *British Journal of Sociology*, 47 (1): 56–67.

Crompton, R. (1998) *Class and Stratification* (2nd edn), London: Polity.

Crompton, R. and Sanderson, K. (1990) *Gendered Jobs and Social Change*, London: Unwin Hyman.

Crompton, R. and Scott, J. (2000) 'Introduction: The State of Class Analysis', in R. Crompton, F. Devine, M. Savage and J. Scott (eds) *Renewing Class Analysis*, Oxford: Blackwell.

Crook, S., Pakulski, J. and Waters, M. (1992) *Postmodernization*, London: Sage.

Crossick, G. (1991) 'From Gentlemen to the Residuum: Languages of Social Description in Victorian Britain', in P. J. Corfield (ed.) *Language, History and Class*, Oxford: Basil Blackwell.

Davey-Smith, G., Charlsey, K., Lambert, H., Paul, S., Fenton, S. and Ahmad, W. (2000) 'Ethnicity, Health and the Meaning of Socio-Economic Position', in H. Graham (ed.) *Understanding Health Inequalities*, Buckingham: Open University Press.

Davidoff, L., Doolittle, M., Fink, J. and Holden, K. (1999) *The Family Story*, London: Longman.

Davin, A. (1996) *Growing Up Poor: Home, School and the Street in London, 1870–1914*, London: Rivers Oram Press.

Davis, A., Gardner, B. B. and Gardner, M. B. (1941) *Deep South: A Social Anthropological Study of Caste and Class*, Chicago: University of Chicago Press.

Davis, K. and Moore, W. E. (1944) 'Some Principles of Stratification', *American Sociological Review*, 10 (2): 242–249.

Denham, J. (2002) *Building Community Cohesion*, London: HMSO.

Devine, F. (1992) 'Social Identities, Class Identity and Political Perspectives', *Sociological Review*, 40 (2): 229–252.

Devine, F. (1998) 'Class Analysis and the Stability of Class Relations', *Sociology*, 32 (1): 23–42.

Devine, F. (2004) *Class Practices*, Cambridge: Cambridge University Press.

Devine, F. and Savage, M. (2000) 'Conclusion: Renewing Class Analysis', in R. Crompton, F. Devine, M. Savage and J. Scott (eds) *Renewing Class Analysis*, Oxford: Blackwell.

Dex, S. (1990) 'Occupational Mobility over Women's Lifetime', in G. Payne and A. Abbott (eds) *The Social Mobility of Women: Beyond Male Mobility Models*, Basingstoke: Falmer Press.

DiMaggio, P. (1987) 'Classification in Art', *American Sociological Review*, 52 (4): 440–455.

DiMaggio, P. and Ostrower, F. (1990) 'Participation in the Arts by Black and White Americans', *Social Forces*, 68 (3): 753–778.

DiMaggio, P. and Useem, M. (1978) 'Social Class and Arts Consumption: The Origins and Consequences of Class Differences in Exposure to the Arts in America', *Theory and Society*, 5 (2): 141–161.

Disraeli, B. (1969) [1845] *Sybil: Or the Two Nations*, London: Oxford University Press.

Duncan, O. (1968) 'Social Stratification and Mobility: Problems in the Measurement of Trend', in E. Sheldon and W. Moore (eds) *Indicators of Change: Concepts and Measurement*, New York: Russell Sage Foundation.

Durkheim, E. (1961) *Moral Education*, Glencoe, IL: Free Press.

Durkheim, E. (1962) *Socialism*, A. W. Gouldner (ed.), New York: Collier Books.

Durkheim, E. (1972) [1897] *Suicide*, London: Routledge.

Durkheim, E. (1984) [1892] *The Division of Labour in Society*, Basingstoke: Macmillan.

Dyer, R. (1997) *White*, London: Routledge.

Dyer, R. (2000) 'The Matter of Whiteness', in L. Back and J. Solomos (eds) *Theories of Race and Racism*, London: Routledge.

Egerton, M. and Savage, M. (2000) 'Age Stratification and Class Formation: A Longitudinal Study of the Social Mobility of Young Men and Women, 1971–1991', *Work, Employment and Society*, 14 (1): 23–49.

Elstad, J. (1998) 'The Psycho-social Perspective on Social Inequalities in Health', in M. Bartley, D. Blane and G. Davey-Smith (eds) *The Sociology of Health Inequalities*, Oxford: Blackwell.

Erickson, B. H. (1996) 'Culture, Class and Connections', *American Journal of Sociology*, 102 (1): 217–251.

Erikson, R. and Goldthorpe, J. (1992) *The Constant Flux: The Study of Social Mobility in Industrial Societies*, Oxford: Clarendon Press.

Evans, M. D. R., Kelley, J. and Kolosi, T. (1992) 'Images of Class: Public Perceptions in Hungary and Australia', *American Sociological Review*, 57 (4): 461–482.

Featherman, D. and Hauser, R. (1976) 'Prestige or Socioeconomic Scales in the Study of Occupational Achievement', *Sociological Methods and Research*, 4 (4): 403–405.

Feld, S. and Carter, W. (1998) 'Foci of Activity as Changing Contexts of Friendship', in R. Adams and G. Allan (eds) *Placing Friendship in Context*, Cambridge: Cambridge University Press.

Feldberg, R. and Glenn, E. (1984) 'Male and Female: Job versus Gender Models in the Sociology of Work', in J. Siltanen and M. Stanworth (eds) *Women and the Public Sphere*, London: Hutchinson.

Floud, R. and Harris, B. (1997) 'Health, Height and Welfare: Britain, 1700–1980', in R. Steckel and R. Floud (eds) *Health and Welfare during Industrialisation*, Chicago: University of Chicago Press.

Floud, R., Wachter, K. and Gregory, A. (1990) *Height, Health and History: Nutritional Status in the United Kingdom 1750–1980*, Cambridge: Cambridge University Press.

Fogel, R. (1994) *Economic Growth, Population Theory and Physiology*, Cambridge, MA: National Bureau of Economic Research.

Forbes, A. and Wainwright, S. (2001) 'On the Methodological, Theoretical and Philosophical Context of Health Inequalities Research: A Critique', *Social Science and Medicine*, 53: 801–816.

Forrest, R. and Kearns, A. (2001) 'Social Cohesion, Social Capital and the Neighbourhood', *Urban Studies*, 38 (12): 2125–2143.

Foster, J. (1998) *Docklands: Urban Change and Conflict in a Community in Transition*, London: Routledge.

Frankenberg, R. (2000) 'White Women, Race Matters: The Social Construction of Whiteness', in L. Back and J. Solomos (eds) *Theories of Race and Racism*, London: Routledge.

Furlong, A. (1997) 'Education and the Reproduction of Class-based Inequalities', in H. Jones (ed.) *Towards a Classless Society?*, London: Routledge.

Gallie, D. (2000) 'The Labour Force', in A. H. Halsey and J. Webb (eds) *Twentieth-century British Social Trends*, Basingstoke: Macmillan.

Galton, F. (1892) [1869] *Hereditary Genius*, London: Macmillan.

Ganzeboom, H., Luijkx, R. and Treiman, D. (1989) 'Intergenerational Class Mobility in Comparative Perspective', *Research in Social Stratification and Mobility*, 8: 3–79.

Giddens, A. (1976) *New Rules of Sociological Method*, London: Hutchinson.

Giddens, A. (1981) *The Class Structure of the Advanced Societies* (2nd edn), London: Hutchinson.

Giddens, A. (1991) *Modernity and Self Identity*, Cambridge: Polity.

Gilroy, P. (1987) *'There Ain't no Black in the Union Jack'*, London: Hutchinson.

Glass, D. (1954) 'Introduction', in D. Glass (ed.) *Social Mobility in Britain*, London: Routledge & Kegan Paul.

Glazer, N. (1999) 'Comment on "London and New York: Contrasts in British and American Models of Segregation" by Ceri Peach', *International Journal of Population Geography*, 5: 347–351.

Goldthorpe, J. (1983) 'Women and Class Analysis: In Defence of the Conventional View' *Sociology*, 17 (4): 465–488.

Goldthorpe, J. (1984) 'Women and Class Analysis – A Reply to the Replies', *Sociology*, 18 (4): 491–499.

Goldthorpe, J. (1996) 'Class Analysis and the Reorientation of Class Theory', *British Journal of Sociology*, 47 (3): 481–505.

Goldthorpe, J. (2000) *On Sociology*, Oxford: Oxford University Press.

Goldthorpe, J. and Hope, K. (1972) 'Occupational Grading and Occupational Prestige', in K. Hope (ed.) *The Analysis of Social Mobility: Methods and Approaches*, Oxford: Clarendon Press.

Goldthorpe, J. and Marshall, G. (1992) 'The Promising Future of Class Analysis', *Sociology*, 26 (3): 381–400.

Goldthorpe, J., Llewellyn, C. and Payne, C. (1980) *Social Mobility and Class Structure in Modern Britain*, Oxford: Clarendon Press.

Goldthorpe, J., Llewellyn, C. and Payne, C. (1987) *Social Mobility and Class Structure in Modern Britain* (2nd edn), Oxford: Oxford University Press.

Gould, R. (1995) *Insurgent Identities*, London: University of Chicago Press.

Gould, S. J. (1984) *The Mismeasure of Man*, London: Penguin.

Granovetter, M. (1995) *Getting a Job*, Chicago: University of Chicago Press.

Grimes, M. (1991) *Class in Twentieth Century American Sociology*, New York: Praeger.

Grusky, D. (1994) *Social Stratification*, Boulder, CO: Westview Press.

Hakim, C. (1996) *Key Issues in Women's Work*, London: Athlone Press.

Halford, S. and Leonard, P. (2001) *Gender, Power and Organisations*, Basingstoke: Palgrave.

Hall, P. (1999) 'Social Capital in Britain', *British Journal of Political Science*, 29 (3): 417–461.

Hall, S. (1980) 'Race, Articulation and Societies Structured in Dominance', in UNESCO, *Sociological Theories: Race and Colonialism*, Paris: UNESCO.

Hall, S. (1991) 'Old and New Identities, Old and New Ethnicities', in A. D. King (ed.) *Culture, Globalization and the World System*, Basingstoke: Macmillan.

Hall, S. (1992) 'The Question of Cultural Identity', in S. Hall, D. Held and T. McGrew (eds) *Modernity and Its Futures*, London: Oxford University Press.

Hamnett, C. (1999) 'The City', in P. Cloke, P. Crang and M. Goodwin (eds) *Introducing Human Geographies*, London: Arnold.

Harris, B. (1994) 'Health, Height and History', *Social History of Medicine*, 7 (2): 297–320.

Hartmann, H. (1981) 'The Unhappy Marriage of Marxism and Feminism', in L. Sargent (ed.) *Woman and Revolution*, London: Pluto.

Hawkins, M. (1997) *Social Darwinism in European and American Thought 1860–1945*, Cambridge: Cambridge University Press.

Heath, A. (1981) *Social Mobility*, London: Fontana.

Heath, A. and Clifford, P. (1990) 'Class Inequalities in Education in the Twentieth Century', *Journal of the Royal Statistical Society*, Series A, 153 (1): 1–16.

Heath, A. and Payne, C. (2000) 'Social Mobility', in A. H. Halsey with J. Webb (eds) *Twentieth-century British Social Trends*, Basingstoke: Macmillan.

Himmelfarb, G. (1983) *The Idea of Poverty: England in the Early Industrial Age*, New York: Alfred Knopf.

Holmwood, J. (1996) *Founding Sociology? Talcott Parsons and the Idea of General Theory*, Harlow: Longman.

Holmwood, J. and Stewart, A. (1991) *Explanation and Social Theory*, London: Macmillan.

Hout, M., Brooks, C. and Manza, J. (1996) 'The Persistence of Classes in Post-industrial Societies', in D. Lee and B. Turner (eds) *Conflicts about Class*, Harlow: Longman.

Ignatiev, N. (1996) *How the Irish Became White*, London and New York: Routledge.

Irwin, S. (1995) *Rights of Passage. Social Change and the Transition from Youth to Adulthood*, London: UCL Press.

Irwin, S. (2000) 'Reproductive Regimes: Changing Relations of Inter-dependence and Fertility Change', in *Sociological Research Online*, 5 (1) www.socresonline.org.uk/5/1/irwin.html.

Irwin, S. (forthcoming) *Reshaping Social Life*, London: Routledge.

Irwin, S. and Bottero, W. (2000) 'Market Returns? Gender and Theories of Change in Employment Relations', *British Journal of Sociology*, 51 (2): 261–280.

Jackson, B. and Marsden, D. (1966) *Education and the Working Class*, London: Routledge & Kegan Paul.

Jenkins, R. (1996) *Social Identity*, London: Routledge.

Jenkins, R. (2000) [1982] 'Pierre Bourdieu and the Reproduction of Determinism', in D. Robbins (ed.) *Pierre Bourdieu*, vol. 2, London: Sage.

Johnston, M. and Jowell, R. (2001) 'How Robust is British Civil Society?', in A. Park *et al.*, (eds) *British Social Attitudes: The 18th Report Public Policy, Social Ties*, London: Sage.

Johnston, R., Forrest, J. and Poulsen, M. (2002) 'Are there Ethnic Enclaves/Ghettos in English Cities?', *Urban Studies*, 39 (4): 591–618.

Jones, G. (1980) *Social Darwinism and English Thought*, Brighton: Harvester Press.

Jones, G. (1990) 'Marriage Partners and their Class Trajectories', in G. Payne and A. Abbott (eds) *The Social Mobility of Women: Beyond Male Mobility Models*, Basingstoke: Falmer Press.

Joyce, P. (1990) *Visions of the People*, Cambridge: Cambridge University Press.

Judge, K., Mulligan, J. and Benzeval, M. (1998) 'Income Inequality and Population Health', *Social Science Medicine*, 46 (4–5): 567–579.

Kalmijn, M. (1991) 'Status Homogamy in the United States', *American Journal of Sociology*, 97 (3): 496–523.

Kalmijn, M. (1994) 'Assortative Mating by Cultural and Economic Occupational Status', *American Journal of Sociology*, 100 (2): 422–452.

Kalmijn, M. (1998) 'Intermarriage and Homogamy: Causes, Patterns, Trends', *American Review of Sociology*, 24: 395–421.

Kalmijn, M. and Flap, H. (2001) 'Assortative Meeting and Mating: Unintended Consequences of Organized Settings for Partner Choices', *Social Forces*, 79 (4): 1289–1312.

Kawachi, I. and Kennedy, B. (2002) *The Health of Nations*, New York: The New Press.

Kawachi, I., Kennedy, B. and Glass, R. (1999) 'Social Capital and Self-rated Health: A Contextual Analysis', *American Journal of Public Health*, 89 (8): 1187–1193.

Kelley, J. and Evans, M. D. R. (1995) 'Class and Class Conflict in Six Western Nations', *American Sociological Review*, 60 (2): 157–178.

Kerr, C., Dunlop, J. T., Harbison, F. H. and Myers, C. A. (1973) *Industrialism and Industrial Man*, Harmondsworth: Penguin.

Kornhauser, R. (1953) 'The Warner Approach to Stratification', in R. Bendix and S. Lipset (eds) *Class, Status and Power* (1st edn), New York: Free Press of Glencoe.

Krivo, L. and Kaufman, R. (1999) 'How Low Can It Go? Declining Black–White Segregation in a Multiethnic Context', *Demography*, 36 (1): 93–109.

Lamont, M. (1992) *Money, Morals and Manners: The Culture of the French and American Upper Middle-class*, Chicago: University of Chicago Press.

Lamont, M. and Lareau, A. (1988) 'Cultural Capital: Allusions, Gaps and Glissandos in Recent Theoretical Developments', *Sociological Theory*, 6 (3): 153–168.

Lamont, M. and Molnar, V. (2002) 'The Study of Boundaries in the Social Sciences', *Annual Review of Sociology*, 28: 167–195.

Lareau, A. (2000) *Home Advantage: Social Class and Parental Intervention in Elementary Education*, Lanham, MD: Rowman & Littlefield.

Laumann, E. O. and Guttman, L. (1966) 'The Relative Associational Contiguity of Occupations in an Urban Setting', *American Sociological Review*, 31 (2): 169–178.

Laumann, E. O., Gagnon, J., Michael, R. and Michaels, S. (1994) *The Social Organization of Sexuality*, Chicago: University of Chicago Press.

Lawrence, E. (1982) 'In the Abundance of Water the Fool is Thirsty: Sociology and Black "Pathology"', in Centre for Contemporary Cultural Studies (eds) *The Empire Strikes Back*, London: Hutchinson.

Lawson, R. and Wilson, W. J. (1995) 'Poverty, Social Rights and the Quality of Citizenship', in K. McFate, R. Lawson and W. Wilson (eds) *Poverty, Inequality and the Future of Social Policy*, New York: Russell Sage Foundation.

Li, Y., Savage, M. and Pickles, A. (2003a) 'Social Change, Friendship and Civic Participation', *Sociological Research Online*, 8 (3): http://www.socresonline.org.uk/8/3/li.html.

Li, Y., Savage, M. and Pickles, A. (2003b) 'Social Capital and Social Exclusion in England and Wales, 1972–1999', *British Journal of Sociology*, 54 (4): 497–526.

Li, Y., Savage, M., Tampubolon, G., Warde, A. and Tomlinson, M. (2002) 'Dynamics of Social Capital: Trends and Turnover in Associational Membership in England and Wales, 1972–1999', *Sociological Research Online*, 7 (3): www.socresonline.org.uk/7/3/li.html.

Lin, N. (1999) 'Social Networks and Status Attainment', *Annual Review of Sociology*, 25: 467–487.

Lin, N. (2001) *Social Capital*, Cambridge: Cambridge University Press.

Lockwood, D. (1958) *The Blackcoated Worker*, London: Allen & Unwin.

Lockwood, D. (1975) 'Sources of Variation in Working-class Images of Society', in M. Bulmer (ed.) *Working-class Images of Society*, London: Routledge & Kegan Paul.

Lockwood, D. (1992) *Solidarity and Schism: 'The Problem of Disorder' in Durkheimian and Marxist Sociology*, Oxford: Clarendon Press.

Longhurst, B. and Savage, M. (1996) 'Social Class, Consumption and the Influence of Bourdieu: Some Critical Issues', in S. Edgell, K. Hetherington and A. Warde (eds) *Consumption Matters*, Sociological Review Monograph Series A, Oxford: Blackwell.

Lupton, R. and Power, A. (2002) 'Social Exclusion and Neighbourhoods', in J. Hills, J. Le Grand and D. Piachaud (eds) *Understanding Social Exclusion*, Oxford: Oxford University Press.

Lynch, J., Davey-Smith, G., Kaplan, G. and House, J. (2000) 'Income Inequality and Mortality: Importance to Health of Individual Income, Psychosocial Environment, or Material Conditions', *British Medical Journal*, 320 (7243): 1200–1204.

Lynch, K. and O'Riordan, C. (1998) 'Inequality in Higher Education: A Study of Class Barriers', *British Journal of Sociology of Education*, 19 (4): 445–478.

Lyons, M. (2003) 'Spatial Segregation in Seven Cities: A Longitudinal Study of Home Ownership, 1971–91', *Housing Studies*, 18 (3): 305–326.

Mac an Ghail, M. (1999) *Contemporary Racisms and Ethnicities*, Buckingham: Open University Press.

McDowell, L. (2003) *Redundant Masculinities?*, Oxford: Blackwell.

McFarland, D. and Brown, D. (1973) 'Social Distance as a Metric: A Systematic Introduction to Smallest Space Analysis', in E. O. Lauman (ed.) *Bonds of Pluralism*, New York: John Wiley.

McGhee, D. (forthcoming) *Intolerant Britain*, London: Routledge.

McLennan, D. (ed.) (2000) *Karl Marx, Selected Writings* (2nd edn), Oxford: Oxford University Press.

McMeekin, A. and Tomlinson, M. (1998) 'Diffusion with Distinction: The Diffusion of Household Durables in the UK', *Futures*, 30 (9): 873–886.

McPherson, M., Smith-Lovin, L. and Cook, J. (2001) 'Birds of a Feather Flock Together: Homophily in Social Networks', *Annual Review of Sociology*, 27: 415–444.

Malik, K. (1996) *The Meaning of Race: Race, History and Culture in Western Society*, Basingstoke: Macmillan.

Mark, N. (1998) 'Birds of a Feather Sing Together', *Social Forces*, 77 (2): 453–485.

Marmot, M. (1996) 'The Social Pattern of Health and Disease', in D. Blane, E. Brunner and R. Wilkinson (eds) *Health and Social Organization*, London: Routledge.

Marmot, M. and Davey-Smith, G. (1989) 'Why are the Japanese Living Longer?', *British Medical Journal*, 299 (6715): 1547–1551.

Marmot, M., Shipley, M. and Rose, G. (1984) 'Inequalities in Death – Specific Explanations of a General Pattern', *Lancet*, 1 (8384): 1003–1006.

Marmot, M., Bosma, H., Hemingway, H., Brunner, E. and Stansfeld, S. (1997) 'Contribution of Job Control and Other Risk Factors to Social Variations in Coronary Heart Disease Incidence', *Lancet*, 350 (9073): 235–239.

Marsh, C. (1986) 'Social Class and Occupation', in R. Burgess (ed.) *Key Variables in Social Investigation*, London: Routledge.

Marshall, G. (1997) *Repositioning Class*, London: Sage.

Marshall, G. and Firth, D. (1999) 'Social Mobility and Personal Satisfaction: Evidence from Ten Countries', *British Journal of Sociology*, 50 (1): 28–48.

Marshall, G. and Swift, A. (1993) 'Social Class and Social Justice', *British Journal of Sociology*, 44 (2): 187–211.

Marshall, G. and Swift, A. (1996) 'Merit and Mobility: A Reply to Peter Saunders', *Sociology*, 30 (2): 375–386.

Marshall, G., Swift, A. and Roberts, S. (1997) *Against the Odds?: Social Class and Social Justice in Industrial Societies*, Oxford: Clarendon.

Marshall, G., Rose, D., Newby, H. and Vogler, C. (1988) *Social Class in Modern Britain*, London: Routledge.

Marx, K. (1852/2000) *The 18th Brumaire of Louis Bonaparte*, in D. McLennan (ed.) *Karl Marx, Selected Writings* (2nd edn), Oxford: Oxford University Press.

Marx, K. (1859/2000) *Preface to a Contribution to the Critique of Political Economy*, in D. McLennan (ed.) *Karl Marx, Selected Writings* (2nd edn), Oxford: Oxford University Press.

Marx, K. and Engels, F. (1848/2000) *Manifesto of the Communist Party*, in D. McLennan (ed.) *Karl Marx, Selected Writings* (2nd edn), Oxford: Oxford University Press.

Massey, D. and Denton, N. (1989) 'Hypersegregation in U.S. Metropolitan Areas: Black and Hispanic Segregation along Five Dimensions', *Demography*, 26 (3): 373–391.

Massey, D. and Denton, N. (1993) *American Apartheid*, Harvard, MA: Harvard University Press.

Mayhew, H. (1968) [1861] *London Labour and the London Poor*, New York: Dover.

Miles, R. (1993) *Racism*, London: Routledge.

Miles, R. (1999) 'Apropos the Idea of "Race" . . . Again', in J. Solomos and L. Back (eds) *Theories of Race and Racism: A Reader*, London: Routledge.

Miles, S. (1998) *Consumerism as a Way of Life*, London: Sage.

Mills, C. W. (1942) 'The Social Life of a Modern Community', in *Power, Politics and People: The Collected Essays of C. Wright Mills*, London: Oxford University Press.

Model, S. and Fisher, G. (2002) 'Unions Between Blacks and Whites: England and the US Compared', *Ethnic and Racial Studies*, 25 (5): 728–754.

Modood, T. (1996) 'If Races Don't Exist, Then What Does? Racial Categorisations and Ethnic Realities', in R. Barot (ed.) *The Racism Problematic*, Lewiston, NY: Edwin Mellon Press.

Modood, T. (1997) 'Culture and Identity', in T. Modood, R. Berthoud, J. Lakey, J. Nazroo, P. Smith, S. Virdee and S. Beishon, *Ethnic Minorities in Britain: Diversity and Disadvantage*, London: PSI.

Morris, L. (1994) *Dangerous Classes*, London: Routledge.

Morris, L. and Scott, J. (1996) 'The Attenuation of Class', *British Journal of Sociology*, 47 (1): 45–55.

Muntaner, C. and Lynch, J. (1999) 'Income Inequality, Social Cohesion and Class Relations: A Critique of Wilkinson's Neo-Durkheimian Research Programme', *International Journal of Health Services*, 29 (1): 59–81.

Muntaner, C., Lynch, J. and Davey-Smith, G. (2001) 'Social Capital, Disorganised Communities and the Third Way: Understanding the Retreat from Structural Inequalities in Epidemiology and Public Health', *International Journal of Health Services*, 31 (2): 213–237.

Muntaner, C., Lynch, J. and Oates, G. (1999) 'The Social Class Determinants of Income Inequality and Social Cohesion', *International Journal of Health Services*, 29 (4): 699–732.

Murphy, R. (1988) *Social Closure: The Theory of Monopolisation and Exclusion*, Oxford: Clarendon Press.

Murray, C. (1984) *Losing Ground: American Social Policy, 1950–1980*, New York: Basic Books.

Nazroo, J. (1998) 'Genetic, Cultural or Socio-economic Vulnerability? Explaining Ethnic Inequalities in Health', in M. Bartley, D. Blane and G. Davey-Smith (eds) *The Sociology of Health Inequalities*, Oxford: Blackwell.

Noble, T. (2000) 'The Mobility Transition: Social Mobility Trends in the First Half of the Twenty-first Century', *Sociology*, 34 (1): 35–52.

Omi, M. and Winant, H. (1994) *Racial Formation in the United States* (2nd edn), New York: Routledge.

ONS (Office for National Statistics) (2001) *2001 Census*: www.statistics.gov.uk (accessed 20 February 2004).

Orwell, G. (1970) [1937] *The Road to Wigan Pier*, Harmondsworth: Penguin.

Ossowski, S. (1963) *Class Structure in the Social Consciousness*, London: Routledge & Kegan Paul.

Pahl, R. (1991) 'The Search for Social Cohesion: From Durkheim to the European Commission', *European Journal of Sociology*, XXXII: 345–360.

Pahl, R. (1993) 'Does Class Analysis Without Class Theory Have a Future?', *Sociology*, 27 (2): 253–258.

Pakulski, J. and Waters, M. (1996) *The Death of Class*, London: Sage.

Park, R. E. (1999) 'The Nature of Race Relations', in J. Solomos and L. Back (eds) *Theories of Race and Racism: A Reader*, London: Routledge.

Parkin, F. (1972) *Class Inequality and Political Order*, London: McGibbon & Kee.

Parkin, F. (1979) *Marxism and Class Theory: A Bourgeois Critique*, London: Tavistock Press.

Parkin, F. (1982) *Max Weber*, London: Routledge.

Parry, G., Moyser, G. and Day, N. (1992) *Political Participation and Democracy in Britain*, Cambridge: Cambridge University Press.

Parsons, T. (1951) *The Social System*, New York: Macmillan.

Parsons, T. (1954a) [1940] 'An Analytical Approach to the Theory of Social Stratification', in *Essays in Sociological Theory*, New York: Macmillan.

Parsons, T. (1954b) [1953] 'A Revised Analytical Approach to the Theory of Social Stratification', in *Essays in Sociological Theory*, New York: Macmillan.

Parsons, T. (1968) [1937] *The Structure of Social Action*, New York: Free Press.

Pawson, R. (1989) *A Measure for Measures*, London: Routledge.

Payne, G. (1992) 'Competing Views of Contemporary Social Mobility and Social Divisions', in R. Burrows and C. Marsh (eds) *Consumption and Class*, Basingstoke: Macmillan.

Payne, G. and Abbott, P. (1990) 'Beyond Male Mobility Models', in G. Payne and A. Abbott (eds) *The Social Mobility of Women: Beyond Male Mobility Models*, Basingstoke: Falmer Press.

Payne, G. and Roberts, J. (2002) 'Opening and Closing the Gates: Recent Developments in Male Social Mobility in Britain', in *Sociological Research Online*, 6 (4): www.socresonline. org.uk/6/4/payne.html.

Payne, G., Payne, J. and Chapman, T. (1990) 'The Changing Pattern of Early Career Mobility', in G. Payne and A. Abbott (eds) *The Social Mobility of Women: Beyond Male Mobility Models*, Basingstoke: Falmer Press.

Peach, C. (1996a) 'Does Britain Have Ghettos?', *Transactions of the Institute of British Geographers*, 21 (1): 216–235.

Peach, C. (1996b) 'Good Segregation, Bad Segregation', *Planning Perspectives*, 11 (4): 379–398.

Peach, C. (1998) 'South Asian and Caribbean Ethnic Minority Housing Choice in Britain', *Urban Studies*, 35 (10): 1657–1680.

Peach, C. (1999) 'London and New York: Contrasts in British and American Models of Segregation', *International Journal of Population Geography*, 5: 319–351.

Peterson, R. (1992) 'Understanding Audience Segmentation: From Elite and Mass to Omnivore and Univore', *Poetics*, 21 (4): 243–258.

Peterson, R. (1996) 'Changing Highbrow Taste: From Snob to Omnivore', *American Sociological Review*, 61 (5): 900–907.

Peterson, R. and Simkus, A. (1992) 'How Musical Tastes Mark Occupational Status Groups', in M. Lamont and M. Fournier (eds) *Cultivating Differences: Symbolic Boundaries and the Making of Inequality*, Chicago: University of Chicago Press.

Pfautz, H. and Duncan, O. (1950) 'A Critical Evaluation of Warner's Work in Community Stratification', *American Sociological Review*, 15 (2): 205–215.

Phillips, D. (1998) 'Black Minority Ethnic Concentration, Segregation and Dispersal in Britain', *Urban Studies*, 35 (10): 1681–1702.

Pick, D. (1989) *Faces of Degeneration*, Cambridge: Cambridge University Press.

Porter, R. (1991) 'History of the Body', in P. Burke (ed.) *New Perspectives on Historical Writing*, Cambridge: Polity.

Portes, A. (1998) 'Social Capital: Its Origins and Applications in Modern Sociology', *Annual Review of Sociology*, 24: 1–24.

Portes, A. and Landolt, P. (1996) 'The Downside of Social Capital', *The American Prospect*, 26.

Power, S., Edwards, T., Whitty, G. and Wigfall, V. (2003) *Education and the Middle Class*, Buckingham: Open University Press.

Prandy, K. (1990) 'The Revised Cambridge Scale of Occupations', *Sociology*, 24 (4): 629–656.

Prandy, K. (1998) 'Class and Continuity in Social Reproduction: An Empirical Investigation', *Sociological Review*, 46 (2): 340–364.

Prandy, K. (1999a) 'The Social Interaction Approach to the Measurement and Analysis of Social Stratification', *International Journal of Sociology and Social Policy*, 19 (9/10/11): 215–249.

Prandy, K. (1999b) 'Class, Stratification and Inequalities in Health: A Comparison of the Registrar-General's Social Classes and the Cambridge Scale', *Sociology of Health and Illness*, 21 (4): 466–484.

Prandy, K. (2000) 'Class, the Stratification Order and Party Identification', *British Journal of Political Science*, 30 (2): 237–258.

Prandy, K. (2002) 'Ideal Types, Stereotypes and Classes', *British Journal of Sociology*, 53 (4): 583–602.

Prandy, K. and Bottero, W. (1998) 'The Use of Marriage Data to Measure the Social Order in Nineteenth-century Britain', *Sociological Research Online*, 3 (1): www.socresonline. org.uk/socresonline/3/1/6.html.

Prandy, K. and Bottero, W. (2000a) 'Social Reproduction and Mobility in Britain and Ireland in the Nineteenth and Early Twentieth Centuries', *Sociology*, 34 (2): 265–281.

Prandy, K. and Bottero, W. (2000b) 'Reproduction Within and Between Generations: The Example of Nineteenth-century Britain', *Historical Methods*, 33 (1): 4–15.

Prandy, K. and Jones, F. L. (2001) 'An International Comparative Analysis of Marriage Patterns and Social Stratification', *International Journal of Sociology and Social Policy*, 21 (4/5/6): 165–183.

Prandy, K. and Lambert, P. (2003) 'Marriage, Social Distance and the Social Space: An Alternative Derivation and Validation of the Cambridge Scale', *Sociology*, 37 (3): 397–411.

Prandy, K., Lambert, P. and Bottero, W. (2003a) 'By Slow Degrees: Two Centuries of Social Reproduction and Mobility in Britain', in *International Sociological Association Research Committee on Social Stratification and Mobility*, Oxford.

Prandy, K., Unt, M. and Lambert, P. (2003b) 'Not by Degrees: Education and Social Reproduction in Twentieth-century Britain', unpublished paper.

Putnam, R. (2000) *Bowling Alone: The Collapse and Revival of American Community*, New York: Simon & Schuster.

Quillian, L. (1991) 'Migration Patterns and the Growth of High-poverty Neighbourhoods', *American Journal of Sociology*, 105 (1): 1–37.

Reay, D. (1997) 'Feminist Theory, Habitus and Social Class: Disrupting Notions of Classlessness', *Women's Studies International Forum*, 20 (2): 225–233.

Reay, D. (1998a) 'Rethinking Social Class: Qualitative Perspectives on Class and Gender', *Sociology*, 32 (2): 259–275.

Reay, D. (1998b) *Class Work*, London: UCL Press.

Reay, D., Davies, J., David, M. and Ball, S. (2001) 'Choices of Degree or Degrees of Choice? Class, "Race" and the Higher Education Choice Process', *Sociology*, 35 (4): 855–874.

Rex, J. and Tomlinson, S. (1979) *Colonial Immigrants in a British City*, London: Routledge & Kegan Paul.

Roberts, K. (2001) *Class in Modern Britain*, Basingstoke: Palgrave.

Rousseau, J.-J. (1984) [1770] *A Discourse on Inequality*, Harmondsworth: Penguin.

Routh, G. (1980) *Occupation and Pay in Great Britain, 1906–1979*, London: Macmillan.

Rubery, J., Smith, M. and Fagan, C. (1999) *Women's Employment in Europe: Trends and Prospects*, London: Routledge.

Rubery, J., Smith, M., Fagan, C. and Grimshaw, D. (1998) *Women and European Employment*, London: Routledge.

Sacker, A., Bartley, M., Firth, D. and Fitzpatrick, R. (2001) 'Dimensions of Social Inequality in the Health of Women in England: Occupational, Material and Behavioural Pathways', *Social Science and Medicine*, 52 (5): 763–781.

Sampson, R., Morenoff, J. and Gannon-Rowley, T. (2002) 'Assessing "Neighbourhood Effects": Social Processes and New Directions in Research', *Annual Review of Sociology*, 28: 443–478.

Saunders, P. (1990) *Social Class and Stratification*, London: Routledge.

Saunders, P. (1995) 'Might Britain be a Meritocracy?', *Sociology*, 29 (1): 23–41.

Saunders, P. (1996) *Unequal but Fair?*, London: Institute of Economic Affairs.

Savage, M. (1997) 'Social Mobility and the Survey Method: A Critical Analysis', in D. Bertaux and P. Thompson (eds) *Pathways to Social Class*, Oxford: Clarendon Press.

Savage, M. (2000) *Class Analysis and Social Transformation*, Buckingham: Open University Press.

Savage, M. (2003) 'A New Class Paradigm', *British Journal of Sociology*, 24 (4): 535–541.

Savage, M. and Egerton, M. (1997) 'Social Mobility, Individual Ability and the Inheritance of Class Inequality', *Sociology*, 31 (4): 645–672.

Savage, M., Bagnall, G. and Longhurst, B. (2001) 'Ordinary, Ambivalent and Defensive: Class Identities in the Northwest of England', *Sociology*, 35 (4): 875–892.

Savage, M., Barlow, J., Dickens, P. and Fielding, T. (1992) *Property, Bureaucracy and Culture*, London: Routledge.

Scott, J. (1996) *Stratification and Power*, Cambridge: Polity.

Scott, J. (2000) 'Class and Stratification', in G. Payne (ed.) *Social Divisions*, Basingstoke: Macmillan.

Scott, J. (2001) 'If Class is Dead, Why Won't It Lie Down?', in A. Woodward and M. Kohli (eds) *Inclusions and Exclusions in European Societies*, London: Routledge.

Seeman, T. (1996) 'Social Ties and Health: The Benefits of Social Integration', *Annals of Epidemiology*, 6 (5): 442–451.

Shilling, C. (1993) *The Body and Social Theory*, London: Sage.

Shilling, C. and Mellor, P. (2001) *The Sociological Ambition*, London: Sage.

Siegrist, J. and Marmot, M. (2003) 'Health Inequalities and the Psychosocial Environment – Two Scientific Challenges', *Social Science and Medicine*, 58 (8): 1463–1473.

Siltanen, J. (1994) *Locating Gender*, London: UCL Press.

Silver, H. (1994) 'Social Exclusion and Social Solidarity: Three Paradigms', *International Labour Review*, 133 (5–6): 531–574.

Skeggs, B. (1997a) *Formations of Class and Gender: Becoming Respectable*, London: Sage.

Skeggs, B. (1997b) 'Classifying Practices: Representations, Capitals and Recognitions', in P. Mahony and C. Zmroczek (eds) *Class Matters*, London: Taylor & Francis.

Smaje, C. (1996) 'The Ethnic Patterning of Health: New Directions for Theory and Research', *Sociology of Health and Illness*, 18 (2): 139–171.

Small, M. L. and Newman, K. (2001) 'Urban Poverty after *The Truly Disadvantaged*: The Rediscovery of the Family, the Neighbourhood and Culture', *Annual Sociological Review*, 27: 23–45.

Social Trends 33 (2003) Office of National Statistics, London: The Stationery Office.

Solomos, J. and Back, L. (1996) *Racism and Society*, London: Palgrave.

Solomos, J. and Back, L. (eds) (1999) *Theories of Race and Racism: A Reader*, London: Routledge.

Sorenson, A. (1994) 'The Basic Concepts of Stratification Research: Class, Status and Power', in D. Grusky (ed.) *Social Stratification*, Boulder, CO: Westview Press.

Sorokin, P. (1927) *Social Mobility*, New York: Harper & Brothers.

Stedman Jones, G. (1984) *Languages of Class*, Cambridge: Cambridge University Press.

Stewart, A. and Blackburn, R. (1975) 'The Stability of Structural Inequality', *Sociological Review*, 23 (3): 481–508.

Stewart, A., Prandy, K. and Blackburn, R. M. (1980) *Social Stratification and Occupations*, London: Macmillan Press.

Swartz, D. (1997) *Culture and Power: The Sociology of Pierre Bourdieu*, Chicago, IL: University of Chicago Press.

Thompson, K. (1982) *Emile Durkheim*, Chichester: Ellis Horwood.

Tillyard, E. M. W. (1963) [1943] *The Elizabethan World Picture*, Harmondsworth: Penguin.

Tomlinson, M. (1994) 'Do Distinct Class Preferences for Foods Exist? An Analysis of Class Based Tastes', *British Food Journal*, 96 (7): 11–17.

Townsend, P. (1993) *The International Analysis of Poverty*, Hemel Hempstead: Harvester Wheatsheaf.

Travers, M. (1999) 'Qualitative Sociology and Social Class', *Sociological Research Online*, 4 (1): www.socresonline.org.uk/socresonline/4/1/travers.html.

Treiman, D. (1994) [1976] 'Occupational Prestige in Comparative Perspective', in D. Grusky (ed.) *Social Stratification*, Boulder, CO: Westview Press.

Wacquant, L. (1994) 'The New Urban Colour Line: The State and Fate of the Ghetto in Postfordist America', in C. Calhoun (ed.) *Social Theory and the Politics of Identity*, Oxford: Basil Blackwell.

Wacquant, L. (1997) 'Three Pernicious Premises in the Study of the American Ghetto', *International Journal of Urban and Regional Research*, 21 (2): 341–353.

Wagstaff, A. and van Doorslaer, E. (2000) 'Income Inequality and Health: What Does the Literature Tell Us?', *Annual Review of Public Health*, 21: 543–567.

Walby, S. (1986) *Patriarchy at Work*, Cambridge: Polity.

Walby, S. (1992) 'Post-post-modernism? Theorising Social Complexity', in M. Barrett and A. Phillips (eds) *Destabilizing Theory*, Cambridge: Polity.

Walby, S. (1997) *Gender Transformations*, London: Routledge.

Wallerstein, N. (1992) 'Powerlessness, Empowerment and Health: Implications for Health Promotion Programmes', *American Journal of Health Promotion*, 6 (3): 197–205.

Warde, A. and Tampubolon, G. (2002) 'Social Capital, Networks and Leisure Consumption', *Sociological Review*, 50 (2): 155–180.

Warde, A. and Tomlinson, M. (1995) 'Taste Among the Middle Classes, 1968–88', in T. Butler and M. Savage (eds) *Social Change and the Middle Classes*, London: UCL Press.

Warde, A., Martens, L. and Olsen, W. (1999) 'Consumption and the Problem of Variety: Cultural Omnivorousness, Social Distinction and Dining Out', *Sociology*, 33 (1): 105–127.

Warde, A., Tampubolon, G., Longhurst, B., Ray, K., Savage, M. and Tomlinson, M. (2003) 'Trends in Social Capital: Membership of Associations in Great Britain, 1991–98', *British Journal of Political Science*, 33 (3): 515–525.

Warner, W. L. and Lunt, P. (1959a) [1941] *The Social Life of a Modern Community*, New Haven: Yale University Press.

Warner, W. L. and Lunt, P. (1959b) [1942] *The Status System of a Modern Community*, New Haven: Yale University Press.

Warner, W. L. and Srole, L. (1959) [1945] *The Social Systems of American Ethnic Groups*, New Haven: Yale University Press.

Warner, W. L., Meeker, M. and Eels, K. (1949) *Social Class in America*, New York: Harper & Row.

Weber, M. (1948) *From Max Weber: Essays in Sociology*, H. H. Gerth and C. Wright Mills (eds), London: Routledge & Kegan Paul.

Weber, M. (1978) [1922] *Economy and Society: An Outline of Interpretative Sociology*, G. Roth and C. Wittich (eds), Berkeley: University of California Press.

Wilkinson, R. (1996) *Unhealthy Societies: The Afflictions of Inequality*, London: Routledge.

Wilkinson, R. (1999a) 'Putting the Picture Together: Prosperity, Redistribution, Health and Welfare', in M. Marmot and R. Wilkinson (eds) *Social Determinants of Health*, Oxford: Oxford University Press.

Wilkinson, R. (1999b) 'Income Inequality, Social Cohesion and Health: Clarifying the Theory – a Reply to Muntaner and Lynch', *International Journal of Health Services*, 29 (3): 525–543.

Wilkinson, R., Kawachi, I. and Kennedy, B. (1998) 'Mortality, the Social Environment, Crime and Violence', in M. Bartley, D. Blane and G. Davey-Smith (eds) *The Sociology of Health Inequalities*, Oxford: Blackwell.

Williams, D. and Collins, C. (1995) 'US Socioeconomic and Racial Differences in Health: Patterns and Explanations', *Annual Review of Sociology*, 21: 349–386.

Wilson, J. and Kelling, G. (1982) 'Broken Windows: The Police and Neighbourhood Safety', *Atlantic Monthly*, March: 29–38.

Wilson, W. J. (1978) *The Declining Significance of Race*, Chicago: University of Chicago Press, 2nd edn.

Wilson, W. J. (1987) *The Truly Disadvantaged*, Chicago: University of Chicago Press.

Wilson, W. J. (1991) 'Studying Inner-city Social Dislocations: The Challenge of Public Agenda Research', *American Sociological Review*, 56 (1): 1–14.

Wilson, W. J. (1992) 'Another Look at *The Truly Disadvantaged*', *Political Science Quarterly*, 106 (4): 639–656.

Wright, E. O. (1979) *Class Structure and Income Determination*, New York: Academic Press.

Wright, E. O. (1985) *Classes*, London: Verso.

Wright, E. O. (1997) *Class Counts*, Cambridge: Cambridge University Press.

Wrightson, K. (1991) 'Estates, Degrees and Sorts: Changing Perceptions of Society in Tudor and Stuart England', in P. J. Corfield (ed.) *Language, History and Class*, Oxford: Basil Blackwell.

Young, J. (2003) 'To These Wet and Windy Shores: Recent Immigration Policy in the UK', *Punishment and Society*, 5 (4): 449–462.

Young, R. J. C. (1995) *Colonial Desire*, London: Routledge.

Index